LIFELONG LEARNING AMONG JEWS

ADULT EDUCATION IN JUDAISM
FROM BIBLICAL TIMES TO
THE TWENTIETH CENTURY

Learning Among Jews—When Young.
Courtesy of Israel Magazine, vol. 6, no. 4, 1974.
Micha BarAm, Photographer.

Learning Among Jews—When Old.
Courtesy of the Museum of the City of New York.

LIFELONG LEARNING AMONG JEWS

ADULT EDUCATION IN JUDAISM
FROM BIBLICAL TIMES TO
THE TWENTIETH CENTURY

By

Israel M. Goldman, D.H.L., D.D.

Rabbi, Chizuk Amuno Congregation
Baltimore, Maryland

Introduction by
Louis Finkelstein

KTAV PUBLISHING HOUSE, INC.
NEW YORK, NEW YORK
1975

Library of Congress Cataloging in Publication Data

Goldman, Israel M.   1904-
   Lifelong learning among Jews.

   Bibliography: p.
   1. Jewish learning and scholarship—History. 2. Jewish
religious education of adults—History. 3. Jews—Intellectual life—History. I. Title.
DS113.G75   296'.07   75-19216
ISBN 0-87068-291-1

PRINTED IN THE UNITED STATES OF AMERICA

DEDICATED
TO MY BELOVED WIFE
MILDRED

לאשתי האהובה
רחל מלכה שתחי׳

תנו לה מפרי ידיה – בזכירת ישועתה
"Give her of the fruit of her hands" ——
by ever-recalling her devoted helpfulness

ויהללוה בשערים מעשיה – בבתי כנסיות ובבתי מדרשים

"and let her works praise her in the gates" ——
because of her labors in the synagogue
and in the halls of Jewish learning

(Yalkut ha-Makhiri on Proverbs 31:31)

v

INTRODUCTION

In this extraordinarily erudite volume, Dr. Israel M. Goldman, my colleague and friend, has given the reader a most delightful, scholarly, and comprehensive account of the role which study played in adult life among Jews across the ages. With amazing assiduity and care, he has sought out the most recondite sources to complete his picture of the historical scene of adult Jews giving their best hours to the study of Torah under all the varied conditions to which Jews have been exposed through the centuries. He has not only brought together all the material available in published books, but has gone to manuscript sources in order to complete the record. With all this material in hand, we are ready, for the first time, to appreciate what Jewish learning meant for our ancestors, as it means for so many of us. From the time we were commanded that "these words which I command thee this day shall be on thy heart (Deut. 6:6)," until the present, adult Jewish education has played a central role, not only in the Jewish religion, but in Jewish life.

The persistence of study of Torah among adults in American Jewish communities is one of the most promising signs for the future of the Jewish tradition. Individuals, who turn to synagogue groups for the pursuit of knowledge of Judaism, often astonish those who knew them in their youth by their gradually acquired thorough mastery of ancient Jewish texts and Jewish history. I have known men and women who in their childhood and youth showed little interest in Jewish studies, and therefore knew comparatively little; and when I met them thereafter in their forties and fifties, I discovered that they had mastered many advanced works, and were at home in Jewish literature, religion and history.

Dr. Israel M. Goldman was one of the great pioneers who made adult Jewish education one of his main concerns. Wherever he served, the synagogue became an adult extension University of Judaism. It was therefore to him that I turned in 1940 with the request that he organize a National Academy for Adult Jewish Studies to help encourage the growth of Jewish study groups in the various communities across the United States and Canada, to discover means for improving the methods used in such groups when necessary, and to give the individual members of each group a sense of being in the mainstream (as Dr. Cyrus Adler used to call it), of the Jewish tradition.

Busy as he was, bearing the load of work of a large congregation which he led with remarkable efficiency, he undertook the assignment without hesitation. He bore the additional burdens placed on him with remarkable patience, and with remarkable results. Under his guidance, the National Academy for Adult Jewish Studies became a significant factor in the lives of men and women throughout the continent, as it still remains.

It is difficult to overestimate the debt which American Jewry owes him for his unstinting labors in this field. Tirelessly, he labored to help raise the standards of adult Jewish education in the United States and Canada, and to stimulate the organization of new Adult Study groups, where they had not previously existed. He thus takes a prominent place in the long chain of Jewish scholars, from Hillel until our own time, who made adult study groups one of the principal aims of their lives.

I believe that it was his experience as builder and Director of the National Academy for Adult Jewish Studies which led him to study with such loving care its antecedents in earlier ages; and that study led to his writing this magnificent and important volume, itself a significant contribution to the field of adult Jewish studies.

As one peruses this volume, one is filled with new respect for the Jewish tradition. One begins to appreciate what it was that helped maintain the faith of the Jews in the long dark ages of persecution to which they were exposed. How is one to understand a people, whose members after a day's manual labor, weary beyond words, would rush to the House of Study, to concentrate on so profound a discipline as the Talmud? To study the Talmud is not easier than to study the philosophy of Spinoza. No one expects a poor day laborer when he comes home from his task to attend classes in philosophy or higher mathematics. But Jewish leaders did expect and demand of their followers that they do what is the equivalent of exactly that. The measure of their success is reflected in the survival of Judaism until our time.

To have transplanted into America this vigorous dedication was almost a miracle. And it is a joy to be associated with a work which records with such clarity the antecedents of this achievement, together with some aspects of the achievement itself.

Louis Finkelstein
Chancellor Emeritus
Jewish Theological Seminary of America

CONTENTS

The schedule of a daily study program for morning, afternoon, and night. It was found on the title page of an old Hebrew Bible. (See pages XVIII-XIX.) Courtesy of YIVO Institute for Jewish Research.

PREFACE

Throughout the ages the Jewish people have been so engrossed in life-long learning that they had no time to write the history of Jewish education. This is true of Jewish education on every level, but especially of adult Jewish education.

It is only in the last century that studies in the history of Jewish education began to appear. The earliest investigations deal exclusively with the biblical and talmudic periods. Since 1872, as the bibliography at the end of this volume will show, no less than thirty-five books in the German, French, English, and Hebrew languages have presented the story of Jewish education during the patriarchal, biblical, tannaitic, and talmudic eras. One scholar, Dr. Sh. Y. Tscharno, carried the story forward into the geonic period up to about the year 1000 C.E.[1] The first student of the subject to go beyond the first millennium of the Common Era was Dr. Moritz Guedemann, the famous chief rabbi of Vienna, who devoted three volumes to the history of Jewish education during the Middle Ages. This great classic, written in German and published in 1888, is titled *Geschichte des Erziehungwesens und der Kultur der Abendländischen Juden während des Mittelalters*.[2] It was translated into Hebrew in 1896. The next great step in writing the history of Jewish education was taken by Professor Simhah Asaf of the Hebrew University, who in 1925 published his monumental four-volume work in Hebrew. Its much broader and fuller scope is indicated in its title, as translated into English: "Sources for the History of Jewish Education from the Beginning of the Jewish Middle Ages to the Haskalah Period." [3] This brings the history of Jewish education down to the nineteenth century. Professor Asaf builds on the work of Dr. Guedemann but goes far beyond it, covering a longer span of time and researching a vaster number of sources. Subsequently, there also appeared specialized and limited studies in this field for Central Europe from the sixteenth to the eighteenth centuries,[4] and for Eastern Europe in the nineteenth and twentieth centuries.[5] Finally, one of the most eminent Jewish educators our own time, Professor Zevi Scharfstein, completed the story of Jewish education in a great three-volume work in Hebrew, which begins with the Haskalah and concludes with the year 1914.[6]

Despite the fact that learning among adults plays so central a role in all of Jewish history, everything that has been written on the history of Jewish education in the last century deals almost entirely with education for children and with learning on the elementary level. Not a single chapter in any of the books referred to above deals exclusively with adult Jewish education. To be sure, there are occasional references to Jewish learning among grown-up Jews, but the subject is not treated as unified and distinct. It is absolutely amazing that this vast and vital subject was treated only in a single eighteen-page pamphlet, the late Rabbi Hyman G. Enelow's *Adult Education in Judaism,* which was published in 1927.

Thus the present volume is the first study devoted exclusively to the fascinating and inspiring story of Jewish learning among adult Jews. Its comprehensive scope is reflected in its title: *Lifelong Learning among Jews: Adult Education in Judaism from Bible Times to the Twentieth Century.*

I have been motivated to write this book by the conviction of a lifetime that American education in general, and Jewish education in America in particular, has been upside down. We have concentrated on the child and forgotten the adult. We have made education almost entirely child-centered. We have been misguided by such slogans as "Youth is the hope of the future!" or "You, boys and girls, will build the world of tomorrow!" These may be beautiful sentiments, but alas, they are not true. This has been our great mistake. We started at the wrong end of the educational process.

It is only recently that American education has awakened with a start to the fact that the affairs of this world are, after all, in the keeping of adults. If adults are ignorant of the problems of the day or indifferent to their adequate solution, what chances are there for building a better future? The world may, as someone has said, "move forward on the feet of little children," but the hands of adults guide those feet. What is more, the world in which the steps are taken is adult-administered, adult-controlled, and adult-manipulated. The shock of this realization has brought into being a strong and growing movement for adult education. The adult has been rediscovered. Education is no longer confined to the short years of childhood. The educational process is being extended beyond youth into the farthest reaches of adult life. Yes, youth can be the hope of the world but only as adults will allow it!

All this has a very direct bearing on American-Jewish life, on synagogal activities, and on Jewish educational programs. In our Jewish tradition, the program of education has always had balance. It was never allowed to develop "upside down." Professor Louis Ginzberg reminds us in one of his famous essays: "In the olden time the opinion prevailed that the fathers were to be educated first and then the children, not in the reverse order." [7]

But we Jews in America have forgotten this vital tradition of our fathers. We have permitted ourselves to be swept along by the currents of prevailing philosophies and practices. We have concentrated as much as we could on the education of childhood. We openly declared that we were building our synagogues "for the sake of our children." The educational activities in our synagogues became exclusively child-centered. This is Jewish education upside down. We have neglected and forgotten the Jewish adult. We have not provided for keeping the mind and interest of the mature Jew and Jewess keyed up to an awareness and understanding of the crying needs of the hour.

Fortunately, the tide has turned. We have noted our mistakes. We are moving in new directions. The Jewish adult and his needs have been rediscovered. There is emerging a nationwide adult Jewish education movement whose purpose it is to inform, to enlighten, to clarify the minds of American Jews, and as a result also to discipline their wills for the work that lies ahead. Many national Jewish organizations, many Jewish communal institutions, and many synagogues have already joined in this great effort of Jewish awakening, and many more will follow their example. The synagogue is at last regaining its educational equilibrium. It is no longer exclusively child-centered. It is fast becoming adult-centered. Many congregations have established institutes or schools of Jewish studies for adults even as there exist religious schools for children and educational programs for young people. If the education of the children of the modern synagogue is the cornerstone, the education of the adult is becoming the capstone.

It is my hope that this book, which presents such a glorious and glowing panorama of the love of learning in the millennial history of our people, will help American Jewry rediscover and revitalize our ancient tradition of lifelong learning. Among the many hundreds of sources I went to, in order to gather material for this study, two especially moving items exemplified for me the central implications of the subject treated in these pages.

The first item is an old Hebrew Bible in the library of the YIVO Institute for Jewish Research in New York City. It came from a Jewish home in

Czernowitz in Rumania. The title page of this old Bible is missing, so it is impossible to ascertain the date of publication, but the fly-leaf brought tears of pride to my eyes. On it an unknown, average Jew in Eastern Europe had written by hand the schedule of his daily study program. Regrettably, we know nothing about the author of this program, except that he had a vision of life and an order of living in which Torah-study occupied the central place. This is patent. His day was long—as a matter of fact it began at midnight—and every moment was put to excellent use. It went like this:

In the Morning

At midnight: *Reshit Hokhmah,* [a moralistic work by Moses de Vidas, first published in Venice, 1579, and frequently reprinted]; Mishnah; *Shaarei Zion* [a compilation of special midnight prayers]; Psalms; *Maamadot* [a compilation of selections from the Bible and Talmud for daily recitation]; *Tzetel Katan* [a list of moral admonitions for daily perusal compiled by Rabbi Zevi Hirsh Elimelekh of Dynow]; *Orhot Hayyim* [ethical precepts]; prayers from the book *Avodat ha-Kodesh;* the Epistle of Nahmanides; *Shulhan Arukh, Orah Hayyim* [the daily duties of the Jew].

At the Table

Scripture, *Midrash Rabbah* and *Midrash Tanhuma* [homilectic compilations], various compilations of Aggadah [legends].

Before Noon

Talmud, *Shulhan Arukh, Yoreh Deah* [instruction on things forbidden and permitted], one sugyah [topic of discussion] a week.

Afternoon

Talmud, *Shulhan Arukh, Hoshen Mishpat* [civil jurisprudence] and *Even ha-Ezer* [laws regulating family life].

After Evening Prayers

Responsa, former and latter.; *Divre ha-Geonim* [a medieval commentary on Job]. *Nahalat Shivah* [a book dealing with the correct forms of marriage certificates, bills of divorce, and other ritual documents].

Keset Sofer [laws governing the writing of a Scroll of the Torah], *Brit Avot* [laws of circumcision].

On the Sabbath

The tractate Shabbat, the laws of Shabbath; *Shulhan Arukh.*

May the example of this unknown and unsung hero of Jewish life cause us to emulate his habit of setting aside fixed periods of time for Jewish study.

The second item is an old manuscript in the library of the Jewish Theological Seminary—the *pinkas,* or minute-book, of the Hevrah Aggadta (Society for the Study of Jewish Lore and Legend) in the city of Bosk in Russia. I came upon a page in this manuscript that contains a description of a siyyum—a feast celebrating both the completion and the commencement of a planned program of Jewish study. These words are just as thrilling today as they were when first recorded more than 130 years ago. Here is what I read:

On Tuesday, the fifth of Nisan 5603 [1843] there was held a great feast by the Hevrah Aggadata. It was both a feast and a festival, and we rejoiced at the *simhah shel mitzvah* that God has aided us to study and to complete the Aggadata. May God further help us to study and to teach, to observe and to do. We celebrated for two whole days. On Tuesday we finished the Aggadata, and we made a party and a festive day. We invited 123 guests, not counting the musicians and the fifteen beadles. Four different and elaborate courses were served. The food was so plentiful that it was left over on the plates. If a man had not eaten in three days, he had more than enough to eat. The musicians were stationed in the women's gallery of the synagogue. Our joy was exceedingly great. Wine poured like water—some pouring it into their throats and others on the floor. On Wednesday we began anew the study of the Aggadata, and we obligated ourselves to study the *Ein Yaakov.* On that day, too, we made a great feast. The people made merry with trumpets and violins until it seemed the earth would split with the noise. The people who stood outside envied us our joy and our *simhah shel mitzvah.*

It is my hope and my belief that we can and must recapture this festive rejoicing, this glowing tradition, in modern form, for American Jewish life today and tomorrow.

ACKNOWLEDGMENTS

1.

It is with profound feelings of admiration and affection that I express my heartfelt gratitude to Dr. Louis Finkelstein, the illustrious and revered Chancellor Emeritus of the Jewish Theological Seminary of America, for his kindness in writing the gracious introduction to this book. He has been my teacher and friend from the days of my youth, as well as my mentor and guide in the course of my rabbinic career.

Dr. Finkelstein, throughout his life, has exemplified the ideals of life-long learning which this book endeavors to expound. From his boyhood, while walking home from high school, he would rehearse and memorize the page of the Talmud he had studied early that morning, thus keeping the commandment: "And these words, which I command thee this day, shall be upon thine heart . . . when thou walkest by the way" (Deut. 6:6–7). Throughout his life up to the present, when, thank God, he is blessed with years of special strength, Dr. Finkelstein has become the living exemplar of the biblical admonition: "The Book of this Torah shall not depart out of thy mouth, but thou shalt meditate therein day and night" (Josh. 1:8). In this respect, as in many others, he has been to me, and to generation after generation of his disciples, a noble model and a source of inspiration. He has, as a brilliant scholar and gifted teacher, devoted his life not only to learning but also to teaching, thereby fulfilling the rabbinic command "to raise up many disciples" (Avot 2:2). Dr. Finkelstein believes, with the great Rabbi Akiba, about whom he has written with such creative insight and sound wisdom, that "even if one has raised many disciples in youth, one must continue to do so even in old age" (Tanhuma, Haye, Sarah 6). The hundreds of disciples of Dr. Finkelstein's, as a mark of respect and love for him, consider it a privilege and an honor to heed the counsel of the Jewish sages to "let reverence for thy Master be like the reverence for Heaven" (Avot 4:15).

2.

For material assistance in the publication of this volume, I want to express my gratitude to the Chizuk Amuno Congregation Publication Fund, and especially to the following, who have generously become the special patrons of this book: Mr. and Mrs. Fred M. Bart, Mr. and Mrs. Allan L. Berman, Mr. Herman Cohen, Mr. Isaac C. Rosenthal, Mr. Isaac H. Taylor, all of Baltimore; Mr. and Mrs. Max Alperin, of Providence, Rhode Island; and Mr. and Mrs. Edward Goldberger, of New York City.

3.

Acknowledgement is herewith gratefully made to the following publishers and authors who have kindly granted permission to use the material indicated:

Bloch Publishing Company for selections from the *Mishneh Torah of Maimonides,* translated and edited by Moses Hyamson.

Commentary, published by the American Jewish Committee, for quotations from: "Learning Among the Hebrews" by Felix Giovanelli, June 1952, vol. 13, no. 6; "Rules for the House of Study" by Nahum N. Glatzer, May 1951, vol. 11, no. 5; and "An Aristocracy of Learning" by Shlomo Katz, June 1947, vol. 3, no. 6.

The Jewish Publication Society of America for quotations from *Morning Stars* by Zalman Shazar and *My Jewish Roots* by Solomon Simon.

Jewish Education, published by the National Council for Jewish Education, for selections from "The Traditional Code of Jewish Education" by David De Sola Pool, May 1945, vol. 16, no. 3.

Rhode Island Jewish Herald for quotations from "A Memorial to Rabbi Rabinowitz" by Beryl Segal, October 15, 1948.

Rhode Island Jewish Historical Notes, published by the Rhode Island Jewish Historical Association, for quotations from "The Pinkas" by Bernard Segal, June 1955, vol. 1, no. 3.

A Word About Transliteration

It is important to note that in the matter of Hebrew transliteration, I have followed the usage in the new *Encyclopedia Judaica.* However, when quoting from the writings of other authors, I have used the Hebrew transliterations found in the sources quoted.

CHAPTER

I

IN BIBLICAL TIMES

Beginning in biblical times, going back to the days of Moses, the commandment of God imposed the duty of constant study upon every adult Jew. In the great passage from the Shema, read twice daily in our prayers, we come upon the divine behest: "And these words, which I command thee this day, shall be upon thy heart; and thou shalt teach them diligently unto thy children, and *shalt talk of them* when thou sittest in thy house, and when thou walkest by the way, and when thou liest down, and when thou risest up" (Deut. 7:6–7).[1] The Torah thus laid the foundations for mass education in Judaism. One of the sages of the Talmud, in order to make sure the implications of this passage are abundantly clear, specifically reminds us that the words "and shalt talk of them" mean: "make these words the subject of study daily during fixed periods of time." [2] The rabbis also interpret the words "and thou shalt teach them to your children" to mean that every male adult is obligated to study Torah in order to teach it to his sons.[3] In the days of Joshua, this commandment was repeated in these strong words: "This book of the law shall not depart out of thy mouth, but thou shalt meditate therein day and night" (Josh. 1:8).

(1) MOSES: THE FATHER OF JEWISH LEARNING

Tradition has it that Moses was the father of adult education, for we read in the Bible: "And Moses assembled all the congregation of the children of Israel . . ." (Exod. 35:1). In commenting on this verse, the rabbis say: "This is to teach us that the Holy One, blessed be He, said to Moses:

1

'Gather large congregations and speak before them about the laws of the Sabbath, so that the leaders of future generations may follow your example and gather congregations every Sabbath in the houses of study to teach unto Israel the words of the Torah.' " [4]

That the adult was the educational concern of Judaism is further evidenced by the Mosaic ordinance requiring that the people be assembled every seven years in order to receive instruction in the words of the Torah:

> And Moses wrote this law, and delivered it unto the priests the sons of Levi, that bore the ark of the covenant of the Lord, and unto all the elders of Israel. And Moses commanded them saying: "At the end of every seven years, in the feast of Tabernacles, when all Israel is come to appear before the Lord thy God in the place which He shall choose, thou shalt read this law before all Israel in their hearing. *Assemble the people, the men and the women and the little ones . . . that they may hear and that they may learn . . .*" [Deut. 31:9–12]

It is significant that "the men and the women" are mentioned first as the object of this educational endeavor. It is to the adults that the teachers of the people first address themselves.

With this command to "assemble the people"—*Hakhel et ha-am,* Moses established an educational institution that endured from his time down to the end of the Second Hebrew Commonwealth—a period of over three thousand years. While the Bible itself does not offer details as to the way in which this septennial national assembly for Torah was celebrated, many fascinating features of its observance are afforded us in postbiblical literature.[5] It is also described by Josephus,[6] and is dealt with by Maimonides[7] and by many other writers down to our own time.[8] Finally, with the approval of the late chief rabbis Abraham Isaac Kook and Isaac Halevi Herzog, the institution of *Hakhel* was revised and renewed in Jerusalem during the week of Sukkot, 1946, and continued with the establishment of the State of Israel.[9]

(2) PRIESTS, LEVITES, AND PROPHETS AS TEACHERS OF THE PEOPLE

Who were the teachers of "the men and the women" in the days of Moses? Who were the pioneer educational agents that gave instruction to the mature minds of the nation? The biblical passage quoted above points to the answer. They were the priests, the Levites, and the elders of Israel. In the Bible, the instruction of the people in the Torah is spoken of as an office of the priesthood. "They [the priests] shall teach Jacob Thine ordinances, and Israel Thy law" (Deut. 33:10). When the prophet Jeremiah chastises the priests of his day for neglect of duty, he declares: "The priests said not: 'Where is the Lord?' And they that handle the law knew me not" (Jer. 2:8). The prophet Malachi holds aloft the ideal of the priesthood, stating that "the priest's lips should keep knowledge, and they should seek the law at his mouth; for he is the messenger of the Lord of hosts" (Mal. 2:7). The masses of the people regarded the priest as a teacher. This is indicated by their assertion, in the days of Jeremiah, that "instruction shall not perish from the priest" (Jer. 18:18),[10] and by Azariah's telling King Asa that "now for long seasons Israel was without the true God, and without a teaching priest" (2 Chron. 15:3).

The priests, most likely, instructed the people in the parts of the Torah that dealt with religious ritual. It was the task of the Levites, however, to expound the Torah in its more general aspects. Thus, the Bible chronicles the appointment by King Jehoshaphat of an education commission consisting of princes and Levites who "taught in Judah, having the book of the law of the Lord with them; and they went about throughout all the cities of Judah and taught among the people" (2 Chron. 17:7-9). In the days of King Josiah, the Levites were also the teachers of the people and the expounders of the Torah, for the Bible tells us: "And he [the king] said unto the Levites that taught all Israel . . ." (2 Chron. 35:3). This was true in the time of the First Temple. But the role of the Levites as teachers grew to even greater proportions in the period of the Second Temple. In the days of Ezra and Nehemiah the Levites are described as being the ones who "caused the people to understand the Law" (Neh. 8:7). When Ezra read the Torah to the people, it was the Levites who taught its contents to the adults. Let that stirring scene come to us through the words of the Bible narrative:

And when the seventh month was come, and the children of Israel were in their cities, all the people gathered themselves together as one man into the broad place that was before the water gate; and they spoke unto Ezra the scribe to bring the book of the Law of Moses, which the Lord had commanded to Israel. And Ezra the priest brought the Law before the congregation, *both men and women.* . . . And Ezra the scribe stood upon a pulpit of wood, which they had made for the purpose. . . .

And Ezra opened the book in the sight of all the people—for he was
above all the people—and when he opened it, all the people stood up
. . . the Levites caused the people to understand the Law . . . and they
read in the book, in the Law of God, distinctly; and they gave the sense,
and caused them to understand the reading. [Neh. 8:1–8]

According to the chronicler, the Levites also served as scribes and thus
helped to preserve and disseminate the sacred word (2 Chron. 34:13).

In the development of Judaism, the figure of the prophet was destined
to tower above both priest and Levite as the religious teacher of adults.
The prophet's life was sacrificially dedicated to the high task of spreading
and deepening the divine education of the people. The first and greatest of
the prophets is known to Jewish history as "Mosheh Rabenu"—"Moses
Our Teacher." In his farewell addresses to his people, before his death,
Moses reviews the underlying purpose of his life: "Behold, I have taught you
statutes and ordinances even as the Lord my God commanded me" (Deut.
4:5). In the classic period of Hebrew prophecy, these great teachers of
Judaism were fully aware of their prime role as teachers. Thus Hosea
exclaims: "My people perish for lack of knowledge" (Hos. 4:6), while
Isaiah opens his majestic arraignment of Israel with the charge: "Israel
doth not know, my people doth not consider" (Isa. 1:3). This is the usual
translation of Isaiah's words, but it does not do full justice to his meaning.
For it is well to note that the Hebrew verb *hitbonan* is grammatically in
the hitpael form, and therefore the passage means: "my people doth not
understand itself." In other words, the Jew can only know himself through
knowledge of the Torah. Isaiah recognizes the prime importance of instructing the elders of his people when he cries out: "Whom shall one
teach knowledge? And whom shall one make to understand the message?
Them that are weaned from the milk, them that are drawn from the
breasts?" (Isa. 28:9). Jeremiah is consecrated to prophecy when God
tells him: "Behold, I have put My words in thy mouth" (Jer. 1:9).
Ezekiel is commissioned by God to "speak My words unto them, whether
they will hear or whether they will forbear" (Ezek. 2:7). Ezekiel was not
only the teacher of the priestly class, to whom he taught their priestly
duties in preparation for the Restoration of Zion, but he also propagated
new theological and messianic concepts to help the people endure the
Exile and get ready for the Return (Ezek., chaps. 18, 33, 36, 37). The
prophecy of the Second Isaiah envisages a future when "all thy children
shall be taught of the Lord" (Isa. 54:13). The prophet believes it is his

duty to hasten such a day, and therefore: "The Lord hath given me the tongue of them that are taught" (Isa. 50:4). The very last of the prophets, Malachi, summarizes this prophetic burden in his admonishment: "Remember ye the Law of Moses My servant, which I commanded unto him in Horeb for all Israel" (Mal. 3:22).

These divinely inspired teachers, unique in the history of mankind, addressed their words to the grown-up men and women of their respective generations—as indeed to those of all generations—interpreting the Word of God and translating it into practical terms of life—both private and national.

While the priests and Levites taught, for the most part, in the Tent of Meeting in the wilderness, and later in the Temple in Jerusalem, the prophets taught in private assemblies, in public forums, and even in their own humble homes. Each of these places of instruction was primarily a place of assembly for adults. It is especially significant that the exiles of the Babylonian captivity regularly gathered in the homes of the prophets to be instructed and inspired. In all likelihood the institution of the synagogue emerged from these antecedents. In such gatherings, states Professor Moore:

We may imagine them listening to the words of a living prophet like Ezekiel [8:1, 14:1, 20:1] or the author of Isaiah 40 ff., or reading the words of older prophets; confessing the sins which had brought this judgment upon the nation and beseeching the return of God's favor in such penitential prayers as ere long became an established type in Hebrew literature, or in poetical compositions of similar content such as are found in the Book of Lamentations and in the Psalter.[11]

Thus we can see that throughout the biblical period, Judaism and its great teachers sought to educate the whole people during the whole of their lives in the principles and practices of Jewish life. That the people responded to these educational endeavors is evidenced by the popular literature of the times. The poetry of the psalmists expresses, no doubt, the attitudes and feelings of many of its contemporaries when it exclaims rhapsodically:

Oh how I love Thy Torah!
It is my meditation all the day [Ps. 119:97]

and when it explains the satisfactions of Jewish study in words like these:

Happy is the man whose delight is in the Torah of
God, and in His Torah doth he meditate day and night. [Ps. 1:1–2]

Great peace have they that love Thy Torah; and
there is no stumbling for them. [Ps. 119:165]

and when it speaks of the rewards of religious knowledge in such lines as:

Unless Thy Torah had been my delight,
I should have perished in my affliction. [Ps. 119:92]

The authors of the Wisdom Literature, addressing themselves to the practical needs of everyday life, counsel their readers:

Happy is the man that findeth wisdom,
And the man that obtaineth understanding.

For the merchandise of it is better than the
merchandise of silver,
And the gain thereof than fine gold.

She is more precious than rubies;
And all the things thou canst desire are not
to be compared unto her.

Length of days is in her right hand;
In her left hand are riches and honor.

Her ways are ways of pleasantness,
And all her paths are peace

She is a tree of life to them that lay hold upon her,
And happy is every one that holdeth her fast. [Prov. 3:13–18]

The same writers also comment on the moral influence of religious study:

They that forsake the Torah praise the wicked;
But such as keep the Torah contend with them. [Prov. 28:4]

From the very beginning, therefore, the Jewish ideal has been to en-lighten and inform the mind of every Jew at every stage of his life in the teachings and observances of his religious culture. Such a practice has no parallel among the peoples of the ancient world, as indeed it has few counterparts in the modern world. Among the nations of antiquity, knowl-edge of the gods and their teachings was scrupulously kept from the masses. It was reserved for the priesthood or for ecclesiastical hierarchies. The people at large were kept in ignorance and darkness. Jewish life is, therefore, unique from the very dawn of its history in that the revelations of God, as contained in the sacred Scriptures, were made the possession of the whole people, whose duty it was, for the sake of their own well-being and for the sake of the welfare of the nation, to study it the whole of their lives. Judaism was to be the heritage of every Jew. This is precisely the sense of the following biblical verse, which is included in our daily morn-ing prayers and is especially taught to children for them to recite upon rising:

Moses commanded us a Torah,
An inheritance of the congregation of Jacob. [Deut. 33:4]

The historian of Jewish antiquity, Josephus, writing in the first century of the common era, truly summarized the place of adult learning in the biblical period of Jewish history:

He [Moses] left no pretext for ignorance; he appointed the Torah to be the most excellent and necessary form of instruction, not that it should be heard once for all or twice or on several occasions, but that every week men should desert their other occupations and assemble to listen to the Torah and to obtain a thorough and accurate knowledge of it, a practice all other legislators seem to have neglected.[12]

(3) BIBLE PERSONALITIES AS STUDENTS OF THE TORAH

It is both interesting and important to note that the rabbis, in their interpretations of the Bible, ascribed the practice of studying the Torah to many biblical figures. They began with Adam, asserting that God had put him into the Garden of Eden "to dress it and to keep it" in order to afford him a means of studying the Torah and fulfilling its commandments.[13] Abraham was portrayed as the head of an academy,[14] who commanded his children to study Torah.[15] He gave special instruction to his son Isaac,[16] who ultimately studied more Torah than Abraham.[17]

Abraham sent Isaac to study Torah at the academy of Shem and Eber. Why did he do this? A talmudic sage offers this explanation:

> It is to be compared to a woman who grows rich from plying her distaff. She says to herself: "Since this distaff has made me rich, it will never leave my hand." In the same way Abraham said to himself: "Everything I gained, I have gained only because I engaged in the study of Torah and in carrying out God's commandments. That is why I do not want such practice ever to leave my seed." [18]

Thereafter Isaac passed three years in the great study house of Shem and Eber.

Jacob followed his father, Isaac, in studying at this same academy,[19] and later he established his own academy.[20] Joseph also emulated the example of his father, Jacob, by frequenting the bet ha-midrash until the age of seventeen.[21] Joseph, in turn, became the teacher of his brothers[22] and kept exhorting them ever to study the Torah.[23]

In the minds of the rabbis, Moses stands supreme among all Bible personalities in his dedication to the study and teaching of Torah. Moses is depicted as having spent the entire forty days in heaven studying the Torah—both the Written Law and the Oral Law. The program of study for the forty days was so planned that God studied the written teachings with him by day and the oral by night. In this way, Moses was enabled to distinguish between night and day, for in heaven "the night shineth as the day." [24] Another tradition states that Moses learned Torah by day and repeated it at night.[25] Moses studied in order to teach,[26] so he read the whole Torah aloud to the Jewish people,[27] he expounded it in seventy languages,[28] he instructed Israel in the laws of Judaism,[29] and he also instituted the practice of preaching in the synagogue.[30] Moses was assisted in spreading the Torah by his brother, Aaron. We are told that "Aaron would go from house to house, and wherever he found one who did not know how to recite the Shema, he taught him the Shema; if one did not know how to pray, he taught him to pray; and if he found one who was not capable of penetrating the study of the Torah, he initiated him into

CHAPTER

II

THE SYNAGOGUE AS SCHOOL OF INSTRUCTION

With this unique heritage, which for a thousand years had sought to make Jewish knowledge "the inheritance of the congregation of Jacob" (Deut. 33:4), it was inevitable that when the synagogue emerged upon the Jewish scene, it would become a school for adults, an institute of religious instruction.

(1) KNOW BEFORE WHOM THOU STANDEST

The tradition of synagogal architecture to this very day prescribes that there be engraved above the holy ark, which is the repository of the sacred Torah scrolls, the talmudic injunction: "Know Before Whom Thou Standest." [1] This admonition greets the worshipper as he enters the synagogue. It looks down at him during his entire stay in the sacred precincts of the House of God. The key word in this message is *know*. The Jew must know! Without knowledge he cannot truly worship God. Without mastering the contents of his people's religious literature, he cannot possibly lead the Jewish good life. From its very beginnings, therefore, one of the supreme functions of the synagogue was to serve not only as a house of prayer but also as a school of instruction.

(2) THE ORIGIN OF THE SYNAGOGUE

It is altogether likely that the synagogue owes its very origin to places of study. The prayer-meetings of the pre-exilic prophets—that is, about the end of the seventh century[2]—and more certainly the assemblies held in

11

the homes of the prophets during the Babylonian Exile—which are alluded to in the writings of the prophet of the exile, Ezekiel (8:1, 14:1, 20:1)— are examples of the meetings for instruction and worship that gradually developed into the synagogue. During the five centuries that followed the Exile, embracing the entire period of the Second Hebrew Commonwealth (515 B.C.E.–70 C.E.), the synagogue grew more and more into an institution of universal public learning. It finally became a veritable people's university.

This development did not come about accidentally. In its unique aim for the religious education of the whole people, and in the special methods it devised for the achievement of that aim, we can see that the synagogue was very conscious of the goal of making "all its children taught of the Lord" (Isa. 54:13). No doubt the greatest impetus in this direction was given to the synagogue by the Pharisees in the second century before the common era. The Pharisees, representing the popular masses and preaching Jewish loyalty, saw in the Maccabean struggle of their day a challenge "to do something for the Lord" (Ps. 119:126). The armies of the Syrian Greeks were not the only threat to Jewish survival; indeed, even more dangerous was the assimilationary trend toward Hellenism, which was rotting the very vitals of Jewish life. Jews were nullifying God's law. Men in high places were guilty of apostasy. Multitudes, lured by the new cult and its way of life, became indifferent to Judaism and to the conduct it prescribed. The Pharisees realized that nothing was more urgent than to inculcate and confirm religious loyalty. If the Hellenistic menace was to be combatted and the Jewish heritage perpetuated, it was imperative for the people to understand Judaism, appreciate its incomparable worth, and devote themselves to its distinctive observances. Methodical instruction in the Torah would be the foundation of everything else, and the synagogue, which combined worship with knowledge, was an institution eminently suited for attaining these ends. The Pharisees, therefore, took hold of the synagogue, used it as a forum to spread their doctrines,[3] and adapted it more completely to the ends of religious education. The slogan of the Maccabees, "Who is like unto Thee, O Lord, among the mighty ones!" (Exod. 15:11), and the cry of Mattathias, "Who is unto the Lord, come unto me!" (Exod. 32:16), are illustrative of the national and religious zeal that were spread among the people. The Pharisees stirred up a religious revival. They brought about a "back-to-the-synagogue movement" whose chief exhortation may well have been: "Back to the Torah!" Through such conditions in Jewish history, and through such insight and foresight of Jewish leadership, did the synagogue grow as the house of instruction in Jewish life.[4]

(3) THE PEDAGOGUES OF THE SYNAGOGUE INSTITUTE TORAH READING

The public reading of the Torah was the synagogue's principal pedagogic technique for achieving its goal of bringing the Jewish heritage nearer and nearer to each individual in the nation throughout his entire life. While it is not possible to state with exactness when this institution arose, yet of this we are certain: the *migdal etz*—"the turret of wood"—from which Ezra the Scribe, in the fourth century before the common era, read the Torah to the people (Neh. 8:4), has survived down to our own times as the central architectural feature of every synagogue edifice. In the more Orthodox synagogues, the wooden turret is represented by the platform in the middle of the synagogue on which the reading desk stands. In modernized congregations, it has been pushed forward closer to the ark or combined with the pulpilt. But no matter where it is situated, it occupies a place of the utmost prominence, and from it, as in the days of Ezra, the Torah is read "in the presence of the men and the women and of those that could understand" (Neh. 8:3).

In the days of Ezra, public reading of the Scriptures was already an established institution and a characteristic feature of the synagogue service. Jewish tradition ascribes the beginning of this practice to Moses. According to the rabbis, it was the great lawgiver himself who ordained that portions of the Torah be read on Sabbaths.[5]

> The Holy One, blessed be He, said to Moses, "Assemble the people in congregations and expound the Torah to them in public that future generations may learn from you to assemble in congregations every Sabbath of the year for instruction in the Torah, and that My great name shall be extolled among My children."[6]

Josephus, the first-century Jewish historian, reiterates this view:

> He [Moses] . . . appointed the Law to be the most excellent and necessary form of instruction, not that it should be heard once for all or twice or on several occasions, but that every week men should desert their other occupations and assemble to listen to the Law.[7]

In another of his writings, Josephus elaborates on the idea of the Sabbath as a day of study and reflection:

> And the seventh day we set apart from labour; it is dedicated to the learning of our customs and laws because we think it proper to reflect on them, as well as on any other good thing, in order that we may avoid all sin. If anyone therefore examine into our observances, he will find that they are good in themselves, and that they are also ancient.[8]

Philo, the first-century Alexandrian Jewish philosopher, states that Moses commanded the Jews to assemble on the seventh day, and being seated, to reverently and decorously listen to the Torah in order that they should not be ignorant of it. This was the practice in the Alexandrian synagogues of his own day, he says, and to demonstrate how the Hellenistic synagogue functioned as an institute of instruction in the Scriptures, he provides us with a brief description of the service. According to Philo, one of the priests who was present, or one of the elders, read the divine laws to the congregation and expounded them in details, continuing till some time in the afternoon; then the congregation dispersed, having acquired knowledge of the divine laws and making much progress in religion.[9] To quote his exact words:

> On the seventh day they all came together . . . and then the eldest of them, who has the most profound learning, comes forward and speaks with a steadfast look and with steadfast voice, with great powers of reasoning and great prudence, not making an exhibition of his oratorical powers like the rhetoricians of old or the sophists of the present day, but investigating with great pains and explaining with minute accuracy the precise meaning of the laws, which sits not indeed at the tips of their ears, but penetrates through the hearing into the soul and remains there lastingly.

In another work Philo writes:

> Innumerable schools of practical wisdom and self-control and manliness and uprightness and the other virtues are opened every seventh day in all cities. In these schools the people sit decorously, keeping silence and listening with the utmost attention out of a thirst for refreshing discourse, while one of the best qualified stands up and instructs them in

what is best and most conducive to welfare, things by which their whole
life may be made better.

The two comprehensive topics of these discourses are first, piety and
holiness toward God, and second, benevolence and uprightness toward
men.[10]

The use of the holy Sabbath day for purposes of study is further elaborated by Philo in his exposition of the meaning of the Fourth Commandment, "Observe the Sabbath day to keep it holy":

The fourth commandment has reference to the sacred seventh day, that
it may be passed in a sacred and holy manner . . . for the sacred historian says, that the world was created in six days, and that on the
seventh day God desisted from His works, and began to contemplate
what He had so beautifully created; therefore He commanded the beings
also who were destined to live in this state, to imitate God in this particular also . . . applying themselves to their works for six days, but
desisting from them and philosophizing on the seventh day, and devoting
their leisure to the contemplation of the things of nature, and consider-
ing whether in the preceding six days they have done anything which
has not been holy, bringing their conduct before the judgment-seat of
the soul, and subjecting it to a scrutiny, and making themselves give an
account of all the things which they have said or done. . . . Moreover,
the seventh day is also an example from which you may learn the pro-
priety of studying philosophy; as on that day, it is said, God beheld the
works which He had made; so that you also may yourself contemplate
the works of nature, and all the separate circumstances which contribute towards happiness.

Let us not pass by such a model of the most excellent ways of life,
the practical and the contemplative; but let us always keep our eyes
fixed upon it, and stamp a visible image and representation of it on our
own minds, making our mortal nature resemble, as far as possible, His
immortal one, in respect of saying and doing what is proper.[11]

Professor Wolfson, in his classic study of Philo, writes:

With the assumption that the study of the Law is a religious duty, evi-
dently prescribed in the Pentateuch, he [Philo] tries to find in the Pentateuch further specifications of this duty in the verse "and ye shall lay

up these my words in your heart and in your soul, and bind them for a sign upon your hand, that they may be movably before your eyes." The first of these three figurative expressions, he says, intimates that the learning of the Law is not to be a matter of mere hearing with the ear but rather one of understanding with the mind. The second expression intimates that learning must be reinforced by action. The third expression intimates that the laws which we learn must be a vital force within us, moving us to action. When a man has achieved this last stage of the knowledge of the Law, he says, "he is no longer to be ranked among learners and pupils but rather among teachers and instructors." [12]

The public Torah reading is also attested by the New Testament writers of the first and second centuries. The author of Acts, for instance, declares that Moses "had from generations of old, in every city, them that preach him, being read in the synagogue every Sabbath," and the New Testament writers often speak of the "teaching in the synagogue" as an established institution.[13]

Ezra increased the number of periods of Torah instruction to four per week. In addition to the readings on Sabbath mornings, he prescribed the reading on Monday and Thursday mornings and at the afternoon service on the Sabbath so that three days could never pass without some public instruction in the Torah.[14] Mondays and Thursdays were market days and also court days. The populace came into the towns to transact legal and other business, and while there they visited the synagogue. Thus these were deemed the best times to obtain audiences for short lessons from the Torah.[15] Torah readings were also ordained for the holy days, the festivals, the intermediate days of the festivals, and the new moons. By the time of the Mishnah there already existed a list of appointed lessons for many occasions of the year.[16] The custom of dividing the Pentateuch into separate sections for each of the Sabbaths of the synagogue year gradually spread; it was authoritatively established not much before the third century of the common era.[17]

The teachers of adults in the synagogue were not content merely to have the prescribed lessons read at the various religious services. What if the people did not understand the Hebrew of the Bible? Should they just sit and listen without grasping the subject of instruction? This became a serious problem, for there came a time, during the Second Commonwealth, when the language of the Bible ceased to be the spoken language of the Jewish people. In Palestine, in Babylonia, and in parts of Syria they spoke dialects of Aramaic. In Egypt, Aramaic eventually gave way to Greek, and in other countries the Jews spoke the languages of their surroundings. The pedagogues of the synagogue, though sharing with the people the greatest reverence for the "sacred tongue" of the Bible, nevertheless had no superstitions about it. Putting the need for understanding above sentiment, they acknowledged the role translation could play in achieving their purposes,[18] and to this end they created a new synagogue functionary, the meturgeman, "translator" or "interpreter." The meturgeman stood beside the Torah reader; as the latter read the Torah in Hebrew, he would translate the verses into Aramaic. The duty thus to translate and interpret the Torah lesson is traditionally derived from Ezra's reading of the Torah to the people, described in the eighth chapter of the Book of Nehemiah, and interpreted by the rabbis as having been accompanied by a translation into Aramaic.[19]

It became necessary to set up rules for the guidance of these translators. Any competent person, even a minor, might serve in this capacity. The Mishnah, in speaking of a person reading the Pentateuch or the Prophets to the congregation, says: "He gives out only one verse at a time to the meturgeman from the Law, and not more than three from the Prophets, provided the subject was the same." [20] The translation was supposed to be extempore; the interpreter listened to the reading of the verse or verses in the Hebrew and then gave the meaning to the congregation in their own language. He could prepare himself beforehand, but in the synagogue he must have nothing written before him.[21] This was to prevent the congregation from thinking the translation a kind of second Scripture. Oral tradition and sacred Scripture were to be sharply distinguished. In order to avoid any possible confusion, the reader was forbidden even to prompt the translator, lest some might think the translation was in the scroll before him. The object of this translation method was not to turn the Scripture word for word into another language, but to give the hearers an understanding of the sense. It was, therefore, a free interpretation rather than a literal translation.[22]

(4) THE SERMON AS AN EDUCATIVE METHOD

But the synagogue was to go even further in the fulfillment of its purpose as a school for adults. Opening the sacred books to all the people, reading from them, and translating them were merely the first steps toward a universal democratic education. For in the course of time there developed still another method of educating the people. This new instrument was the sermon, which became an established and independent part of the synagogue service. How early the sermon evolved in not definitely ascertained. Talmudic tradition ascribes it to the days of Moses, saying: "The sages teach that Moses already laid down the rule that they should inquire and preach about the business of the day; the rules of the Passover on the Passover, the rules of Pentecost on the Pentecost, the rules of the Feast [of Tabernacles] on the Feast." [23] We are on surer ground, however, when we see the sermon as a direct and natural outgrowth of the translation. The translation of the Torah lesson was given orally and in an interpretive vein. This public utterance developed into the sermon,[24] and the meturgeman, the translator, was supplemented or superseded by the maggid (oral teacher) and the darshan (preacher).[25]

If we carefully examine the sermon as an educative device of the synagogue, we shall see how it helped a whole people to study and think creatively. The original purpose of scriptural reading and scriptural translation was, as stated, to give the people a knowledge of the Law. This purpose could have been achieved merely by the public reading and its translation into the vernacular, but already in the earliest days the Levites were not content with proclaiming the Law to the people for their blind acceptance. They endeavored, as the text reads, "to cause the people to *understand* the Law" (Neh. 8:7), "and they read in the book, in the Law of God, *distinctly; and they gave the sense, and caused them to understand the reading*" (Neh. 8:8).[26] The first phrase, "they gave the sense," may refer to literal explication of the words of Scripture; the second phrase, "and caused them to understand," may refer to exposition in depth in order to reveal the great moral and religious truths implicit in the Torah reading. The latter was the homiletical enlargement, or the sermon as we know it today. Thus there emerged a new religious functionary in the synagogue, the darshan ("preacher"). Dr. Israel H. Levinthal, a master in the art of the classic Jewish sermon, states:

> The term used by the rabbis for preachers, *darshanim,* gives us an insight into the unique characteristics of the Jewish sermon. In the days of Ezra this method of preaching began. "And Ezra had set his heart *lidrosh,* to interpret the law of the Lord, and to do it, and to teach in Israel statutes and ordinances" [Ezra 7:10]. The word *lidrosh* is significant. Ezra not only read the words of Torah to the people, but also

interpreted them, to make the words relevant for the teaching and performance of God's Law.[27]

The importance of the sermon as an educative force, is fully developed by Dr. Solomon Freehof. He points out that, through the sermon, a new and higher turn was given to the entire instructional activity of the synagogue. Since the sermon was intended to make the people understand, sermonic interpretations were so couched and selected as to arouse active understanding. The primary purpose of the sermon had been to inform, but in time another purpose was added. The darshan undertook the task of awakening the mind of the average man and training him to think. To this end the preacher would distinctly and carefully read the scriptural verses, arousing congregational interest by pointing out difficulties and indicating contradictions between verses, then resolving them. To prevent the process of close reasoning from becoming too arduous for minds unaccustomed to such exertions, he gave his listeners frequent respites through anecdotes, fables, myths, and legends. But always, by every possible pedagogic device, the effort was made, week after week, to stimulate each individual not merely to listen to Scripture, but actively to meditate upon it and to try to derive the deeper meaning inherent in the texts.[28]

Thus the sermon developed active thinkers, and the synagogue service became an actual intellectual participation on the part of the worshipper. This is the highest form of democracy in religion, when the active intellectual effort of every individual is equally required. The spirit of intellectual democracy generated by the sermon is further evidenced by the fact that preaching in the synagogue was not the prerogative of any one individual or class. At least in the early days, almost anyone who had the gift of creative expression was permitted to preach. The New Testament describes the various apostles, who were all Jews, speaking and preaching in the synagogue. It is only natural, however, that in the course of time, those whose life study had been the Scriptures and the religion of their people should be found more profitable for instruction and preferred above all others.

We see, therefore, that from the very beginnings of its history the sermon was a pioneer achievement in the realm of democratic education; it intended not only to provide knowledge of the Law, but to awaken the hitherto slumbering intellect of man, to teach a whole people to study and to think creatively. Thus it helped develop a religious service unlike any service hitherto known. Now the worshipper was no mere spectator of ecclesiastical pageantry or religious ritual, no mere obedient conformant to laws pontifically promulgated, but an active, intelligent participant in the great personal and social quest of discovering and understanding the ways and the will of God.[29]

An appraisal of the sermon's place in the synagogue service, and the story of its development through the centuries, is a fascinating subject in itself. No less a scholar than Dr. Leopold Zunz, who about one hundred years ago founded the modern school of scientific research in all branches of Judaism, devoted a very weighty volume to his classic study of this problem—bearing the ponderous German title: *Die Gottesdienstliche Vorträge der Juden*. Only thirty years ago, in a very comprehensive volume in Hebrew entitled *Ha-Derashah be-Yisrael*, a Palestinian scholar, Rabbi Shimon Glicksberg, treated the history of sermonic literature from its beginnings to our own times. For our immediate purpose, however, we need not delve too deeply. It will suffice to dwell briefly on the development of the sermon through the first centuries of the common era.

During the tannaitic period, which embraces, roughly speaking, the first two centuries of the common era, the rabbis delivered sermons twice on every Sabbath, one at the Friday evening service or shortly thereafter, and the other at the Saturday morning service.[30] Public discourses were also held on holidays, dealing mainly with the laws pertaining to those occasions. Because of the many laws dealing with Passover, such discourses were given several times during the thirty-day period preceding that festival.[31]

By the very nature of the case, the sermon was the freest and most variable part of the service, and sermonic fashions changed greatly with changing times and circumstances. In early rabbinic literature we find no attempt to regulate either the matter or the method. This, however, is not to say that the sermon "just grew." It took definite shape and form and developed a classic structure all its own. We know that from the days of Ezra the Scribe to the times of Rav Ashi, the editor of the Babylonian Talmud, a period covering about eight hundred years, the preachers built their sermons entirely on verses from Scripture—either from the Pentateuch, the Prophets, or the Hagiographa.[32] After the compilation of the Talmud, the preachers found it necessary to base their discourses not only on scriptural verses but also on rabbinic dicta.[33]

We have seen how the synagogue, through the Torah reading, the practice of translating the reading into the vernacular, and the interpretations afforded by the sermon, served as a school of popular instruction for adults. In truth, the "turret of wood" erected in the days of Ezra, from which the Torah was read and expounded, has stood at the very center of our existence for twenty-four hundred years. The synagogue has benefited and enhanced Jewish life beyond all measure. The joyous and salutary effect Ezra's reading from the Torah had on the people standing before him is symbolic of the experience of the Jewish people through the centuries. "And all the people went their way to eat, and to drink, and to send portions, and to make great mirth, because they had understood the words that were declared unto them" (Neh. 8:12).

CHAPTER

III

"FROM STRENGTH TO STRENGTH": FROM SYNAGOGUE TO HOUSE OF STUDY

According to the rabbis, the biblical verse, "They shall go from strength to strength" (Ps. 84:8), refers to those "who go from the synagogue to the house of study—the bet ha-midrash." [1] Indeed, the Jewish thirst for knowledge and love of learning, coupled with the high religious-cultural requirements of the synagogue service, brought forth the second great institution for adult education in Jewish life—the bet ha-midrash. It arose in response to a compelling need. The synagogue provided an educational program, but its "curriculum" was broad and popular in character. Many in Israel hungered for a deeper and more profound approach to Jewish knowledge. This could only be obtained in a more specialized educational institution—the study house.

(1) THE EMERGENCE OF THE BET HA-MIDRASH

Just when the bet ha-midrash arose as a living force in Judaism is not easy to determine with exactness. Rabbinic tradition claims high antiquity for it, tracing its beginnings as far back as the patriarchal period and also to prophetic times. The rabbinic mind, reflecting a later mode of life, refers to a bet ha-midrash of Shem and Eber, which was attended by Isaac, occasionally also by Rebecca, and regularly by Jacob. [2] To the Jewish sages, Jacob is the exemplar of love of learning, and they interpret the words of the Bible, "and Jacob was a quiet man, dwelling in tents" (Gen. 25:27), as meaning that Jacob's abode was a house of study. [3] They also

23

claim that Jacob served as teacher in a house of instruction,[4] and some assert that he built a bet ha-midrash.[5] The rabbis also speak of a bet ha-midrash which Judah was sent to build for his father, Jacob, in Egypt,[6] and of a house of learning of Moses in which he and his brother, Aaron, taught the Law,[7] and in which Joshua arranged the chairs for the scholars.[8] Similarly the prophet Samuel had his *bet ulfana,* which is Aramaic for bet ha-midrash, in Ramah.[9] King Solomon built synagogues and houses of study,[10] and King Hezekiah furnished the oil for lamps to burn constantly in the synagogues and houses of study.[11] However, while the tradition of intense learning does go back to the earliest beginnings of Jewish nationhood, the emergence of the bet ha-midrash as a distinct institution must be looked for in a much later period in Jewish history.

The term *bet ha-midrash* literally means "house of study," or the place where students gather to listen to Midrash, the discourse on, or exposition of, the Torah. It is used in contradistinction to the term *bet ha-sefer,* the primary school which children under thirteen attend to learn the Scriptures. Thus it is said that Esau and Jacob went together to the bet ha-sefer until age thirteen, when they parted, the former entering the houses of idols and the latter the battei ha-midrashot.[12] Elsewhere we are told: "There were 480 synagogues [battei kenesiyot] in Jerusalem, each containing a bet ha-sefer [primary school] for the Scriptures and a bet talmud [the same as bet ha-midrash] for the study of the Law and the tradition; and Vespasian destroyed them all." [13] It is important to note that the bet ha-midrash came into being before the bet ha-sefer, indicating clearly, as Professor Ginzberg has stated, that "in the olden times the opinion prevailed that the fathers were to be educated first and then the children, not in the reverse order." [14] The school for children was first introduced by Simeon ben Shetah about the year 100 B.C.E. at Jerusalem,[15] and later was introduced generally, for the benefit of all children, by Joshua ben Gamala in the first century.[16]

(2) THE BET HA-MIDRASH AS A LIVING FORCE

The origins of the organized school of higher learning that came to be known as the bet ha-midrash are probably to be seen in the injunction of Yose ben Joezer (early second century B.C.E.): "Let thy house be a regular meeting place for learned men"—a *bet vaad la-hakhamim.*[17] The term *bet vaad,* "a stated place of meeting," occurs frequently, especially in the Palestinian Talmud, apparently always to denote a meeting place of scholars, or a school, not the place where a congregation gathered for prayer or worship.[18]

The sayings of the oldest authorities in the Pirkei Avot revert frequently to study and teaching as fundamental institutions of Judaism. The Men of the Great Assembly issued an educational ordinance "to raise up many disciples," [19] thus imposing upon the great teachers in Israel the duty of establishing academies and disseminating higher Jewish learning. Simeon the Righteous taught that the study of Torah is one of the three pillars upon which the world rests.[20] Joshua ben Perahyah, in the middle of the second century B.C.E., admonished: "Provide thyself a teacher and take to thyself a fellow student," [21] implying that one should not try to learn by himself. The term bet ha-midrash occurs for the first time in Ben Sira about the beginning of the second century B.C.E., and may freely be translated in that context as "lecture hall." [22] In the preceding generation, at the time of the attempt of Antiochus IV on the Jewish religion—that is, the end of the third century B.C.E.—the school, in all likelihood, was already an established institution. The existence of many biblical scholars—the soferim—from the third century before the common era shows that regular provision was made for transmitting the learning of former generations and adding to it.[23] By the end of the soferic age, there was a separate edifice called a beth ha-midrash on the Temple Mount. While this house of study seems to have been intended chiefly for the members of the Sanhedrin and the priests and Levites connected with the Temple, it is not unlikely that others were also admitted.[24] From the story of Hillel's wandering from Babylon to Palestine to satisfy his eagerness for more learning, it is clear that by Hillel's time academies for higher learning had long been flourishing in both countries.

In Palestine, and probably elsewhere, the bet ha-midrash was frequently adjacent to the synagogue, and most likely each synagogue had its own. "Rabbi Pinchas said in the name of Rabbi Hoshaiah that there were 480 synagogues in Jerusalem and each had a bet sefer and a bet talmud, the former for the Mikra [for the teaching of the Scriptures], the latter for the Mishnah [for teaching the oral tradition]." [25] This clearly implies that these schools were not for professional scholars alone, but provided instruction for the whole community. As noted above, it was regarded as normal for each community to maintain, in addition to a synagogue, an elementary school (a bet sefer) and an advanced school (a bet ha-midrash). During the Hadrianic persecutions, Rabbi Simeon ben Yohai, a disciple of Rabbi Akiba, said: "If you see cities in the land of Israel that are destroyed to their very foundations, know that it is because they did not provide pay for teachers of the Bible and of oral tradition, according to Jeremiah [9:12], 'because they abandoned My Law.' " [26] In the same context it is related that the Patriarch Judah sent out a commission headed by Rabbi Hiyya to tour the cities of the land of Israel and establish in each one a teacher of Bible and a teacher of the oral tradition. In one small place, where there was a village watchman but no teacher, they proceeded to impress on the townsmen that the true keepers of a city are the teachers of the Bible and the oral tradition.[27]

The very building in which the bet ha-midrash was housed acquired a sanctity all its own and was ranked higher than the synagogue. Thus, a synagogue structure may be transformed to a house of study, but not the other way around, since it would be a descent in holiness.[28] A sage of the first half of the third century of our era, Rabbi Joshua ben Levi, makes the distinction that the bet ha-midrash is a place where the Torah is magnified and the synagogue is a place where prayer is magnified.[29] Rules for proper decorum in the house of study received early formulation. Thus it was believed to bring misfortune to take food to eat during the time that the discourse was being held in the bet ha-midrash;[30] it was forbidden to sleep in the bet ha-midrash;[31] and wives received special merit by waiting for the return of their husbands from the house of learning.[32]

The rabbis attach the greatest importance to the bet ha-midrash, and there are many aggadic allusions to testify to this fact. They state that the bet ha-midrash is meant in such biblical verses as "Thou hast been our dwelling place in all generations" (Ps. 90:1) and "God standeth in the midst of the congregation of [those who seek] God" (Ps. 82:1),[33] and also in Balaam's words: "How lovely are thy tents, O Jacob, thy tabernacles O Israel" (Num. 24:5).[34] The verse in the Song of Songs, "Hark, hark my beloved! behold he cometh leaping . . . my beloved is like a gazelle" (2:8–9), is made to mean that God proceeds from one synagogue to another and from one house of study to another to bless Israel.[35]

This attitude of reverence to the bet ha-midrash[36] became so prevalent in Jewish life that Maimonides, writing nearly one thousand years later, states in his great code: "The sanctity of the bet ha-midrash is greater than that of the houses of prayer," and he further teaches that the bet ha-midrash is not a place for slumbering or for any conversation except discourse on the words of the Torah. If someone sneezes in the halls of learning, the others should not interrupt their studies to offer the customary wishes for good health.[37]

This inner and innate reverence for the house of study was soon translated into codes of law and into legally required modes of behavior within its precincts. Thus the *Shulhan Arukh* has a whole section entitled: "The Laws of Sanctity Pertaining to the House of Prayer and the House of Study." Among these laws are: One should not enter the house of study with muddy shoes or soiled clothing, nor should one enter for such trivial reasons as keeping out of the heat or the rain, or calling someone to come out. If one must enter for such purposes, he should at least stay long enough to recite some psalms, or prayers, or take time for a little learning. One is not permitted to eat or sleep in the house of study except those who spend their days and nights in study.[38]

(3) THE SUBJECTS STUDIED IN THE BET HA-MIDRASH

What subjects were taught in these institutions for higher religious education? The answer may be given in one all-inclusive word: *Mishnah.* This embraced all subjects pertaining to the oral tradition, as distinguished from *Mikra,* which denoted the study of Scriptures. Mikra was the main subject in the elementary-school system, while Mishnah, the science of oral tradition, comprised the curriculum of the bet ha-midrash. During the period of the tannaim it included the following three branches of study: (1) Midrash (also called Talmud), the higher investigation of the meaning of Scripture, (2) Halakhah, the formulations of Jewish oral law; and (3) Aggadah. The attainment of any degree of proficiency in such an intensive program required patience and years of study. It is not to be assumed that every Jew devoted so much of his life to such intensive intellectual pursuits. Only a small proportion of those who went through the elementary school, or even of those who took time for the study of Mishnah—the oral tradition—had either the ability or the opportunity to become masters of the Law. The Midrash probably gives a good summary of the situation when it declares: "Such is the usual way of the world; a thousand enter the Bible school, and a hundred pass from it to the study of Mishnah; ten of them go on to Talmud study, and only one of them arrives at rabbinic ordination." [39] For the sake of the many who did not reach such plateaus, the bet ha-midrash offered popular-level instruction in Scripture and the oral tradition on Sabbath afternoons.[40]

(4) THE TEACHERS OF THE BET HA-MIDRASH

Who were the teachers in these houses of study? Two groups must be mentioned. The men who took the lead in the first few centuries of the

existence of the bet ha-midrash are called the soferim—commonly translated "scribes," more exactly "biblical scholars." The ideal of such a
scholar is well expressed in the description of Ezra: "Ezra had set his
mind intently to study the law of the Lord and to do it and to teach in
Israel statutes and ordinances" (Ezra 7:10). In other words, the sofer
was a teacher who was expert in the Scriptures and in the religious learning of the Jewish people.[41] At the close of the soferic age, the teachers of
the bet ha-midrash were the rabbis. Among the most renowned were
Shemaiah and Avtalyon, Hillel and Shammai, Rabbi Akiba, and Rabbi
Meir. The obligation of the rabbis to teach was strongly expressed by
Rabbi Yose ben Halafta in the second century of the common era: "To
learn and not to teach—there is nothing more futile than that." [42] Rabbi
Yohanan declared: "One who studies the Torah but does not teach it is
like the myrtle in the wilderness, whose fragrance is completely wasted." [43]

After the destruction of the Temple, the rabbis presented study of the
Torah, both the written and the oral law—in other words, the sum total
of Jewish culture—as a substitute for the old-time sacrifices and, together
with prayer and generous acts, as even preferable to them. Study was made
part of everyday religious life. Those were considered devout who morning
and evening devoted some time to study. Those were praised who made a
habit of early going to the house of study—*hashkamat bet ha-midrash*—
while he who from prayer hastened to the place of study not only went
"from strength to strength"—but upon him rested the Divine Presence.

We have seen how the bet ha-midrash evolved in Jewish history. It
left an indelible impression on the mind and character of the Jew, and its
method and program of adult Jewish education helped perpetuate the
Jewish people to our day. The greatest Hebrew poet of modern times,
Hayim Nahman Bialik, immortalized the place of the bet ha-midrash in
Jewish life in these glowing lines:

> And shouldst thou wish to know the Source
> From which thy tortured brethren drew
> In evil days their strength of soul
> To meet their doom, stretch out their necks
> To each uplifted knife and axe,
> In flames, on stakes to die with joy,
> And with a whisper, "God is One,"
> To close their lips?

And shouldst thou wish to find the Spring
From which thy banished brethren drew,
'Midst fear of death and fear of life,
Their comfort, courage, patience, trust,
An iron will to bear their yoke,
To live bespattered and despised,
And suffer without end?

And shouldst thou wish to see the Lap
Whereon thy people's galling tears
In ceaseless torrents fell and fell,
And hear the cries that moved the hills,
And thrilled Satan with awe and grief,
But not the stony heart of man,
Than Satan's and than rock's more hard?

And shouldst thou wish to see the Fort
Wherein thy fathers refuge sought,
And all their sacred treasures hid,
The Refuge that has still preserved
Thy nation's soul intact and pure,
And when despised, and scorned, and scoffed,
Their faith thy did not shame?

And shouldst thou wish to see and know
Their Mother, faithful, loving, kind,
Who gathered all the burning tears
Of her bespattered, hapless sons,
And when to her warm bos'm they came,
She tenderly wiped off their tears,
And sheltered them and shielded them,
And lulled them on her lap to sleep?

If thou, my brother, knowest not
This mother, spring, and lap, and fort,
Then enter thou the House of God,
The House of Study, old and gray,
Throughout the sultry summer days,
Throughout the gloomy winter nights,

At morning, midday, or at eve;
Perchance there is a remnant yet,
Perchance thy eye may still behold
In some dark corner, hid from view,
A cast off shadow of the past,
The profile of some pallid face,
Upon an ancient folio bent,

Who seeks to drown unspoken woes
In the Talmudic boundless waves;
And then thy heart shall guess the truth
That thou hast touched the sacred ground
Of thy great nation's House of Life,
And that thy eyes do gaze upon
The treasure of thy nation's soul.

And know that this is but a spark
That by a miracle escaped
Of that bright light, that sacred flame,
Thy forebears kindled long ago
On altars high and pure.[44]

CHAPTER
IV
STUDY AS A MODE OF WORSHIP

(1) JEWISH STUDY AS DIVINE WORSHIP

In his famous book, *The Varieties of Religious Experience,* Professor William James enumerated the many ways in which the peoples of the world worship God. One form of worship is not listed. It is peculiar to Judaism among all the religions of mankind. That mode of worship is study.[1] Judaism has made of study not merely an intellectual activity but a religious experience—an act of worship through which God is praised and honored. This conception of individual and collective study as a form of divine service has persisted, inspiring Jews through the ages to become lifelong learners in order more adequately to commune with God. In Judaism, Torah—the study of religious literature—has become Avodah— a mode of religious worship.

This unique attitude towards study, although inherent in Jewish life from the earliest times, became especially entrenched in Judaism after the destruction of the Second Temple in the year 70 of the common era. As a result of this calamitous experience, the Jewish people were bereft of their national independence, of their native land, of the sanctuary in Jerusalem, of the meaningful sacrificial rituals, and of the ministrations of the priests and Levites. Jewish national and religious life was in collapse. The outlook for Jewish survival was dark indeed. It was precisely at such a dire moment that the Jewish will to live and the undying spirit of Judaism gave new emphasis to the study of Torah as a substitute for the Temple sacrifices and as a means of worshipping God. True, the Temple on Mount

31

Zion was in ruins, the priesthood annihilated, the sacrificial system a thing of the past, but when the Jew sat down to study the sacred writings and to meditate on their oral interpretations, he was creating for himself a veritable sanctuary at which he became both ministering priest and communicant with God. He was performing a divine service at the new altar of Judaism. It is in this connection that we must see the real significance of what Rabbi Yohanan ben Zakkai did when he established the academy of Yavneh. Though Jerusalem had fallen, though the sacrificial system was terminated and thus no longer afforded a means of divine worship, he saved both the Jew and Judaism by founding a school for the study of Torah, which henceforth became the unifying symbol of Jewish nationhood. In this manner study became the substitute for the Temple service.

(2) THE BOOK OF PRAYER BECOMES A BOOK OF STUDY

Ever conscious of history, however, the Jewish people did not permit the glories of the Temple and its awe-inspiring ritual to fade from their memory. The religious and national splendor of Judaism, as represented by the sanctuary on Mount Zion for a thousand years, is kept alive through daily allusions to it in the prayers of the synagogue, for passages from the Bible, the Mishnah, and the Gemara that deal with the Temple sacrifices were incorporated in the Prayer Book. The study of these passages was accounted to be the equivalent of performing the rituals they described. A prayer of the daily morning service gives voice to this holy sentiment:

Sovereign of the Universe, Thou didst command us to offer the daily sacrifice at its appointed time; and that the Priests be at their service and the Levites on their platform, and the Israelites at their station. But now, because of our sins, the Temple is laid waste and the daily sacrifice is discontinued, we have no Priest at his service, no Levite on the platform, no Israelite at his station. But Thou hast said of us, "We shall render for bullocks the offering of our lips" [Hos. 14:3].

Therefore, may it please Thee, O Lord our God and the God of our fathers, that the word of our lips be accounted, accepted and esteemed before Thee as the equivalent of having offered the daily sacrifice at its appointed time and having stood at our station.

Rabbinic doctrine assured the Jew that studying the portions of the Torah describing the Temple ritual would be as efficacious as the ritual itself;[2] indeed, the rabbis likened the study of Torah in general to the offering of incense on the Temple altar, asserting that it was tantamount to actually rebuilding the Temple.[3]

The synagogue, responding to such holy sentiments and to such doctrinal views, inserted many passages from the Written and Oral Law into the Prayer Book. In this way Judaism developed a Siddur—an Order of Worship—that is distinctive among the prayer books of humanity in that it is not only devotional in spirit but instructional in content—a prayer book that combines and harmonizes prayer with study. Learning became part of the liturgy. In truth, study had become a mode of worship. Such a development had the added advantage of further enhancing the educational function of the synagogue as a school of instruction, for the Jew in the very midst of his devotions would be engaged in Jewish study. A minimum of Torah study on the part of every Jew was thereby insured, and reality was thus given to the words of the evening prayer: "We rejoice in the words of Thy Torah and we meditate on them by day and by night." This unique aspect of Jewish life was aptly summarized by Dr. Leopold Zunz in his monumental history of Jewish worship: "After the national life [of the Jewish people] ceased to be . . . prayer and instruction appeared in combination as the goal and content of public worship." [4] A modern writer, Rabbi Abraham Millgram, states that teaching the Torah is a "core unit of the Jewish liturgy." [5]

Let us now turn to the traditional Siddur and see how the sages of Israel made of it not only a book of prayer but also a book of study. Among the benedictions that precede the passages for study in the morning service is the following, attributed to Samuel, a Babylonian rabbi of the third century:

Blessed art Thou, O Lord our God, King of the Universe, who hast sanctified us by Thy commandments and commanded us to occupy ourselves with the words of the Torah.[6]

There follows the beautiful meditation of Rabbi Yohanan bar Nappaha, also a talmudic teacher of the third century:

Make pleasant, therefore, we beseech Thee, O Lord our God, the words of Thy Torah in our mouth and in the mouth of Thy people, the house of Israel, so that we with our offspring, and the offspring of Thy people, the house of Israel, may all know Thy name and learn Thy Torah.

Blessed art Thou, O Lord, who teachest Thy Torah to Thy people Israel.[7]

The concluding benediction, the well-known blessing recited upon being called to the Torah, was described by Rabbi Hammunah, a contemporary of the teachers just quoted, as the finest of all.

Blessed art Thou, O Lord our God, King of the universe, who hast chosen us from all peoples and given us His Torah. Blessed art Thou, O Lord, who givest the Torah.[8]

Since this benediction is recited only before a reading from the Torah, there immediately follows the Priestly Benediction, consisting of three biblical verses (Num. 6:24–26), the minimum number required to constitute a Bible passage over which this benediction may be recited.

Next come the glowing sentences of the opening chapter of the Mishnah Peah, in which the study of Torah is not merely declared to be one of the functions of the Jewish life for which there is no fixed limit, such as acts of loving-kindness, but is said to be equal in importance to all the others taken together. The full passage reads as follows:

These are the things which have no fixed measure [by enactment of the Law]: the corners of the field, the first fruits, the offerings brought on appearing before the Lord at the three festivals, the practice of charity, and the study of the Law. These are the things, the fruits of which a man enjoys in this world, while the stock remains for him for the world to come: viz., honoring father and mother, the practice of charity, timely attendance at the house of study morning and evening, hospitality to wayfarers, visiting the sick, dowering the bride, attending the dead to the grave, devotion in prayer, and making peace between man and his fellow; but the study of the Law is equal to them all.[9]

All the above is a prelude, devotional and heartwarming in character, which leads the worshippers into the intellectual effort of Jewish study. In accordance with the rabbinic prescription that learning should be unified by the triple cord of passages from the Torah, the Mishnah, and the Gemara,[10] there follow selections from each of these three sources. The first is a section from the Bible (Num. 28:1–8) dealing with the daily sacrifices. The second is a chapter from the Mishnah that poses and answers the question: "Which are the places where the sacrifices were offered [in the Temple]?" [11] The third is a selection from the Gemara, the baraita in which Rabbi Ishmael sets forth his thirteen principles of expounding the Torah.[12]

The Order of Worship then returns to prayers of devotion, praise, and meditation with the Pesukei de-Zimrah, "verses of praise," and soon comes upon another high point of Torah-study in the three Bible passages that constitute the Shema section of the daily morning service. Before entering upon the weighty contents of the Shema paragraphs, the worshipper is uplifted by the two beautiful benedictions that precede it. The first of these praises God the creator and the bringer of light. The second praises God for His choice of Israel. This benediction begins as follows:

> With abounding love hast Thou loved us O Lord, our God. Great and exceeding compassion hast Thou had for us. O our Father, our King, for our fathers' sake who trusted in Thee, and whom Thou didst teach the statutes of life, be also gracious to us and teach us.

The real intent of these words, explains Dr. Max Kadushin, is indicated by the name the Jerusalem Talmud gives to it, namely Birkat Torah,[13] praising God not only as giver of the Torah but also as teacher of the Torah. Kadushin amplifies this by saying: "When we study Torah, and understand what we study, it is God Himself who is our Teacher: Thou didst teach the statutes of life"; "Be gracious to us and teach us"; and further on, "Enlighten our eyes in Thy Torah, and let our hearts cleave to Thy mitzvot." When we study and acquire knowledge of Torah, therefore, we are the objects of God's "abounding love." This benediction is a most appropriate prelude to the Keriat Shema—the Recitation of the Shema, which is then spoken with great devotion and concentration.

The reading of the Shema, besides being a liturgical act, is also an act of studying the Torah. The study function of these three great biblical passages is stressed no less than their liturgical function.[14] Thus the rabbis of the Midrash tell us that when Rabbi Eliezer asked Rabbi Joshua: "In what way can the words, 'In His Law [Torah] doth he meditate day and night [Ps. 1:2]' be obeyed?" Rabbi Joshua answered: "By the reading of the Shema, for when a man reads the [three paragraphs of the] Shema morning and evening, the Holy One, blessed be He, reckons it for him as if he had labored day and night in the study of the Torah." [15] Dr. Kadushin, explains it as follows:

The very term *Keriat Shema* itself indicates that the Recital of the Shema is the study or reading of Scripture, for the root of the Hebrew verb "Karo" refers specifically to Scriptural Study. By reciting the Shema a Jew fulfills the minimum that is required by the duty to study Torah. A man who does no more than recite the Shema morning and evening, says R. Jochanan in the name of R. Simeon ben Yochai, already fulfills the charge, "This Book of the Torah shall not depart out of thy mouth, but thou shalt meditate therein day and night" (Josh. 1:8).[16]

(3) THE LITURGY ENRICHED BY PARTS OF THE BIBLE AND TALMUD

After the formal conclusion of the prescribed order of morning prayers, the Prayer Book offers, for those interested in further study, the Bible passage containing the Ten Commandments (Exod. 20:1–17) and Moses Maimonides' famous formulation of the Thirteen Articles of the Jewish Faith. The very pious would often linger still longer to recite the Maamadot, a group of special passages from the Bible and rabbinic literature.

At the services on Sabbaths and festivals, immediately after the hymn Ein Keloheinu, three passages from the Talmud are added for purposes of study. The first of these, the Pittum ha-Ketoret, sets forth by weight and measure the composition of the incense burnt in the Temple service.[17] The second, Ha-Shir she ha-Leviim, tells which psalm the Levites sang on the steps of the Temple each day.[18] The third is the oft-quoted Amar Rabbi Eleazar,[19] which speaks words of praise for men of learning. This passage merits quotation in full:

> Rabbi Eleazar said in the name of Rabbi Hanina, "The disciples of the sages increase peace throughout the world, as it is said, 'And all thy children shall be taught of the Lord; and great shall be the peace of thy children [Isa. 54:13].' Read not here *banayikh,* thy children [or disciples], but *bonayikh,* thy builders."—Great peace have they who love thy Law; and there is no stumbling for them. Peace be within thy rampart, prosperity within thy palaces. For my brethren and companions' sake, I would fain speak peace concerning thee. For the sake of the house of the Lord our God I would seek thy good. The Lord will give strength unto his people; the Lord will bless his people with peace.

At the Sabbath Eve service, the whole second chapter of the Mishnah Shabbat is inserted, opening with the question: *Bameh madlikin uvamah ein madlikin?*—"With what materials may the Sabbath lamp be lighted, and with what may it not be lighted?" The rest of the chapter gives the answer, and proceeds also to other essential Sabbath laws. Since the concluding passage is the saying of Rabbi Eleazar quoted above, this brief study period closes on a note of praise for men of learning who bring peace to the world. When the Sabbath is ushered out with the evening service on Saturday night, a highly interesting selection from the Talmud is inserted, which opens with the words: "Rabbi Yohanan said: 'In every passage where thou findest the greatness of God mentioned, there thou findest also his humility.' " [20]

Since the Sabbath is especially dedicated to Jewish study, the Siddur has incorporated a complete book of the Bible for recitation on Friday afternoons, and a complete treatise of the Talmud for study on Sabbath afternoons. On Friday evening, prior to the inauguration of the Sabbath, the Song of Songs is chanted. On Sabbath afternoon, as part of the afternoon service, the Pirkei Avot (Ethics of the Fathers) is studied, one chapter each Sabbath from the Sabbath after Passover to the Sabbath before Rosh Hashanah. On the other Sabbaths of the year—that is, from the Sabbath after Simhat Torah until the Sabbath before Passover—the Sabbath afternoon psalms are read. They begin with Psalm 104 and continue with the fifteen Songs of Degrees, Psalms 120–134.

Not only in the daily and Sabbath liturgy did study become part of the service of worship but also on many other occasions throughout the synagogue year. Thus, each of the five Megillot is read in the synagogue: the Song of Songs on Passover, the Book of Ruth on Shavuot, the Book of Ecclesiastes on Sukkot, the Book of Lamentations on Tisha be-Av, and the Book of Esther on Purim. The Book of Job is assigned for afternoon reading on Tisha be-Av, and also for houses of mourning. Selections from the Mishnah are studied at the prayer services on Yahrzeits. Elaborate readings called tikkunim, (literally, arrangements), consisting of passages from biblical and rabbinic literature, are recited and studied in the synagogue in a festive spirit on the nights of the seventh day of Passover, Shavuot, and Hoshana Rabba.

(4) SYNAGOGUE HYMNS AS VEHICLES OF INSTRUCTION

The synagogue also developed an extensive literature of additional hymns, called piyyutim, which were inserted at appropriate places in the regular liturgy on special Sabbaths, on festivals, and on the High Holy

Days. This literature began in the talmudic period and continued on into the Middle Ages. Many of the piyyutim were instructional in character. This was made necessary by the fact that during the many persecutions in the Roman, Byzantine, and Christian eras, official edicts often forbade Torah study. The government would send spies and censors into the synagogues during the hours of worship to make sure that these edicts were obeyed. In order to circumvent the prohibitions, poets incorporated biblical and talmudic teachings into the synagogue hymns in the form of involved metaphors or pointed allusions that would be clear to the Jewish worshippers but meaningless to the government spies.

We have seen how study became both a mode of worship and a part of worship. Such study gave real value to the individual worshipper's prayers, for mechanical, unenlightened prayer has no worth. "He that turneth away his ear from learning the Torah," the rabbis quoted from the Book of Proverbs (28:9), "even his prayer is an abomination." Through the synagogue, Judaism was so successful in fusing devotional zeal with intellectual ardor that the Jew's heart and mind were as one in the worship of God. This fusion is beautifully exemplified in the way the Gaon of Vilna prayed and studied. He wore his tefillin and his tallit for both prayer and study. The significance of this practice was explained by Solomon Schechter:

> To learn Torah meant for the Gaon . . . a kind of service to God. Contemporaries who watched him when he was studying the Torah observed that the effect wrought on the personality of the Gaon was the same as when he was praying. With every word his countenance flushed with joy; with every line he was gaining strength for proceeding further.[21]

(5) STUDY AND PRAYER: WHICH IS HIGHER?

While the preeminence of Torah study was fully established in the Jewish tradition, yet there was a time in Jewish history when this basic precept of Judaism was seriously challenged. This occurred with the rise of Hasidism. One of the grievous points at issue between the Hasidim and their opponents, the Mitnaggedim, was the relative values to be assigned to the study of Torah and to prayer. To the Hasidic masters and their followers, prayer was even higher in importance than the study of Torah. Thus, an early Hasidic text, speaking of the dialogue of the Baal

Shem Tov (d. 1760), the founder of the Hasidic movement, with his own soul, states:

> The soul declared to the rabbi, may his memory be for a blessing for the life of the world to come, that the reason why the supernal matters were revealed to him was not because he had studied many Talmudic tractates and Codes of Law but because of his prayer. For at all times he recited his prayers with great concentration. It was as a result of this that he attained to an elevated state.[22]

An early Hasidic master, R. Meshullam Phoebus of Zhabaraz, a disciple of the Maggid of Mezeritch, accused the learned of his day of totally lacking real religious fervor even though they were well versed in Torah. He attacked such scholars sharply:

> They know nothing of what attachment to God means and nothing of what love and fear mean. For they imagine that their studies themselves constitute attachment to God and that these are themselves the love and fear of God. But how can this be? It is well known that many of the scholars are notorious sinners. It is also true that many Gentiles study our Torah. How, then, can this be considered attachment to God? For one who is attached to God in love and fear cannot possibly commit even the slightest sin.[23]

Later Hasidic teachers took a more moderate view. While they were not unaware that the elevation of prayer over study was an innovation, they tried to show that both Torah and Tefillah are essential and that one without the other is inadequate. This was the position of Rabbi Kalonymus Kalman Epstein of Cracow (d. 1827), and yet he urges the primacy of prayer:

> There is no doubt that a man who studies the Torah for its own sake can attain to great sanctity, provided always that he studies for its own sake and attaches all his vitality, spirit and soul to the letters of the Torah. For all that, the only way he can attain to real fear and love of God, to the longing for the worship of God, and to comprehension of His divinity, is through prayer offered with self-sacrifice and burning enthusiasm. All this is well known and is stated in all the holy books.[24]

Among the chief proponents of the moderate point of view was Rabbi Shneor Zalman of Liady (1747–1813), the founder of the Habad movement in Hasidism. He does not yield the primacy of prayer, but he declares that such primacy stems from knowledge of the Torah:

> Those who argue that prayer is only binding by Rabbinic law have never seen the light. It is true that the forms of the prayers are Rabbinic, and that prayers must be recited three times a day, but the concept of prayer and its essential idea belong to the very foundation of the Torah, namely, to know the Lord, to recognize His greatness and His glory with a serene mind, and, through contemplation, to have these fixed firmly in the mind.[25]

The latter part of the eighteenth century and the early part of the nineteenth was a period of bitter polemics between the Hasidim and the Mitnaggedim. One of the more moderate polemicists with Rabbi Shneor Zalman of Liady was Rabbi Hayyim of Volozhin, the favorite disciple of the Vilna Gaon, who was himself a strong opponent of Hasidism. In the year 1803, Rabbi Hayyim founded the yeshivah of Volozhin; in his proclamation announcing the formation of the yeshivah, he stresses the supremacy of study over all other precepts. A modern scholar, Rabbi Norman Lamm, states:

> Perhaps the most succinct expression of R. Hayyim's views consists of a double entendre of a key word in a famous passage in *Avot*: "R. Meir said, everyone who is occupied with Torah for its own sake is worthy of many things," and here follows a list of felicitous consequences of the selfless enterprise of Torah study, the concluding and climactic of which is, "it makes him great and lifts him above all things." This last word is, in the Hebrew, *maasim*, which in this context means, "things," but which can also mean "deeds," i.e., sacred deeds or practical *mitzvot*. It is this meaning that is preempted by R. Hayyim: "That is to say, (it makes him great and lifts him) above all the deeds of *mitzvot*."
>
> All the other *mitzvot* together, R. Hayyim maintains, do not have the value of one word of the Torah. Torah, even if it is studied not for its own sake but for some ulterior motive (she'lo lishmah), is superior to the practical precepts performed for their own sake. R. Hayyim appeals to the earliest source for the supremacy of Torah, the Tannaitic assem-

bly in Lydda during the Hadrianic persecutions. The question of study vs. practice was there decided in favor of study. Halakhically, the study of Torah has a double function: it instructs in the performance of the other precepts, and it is in itself the fulfillment of a commandment. Moreover, Torah is not only more significant functionally or halakhically, but it is totally inclusive. Torah is the whole of which the *mitzvot* are the individual parts. The commandments are the individual organs; Torah is the hypostasized mystical organism. The *mitzvot,* therefore, have no autonomous significance; they derive their sanctity from the fact that they are inscribed in the Torah. Torah, in turn, has a significance over and above the combined and cumulative sanctity of its various *mitzvot;* the whole is greater than its parts. . . .

Even as R. Hayyim considered all the other precepts totally dependent upon Torah study, which comprehends them, so with prayer. What, however, of the famous statement in the Mishnah that the world stands on three things: Torah, worship, and acts of kindness? Does this not place prayer and good deeds on a par with study?

R. Hayyim, in interpreting this Mishnah, maintains that the equality of these three institutions, as separate entities, held true only for the times before the Sinaitic revelation. Once the Torah was given, however, prayer and good deeds lost their autonomy and derived, as does all else, from Torah, the repository of that revelation. The equivalents of Torah as pillars of the world, are, since Sinai, inauthentic, even prohibited. Hence, natural expressions of piety and ethics are invalid unless they issue from Torah. The study of Torah is, therefore, indispensable to both worship and social ethics.[26]

ward finding a solution
minority group could
e engulfing nations of
ed by the compulsion
oncerning the Jewish
Num. 23:9).

VIVAL

mud laid such great
hey considered to be
vould be enabled to
study of the Torah
petuate the existence
ressed by the sages
h-study in the days
shall be destroyed
synagogues and in
ed a sword by the
will not study the
rah and its study
mies of the Jewish
almudic sages ex-
e good gifts that
and if not for the
ld not be distin-
s the message of
e fishes and the
he Roman Em-
been forbidden
rned him to give

f a river looked
e water. "Why
nd nets of the
unseled them.
"You foolish
mal you claim

ALMUD
NING

a period of nearly seven
g the philosophy, function,
mud, which comprises the
e Bible, the second greatest
esents the best thought of the
centers of Jewish life in all
he tannaim, the great teachers
entury B.C.E. to the middle of
academies of Jerusalem, Yav-
n, Usha, and Sepphoris, pro-
aboraim, the masters of Jewish
Sura, Pumbedita, and Nehardea
ears, reaching down to the sixth
he Gemara. Thus the scholastic
re than a thousand scholars, was

hich the tannaim and the amoraim
their teachings. The tannaim lived
lependence was destroyed by Rome.
to preserve Jewish life even after it
vish statehood. The amoraim lived in
midst of a gentile nation. It became
vish life in such a manner as to enable
The views and doctrines of the rabbis

of the Talmud were therefore constantly directed to
to the ever-pressing problem of how the Jewish
perpetuate itself and its religious heritage among t
the world. Their teachings were always condition
to insure the fulfillment of the biblical promise
people: "Lo, it is a people that shall dwell alone" (

(1) STUDY AS A WEAPON FOR JEWISH SUF

It is no wonder then that the rabbis of the Tal
stress on the importance of Jewish learning, which t
the supreme method by which the Jewish people v
survive. Thus, the primary goal to be achieved by the
was national in character, and its purpose was to per
of the Jewish people. This thought is powerfully exp
of the Talmud, who praised the glorious era of Tora
of King Hezekiah, saying: "The yoke of Sennacherib
on account of the oil of Hezekiah, which burnt in the
the houses of study. What did Hezekiah do? He plant
door of the house of study and proclaimed: 'He who
Torah will be pierced by the sword.' " [1] Here the T
are depicted as the weapon with which to defeat the ene
people who are bent on its destruction. One of the t
pressed himself in a similar vein when he said: "All t
were granted to the Jews were taken away from them,
Book of the Torah that remained with them, they wou
guishable from the nations of the world." [2] This, too, i
the martyred Rabbi Akiba in his famous parable of th
fox, which he propounded during the persecutions of
peror Hadrian. The study and teaching of the Torah had
on the pain of death. When his old antagonist Pappias wa
up this dangerous activity, Akiba replied:

Let me tell you a story. A fox walking along the banks o
down in pity at the agonized struggles of the fish in t
are you so restless?" he asked. "We fear the hooks a
fishermen," they replied. "Then come on land," he c
"We shall dwell together here in peace and security."
fox!" exclaimed the fish. "Can you really be the wise an

to be? If we are not safe in the element in which we live, how much greater will be our peril out of it!"

"Our element," concluded Rabbi Akiba, "is the Torah. If we forsake it, we destroy ourselves." [3] When Rabbi Eleazar in the name of Rabbi Haninah interpreted the verse from Isaiah, "And all thy children shall be taught of the Lord" (Isa. 54:13), by saying, "Read not here *banayikh,* thy children, but *bonayikh,* thy builders," he implied that only those who were educated in the Torah could be counted on to be the builders of a separate and enduring Jewish national life.[4]

(2) STUDY AS A MEANS TO MORAL PERFECTION

If the first goal of Jewish learning was national in character, the second goal was entirely religious in scope. The Jewish people was to be perpetuated in order to fulfill its destiny, as expressed in the Bible, to be "a kingdom of priests and a holy nation" (Exod. 19:6). Jewish learning is the indispensable means to the achievement of this noble end and is directly related to the high goals of Jewish living.

There is a lofty and practical purpose to the study of Torah. It must not become mere intellectual exercise, and must not be used for cultural self-adornment or personal aggrandizement. Rabbi Zadok warned: "Make not of the Torah a crown wherewith to aggrandize thyself, nor a spade wherewith to dig." [5] Hillel echoed this view when he taught: "He who makes a worldly use of the crown of the Torah shall waste away; hence thou mayest infer that whosoever derives a profit for himself from the words of the Torah is helping on his own destruction." [6] The acquisition of Jewish knowledge must lead to good deeds, to the practice of the will of God. It must find practical expression in Jewish living. Rabbi Simeon ben Rabbi Gamaliel declared that "not learning but doing is the chief thing." [7] This categorical assertion is fully supported in a famous discussion that was held in the academy at Lydda: "The following question was raised before them: 'Is study greater or is action greater? Rabbi Tarfon replied: 'Action is greater.' Rabbi Akiba replied: 'Study is greater.' Thereupon all of them responded: 'Study is greater for study leads to action.'" [8] The School of Hillel amplified this view by declaring: "When there were many sinners in Israel, and when they came closer to the study of the Torah, many were transformed into righteous men, pious men, and observant men." [9]

The books of Jewish learning are regarded as an "enabling literature" which helps the Jew to attain the benefits of Jewish spirituality. Thus, Rabbi Ishmael taught: "He who learns in order to practice, to him the means will be vouchsafed to learn and to teach, to observe and to practice." [10] Rabbi Eleazar ben Azariah reinforced this sentiment with the following parable:

> He whose wisdom exceeds his works, to what is he like? To a tree whose branches are many, but whose roots are few; and the wind comes and plucks it up and overturns it upon its face, as it is said, "And he shall be like a lonely juniper tree in the desert, and shall not see when good cometh; but shall inhabit the parched places in the wilderness, a salt land and not inhabited" [Jer. 17:6]. But he whose works exceed his wisdom, to what is he like? To a tree whose branches are few, but whose roots are many, so that even if all the winds in the world come and blow upon it, it cannot be stirred from its place, as it is said: "And he shall be like a tree planted by the waters; and that spreadeth out its roots by the river, and shall not perceive when heat cometh, but his leaf shall be green; and shall not be troubled in the year of drought, neither shall cease from yielding fruit" [Jer. 17:8].[11]

Just as Torah-study trained the Jew to choose the good and shun evil, so, too, it directed him to penitence. While the heart of man is prone to evil, the Torah can bring guidance to the evil inclination so as to help man habituate himself to the good life.[12] A superb statement of this view is found in this favorite saying of Raba: "The goal of wisdom is repentance and good deeds, so that a man should not study Torah and Mishnah and then despise his father and mother and teacher." [13] The life of penitence and piety is therefore the goal of Jewish learning. The scholar who is not so motivated is scorned, as expressed in words of Rabbi Shimon ben Halafta: "He who studies the words of the Torah, but does not fulfill them, his punishment is more severe than that of the one who never studied." [14]

The indispensable relationship between Jewish learning and Jewish living is well expressed in this passage from the Ethics of the Fathers: "There are four characters suggested by those who attend the house of study: he who goes and does not practice secures the reward for going; he who practices but does not go, secures the reward for practicing; he who goes and practices is a saint; but he who neither goes nor practices is a wicked man." [15]

The ultimate test of the value of Jewish learning is whether it leads to better Jewish living in one's daily life. So Abbaye explained:

As it was taught, "And thou shalt love the Lord thy God" [Deut. 6:5], this implies that the Name of Heaven be beloved because of you. If someone studies Scripture and Mishnah, and attends on the disciples of the wise, is honest in business, and speaks pleasantly to persons, what do people then say concerning him? "Happy the father who taught him Torah! Happy the teacher who taught him Torah! Woe unto people who have not studied Torah! Behold this man who has studied Torah; look how fine his ways are and how righteous his deeds!" Of him does Scripture say, "Thou art my servant, Israel, in whom I will be glorified" [Isa. 49:3]. But if someone studies Scripture and Mishnah, attends on the disciples of the wise, but is dishonest in business and discourteous in his relations with people, what do people say about him? "Woe unto him who studied the Torah! Woe unto his father who taught him Torah! Woe unto his teacher who taught him Torah! Behold this man who studied the Torah and yet how corrupt are his deeds, how ugly his ways; of him Scripture says, "In that men said of them: These are the people of the Lord and are gone forth out of his land" [Ezek. 36:20].[16]

(3) THE REWARDS OF LEARNING

It is evident from all the foregoing that the rabbis saw the rewards of the learning process in terms of a deeper and stronger spiritual life. The aphorisms of Hillel were therefore most apt: "An ignorant person cannot be truly pious," [17] and "The more Torah, the more life; the more schooling, the more wisdom." [18] Rabbi Eleazar ben Azariah said: "Where there is no Torah, there is no right conduct." [19] Other sages expressed themselves in a similar vein: "There is no one so poor as the man who is wanting in knowledge";[20] "He who guards the study of Torah, his soul is preserved";[21] "He who has acquired for himself words of Torah has acquired for himself life in the world to come";[22] "Great is the Torah, which gives life to those that practice it in this world and in the world to come";[23] "If thou hast studied Torah, much reward will be given thee . . . and know that the grant of reward unto the righteous will be in the time to come." [24] The Jewish teachers also held that making study the main concern profits both the realm of the spiritual and the realm of the material, for "the earlier generations made the study of the Torah their main concern and their ordinary work subsidiary to it, and both prospered in their hands. The later generations made their ordinary work their main concern and their study of the Torah subsidiary, and neither prospered in their hands." [25]

(4) THE DUTY OF THE JEW TO LEARN

Since the study of Torah was so vital to Jewish life, and its rewards so great, the rabbis incessantly urged the Jew to devote himself to it. Rabbi Yose admonished: "Qualify thyself for the study of the Torah, since the knowledge of it is not an inheritance of thine." [26] Rabbi Yohanan ben Zakkai, quoting a tradition of the great Hillel and Shammai, said: "If thou has learned much Torah, ascribe not any merit to thyself, for thereunto wast thou created." [27] Neither riches nor poverty may stand in the way of acquiring Jewish knowledge. Rabbi Meir, turning to the well-to-do, counseled: "Lessen thy toil for worldly goods and be busy in the Torah; many causes for neglecting it will present themselves to thee, but if thou laborest in the Torah, He has abundant recompense to give thee." [28]

The sages, directing their message to the whole people, held the view that one can best achieve the mastery of learning when he is entirely unencumbered by material goods. They said: "This is the way that is becoming for the study of the Torah: a morsel of bread with salt thou must eat, and water by measure thou must drink; thou must sleep upon the ground and live a life of trouble the while thou toilest in the Torah. If thou doest thus, happy shalt thou be and it shall be well with thee in the world to come." [29] The example of Hillel is cited to show that poverty is no excuse for neglecting the study of Torah. Hillel worked daily as a woodcutter so as to earn a small coin. Half of it he used for his bare needs and half for the admission fee to the academy of Shemaiah and Avtalyon. One wintry day, Hillel had not earned any money, and not having the required admission fee, he climbed to the roof of the academy in order to listen to the words of instruction. That day, a heavy snow fell on Jerusalem. After a while, Hillel was discovered covered with snow on the skylight of the building. Seeing Hillel's yearning for Torah, he was henceforth admitted to the academy daily and ultimately became one of the great sages in Israel.[30] Rabbi Jonathan issued a word of comfort to the poor and a word of warning to the rich when he said: "Whoso fulfills the Torah in the midst of poverty shall in the end fulfill it in the midst of wealth; and whoso neglects the Torah in the midst of wealth shall in the end neglect it in the midst of poverty." [31]

The Torah is extolled as the Great Pedagogue who educates God's creatures. [32] The student can find everything in the Torah. "If thou wantest advice—even in matters secular or in questions regarding behavior and good manners—take it from the Torah, even as David said: 'From Thy precepts I got understanding' [Ps. 119:104]." "Turn it [the Torah] and turn it over again," conclude the rabbis, "for everything is in it, and contemplate it, and wax gray and old over it, and stir not from it, for thou canst have no better rule than this." [33]

The Torah is exalted above all things. It is greater than the priesthood and royalty. [34] It is the true source of all honor and goodness. [35] It is the choicest possession of God in the whole world. [36] "Daily a heavenly voice goes forth from Mount Sinai, proclaiming these words: 'Woe to mankind for contempt of the Torah,' for whoever does not labor in the Torah is said to be under the divine censure." [37]

(5) UNIVERSAL AND DEMOCRATIC EDUCATION

If adult learning was so important to the rabbis of the Talmud, then it follows logically that they also believed in universal, democratic adult education. Basing themselves on the biblical verse, "The Torah that Moses commanded us is the heritage of the congregation of Jacob" (Deut. 33:4), the talmudic teachers insisted that the Torah is the inalienable property of every Jew, and belongs by ancestral right to every son of Israel. Hence the dictum that "anyone who withholds the knowledge of a law from any student is as though he robbed him of his patrimony." [38] A famous anecdote in the Talmud shows how seriously both laity and scholars held to this belief.

Rabbi Yannai once met a very respectable-looking man in the street. "Would you do me the honor of dining with me?" he asked him. The man replied: "As you wish," so Yannai brought him home. Conversing with him, Rabbi Yannai probed his knowledge of Bible, and found none; of Mishnah, and found none; of Talmud, and found none; of haggadah, and found none. He then said to him: "Recite the grace," to which the man evasively replied: "Let Yannai say grace in his own home." Disgusted, Yannai said: "Can you repeat what I say?" "Yes," said the man. "Say, then: a dog has eaten at Yannai's table." At that, the man sprang up and seized Yannai, crying: "My inheritance is with you and you insult me?!" "And what inheritance of yours is with me?" asked Yannai. The man replied: "Why, every child says 'The Torah that Moses commanded us is the heritage of the congregation'—not of Yannai—but of Jacob." [39]

The study of the Torah was not restricted to any special group. It had to be open to all. Was not the Torah given by God in the free desert, in the open places, so that everyone feeling the desire for it might receive it? Even as the desert is open to all and is not privately possessed, so is the Torah accessible to all and the private property of none! [40] When the School of Shammai ventured the opinion that only those should be taught "who are wise, modest, of good family, and wealthy," the School of Hillel objected, countering with the prevailing view to "teach everyone, for when there are sinners in Israel and they are brought to the study of the Torah, many righteous, pious, and worthy Jews will come from them." [41]

Thus Judaism fostered the democratic ideal in education. In fact, learning that was coupled with a worldly occupation or with labor was especially esteemed. No less a high-born personage than Rabban Gamaliel, the son of Rabbi Judah the Prince, said: "An excellent thing is the study of the Torah combined with some worldly occupation, for the labor demanded by them both makes sin to be forgotten. All study of the Torah without work must in the end be futile and become the cause of sin." [42] Many of the outstanding scholars and rabbis were artisans, laborers, or tradesmen.

(6) TEACHERS AND STUDENTS

In order to make learning universal, it became the duty of every rabbi to teach and "to raise up many disciples." [43] It was obligatory upon every learner also to be a teacher. Rabbi Yohanan maintained that "everyone who learns the Torah but does not teach it is like a myrtle in the desert, whose fragrance is wasted in the emptiness of the desert air." [44] Rabbi Aha said: "He who studies Torah but does not teach, there could be no greater vanity than this." [45] In a similar vein, a very meaningful interpretation is given to the Seventh Commandment: "Thou shalt not take the name of the Lord thy God in vain" (Exod. 20:7). In Hebrew, the first word is *lo*. The rabbis interpret the letter *lamed* in *lo* as standing for *lemod*, which means "to study," and the letter *alef* in *lo* as standing for *allef,* which means "to instruct." This, then, conveys the message that we must study in order to teach, for if you do not, you take the name of the Lord in vain.[46] Rav Yehudah in the name of Rav is even more forceful when he asserts that "any teacher who withholds the teaching of the law from his pupil, it is as if he had robbed him of the inheritance of his fathers, for it is written in Scripture: 'Moses commanded us a law, an inheritance of the congregation of Jacob' [Deut. 33:4]. This means that the law is the inheritance of all Israel." [47] Rabbi Akiba believed that "even if one had raised many disciples in youth, one must continue to do so even in old age." [48]

Every serious student could aspire in time to become a teacher of others. Raba, pointing to a discrepancy in the two scriptural verses, "Upon the high places" (Prov. 9:3), and "On a seat [in the high places]" (Prov. 9:14), states that "at the beginning the student occupies any place, but ultimately he will occupy a seat—as a teacher to disciples." [49] Ulla derived the same thought from the contradiction between the biblical verses, "Drink water out of thine own cistern" (Prov. 5:15), and "and running waters out of thine own well" (Prov. 5:15), by saying: "At first drink from thy cistern, and latterly running waters from thine own well." [50] By this he meant that at first one should imbibe knowledge drawn from other sources, and in time one will become an inexhaustible source of learning.

The duty of the teacher is to stimulate and guide his students. The rabbis, commenting on the verse, "The words of the wise are as goads" (Eccles. 12:11), ask: "Why as goads?" They give these answers: Because as a goad directs the heifer to plow on the furrow it is meant to plow, so the words of the wise direct a man in the ways of the Holy One, blessed be He. As for the word *goad,* the Mishnah, in tractate Ohalot, calls a goad *mardea,* while the Bible calls it either *darban* or *malmad,* as it is written, "with an ox-goad [*malmad*]" (Judg. 3:31), and "to set the goads [*darban*]" (2 Sam. 13:21). Why, Rabbi Nathan asked, is the goad called *mardea?* Because it imparts sense (*moreh deah*) to the heifer. And why is a goad called *darban?* Because it lodges understanding (*madir binah*) in the heifer. *Malmad?* Because it trains (*melammed*) the heifer to plow in the furrow it is supposed to plow. Even so the words of the wise lodge understanding in men, impart sense to them, and teach them the ways of the Holy One, blessed be He. So you see, "The words of the wise are as goads." [51]

The teacher has his reward in that "he who learns acquires only one portion [of what he learns], while he who teaches acquires five portions." [52]

Even more, the teacher is rewarded with immortality and everlasting remembrance and influence. In commenting on the verse, "They sing for
joy upon their beds" (Ps. 149:5), the question is raised: How can it be
said of them who are sleeping upon their beds in the beyond that they
are singing for joy? Rabbi Yohanan explained: "Whenever an elder expounding from a teacher's chair says, 'Thus taught Rabbi Akiba,' or 'Thus
taught Rabbi Simeon ben Yohai,' the lips of such sages in the beyond
move; the elders' citation of their words has the power of 'moving gently
the lips of those that are asleep' [Song of Songs 7:10] so that it may be
said of them, 'They sing for joy upon their beds' [Ps. 149:5]." [53]

The ideal of being a teacher of others in order to transmit the Torah
to the next generation is fully evidenced in all of talmudic literature.
Countless dicta show that the rabbis regarded this responsibility of teaching
their fellow-Jews as most sacred. They declared: "He who studies in order
to teach, Heaven will grant him the opportunity both to learn and to
teach." [54] The verse, "She openeth her mouth with wisdom and the Torah
of lovingkindness is on her tongue" (Prov. 31:26), is interpreted to mean:
"Torah studied in order subsequently to teach is a 'Torah of lovingkindness,' but Torah not studied subsequently to teach is a Torah which is not
of lovingkindness." [55] The verse in the Psalms (112:3), "Wealth and
riches are in his house," refers "to the one who both learns the Torah and
teaches the Torah," for he is blessed with wealth and riches.[56] So, too,
the verse in Numbers (15:31), "He hath despised the word of the Lord,"
is interpreted by Rabbi Meir to allude to him "who studies the Torah
but does not teach it." [57] Once again, the well-known biblical term
ve-shinantam ("thou shalt teach") in Deuteronomy 6:7 is interpreted to
mean "that the word of the Torah shall be sharp in your mouth, so that
if a person asks you something you will not hesitate and stammer but
rather you will tell him immediately and clearly." [58] In interpreting
Malachi 2:27, Rabbi Yohanan declares that the people will seek the law
at his mouth if he will be "like an angel of the Lord." [59]

But more than just professing such dedication to teaching, they actually
lived by these principles. Of Rabbi Yohanan ben Zaccai, it is related that
he studied for forty years and taught for forty years.[60] It is also recorded
that a disciple turned apologetically to Rabbi Akiba while he was im-
prisoned with the plea, "Master, teach me Torah." "My son," answered
Rabbi Akiba, "more than the calf wishes to suck does the cow desire to
suckle." [61]

In return for such zealous devotion to teaching, great respect was due the teacher from the student. "He who learns from his fellow a single chapter, a single rule, a single verse, a single expression, or even a single letter, ought to pay him honor." [62] The talmudic teaching is that "one's teacher takes precedence over one's father." [63] This is not mere verbal fancy, but was actually enacted into law, for the Talmud prescribed: "If a man's own lost article and his father's lost article need attention, his own takes precedence. His own and his teacher's, his own takes precedence. His father's and his teacher's, his teacher's takes precedence, because his father brought him into the world, whereas his teacher, who instructed him in wisdom, brings him to the future world." [64] Similarly, the student is to help his teacher with putting down a burden before he helps his father. But even more astonishing is the regulation providing that in case his father and his teacher are held captives, the teacher is to be redeemed first.[65]

These views are all the more remarkable when one considers the basic teaching of Judaism, stemming from the Decalogue itself, that one should honor one's father. But the respect due a teacher is on an even higher plane, for it reaches the level of reverence one feels toward the divine. So we are taught: "Let reverence for thy master be like the reverence for Heaven." [66] We are also told: "Whoever contends again the ruling of his teacher is as though he contended against the Divine Presence. Whoever quarrels with his teacher is as though he quarreled with the Divine Presence." [67] Even such a seemingly minor matter as failure to include the words "my teacher" in the greeting addressed to him "cause the Divine Presence to remove itself from Israel." [68]

Many are the regulations scattered through the Talmud concerning the respectful conduct of disciples toward their teachers. Here are some of them:

All manner of work that a servant performs for his master, a disciple shall perform for his teacher except the untying of his shoestrings.[69]

A disciple must not bathe with his teacher, but if his teacher needs him, it is permitted.[70]

Who is an epikoros [heretic]? Rab and Rabbi Haninah both taught that this means one who insults a scholar. Rabbi Joseph said that this refers to those who mock, saying: "Of what use are the rabbis to us?" Rabbi Nahman said: "one who calls his teacher by name." [71]

One who walks at his master's right hand is a boor. Of three walking together the teacher should walk in the middle. One who walks in

front of his teacher is a boor. One who walks behind his teacher is arrogant (for he should be walking to the left of his teacher).[72]
A disciple who takes leave of his master should not turn on his heels to walk away.[73]

While students must respect their teacher, the Talmud also requires the teacher to have proper regard for his students. Rabbi Elazar ben Shamua expressed this thought as follows: "Let the honor of your student be as dear to you as your own, and the honor of your associate be like the reverence for your teacher, and the reverence for your teacher like the fear of Heaven." [74] This admonition is made more specific by Rabbi Abahu: "From where do we know that the teacher shall not sit on a couch and teach his students who are sitting on the floor?" He answers by pointing to the verse in Deuteronomy 5:28, "But you stand here with me," which implies that God was standing while He instructed Moses in the laws of the Torah. Therefore, all teachers were to emulate the example of the Almighty and stand before their students.[75]

The teacher must exert himself to the utmost in behalf of his students. Instruction should be interesting so that the learner will be anxious to acquire knowledge. Rabbah, before he began to teach his pupils, was in the habit of introducing his remarks with something bright and sparkling; by this means he put the students in a joyous mood. Then he proceeded in all gravity to the subject of his discourse.[76] Rabbi Akiba, Rabbi Meir, and others would cross-question their pupils so as to sustain their attention and sharpen their wits.[77] It was urged that instruction be properly graded so that the teacher should teach from the known to the unknown, from the near to the distant, from the simple to the complex. "He who observes this method is like a tree which yields its fruit in due season; but he who does not observe such order is like chaff which the wind blows away." [78] "If what has been learned has been well ordered in the mind, you will be able to add new knowledge." [79]

A teacher should have patience and perseverance. He should teach and explain the lesson at least four times; and if this be insufficient, he has to repeat it even more times, until the student knows it well. Teachers were reminded that they must emulate the master teacher of Judaism, Moses, who repeated to Aaron four times the explanation of the Torah he had received from God. Aaron did the same to his sons, they to the elders, and the elders taught these unto the whole people four times.[80] The biblical injunction "And thou shalt teach them diligently" (Deut. 6:7) is made to refer to the teacher, who must teach so many times until he understands the subject.[81]

Teachers were looked upon as the guardians of Jewish life. This is brought out in the following famous story:

Rabbi Judah the Prince sent Rabbi Hiyya, Rabbi Yose, and Rabbi Ami to visit cities in the land of Israel and to set up in them teachers of Scripture and instructors of Oral Law. Coming to one city where they found no teacher of Scripture and no instructor of Oral Law, they said to the people: "Fetch us the chief watchmen of the city." The people brought the watchmen of the city to the rabbis, and the rabbis said: "Are these the watchmen of the city? In truth, they are the destroyers of the city!" And when the people asked the rabbis: "Who, then, are the watchmen of the city?" the rabbis answered: "The watchmen of the city are the teachers of Scripture and the instructors of the Oral Law." [82]

It is evident that in the talmudic period the teacher was held in great esteem because of his dedicated labors, and found great satisfaction and reward in his sacred calling. The Mishnah speaks of one such teacher, who must have been typical of his colleagues in Jerusalem—Rabbi Nehunya ben Hakanah, who, when he left the house of study, would offer the prayer, "I give thanks for my lot." [83]

(7) METHODS OF ACQUIRING KNOWLEDGE

In their philosophy of adult education, the rabbis expanded considerably on the methods by which learning can best be acquired. To begin with, one must have the will to learn. "Make thy ear," urged the rabbis, "like the hopper [the grain-receiver on top of the millstone] to receive the teachings." [84] Everyone had to qualify himself for study, since it does not come by inheritance.[85] Then again, the learning process must have regularity and continuity. This view is reinforced by the question: "Why were the words of the Torah compared to the fig tree?" The answer is: "The more one searches in the fig tree, the more figs one finds in it, so it is with the words of the Torah, the more one studies them, the more relish he finds in them." [86] Another answer in the same vein: "From most trees one plucks the fruit all at once, but from the fig tree, the fruits are plucked slowly over a period of time. So, too, with the study of the Torah, one studies a little today, some more the next day, for the Torah cannot be learned all at one time; neither in one year nor in two years." [87] Hillel warned: "Don't say: When I have leisure I will study; perchance thou wilt have no leisure." [88] Shammai counseled: "Fix a period for thy study of the Torah." [89] The scholars of the Jerusalem Talmud echo these sentiments: "If you forsake the Torah for one day, the Torah will forsake you for two days." [90]

Great importance was attached to repetition in study, for "he who studies and does not go over it again is like a man who sows but does not reap," [91] and "he who repeats his chapter a hundred times is not to be compared to him who repeats it a hundred and one times." [92] It is best to repeat something that has been recently studied, for "it is harder to remember well something old than to commit to memory a fresh thing, your analogy being a cement made out of old cement." [93] Constant repetition is urged especially because one can so easily forget what has been studied. Rabbi Meir stated that "the words of the Torah, like vessels of fine gold, are hard to acquire, but, like vessels of silver, are easily destroyed [by forgetfulness]." [94] The sages taught that "he who studies Torah and forgets it is like a woman who gives birth and then buries her offspring." [95] To remedy forgetting, Raba admonished constancy in study: "Let one by all means learn, even though he is liable to forget; yea, even if he does not fully understand all the words he studies," [96] and it was held that "the words of the Torah are not forgotten except for inattention in study." [97]

On the other hand, "the more one meditates upon the words of the Torah, the more meaning they acquire," [98] and "the more the words of the Torah age and ripen in the mind and body of the learner, the more they improve." [99] Praise is therefore given to incessant study, and the case is cited of "Rabbi Isaac, who studied from Rabbi Abahu forty times, and it seemed to him as though it were lying in his wallet"; that is, he knew it perfectly and would not forget it. [100]

As an aid to memory and to effective study, it was held that study should be out loud. The story is told of "Beruriah, the wife of Rabbi Meir, who once discovered a student who was learning silently. She rebuked him, exclaiming: 'Is it not written: ordered in all things and sure' [2 Sam. 23:5]. If it is ordered in all your 248 limbs, it will be sure, otherwise it will not be sure." [101] The case is also cited of Rabbi Eliezer, "who had a disciple who learned in a low voice and after three years he forgot his learning." [102] The most interesting illustration of this point is the following incident recorded in the Talmud:

Samuel said to Rab Judah: "Keen scholar! Open your mouth and read the Scriptures; open your mouth and learn the Talmud that your studies may be retained and that you may live long, since it is said, 'For they [the words of the written and oral Torah] are life unto those that find them and a healing to all their flesh' [Prov. 4:22]; read not 'to those that find them' but 'to him who utters them with his mouth.' " [103]

It was held that chanting was a further aid to study. "Rabbi Shefatiah said in the name of Rabbi Yohanan: 'If one reads the Scripture without a melody [i.e., as indicated by the singing accents] or repeats the Mishnah without a tune [i.e., to aid the memory], of him the Scripture says, "Wherefore I gave them also statutes that were not good and ordinances whereby they should die" [Ezek. 20:25].' " [104]

Since books and manuscripts were scarce, it was necessary to rely upon memory a great deal. Therefore, a whole system of mnemonics was developed as an aid to memory. This was so essential that Rabbi Hisda stated: "The Torah can only be acquired with the aid of mnemonic signs, for it is said in the Scripture, 'Put it in their mouths' [Deut. 31:19], read not 'put it' [simah] but 'its mnemonic sign' [simana]." [105] However, where texts were available, visual aid in the learning process was strongly advocated, for "he who learns [Haggadah] from a book will not forget it quickly," [106] and "seeing is an aid to remembering." [107]

Furthermore, one should study under proper guidance. "Lean not upon thine own understanding"; [108] "provide thyself with a teacher and get thee a companion" [109] with whom to study; "provide thyself with a teacher and be free of doubt"; [110] "warm thyself by the fire of the sages"; [111] are some of the rabbinic utterances on this subject.

It was even urged that one should study under more than one master, for "he who learns Torah from only one master will never achieve great success." [112] The Talmud records an incident in which this sentiment plays an important part.

Rabbi Hisda said to his students: "I have a mind to tell you something though I fear that you might leave me and go elsewhere. 'Whoever learns Torah from only one master will never achieve great success.' " The students did leave him and went to sit before Rabbah, who, however, explained to them that the maxim only applies to lessons in logical deduction [dialectics] but as to oral traditions it is better to learn from only one master so that one is not confused by the variation in the terms used. [113]

Both teacher and student must be dedicated to the mastery of Jewish learning.

> Rabbi Akiba stated: "Whence is it deduced that a man must go on teaching his pupils until he has mastered the subject? From Scripture, where it says, 'And teach thou it to the children of Israel' [Deut. 31:19]. And whence is it deduced that it must be taught until the students are well versed in it? From Scripture, where it says, 'Put it in their mouths' [Deut. 31:19]." [114]

(8) PRIVATE OR GROUP STUDY?

The greatest value was attached to group study, for "the words of the Torah do not endure with one who limits himself to private study alone." [115] "Form yourselves into bands to study the Torah," urged the rabbis, "for the Torah is not acquired except in groups." [116] This thought was poetically emphasized in such similes as: "Just as fire cannot ignite by itself, so the words of the Torah cannot endure with him who studies alone";[117] "Just as one piece of iron sharpens another, so do two students of the Law stimulate one another in the study of the Law";[118] "Just as a small piece of wood kindles the larger piece, so do lesser scholars, by their inquiries, sharpen the scholarship of the greater scholars." [119] It is also pointed out that private study often stultifies and leads to folly.[120] The importance of group as well as individual study is urged in such passages as "When ten people sit together and occupy themselves with the Torah, the Shekhinah abides among them," [121] and the same applies to five or three or two, and "whence can it be shown that the same applies even to one? Because it is said: 'In every place where I cause my name to be remembered, I will come unto thee and I will bless thee' [Exod. 20:24]." "If two sit together and words of the Torah are spoken between them, the Divine Presence rests between them . . . even if one person occupies himself in the study of Torah, the Holy One, blessed be He, appoints unto him a reward." [122] "If three have eaten at one table and have spoken over it words of the Torah, it is as if they had eaten from the table of the All-present." [123]

(9) THE QUALITIES OF THE LEARNER

What qualities must the learner possess to acquire knowledge of Judaism? The rabbis enumerate forty-eight qualifications:

by audible study, by distinct pronunciation; by understanding and dis-
cernment of the heart; by awe, reverence, meekness, cheerfulness; by
ministering to the sages, by attaching oneself to colleagues, by discussion with disciples; by sedateness; by knowledge of the Scripture and
of the Mishnah; by moderation in business, in intercourse with the
world, in pleasure, in sleep, in conversation, in laughter; by long-
suffering; by a good heart; by faith in the wise; by resignation under
chastisement; by recognizing one's place, rejoicing in one's portion,
putting a fence to one's words, claiming no merit for oneself; by being
beloved, loving the All-present, loving mankind, loving just courses,
rectitude and reproof; by keeping oneself far from honor, not boasting
of one's learning, nor delighting in giving decisions; by bearing the
yoke with one's fellow, judging him favorably, and leading him to truth
and peace; by being composed in one's study; by asking and answering,
hearing and adding thereto [by one's own reflection]; by learning with
the object of teaching, and by learning with the object of practicing;
by making one's master wiser, fixing attention upon his discourse, and
reporting a thing in the name of him who said it.[124]

The qualities of humility and meekness are regarded as prerequisites
to study. The following passage from the Talmud illustrates this point:

Rabbi Hanina ben Ida said: "Why are the words of the Torah likened
unto water—as it is written, 'Ho, everyone that thirsteth, come ye for
water'? This is to teach you, just as water flows from a higher level
to a lower, so too the words of the Torah endure only with him who
is meek-minded." Rabbi Oshaia said: "Why are the words of the Torah
likened unto these three liquids; water, wine, and milk—as it is written,
'Ho, everyone that thirsteth come ye for water'; and it is written, 'Come
ye, buy and eat; yea, come buy wine and milk without money and
without price'? This is to teach you, just as these three liquids can only
be preserved in the most inferior of vessels, so too the words of the
Torah endure only with him who is meek-minded. This is illustrated
by the story of the daughter of the Roman emperor, who addressed
Rabbi Joshua ben Hanina: 'O glorious wisdom in an ugly vessel.' He
replied: 'Does not your father keep wine in an earthenware vessel?'
She asked: 'Wherein else shall he keep it?' He said to her: 'You who
are nobles should keep it in vessels of gold and silver.' Thereupon
she went and told this to her father, and he had the wine put into

vessels of gold and silver and it became sour. When he was informed of this, he asked his daughter: 'Who gave you this advice?' She replied: 'Rabbi Joshua ben Hanania.' Thereupon the emperor had him summoned before him and asked him: 'Why did you give her such advice?' He replied: 'I answered her according to the way that she spoke to me.' But are there not good-looking people who are learned? If these very people were ugly they would be still more learned." [125]

(10) THE PLACE OF STUDY

Even as it was necessary to have a fixed time for study, so was it desirable to have a fixed place. for study. This was the view of Rabbi Simeon ben Yohai, who said: "He who fixes a place for his study of the Torah, his enemies shall fall before him, as it is said in Scripture, 'And I will appoint a place for thy people Israel, and will plant them, that they may dwell in their own place, and be disquieted no more; neither shall the children of wickedness afflict them any more, as at first' [2 Sam. 7:10]." [126]

While everyone was urged to make his own home "a meeting place for the wise," [127] yet if that did not prove possible, or if the community in which one lived did not afford opportunities for Jewish study, the Jew was urged "to wander forth to a home of the Torah," and he was admonished: "Say not that the Torah will come after thee." [128] Such extraordinary exertion in seeking the association of fellow-learners will be amply rewarded in that "thy companions will establish thee in the possession of it [the Torah]." [129] The following incident in the life of Rabbi Yose ben Kisma is illustrative of these views. Rabbi Yose relates:

I was once walking by the way, when a man met me and saluted me, and I returned the salutation. He said to me, "Rabbi, from what place art thou?" I said to him: "I come from a great city of sages and scribes." He said to me: "If thou art willing to dwell with us in our place, I will give thee a thousand golden dinars and precious stones and pearls." I said to him: "Wert thou to give me all the silver and gold and precious stones and pearls in the world, I would not dwell anywhere but in a home of the Torah." [130]

(11) TIME AND DAYS OF STUDY

What time of day and what days of the week were preferable for study? While every Jew was enjoined to appoint some fixed time for daily study,[131] as it is said, "And thou shalt meditate thereon both by day and by night" (Josh. 1:8), there was difference of opinion as to whether the day or the night is more suitable for study—with the major emphasis favorable to study at night. Rab Judah held that "night was created for naught but sleep." When Rabbi Zera was told, "You are exceedingly well versed in your studies," he replied, "They are the result of day work." [132] Rabbi Simeon ben Lakish, on the other hand, maintained that "the moonlight was created only for purposes of study," [133] and others maintained that "there can be no true joyous song of the Torah except in the nighttime." [134] The opinions were also expressed that "every house in which the words of the Torah are studied in the nighttime shall never be destroyed," [135] and that "every house which does not resound each night with the words of the Torah will be consumed with fire." [136] There were others, however, who held that it is important to study the Torah both day and night. They maintained that Moses himself set the Jewish people such an example. He studied the Torah in the daytime and would review it at night. This he did in order to teach the children of Israel that they should labor in the study of the Torah both day and night in order to fulfill the verse in Scripture, "The book of the Torah shall not depart from your mouth day and night" (Josh. 1:8).[137]

While every day was adequate for study, yet the Sabbath was held to be especially suitable for that purpose. In commenting on the verse, "And Moses assembled all the congregation of the children of Israel" (Exod. 35:1), the rabbis say:

From the beginning of the Torah unto its end, there is no portion in which is found the phrase "and he assembled" except here, in connection with the Sabbath. This is to teach us that the Holy One, blessed be He, said to Moses: "Gather large congregations and speak before them about the laws of the Sabbath so that future generations shall follow your example to assemble congregations every Sabbath and gather in the houses of study to teach the children of Israel the words of the Torah and to instruct them in what is permissible and what is prohibited. By doing so they will glorify My great Name among My children." [138]

The Sabbath and the Torah are mated one to the other. According to the rabbis, the Torah complained to God: "Lord of the Universe, if every Israelite goes about his work ploughing and sowing his field, what

will become of me?" To which God replied: "You will not be forsaken,
for I have provided a mate for you, the Sabbath day." "This is why,"
conclude the rabbis, "on the Sabbath Israelites desist from work to enter
the synagogues and houses of study and occupy themselves with Torah." [139]
In answer to the question "How shall one hallow the Sabbath?" the rabbis
reply: "By study of the Bible and Mishnah." [140] Such occupation with the
Torah was part of the Sabbath delight. Rabbi Berechya, in the name of
Rabbi Hiya ben Abba, said: "The Sabbath was not given except for
pleasure." Rabbi Hagi, in the name of Rabbi Samuel ben Nahman, said:
"The Sabbath was not given except for the study of Torah." The sages
conclude that there is no contradiction in these two views. For the first
applies to the students of the Torah, who engage in the study of the Torah
every day of the week, but on the Sabbath came together for group study
and therein find pleasure. The second refers to workmen, who each day
of the week engage in their daily toil but on the Sabbath came together
for the study of the Torah.[141] Instances are cited of renowned talmudic
teachers who studied and taught on the Sabbath. Rabbi Meir studied and
dispensed instruction on the eve[142] and the afternoon of the Sabbath.[143]
Rabbi Yohanan and Resh Lakish would delve into aggadic books on the
Sabbath.[144]

It was recognized that study was a strenuous matter, for the sages held
that through constant study "the Torah weakens the strength of man." [145]
That is why Rabba, reiterating the opinions of several scholars, urged that
studies should be pursued a little at a time. He explained the verse "Wealth
gotten by vanity shall be diminished, but he that gathereth little by little
shall increase" (Prov. 13:11) by saying: "If one takes his studies by
heaps at a time, he will benefit but little, but if one gathers knowledge
little by little he will gain much." [146] Students were also advised to learn
that for which they had an aptitude or to which their mood was attuned.
No less a teacher than Rabbi, the compiler of the Mishnah, counseled:
"A man can learn well only that part of the Torah which is his heart's
desire, for it is said 'but whose desire is in the Law of the Lord' [Ps.
1:2]." [147] An interesting story is related in which this maxim was applied.
The Talmud relates:

> Levi and Rabbi Simeon the son of Rabbi were once sitting before Rabbi
> and were expounding a part of Scripture. When the book was con-
> cluded Levi said: "Let the Book of Proverbs now be brought in." Rabbi
> Simeon the son of Rabbi, however, said: "Let the Psalms be brought,"

and Levi having been overruled, the Psalms were brought. When they came to this verse, "but whose desire is in the Law of the Lord," Rabbi offered his comment: "One can only learn well that part of the Torah which is his heart's desire." Whereupon Levi remarked, "Rabbi, you have given me the right to rise [and leave]." [148]

Rabba felt, as did Rabbi, that one can study best what is close to his heart, and he added: "At the beginning of the above-quoted verse, the Torah is assigned to the Holy One, blessed be He, but at the end it is assigned to him who studies it, for it is said 'whose desire is in the Law of the Lord and in his [own] Law doth he meditate day and night.' " [149] In other words, by interested and diligent study the student makes the subject his own.

(12) NEW INTERPRETATIONS

The Torah is a continuous guide to life. It is capable of producing new insights into the ever-changing conditions of life. The aged Rabbi Joshua ben Hananiah inquired of his two younger colleagues, Rabbi Yohanan ben Beroka and Rabbi Eleazar Chisma, when they called upon him: "What new teaching was there at the college today?" When, out of deference to him, they gave an evasive answer, implying that they could bring nothing new to so eminent a scholar, he challenged them with the statement: "It is impossible for a college session to pass without some new teaching!" [150] The purpose of learning was not to be merely a "basketful of books" [151]—a phrase used in the Talmud in a derogatory sense— but as the popular saying had it: "Better is one grain of sharp pepper than a basketful of pumpkins." [152] By this it was meant that a real student of Torah should sharpen his mind in order properly to interpret and extend the meaning of the Law. So, too, it was believed that among the questions the dead are asked on appearing before the Throne of Judgment is the following: "Hast thou been a searcher after wisdom?" [153]

The sages of a later age taught: "Let the teachings of the Torah be new to thee every day so that thou shalt not consider the Torah an ancient document that is no longer regarded by men." [154] Rabbi Joshua ben Karha said: "Whosoever studies the Torah and does not revise it is likened unto one who sows without reaping." [155] The intent of all these rabbinic teachings is to make the Jewish law, the halakhah, a living, growing tradition that both responds to and creates "the way in which the people walk." This concept is expressed in the talmudic aphorism: "Read not *halikhot* but *halakhot*," [156] implying that what is going on among the people should be related to the development of Jewish law.

(13) WHAT TO STUDY: THE SUBJECT MATTER OF LEARNING

The student of the Torah must acquire knowledge of the twenty-four books of the Bible, even as a bride adorns herself with the twenty-four different kinds of ornaments.[157] In addition to the Written Law, he must also study the Oral Law. The rabbis express this thought beautifully:

When God revealed Himself at Sinai to give the Torah unto Israel, He promulgated it unto Moses in the following order: the Scriptures, the Mishnah, the Talmud, and the Aggadah. After God had taught them to Moses, He said to Moses: "Teach them unto Israel." Moses then said: "I will write it down for them." God replied: "I do not want all of it given unto them in written form, for in ages to come the nations of the world will rule over my people and will take it away from them; therefore I shall give them the Scriptures in written form, but the Mishnah, the Talmud, and the Aggadah I will give them in oral form so that my people shall be distinct from the other nations of the world." [158]

The importance of studying both the Written Law and the Oral Law is expounded in different ways. Thus we are told: "Our rabbis taught, 'Those who occupy themselves with the Bible alone are but of indifferent merit; with Mishnah, are indeed meritorious and are rewarded for it; with Gemara, there can be nothing more meritorious." [159] Expounding on the words in the Book of Proverbs, "Prepare thy work without, and make it ready for thee in the field, and afterward built thine house" (Prov. 24:27), the talmudic masters state:

"Prepare thy work without"; that is Scripture, "and make it ready for thee in the field," that is Mishnah; "and afterward build thine house," that is Gemara. Another explanation is, "Prepare thy work without," that is Scripture and Mishnah; "and make it ready for thee in the field," that is Gemara; "and afterward build thine house," that is good deeds. Rabbi Eliezer ben Rabbi Yose the Galilean says: " 'Prepare thy work without,' that is Scripture, Mishnah, and Gemara; 'and make it ready for thee in the field,' that is good deeds; 'and afterward build thine house,' that is: make research in the Torah and receive the reward." [160]

Similar thoughts are also expressed in metaphorical form; for instance, it is taught that "the Torah is likened to salt, the Mishnah to pepper, and the Gemara to spices. For purposes of good living, salt, pepper, and spices are necessary. A rich man uses all three. So it is impossible to live without Scripture, without Mishnah, and without Gemara. Fortunate is the man who studies the Gemara and does not skip over the Scriptures and the Mishnah." [161]

It is evident that the subject matter of Jewish studies incorporated the whole of the national literature of the Jewish people, which included, up to the talmudic period, the Bible, the Mishnah, and the Gemara. The question arose as to how the learner should divide his time among these branches of Jewish knowledge. The answer is expressed in these words: "One should divide his years into three: devoting a third to Mikra [the study of the Bible]; a third to Mishnah; and a third to Talmud." [162] This passage obviously needs clarification. Rashi interprets it to mean that two days in the week one should study Bible, two days Mishnah, and two days Talmud. The Tosafists hold a different view. They state that each day itself should be divided into three parts. In practice, however, Jewish scholars have traditionally confined themselves to the Talmud, but since the Babylonian Talmud is an amalgam of all three branches of study, this rabbinic dictum is held to be fulfilled. [163]

(14) TORAH LISHMAH

The rabbis of the Talmud developed a new concept for motivating the study of Torah. They called it *Torah Lishmah*—"the study of Torah for its own sake." By this they meant that one should not occupy himself with study for the purpose of receiving material reward or achieving personal glory, or for any other ulterior motive. One learns just because of the love of learning. Thus the biblical phrase "to love the Lord your God" (Deut. 11:13) is explained to mean: "Say not I will study the Torah with the purpose of being called sage or rabbi, or to acquire fortune, or to be rewarded for it in the world to come; but do it for the sake of thy love of God, though the glory will come in the end." [164] This sentiment runs through all of rabbinic literature. In commenting on the words, "that thou mayest love the Lord thy God" (Deut. 30:20), the rabbis declare: "One should not say, I will read Scripture that I may be called a sage; I will study that I may be called rabbi; I will study to be an elder and sit in the assembly of elders; but learn out of love, and honor will come in the end." [165] And again: "Whosoever occupies himself with the Torah for its own sake, his learning becomes an elixir to life to him, for it is said, 'It is a tree of life to them that grasp it' [Prov. 3:18], and it is further said, 'It shall be a health to thy navel' [Prov. 3:8], and it is also said, 'For whoso findeth me findeth life' [Prov. 8:35]." [166] It can therefore be seen that occupation with the study of Judaism was not calculated to produce men of world success or renown, but saintly lives and devout spirits. "Whosoever labors in the Torah for its own sake merits many things," declared Rabbi Meir. And what are these things? This sage lists them as follows:

> He is called friend, beloved, a lover of the All-present, a lover of mankind; it clothes him in meekness and reverence; it fits him to become just, pious, upright and faithful; it keeps him far from sin, and brings him near in virtue; through him the world enjoys counsel and sound knowledge, understanding and strength . . .; and it gives him sovereignty and dominion and sound judgment; to him the secrets of the Torah are revealed; he is made like a never-failing fountain and like a river that flows on with ever-sustained vigor; he becomes modest, long-suffering, and forgiving of insults; and it magnifies and exalts him above all things.[167]

Rabbi Sifra was accustomed to pray: "May it be Thy will that You bring peace . . . among those students who are occupied with the study of the Torah, both those who do it for its own sake and those who do not do it for its own sake. And that these latter may come ultimately to occupy themselves for its own sake." [168]

This high motivation of "study for its own sake" enables one to touch the very essence of the Torah, and thereby he brings peace to the world and hastens the coming of God's Kingdom. This is indicated in the following two passages:

> Rabbi Eleazar stated: "What is the purport of what was written, 'she openeth her mouth with wisdom, and the Torah of lovingkindness is on her tongue'? [Prov. 31:26]. Is there then a Torah of lovingkindness and a Torah not of lovingkindness? But the fact is that Torah studied for its own sake is a 'Torah of lovingkindness' whereas Torah studied for an ulterior motive is a Torah not of lovingkindness." [169]

Rabbi Alexandri said: "He who studies the Torah for its own sake makes peace in the Upper Family—among the angels, and the Lower Family—among men." Rab said: "It is as though he built the heavenly and the earthly temples." Rabbi Yohanan said: "He also shields the whole world from the consequences of its sins." Levi said: "He also hastens the redemption." [170]

(15) THE EDUCATION OF WOMEN

Although women were not obligated to study Torah, they attended, especially on Sabbaths and holidays, the divine services at the Temple in Jerusalem, and at synagogues in Palestine and in the lands of the Diaspora. In the special galleries or halls provided for them, they participated in all the prayers and listened to the readings and translations of the portions of the Pentateuch and the Prophets. They were also present at the sermons of the rabbis on Friday evenings and Saturday mornings. In fact, some women attended these sermons more regularly than their husbands.[171] There were times when women did attain great learning. Thus we are told about the Jewish women in the days of King Hezekiah, when Torah study flourished greatly. The rabbis state that in those days "search was made . . . and no ignoramus was found . . . and no boy or girl, man or woman, was found who was not thoroughly versed in the laws of cleanliness and unclean lives." [172] These particular laws are probably mentioned on account of their difficulty, and the girls and the women are mentioned to show how they, too, attained to higher Jewish learning.

The most important role of women was to inspire their children and husbands to be students of the Torah. So did Rab say to Rabbi Hiyya: "Whereby do women earn merit? By making their children go to the synagogue to learn Scripture and their husbands to the bet ha-midrash to learn Mishnah, and waiting for their husbands till they return from the bet ha-midrash." [173]

Some women were so imbued with love of Torah that they encouraged their husbands to devote themselves solely to Jewish learning for a number of years, and willingly shouldered the economic responsibilities. The wife of Rabbi Akiba is an illustration of such a case. The Talmud records that this famous scholar, in the presence of his many disciples, publicly acknowledged the debt he owed his wife with these frank words: "All that I am, and all that you are, is owing to her." [174]

(16) PRAYERS IN GRATITUDE FOR LEARNING

We can give no better summary of the place occupied by the religious education of the adult in talmudic times than by turning to some of the recorded prayers of the great leaders of those centuries. There is the beautiful meditation of Rabbi Yohanan bar Nappaha, who lived in the latter half of the third century: "Oh, make pleasant, O Lord our God, the words of Thy law in our mouth and in the mouth of Thy people, the house of Israel, so that we with our offspring, and the offspring of Thy people, the house of Israel, may all know Thy name and learn Thy law. Blessed art Thou, O Lord, who teacheth the Torah to His people Israel." [175] After his prayers, Rabbi Elazar would utter this private devotion: "May it be Thy will, O Lord our God, that there abide in our destiny love, brotherhood, peace, friendship, and that there shall be multiplied in our borders many disciples." [176] Rabbi Hiyya, after his prayers, would say: "May it be Thy will, O Lord our God, that the study of Thy Torah shall be our occupation:" [177] Rav used to pray, "that there abide within us the love of Torah." [178] Mar ben Rabina prayed: "Open my heart to Thy Torah." [179] Rabbi Yohanan's words were: "Happy is he who has been raised in the study of the Torah and who has labored in it." [180] Rabbi Meir's favorite saying was: "Study with all thy heart and with all thy soul to know My ways and to watch at the doors of My law. Keep My law in thy heart, and let My fear be before thine eyes. Keep thy mouth from all sin and purify and sanctify thyself from all trespass and iniquity, and I shall be with thee in every place." [181] To this day, whenever a celebration —called a *"siyyum"*—is held to mark the completion of the study of a tractate of the Talmud, the following prayer is recited:

> I give my thanks to Thee, O Lord, my God and God of my fathers, that Thou hast placed my portion among those who sit in the house of study and the house of prayer, and didst not cast my lot among those who frequent theaters and circuses. For I labor and they labor; I wait and they wait; I to inherit paradise, they the pit of destruction.

This prayer is based in part on some of the sentiments expressed above, and also on the following teaching found in the Midrash: "Six things," said Rabbi Levi, "serve man: three beyond his control, and three within his control to do good or evil. Of these, his foot can take him to the theaters or circuses, or to the synagogues or houses of study." [182]

CHAPTER
VI

IN THE DAYS OF THE GEONIM:
A NATIONAL ASSOCIATION FOR
ADULT JEWISH STUDIES

In Babylonia, during the amoraic and geonic periods, there flourished for about eight hundred years—in various stages of development, from the third to the eleventh centuries—an unprecedented institution for the widespread dissemination of Jewish learning among adults. This institution was known as the *kallah*. While the precise meaning of the term is still a subject of speculation, a modern scholar, Professor Jacob Z. Lauterbach, has brilliantly suggested that it is an acronym made up of the initials of the three Hebrew words *kenesset lomedei ha-Torah,* meaning "assembly of students of the Torah." [1] Possessed of a truly remarkable purpose, program, organizational structure, and range of activity, the kallah might well be designated the first "National Association for Adult Jewish Studies."

(1) THE BABYLONIAN SYSTEM OF BRANCH SCHOOLS FOR ADULTS

Jewish learning in Babylon was centered in the great academies, the most renowned among them being Sura and Pumbedita. In these, as in the great modern universities, were concentrated the most famous and authoritative scholars. At their head stood the great spiritual leaders of Babylonian Jewry. The academies attracted many students, but because of the great expanse of Babylonia, only a small fraction of the total Jewish community could be reached. As a result, the kallah organization was brought into being to provide a stimulus and a program for Jewish study in every part of the land, to extend the influence of the academies, and to establish a point of contact between the local communities and the central seats of learning. Through the kallah organization the academies created extramural centers for Jewish learning, or branch-schools, which received direct inspiration and guidance from the out-standing scholars of the day.

These branch-schools were study-groups, or associations, of adult learners. Since their members, both teachers and learners, were un-ordained, the groups did not have the authoritative character of an academy or yeshivah, and thus they had to be designated by a special name to distinguish them from the academies. The name given the study-groups was *kenesset*, which means "assembly," but since this term was too general and not sufficiently descriptive of the nature and purpose of such organizations, the phrase *lomedei ha-Torah* ("learners of the Torah") was added. Thus, as mentioned above, the full designation of the study-groups was *kenesset lomedei ha-Torah,* which was abbreviated as kallah.

The minimum number for the formation of a kallah was ten, probably because the members held religious services in their places of study and ten men constituted the minyan, or quorum, required for public worship. Hence the rule was established that "one does not form or open a kallah organization with less than ten members." [2] The leader of the group was called *resh kallah* ("head of the assembly"), and the same title was given to one who was the leader of several study-groups in one locality or united into one school. Some of the study-groups were more advanced and some less advanced; the latter were called *kallei zutra*—junior groups.

It is fascinating to observe how the local kallah assemblies were tied up with the mother institutions. The academies set aside one month every half-year for the purpose of bringing together their branch-schools and extension students. These *yarhei kallah* ("kallah months") were stra-tegically held in Adar and Elul, just prior to the Passover and High Holy Day seasons, in order to utilize the heightened devotion of the Jewish people at these times of the year, and in order to return them to their homes and communities better instructed in the significance and observances of these major occasions in the Jewish calendar. We are told that in the days of Rab, who in the first half of the third century intro-duced this form of organization into Babylonian Jewish life, no less than twelve thousand students came day in and day out, from morning till evening, during the kallah months. The attendance was especially great in the weeks immediately preceding Passover and Rosh Hashanah, when public discourses on matters of Jewish law, probably pertaining to the festivals and the Solemn Season, were delivered before enormous crowds of laymen. In the days of Ashi, who was the head of the Sura academy for more than fifty years, from 375 to 427 c.e., one tractate of the Talmud after another was taken up, under his direction, at each of the semiannual kallah sessions. In this way, the entire Talmud was studied two times during the period of his leadership.

(2) THE CENTRAL NATIONAL ASSEMBLIES AT THE GREAT ACADEMIES

Just what transpired at the great national assemblies of students of the Torah, how they were organized and the procedure followed, what was studied, and the kind of guidance the students received from the great masters at the academies in order to pursue their studies back home, are all graphically described in a document written in the tenth century by the Babylonian Jewish historian Rabbi Nathan ha-Kohen who was also known as Rabbi Nathan the Babylonian.[3] While this chronicle only describes the kallah assemblies of the geonic period, much of what it says extends far back to the earlier centuries of the institution.

We learn from it that the outstanding scholars at the national assemblies were divided into two separate groups, the "Great Sanhedrin" and "Small Sanhedrin." The members of the upper body assisted the gaon in his instructional duties in the various fields of talmudic knowledge. The elders and the more renowned scholars had, as in the earlier talmudic period, a section reserved for them. The others sat in unassigned seats. The reserved section consisted of the first seven rows, in each of which there were ten seats. This section constituted the Sanhedrin. In these rows, each had his assigned seat and no one sat in the seat of his colleague. The first row was especially important, and seven of the scholars seated in it were each in charge of one of the seven rows occupied by the Sanhedrin. These scholars were called the roshei kallot—"heads of the kallah." They assisted the head of the academy in the work of instruction, whereas the other scholars were permitted to act only as participants in discussions and not as lecturers. The remaining three scholars seated in the front row were the assistants to the heads of the kallah, serving only in the absence of their superiors. Rabbi Nathan ha-Kohen relates:

This is the order in which the scholars are seated: The head of the academy sat in front. Facing him sat ten scholars on a bench called

"The First Row." Seven of these were the roshei kallot and three were
haverim—associates. And why was their name called roshei kallot?
Because each one of them is in charge of ten scholars of the Sanhedrin
who are called alufim—"masters." [4]

The seats in the first row, like the seats in the whole Sanhedrin section,
were transmitted from father to son if the heir was worthy of it. The
seating was assigned in accordance with the prominence and importance
of each scholar. The prevailing practice was as follows: If one of the
roshei kallot died and his son merited to succeed him, he did so. The
same was true of the haverim. If the son did not merit succession to his
father's place, he would be seated in one of the seven other rows, and if
he was not qualified for such distinction, he would be seated in the
general assembly of scholars.

The scholars who constituted the Sanhedrin are designated by different
titles in the geonic responsa. Those who had received rabbinic ordination
are called *semuhim,* meaning "ordained"; others were honored with the
titles *zaken* or *kashishai,* both meaning "elders," or with *raban dedoro
rabba,* "rabbi of the main bench." The scholars of lesser rank who were
members of the small Sanhedrin also had special titles conferred upon them,
such as *beni kiyumei*[5] and *raban dedoro desiyumei,* more generally *raban
desiyumei.* These titles are of less definite character, and their exact
meaning is not clear.

The Gaon Rabbi Amram thus opens one of his responsa addressed to
the Jewish community of Barcelona:

Receive now greetings from me, from Rabbi Zemach, the judge in the
gates, from the heads of the kallah, from the ordained scholars, who
are in the place of the Great Sanhedrin, from the *benei kiyumei* who
are in the place of the Small Sanhedrin, and from the other scholars
and sages who are in the sessions of the kallah.

Rabbi Zemach the Judge writes:

Accept the salutations of peace from me, from the alufim [i.e., the reshei
kallah], from the *rabanan kashishai dedoro rabba* [the elders of the
main bench (i.e., from the Sanhedrin who occupy the first seven rows)]
who are in the place of the Great Sanhedrin, and from the *rabanan
dedoro desiyuma* who are in the place of the Small Sanhedrin.

Rabbi Sherira Gaon and Rabbi Hai Gaon begin a joint responsum with the words:

> Receive the greetings from us, from the roshei kallah, from the *roshei midrashei* and the *roshei pirkei,* from the scholars of the main bench and the *rabanan desiyuma.*[6]

From the above we may get some idea as to the function of the *rabanan deseyumei.* While the elders who were ordained could expound the law and give instruction in it as well as render legal decisions, the *rabanan desiyumei* could only review, repeat, and summarize, for instructional purposes, the teachings of the more competent and authoritative scholars.

In addition to those already mentioned, there were other officers of instruction at the kallah assemblies. The *roshei sedarim,* "heads of orders," supervised the instruction in whole tractates and orders of the Talmud. The *roshei perakim* were in charge of smaller units of instruction— namely, separate chapters of the tractates. The *roshei midrashim* took care of instruction in Midrash. There were also *tannaim* or *mishnaim,* who recited and taught various parts of the Mishnah and the Baraita. A special function was served by the scribe of the academy, who would expound the written responsa of the gaon. The Judicial Court was in session during the kallah months to render decisions on questions of Jewish law or to uphold the decisions of the exilarch, or rosh ha-golah. It is in this connection that the chief judge, the *dayana debovo,* who was also called the *av bet din,* was of greatest assistance to the gaon, who was the head of the academy. The chief judge would also be in charge of the affairs of the academy in the absence of the gaon. The position of gaon was hereditary if the son was considered worthy of succeeding his father. Otherwise the gaon would be chosen from the scholars of the academy, preference being given to those who were ranked as elders. This is evidenced by the fact that with the exception of Rabbi Sherira and Rabbi Hai, no other geonim were in office as much as thirty or forty years. Most of the geonim "reigned" for less than ten years each. As a rule, the gaon was chosen from among the scholars of the academy; only when conditions made it absolutely necessary did they elect a gaon from a distant place. This was the case with Rabbi Saadia Gaon, who was brought from Egypt because the academy at Sura had become greatly impoverished both spiritually and materially.

(3) THE PROGRAM OF STUDIES AT THE KALLAH

The writings of Rabbi Nathan the Babylonian give us a picture of the order of study during the kallah months. Every morning, after the entire assembly had convened, each of the occupants of the first row would recite and expound part of the tractate that had been assigned at the previous assembly, which the constituent groups had all been studying in their respective communities. Following this came a discussion period during which the occupants of the other six benches could ask questions, raise objections to what had already been said, or offer their own explanations of the texts and problems under consideration. The head of the academy would then rise to speak. Standing before the silent and attentive assembly, he would explain difficult points, resolve conflicting views, and clarify any other complicated matters, instructing the assembly in the correct rendition and meaning of the part of the tractate being studied. From time to time he would interrupt his lecture to ask pointed questions of his auditors, determining from their answers whether they understood his exposition of the text. After the gaon concluded his address, one of the members of the first row would repeat and review the portion of the tractate in accordance with the explanations and conclusions just listened to. Then there would follow a question-and-discussion period in which all of the members of the assembly could participate. This procedure was followed for the first three weeks of the kallah assembly. In the fourth week, examinations were held on the talmudic tractate that had been studied for the preceding six months. Every member of the assembly was subject to these examinations.

From this description, the twofold objective of the kallah's program and method of study becomes clear: first, to explain all difficult passages and to clarify complex problems in the tractate the head of the academy had assigned for study during that half-year; second, to check on the constancy of the students and stimulate them to more devoted study. Such objectives fitted in well with the widespread organizational structure of the kallah. Only in this way could some semblance of unity and uniformity in the course of study be maintained among the distant and far-flung local assemblies of students of the Torah. The method of instruction was well suited to the nature of the gathering. Despite the large numbers in attendance, every student was afforded an opportunity to participate actively, in a prescribed and orderly manner. After the set lectures and addresses of the leading scholars—among which the address of the gaon held a central position—the students had ample opportunity to ask questions and engage in the discussion. During the first three weeks participation was voluntary, but in the final week, during the examination period, everyone had to recite and answer questions. From this account we see the serious purpose and zealous spirit underlying the semiannual kallah assemblies, in which the whole of Babylonian Jewry, together with many neighboring and distant Jewish communities, participated.

The national assemblies of students of the Torah continued down to the end of the gaonic period. In the days of Rabbi Nathan the Babylonian, the number in attendance had fallen to about four hundred. When the Jewish community of Babylon began to decline, and with it the greatness of the academies, it was natural that these national assemblies should also diminish in numbers and importance. Thus, in his famous letter to the Jews of Kairouan, Rabbi Sherira Gaon speaks in heart-rending tones of the low estate to which the semi annual assemblies had fallen. He tells the new Jewish communities of the Western countries that he lacks the financial resources to maintain these gatherings adequately; that his son, Hai, has had to take the place of many absent scholars in the work of instruction; moreover, Sherira says, since he does not receive sufficient funds to support the students who come, he has to take monies from his own meager private income to aid them. In so doing he was depriving his family; to quote his words: "Out of the mouths of my own dependents and children, we take and give to them."

Apparently, the students who came to the kallah, were maintained without charge, and they were exempt by the Persian government from paying taxes during their stay there.[7]

(4) JEWISH LEARNING FOR THE MASSES

The kallah assemblies were not the only means used by the academies to disseminate Jewish knowledge among the people. They also maintained special schools known as *tarbitzot,* "school-halls," or places for the spread of learning.[8] While the regular sessions of the academies were for advanced students in regular attendance who were pursuing a prescribed course of studies, the *tarbitzot* were for students who could not qualify for admission to the regular courses, or who had sufficient knowledge to qualify but did not want to submit to the regimen and fixed program of the academies. The *tarbitzot* were characterized by a more free and elective system. Students did not have to follow the prescribed course of study laid down by the head of the academy, but could pursue whatever interests their spirits dictated. However, the geonim did not consider the versions of the talmudic texts used in the *tarbitzot* to be as authoritative as the ones used in the regular sessions of the academy, and while students of the *tarbitzot* could attend academy sessions as auditors, they were not permitted to participate in the discussions.

Finally, in order to provide instruction to those who were engaged in earning a living during the day, the great Babylonian teachers regularly gave early-morning public lectures. This gave those residing at great distances from the academies, especially farmers and artisans, an opportunity to learn from the most renowned teachers.

Through all these methods, which established a virtual network of Jewish educational activity throughout Babylonia, the amoraim and geonim sought to disseminate Jewish learning among the masses of the people.

It is interesting to note that in modern Israel there has been a revival of the *yarhei kallah,* the kallah months, initiated by Rabbi Abraham Cahanaman at his yeshivah in Benei Berak. The Poel Hamizrahi have likewise instituted such programs in some of their settlements.[9]

(5) THE BABYLONIAN HERITAGE TRANSFERRED TO EGYPTIAN JEWRY

As the Babylonian Jewish community began to decline, during the closing centuries of the geonic period, the Jewish community in Egypt took on greater and greater importance. Among the religious and cultural treasures Egyptian Jewry inherited from Babylonian Jewry was the vital tradition of Jewish learning among adults. In the genizah sources, Professor S. D. Goitein has discovered new materials from geonic times that shed much light on the ways in which the Jews of Egypt engaged in activities for Jewish learning among young and old.[10]

His findings reveal that the chief officer in the instruction of adults was the spiritual leader of each community.[11] There were learning periods on Sabbaths and festivals and also fixed periods for learning on weekdays, especially in the evenings. The study groups were attended by all elements of the population, including the well-to-do, the workingmen, and the tradesmen.[12] In the days of the Nagid Mevorach ben Saadia (ca. 1079–1110), a communal quarrel compelled the spiritual leader of a certain community to leave his post, and as a result, we learn, "there had to be discontinued the regular and customary study sessions for young and old." [13] When Rabbi Abraham, the son of Maimonides, was nagid in Egypt, the Jews of Alexandria sent him a letter stating that they were moving to his city, Fostat, because their rabbi, "who illumined our world and rejoiced our hearts with his instruction," had left them.[14] Not only in the capital city, where Rabbi Abraham resided, but also in a neighboring city, where his son, Rabbi David, was the spiritual leader, we find that the local dayan "conducted the study session on the Sabbaths and on Monday and Thursday evenings." [15] While the traditional subjects of Jewish study were in general vogue, we come upon a group of Jewish men, all of whom were priests—kohanim—who met regularly to study the Bible with the commentary of Rabbi Saadia Gaon.[16] Some of the students were very advanced in their studies, delving into the geonic writings on the Talmud.[17]

CHAPTER

VII

LIGHT IN THE DARKNESS OF
OF THE MIDDLE AGES

The ten tragic centuries overshadowed by the Crusades, the Inquisition, and the innumerable Jewish expulsions are known as the "Dark Middle Ages." It is indeed an apt term for a period in human history that was marked by the blackness of ignorance, bigotry, and fanaticism, and expressed itself in acts of intolerance, cruelty, and bloodshed. During the medieval era, European civilization—if such it can be called—imposed upon the Jew the staff of the wanderer, the indignity of the ghetto, the misery of the blood-libel, and the death sentence of the auto-da-fé. Those were in truth dark ages for the intellectual life of the people of Europe. The minds of men were destitute of knowledge and darkened by illiteracy, for it was in the interest of the secular and religious ruling castes to enshroud the thought-life of man in utter ignorance.

(1) THE BEACON LIGHT IN A SEA OF DARKNESS

How different it was among the Jewish people of the self-same period. To them, the biblical words do fittingly apply: "all the children of Israel had light in their dwellings" (Exod. 10:23). Their lives were illuminated by the light of the Torah. Their leaders were constantly endeavoring to spread enlightenment among the Jewish masses, and they never ceased urging the importance of acquiring more and more Jewish knowledge. The Jew of the Middle Ages represented a beacon of light in a sea of darkness. The writings of the rabbis and religious leaders of practically every country in Europe and the Middle East during this thousand-year

79

period picture the high place occupied by Jewish learning and the great importance attached to it.

(2) THE LIGHT OF LEARNING IN FRANCE: RASHI THE GREAT PEDAGOGUE

Among the European Jewish communities of the Middle Ages, the Jews of France achieved a very high level of Jewish literacy. This was especially true in the tenth and eleventh centuries. The impulse to such high standards of Jewish learning was given by a series of powerful personalities, such as Rabbenu Gershom (960–1040) and his disciples. Most notable among these was a pupil of one of Rabbenu Gershom's disciples, Rabbi Shelomoh Yitzhaki, commonly known as Rashi (1040–1105).[1]

By his commentaries on the Bible and Talmud, Rashi became the commentator par excellence and the master pedagogue, not only of his generation but also of all subsequent generations. From the testimony of Rashi and his immediate descendants we obtain a first-hand knowledge of the status of Jewish learning in France at that time. Rashi informs us that "there is no 'empty one' [i.e., an ignoramus or illiterate] in Israel who does not have some knowledge of the Torah and the commandments"[2] He further tells us that "the learned men hold the ignorant ones in contempt and are looked down upon by the people,"[3] and also "that among all classes of the Jewish populace, whether they be students or the common people, there are present these two elements: the sanctification of God's name and the study of the Torah."[4] Rashi speaks of a custom in his day "to study Torah between vesper and evening services on Saturdays,"[5] and of preachers who addressed congregations on Sabbaths,[6] and of men and women who would come to listen to them.[7] Rashi's grandson, Rabbenu Tam, speaks of the prevalence of learning, for "every Jewish man sets aside time for study. If he cannot study the Talmud, he studies the Bible, or the Portion of the Week, or the Midrash,"[8] and another Tosafist states that "everyone knows the Eighteen Benedictions perfectly."[9]

If Jewish literacy was so prevalent in medieval France, this was due not only to the monumental labors of Rashi, the popular expounder of the Bible and Talmud, the two classic texts of Judaism, but also to the repeated emphasis in these commentaries on the need for constant Jewish study. In his valuable book, *Master of Troyes: A Study of Rashi the Educator,* Rabbi Samuel M. Blumenfield has collected most all of the passages on education found in Rashi's commentaries on the Bible and the Talmud. From these selections, which number more than three hundred, there emerges a clear picture of Rashi's views on the meaning and importance of lifelong learning.

Concerning the duty of transmitting the Jewish cultural heritage, Rashi naturally repeats and fully endorses the rabbinic thought that "he who teaches someone is as though he gives him birth," for by the act of teaching one re-creates the personality of the learner and thus makes him a new man. With this idea in mind, Rashi interprets the verse "Thou shalt teach them to thy sons" (Deut 6:7) to mean "thy students," and emphasizes the rabbinic admonition to address one's teacher as "father." [10] Rashi further suggests that one cannot be a true son without having received the instruction given by the father. Commenting on Proverbs 2:1, "My son, if you will take my words," Rashi says: "You will be my son if you will take my words"; also, "He who raises a righteous son is as though he never dies" (ad loc. Gen. 18:19). Time and again Rashi speaks of priests and prophets as teachers and scholars (ad loc. Ezek. 7:26), [11] and of students as their beloved children (ad loc. Isa. 8:18). He emphasizes the rabbinic dictum that study surpasses in importance the bringing of sacrifices, for "a day that you stand in my court engaged in [the study of] Torah is better than a thousand burnt offerings that your son Solomon shall bring up [on the altar]." [12] One can best appreciate the deeper meaning education holds for Rashi from the fact that he speaks of God Himself as educator and interprets the term "your teacher" in Isaiah 30:20 to mean "The Holy One, blessed be He" (See also Rashi ad loc. Prov. 4:1 and Job 36:22).

Precious as the ideal of learning is to Rashi, it does not become an end in itself until it is integrated with man's everyday life and conduct. Rashi calls one who intends to "study Torah merely to gain prestige" a fool or a rogue (ad loc. Prov. 17:16), and he cautions: "You must not say: 'I shall study in order to be rich or in order that I may be called rabbi or that I may receive a reward,' but all that you do should be done out of love; recognition will follow as the end reward." [13] Rashi further admonishes: "He who studies and does not practice, it is like unto a woman who gives birth and buries, or like one who sows and does not reap." [14] It is significant that while this statement is taken from the Talmud, [15] Rashi does not hesitate to amend the original text, which reads: "he who studies and does not review it," in order thereby to express his own view concerning the importance of practice.

Great pedagogue that he was, Rashi offers much sound advice on the basic principles of the learning process. To begin with, he touches on the need for proper motivation. He stresses the point that learning can best be achieved through love and joy rather than fear and pain. "He who does not care for the words of the Torah, even reasonable explanations do not appeal to him; but he who desires them, even those parts which he learns with effort and bitterness, become sweet to him" (ad loc. Prov. 27:7). He also underscores the rabbinic thought that "there is no comparison between one who does things out of love and one who does things out of fear. He who does things for his teacher out of fear leaves him the moment the studies become burdensome" (ad loc. Deut. 6:5). Rashi goes further, advising the teacher to "teach only the tractate that the learner requests; for if the teacher uses another tractate, the student will not master it, for his heart is set upon the subject of his own choice." [16] Commenting on the expression "early rain which falls gently," Rashi suggests that it refers to "a person who teaches his students gently." [17] Rashi also maintains that "when a master explains the subject clearly and pleasantly, the disciple will succeed in his studies, otherwise he will not benefit from his master." [18] He exhorts all: "Learn out of joy and good cheer in accordance with your heart's dictates and desires." [19]

Rashi likewise offers helpful advice on the methodology of teaching and learning. He urges a number of methods, namely *enunciation, memorization, drill, concentration and discussion,* and *systematic learning,* stressing the talmudic thought that the words of the Torah cannot be acquired except through the vocal utterance of the mouth.[20] Rashi states: "You must arrange the words of the Torah and utter them well and not stammer or whisper." [21] Again taking his cue from a rabbinic dictum—"One who repeats his lesson a hundred times is not like one who repeats a hundred and one times" [22]—Rashi says: "The scholar who keeps on reviewing succeeds in preserving his studies";[23] also: "If you repeat your course of study, you will be wise enough to understand new things from old." [24] Commenting on Proverbs 12:11, "He that tilleth the ground shall have plenty of bread," Rashi offers the figurative interpretation that it refers to "one who continually reviews his studies." Time and again he advises: "Recite your learning even though it may already be as familiar to you as a song." [25] Also, in commenting on Proverbs 3:13,[26] he declares that when the Book of Proverbs speaks of "the slothful" (Prov. 24:30), it refers to the learner "who does not review the text of his studies." But "the wise man studies a little today and a little tomorrow" (ad loc. Prov.

24:7). Moreover, "like the forest that sprouts, so are the words of the Torah; he who meditates upon them continually discovers new meanings" (ad loc. Song of Songs 5:10). Once again in keeping with a talmudic teaching, Rashi counsels: "One should take the trouble of effecting reminders and inventing special devices in order to remember his studies," [27] and also: "One must take the trouble to set up mnemonics and devise tricks in every way in order that the Torah be retained by those who study it." [28] He recommends the habits of regularity and concentration. To teachers he says: "Fix regular times for your students so they will know when it is time to come and study." [29] To students, commenting on the talmudic dictum, "Do not sit and study at the highest point in town," [30] he says: because it is "a place where the people of the city continually pass; perhaps when they pass they will disturb you from your studies." He warns students to be on guard and very careful lest they forget what they have learned (ad loc. Deut. 11:12), for "if you have begun to forget you will ultimately forget all of it, as it is written, 'If thou forgettest Me one day, I will forget thee two days' [Deut. 11:13]." [31]

Drill and review are not ends in themselves. They must lead to greater understanding. Commenting on Exodus 21:1, "Now these are the ordinances . . . which thou shalt set before them," Rashi declares:

God said to Moses, it should not enter your mind to say, I shall teach them the law of the Torah twice or three times until it becomes current in their mouths exactly according to its wording, but I shall not take the trouble to make them understand the meaning and the reasons of these teachings; therefore Scripture says, "which thou shalt set before them," like a table fully laid and prepared for a person that he may eat.[32]

While he sees drill and repetition as important, Rashi fully appreciates the value of the discussion method. Commenting on "Happy is the man that hath his quiver full of them; they shall not be put to shame" (Ps. 127:5), Rashi suggests that it refers to "scholars who argue with one another in halakhahs as though they were enemies." He notes that "there are many disputations in the houses of learning, but all scholars have their hearts set on one thing—to understand the Torah properly and truly" (ad loc. Song of Songs 6:9). He encourages students to ask as many questions as they want, "even though his fellow-students will mock him," [33] and he adds: "If you have lowered yourself, for the sake of the Torah, to inquire and present your doubts to your teacher, even if you seem to him like a fool without understanding, you will in the end be elevated" (ad loc. Prov. 30:33). He confirms the right of the learner "to question the reasons why scholars issued certain regulations or provided for certain enactments" (ad loc. Prov. 25:27). In addition to all these observations on methodology, Rashi emphasizes the importance of systematic and constant study. He makes a distinction between the foolish man, who is disorganized and helplessly asks: "How can I ever study Torah? When will I ever succeed in my learning?" and the wise man, "who systematically studies a little today and a little tomorrow" (ad loc. Prov. 24:7). Commenting on Avot 1:15, Rashi says: "You should establish fixed times for study every single day and study four or five chapters," [34] and in the same vein he writes: "Because one must busy oneself with worldly matters, for without worldly pursuits there can be no Torah; therefore it is all the more necessary to set aside certain times for the study of the Torah, a fixed period of time so as not to spend the entire day on worldly matters." [35]

While the study of Torah should be engaged in for its own sake, Rashi nevertheless points often to the rewards of learning and the penalties for not learning. He who learns grows in mental and emotional maturity for, says Rashi, "as the winds uphold the grasses and promote their growth, so too the words of the Torah promote the growth of those who study them," [36] and the learner "has a warm heart because of his studies, and he takes things to heart more than other people." [37] Of course the ultimate reward of study is that it strengthens man's moral nature and helps him to lead the good life, for "when you engage in the study of the Torah, you will learn to walk in the good way and to overcome evil inclinations" (ad loc. Hos. 10:12). The opposite is the case with the ignorant who do not study. The greatest punishment that could possibly be visited upon them is the weakening of the moral fiber, which leads to sin and ultimately to the denial of God. Rashi warns that "there are seven sins. The first leads to the second, and so on to the last. The very first sin is: He does not learn. The others follow inexorably: He does not practice. He despises others who practice. He hates scholars. He prevents others from studying. He rejects the basic principle concerning belief in God" (ad loc. Lev. 26:15). In another connection, Rashi bluntly states that "when a man departs from the study of Torah, he attaches himself to idol worship" (ad loc. Deut. 11:10).

Two generations later, Rabbenu Tam and his school of Tosafists issued their famous takkanot, which state: "Every man shall fix times for study. If he is not able to study Talmud, let him study Bible, or the Portion of the Week, or Midrash. Each man according to his abilities—some more, some less." One of the Tosafists offers a brilliant answer to the question why we are not required to recite the blessing over the Torah every time we begin to study Torah, explaining:

You cannot compare this to the law pertaining to eating in the Sukkah, which requires that the blessing over bread must be recited every time you partake of a meal in the Sukkah. It is entirely different with Torah study because this is a continuous and constant occupation for a Jew, since he is obligated to study Torah all the time without interruption, as it is written, "Thou shalt meditate upon it day and night" (Josh. 1:8).[38]

(3) THE LIGHT OF LEARNING IN THE GERMAN COUNTRIES

Turning from France to the German countries, we come upon the famous Rabbi Judah the Pious of Regensburg, writing at the end of the twelfth century and reflecting the views of Franco-German Jewry in the early Middle Ages.[39] He wrote:

The Talmud states one should always divide his years into three; devoting a third to Mikra, a third to Mishnah, and a third to Talmud.[40] This means (quoting the view of Rashi) that he shall devote two days a week to the study of the Bible, two days to the Mishnah, two days to the Talmud, all three together on the Sabbath day; some hold that the Aggadah should be studied on the Sabbath. There are others (quoting the view of the Tosafists), who interpret the talmudic dictum to mean that every day should be divided into three parts so that four hours each should be devoted to Bible, Mishnah, and Talmud. There are still others who accept the talmudic injunction more literally, maintaining that the years should be divided into three, with one year each devoted in turn to the study of the Bible, the Mishnah, and the Talmud. . . . If a man has the means to hire a teacher for his son, he should not instruct his child himself, so that he should be able to devote more time to his own studies. When a man sees that he is earning a good living, and that if he devoted only part of his time to his occupation he would still have enough for his needs, then he should not say: "Where there is no meal there is no Torah," making the study of Torah a temporary occupation and his business a full-time occupation. On the contrary, the study of the Torah should receive a fixed time and his business part-time. Nor should anyone idle away even a single moment without studying Torah, for the punishment meted out to one who sits idly is greater than to one who devotes all his time to his business, even if he is a man of means. When a man employs a manager or an assistant in his business whom he can trust, then he should follow the example of Rabbi Simeon bar Yohai (who held that when Israel obeys the will of God their labors are performed by others)[41] in order to fulfill the biblical command: "Thou shalt meditate therein day and night" (Josh. 1:8), and not occupy himself with his business affairs. When a man only has to provide for his own immediate family, then he should not make his business a full-time occupation, except when, in addition, he has to provide for orphans and widows, or the poor, or the aged who are not able to earn for themselves but are dependent on him—then he is permitted to devote himself fully to his business. He who has money, rather than donate it for the building of a synagogue or a bet ha-midrash, should donate it for the support of righteous men who will occupy themselves in the study of Torah, and preferably scholars who study in a God-fearing spirit because they want to fulfill God's commandments, rather than scholars who want the world to know of their intellectual prowess.[42]

Rabbi Sheftel Hurwitz, the famous son of a famous father, who edited his father's great work, *Two Tables of the Covenant,* and was the rabbi of Frankfurt on the Main in the middle of the seventeenth century, paints a glowing picture of Jewish learning in his time:

It is incumbent upon every Jew to engage in the study of Torah. Even if he is occupied with business affairs, he should set aside one hour each day and join a study group. When I was the rabbi and head of the academy in Frankfurt, the custom prevailed for people to gather at midday, flock by flock, group by group, society by society. Each group had a scholar at its head who served as instructor. After the period of study a Kaddish D'Rabbanan was recited and a donation was made to the treasury. From these funds festive occasions were arranged. Happy is the eye that has seen these things, and happy the generation in which men of prominence and renown received instruction from the humble—for so humble a man as myself was listened to. This practice prevailed in each place and in each community—whether large or small.[43]

At the end of the seventeenth century, another rabbi in Germany, Rabbi Chanoch Henech, admonished his people in these words:[44]

Since every man is obligated to study Torah, therefore he should set aside fixed periods of time for it. He who is too preoccupied with earning a livelihood is in duty-bound to study immediately after the morning prayers. If a man does not know the Hebrew tongue sufficiently to understand it, he is not excused from this obligation since he can study in the vernacular, which in this country is German. The all-important thing is to understand what one learns and to obey what one is taught. This is easy to accomplish in our day since many of the branches of Torah-study which are to be transmitted to the masses are available in Judeo-German. The following books must be mastered thoroughly by those who do not know Hebrew: *Lev Tov*,[45] *Mitzvat Nashim*,[46] *Brant Spiegel*,[47] *Sefer ha-Musar*,[48] and the like. After he has mastered these books, he should also read the *Tze'ena u-Re'ena*,[49] the twenty-four books of the Bible, the Festival and Holy Day Prayer Books, and the Penitential Prayers. The latter books are not as compulsory as the former.[50]

(4) THE LIGHT OF LEARNING IN BOHEMIA AND POLAND

Similar views were expressed in other European centers of Jewish life. Thus Rabbi Ephraim Luntshitz, the chief rabbi of Prague toward the end of the sixteenth century and the beginning of the seventeenth, and one of the greatest preachers of his time, wrote:[51]

I have seen the great good that has come from the study of Mishnah—a practice established by Rabbi Leib[52], of blessed memory, here in Prague in all the congregations to study in groups one chapter of the Mishnah after the morning services. As a result, even those men who, because they lack the knowledge to study the Talmud daily, or because they haven't too much time, at least learn a chapter of the Mishnah each day. I am therefore determined to strengthen this practice with all my might, especially since there has been published the commentary of the *Tosafot Yom Tov* on the Mishnah [first published in the years 1614–17]. This practice has been followed in every city and in every community.

A contemporary of Rabbi Ephraim was Rabbi Isaac ben Eliakim of Posen in Poland, whose popular book, *Lev Tov,* was printed in Prague in 1620. In it he states:

Each Jew is duty-bound to make the study of Torah a principal and fixed occupation and his worldly occupation minor and temporary. . . . He who fixes times for Torah, even if only for one hour a day, and does not interrupt his studies during this hour even for the greatest profit in the world, such a man is one who makes the Torah his principal occupation. But he who does not put aside a fixed time for the study of Torah, but looks into a book when he has free time from his business, and closes the book when some business matter comes along, such a one does not make the Torah his principal occupation. Therefore, each man must set aside a definite time each day for Torah, even if it be only a short period of time. The important thing is: not to interrupt his studies no matter what business affair should come along. It is better to study a little with concentration than a great deal without concentration. Even he who is not learned should set aside a fixed time for study, and if he is poor and cannot engage a teacher, then let him read the *Teitch Humash* or the *Teitch Tehillim* or the books written in Judeo-German, or he should listen daily to the exposition of one or two regulations of the Jewish law and should repeat them.

Another witness to the aristocracy of Jewish learning in seventeenth-century Poland is Rabbi Nathan Nata Hanover. In the final chapter of his classic *Yeven Metzulah* ("The Abyss of Despair"), published in Venice in 1653 against the background of the slaughter of the Jews during the bloody days of the Cossack pogroms under Bogdan Chmielnicki, he describes the zealous dedication of Polish Jewry to Jewish learning. In the part of his book called "The Pillar of Torah" he writes:

Matters that are widely known need not be proved, for throughout the dispersions of Israel there was never so much learning as in the Kingdom of Poland. There each and every community maintained yeshivot, and they lavished great compensation on the master of each yeshiva that he might maintain his yeshiva without worry and that the Torah might be his trade. And the master of the yeshiva would not leave his house the entire year except to go to the house of prayer or the house of study, and he was engaged day and night in the study of the Torah. Furthermore each community maintained young men and provided them with a weekly allotment of money that they might study with the master of the yeshiva, and for each young man they also maintained at least two boys who should study under his supervision so that he should orally explain the *Gemara, Rashi,* and *Tosafot* [the Talmud and its exegeses and commentaries] which he had learned, and thus they should become adept at argumentation.

The boys were provided with food from community funds or public kitchens. A community of fifty households maintained not less than thirty young men and boys, and one young man and his two pupils would be in the same household, and the young man at least sat at table as one of the sons. And although the young man had an allotment from the community, his host provided him with food and drink as he needed. Some of the more generous householders also permitted the boys to eat at their tables, thus providing food and drink to three persons the entire year.

And there was scarcely a house in all the Kingdom of Poland where they did not engage in the study of the Torah: either the head of the household was a scholar, or his son, or his son-in-law, or a young man eating at the table, and at times all of these were in the same house. Thus they realized the three things which Rava listed in the Tractate *Shabbat,* Chapter I: "Rava said he who loves scholars will have scholarly sons; he who honors scholars will have scholarly sons-in-law; he who fears scholars will be himself a scholar." Thus it came about that there were many learned men in each community and if there was a community of fifty householders it contained twenty scholars who were called *morenu* [our master] or *haver* [friend]. [These were honorary titles accorded by the rabbi to scholarly members of his congregation. Communal regulations defined the conditions to be met in order to obtain such titles.] The master of the yeshiva was over all these and the scholars were obedient toward him and went to hear his discourses at the yeshiva.

And this was the order of study in the Kingdom of Poland: the

term of study was that time during which the young men and the boys
had to study with the master of the yeshiva. In the summer it extended
from the first day of the month of Iyar till the fifteenth day of the
month of Ab; in the winter from the first of the month of Heshvan
till the fifteenth day of Shevat. After the fifteenth of Shevat or the
fifteenth of Ab the young men and the boys were free to study wherever
they chose. From the first day of Iyar till the feast of Pentecost, and
in the winter from the first day of Heshvan till Hanukah, all the students at the yeshiva studied *Gemara, Rashi,* and *Tosafot* with great
diligence. Each day they studied a *halachah*—a page of *Gemara* with
its commentaries was called a *halachah.*

All the scholars and young men of the community and anyone with
a penchant for learning would go to the yeshiva. The master of the
yeshiva alone would be seated in a chair and all the others stood about
him. They would dispute with each other in matters of Law before
the master of the yeshiva arrived, and when he came each would ask
him that which he had found difficult in the Law and he would answer
their questions. Then they were all silent and the master of the yeshiva
discoursed about his new interpretations of the Law, and after he had
stated his innovations the master of the yeshiva would state a contradiction, i.e., he would cite from the *Gemara* or *Rashi* or *Tosafot* things
that are contradictory, he would question abbreviations and provide
answers which might also be contradictory; thus he would find answers until the Law emerged clearly.

In the summer they would not leave the yeshiva earlier than noon.
From the feast of Pentecost till the New Year, and from Hanukah till
Passover, the master of the yeshiva would not engage in so many
disputatious subjects, but taught the scholars *Arba'ah Turim* [a collection of laws compiled by Rabbi Jacob ben Rabbi Asher]; the young
men he taught *Rav Alfas* [the compilation of laws by Rabbi Yitzchak
Alfasi] and other works. In any case they also studied *Gemara, Rashi,*
and *Tosafot* till the first day of Ab or the fifteenth day of Shevat. From
then on until Passover or the New Year they studied solely compilations
of Law and other works.

Some weeks before the fifteenth day of Ab or the fifteenth day of
Shevat the master of the yeshiva would honor each one of his students
by allowing him to conduct the discourses in the yeshiva in his stead;
both scholars and young men were thus honored. They would hold

forth and the master of the yeshiva disputed with them so that they should sharpen their wits.

Thus they studied the same tractate throughout the Kingdom of Poland in sequence through the six orders [of the *Mishna*]. And each master of a yeshiva had one attendant who went daily to all the schools to look after the boys, both rich and poor, that they should study; and he would warn them every day in the week that they should study and not roam the streets. On Thursdays all the boys had to go in a group to the director in charge of the Talmud Torahs who questioned them on what they had learned during the week, and he who knew nothing of what he had studied or made one error was flogged by the attendant at the order of the director and was otherwise chastised before the other boys so that he should remember and study more diligently the following week. Likewise on the eve of Sabbath all the boys went in a group to the master of yeshiva, who questioned them on what they had learned during the week. In this manner there was a great fear upon the boys and they studied with diligence.

Also during the three days before Pentecost and during Hanukah the young men and the boys reviewed what they had studied during the term, and the heads of the community gave them allotted gifts of money. Such was the custom till the fifteenth day of Ab or the fifteenth day of Shevat. After that the master of the yeshiva, together with all his pupils, young men and boys, traveled to the fair.

In the summer they traveled to the fairs in Zaslav and Jerislav; in the winter to the fairs in Lvov and Lublin. There the young men and boys were free to study in any yeshiva they chose. And at each fair there were some hundreds of masters of yeshivot, some thousands of young men, tens of thousands of boys and Jewish merchants, and Gentiles like the sands on the shore of the sea, for people would come to the fair from one end of the world to the other. And whoever had a son or a daughter to marry off went to the fair and there chose a match, for there everyone found his like and his mate. And there would be hundreds of matches made at each fair, and sometimes thousands. Jews, men as well as women, went about the fair dressed in royal garments, for they were held in esteem by the rulers and by the Gentiles, and the children of Israel were numerous as the sands of the sea, but now, because of our sins, they have become few, may the Lord have mercy upon them.

And great honor was accorded to the master of the yeshiva in each community, and his words were heard by rich and poor alike, none gainsaid him, without him no man raised his hand or foot, and as he commanded thus it came to be. In his hand he carried a stick and lash to flog and to punish and to chastise transgressors; it was his to formulate regulations, establish safeguards and declare the forbidden. Nevertheless the master of the yeshiva was loved and one who had a good portion such as fatted fowl or good fish would honor the master of the yeshiva with half or all of these, and with other gifts of money or silver and gold without measure. In the synagogue, too, most of those who bought honors shared them with the master of the yeshiva, who was called up at least third to the reading of the Torah on Sabbaths and the first day of the holidays. And if the master of the yeshiva was a Kohan or a Levite, the honors that belong to these were accorded to him, despite the fact that there may have been many other Kohanim or Levites in the congregation. And no man walked out of the synagogue on Sabbaths or holidays until the master of the yeshiva went out first and his pupils after him, then the whole congregation accompanied him to his home. On holidays the entire congregation went to his home to greet him. For this reason all scholars were envious and studied diligently that they, too, might reach this state and become masters of yeshivot in some community, and through study for extraneous motives they came to study the Torah for its own sake, and the land was filled with knowledge.[53]

(5) THE LIGHT OF LEARNING IN ITALY

When we turn to the Italian Jewish community, we find the importance of Jewish learning for its own sake being urged by a rather unexpected source—the secular Hebrew poem *Ha-Tofet ve-ha-Eden* ("Hell and Heaven") by the Jewish poet and friend of Dante, Immanuel of Rome (1270–1330). While on an imaginary descent to the nether-world, the author tells us, he came upon

people for whom the light had become darkness, the sun and moon had set for them . . . and they dwelt in a low estate. . . . When I saw them sinking in such anguish, I inquired into the reasons that had brought them to such a pitiful condition, and I was told: These are the transgressors [*shovavim*]. They had studied the Pentateuch, the Prophets, the Hagiographa; and also the Mishnah, the Gemara, the Sifre, the Sifra; and also the Tosafot, the commentaries, the compendia, and the novellae; but they made of their Torah crowns and spades. Crowns for self-exaltation, and spades for material self-improvement. They did not love the Torah and its wisdom for the sake of their intrinsic majesty and greatness, but rather used them as means to achieve their own ends. They faultily and foolishly thought that by means of the Torah they would mount to heights greater than the Torah itself. Therefore he who intends to utilize the Torah, which is the word of the living God and is spiritual, for ends that are material, has dreamed a false dream and will never find the way of peace. His deeds will not be acceptable to God. . . . Thus did King Solomon teach: "For whoso findeth me findeth life" [Prov. 8:35]. He did not say: "Whoso findeth me shall find something by means of which he will attain his desires." [54]

Our source for the state of Jewish learning in sixteenth-century Italy is Rabbi Judah Leib ben Naphtali Bresh. In the introduction to his translation of the Pentateuch into Judeo-German, printed in Cremona in 1560, he tells us:

I have seen the great need for the study of Torah in our generation. Every man craves for it, especially in our land [Italy] where, because of our sins, we do not busy ourselves overmuch with its study. Seeing that the men do not learn, the women, young women, and girls do not learn either. Many men, who were unable or unwilling to learn in their youth, now, in their maturity, want to learn, but they are ashamed at this age to learn the sidrah of the week with a teacher. I have observed all this, and I therefore hope to bring benefit to our people by printing this Pentateuch in the German language.[55]

In seventeenth-century Italy, Rabbi Simone ben Isaac Luzzatto (1583–1663), who was a rabbi in Venice, wrote a work of apologetics in Italian entitled *Discourse on the Situation of the Hebrews*. Its section on "Learning Among the Hebrews," first translated into English in 1952, says much of relevance to our theme of adult Jewish learning.

Rabbi Luzzatto begins by stating: "As long as it was protected by Divine favor, the Hebrew Nation was celebrated by both Arms and Learning amongst all the peoples coeval with it." He then recounts the military defeat of the Jewish people by the Romans and the dispersion of the Jews to all the lands of the world. This sad circumstance, he explains, only increased the Jewish zeal for learning. After describing the three main categories of Jewish learning—Talmud, philosophical theology, and kabbalah, citing the names and writings of the leading figures in each field—Rabbi Luzzatto concludes with these words of glowing tribute to the Jewish ardor for secular as well as sacred knowledge:

> This is what I have bethought me to say concerning the learning of Hebrews in matters of Holy Writ. As for their application to human sciences, not only are they under no ban, but they are enjoined by Legal precept to dedicate themselves to the contemplation of natural things, the end proposed being a probable recognition of God's greatness. Even more do they deem themselves bound to address themselves to the study of Astronomy, both in virtue of the need to determine the Institution of Feast Days, and because that science is a kind of introduction to the apprehension of Divine power and wisdom; this last in conformity with the saying of the Psalmist: *In coelis praeparabitur veritas* [or *fides*] *tua in eis.* That is, the heavens are the place and the means whereby God prepares the souls of men for faith; this, through a contemplation of their vastness, celerity of motion, constancy of periods, and immutability of cycles.
>
> Of a truth, the Hebrews being in their present state of subjection and free only to give a scholarly employment to their minds, ought to apply themselves thereto single-mindedly and assiduously. And they ought to hold for a certainty that the unity of dogmas, the Princely protection with which they have been favored, and the self-preservation which through so long a course of time they have against so much oppression assured themselves, have, humanly speaking, been a consequence of the virtue and learning of some few of them, who had acquired credit and authority before Ruling sovereigns. Since they have no other means whereby to aspire to the favors and graciousness of the Powerful, they must take heed that, failing an appreciation of Letters and the esteem of the judicious, they stand on the brink of some notable declination and despised oppression greater than any they have ever suffered in the past.[56]

(6) THE LIGHT OF LEARNING IN BABYLONIA, SPAIN, AND NORTH AFRICA

From the writings of three of the leading Jewish figures of the ninth through the eleventh centuries, we get an extremely interesting description of the devotion of the Jewish communities of Babylon, Spain, and North Africa to Torah study.

Let us begin by examining the responsum of Rabbi Natronai, the gaon of the academy at Sura from 852 to 856, to a question posed by the Jewish community of Spain.

Concerning your inquiry about those synagogues in which the public gathers to recite chapters from the Psalms on the Sabbaths and Festivals; and on Rosh Hashanah and Yom Kippur they recite additional Psalms; and while the congregation chants the Psalms, students begin to study and busy themselves in the study of Torah, until two hours after sunrise; and then they begin the morning prayers. You inquire whether it is permitted to do so, since, by not reciting the Shema at sunrise, they are studying prior to having accepted the yoke of God's kingdom. . . .

Thus have we been shown from Heaven that when Israel rises early and comes to the synagogues on the Sabbaths and Festivals to study— it is a good practice that they follow. And this has been the minhag [established custom] in Babylon from the time of the first Exile. Since the Jewish people were exiled to Babylon and the study of the Torah, together with the number of teachers, has lessened, the Children of Israel have been coming to the Prophets and to the masters of Torah and said to them: "We are not able to study Mishnah and Talmud every night since we are burdened with the responsibility of earning a livelihood; at least on the Sabbath and Festivals, when we do have time, shall we be idle and waste the night in sleep?" Therefore they have established the practice of rising early to go to the synagogue to study until morning.[57]

This was also the custom in Kairouan in North Africa, as seen from a question sent to Rabbi Hai (939–1038), the gaon of Pumbedita. As quoted in Rabbi Hai's responsum, the questioner wrote: "It is our custom here in Kairouan for people to gather in the synagogues during the night of Yom Kippur, and sometimes on the nights of the Sabbath also, to recite the Psalms by the light of the candelabra."[58]

Rabbi Samuel Ha-Nagid (993–1055) of Spain writes: "The people would gather in the synagogues on the Sabbaths and set aside fixed periods of time for study until about two hours before sunrise. An inquiry was sent to the heads of the academies, who permitted them to delay the recitation of the Shema even after sunrise for the sake of spreading the Torah." [59]

A number of Jewish leaders in Spain, probably men of Babylonian origin, were troubled by the Spanish custom of omitting the Targum translation during the Torah Reading. They expressed their concern in a question addressed to Rabbi Hai Gaon in Babylon as follows: "The Spanish Jews abandoned the use of the Targum translation during the Torah Reading. We find, however, in many passages of the Torah, that this is a positive commandment." Rabbi Hai, replying that it is a duty to read the Targum and an ordinance going back to prophetic times, expressed surprise: "We did not know that in Spain they have set the Targum aside."

In geonic times it was the practice in many countries to translate the Torah Reading, verse by verse, from Hebrew into Aramaic. But since the Aramaic tongue, in which the Targum is written, was not too well understood by the Jews of Europe and Africa, this practice began to fall into disuse. The geonim of Babylon, naturally, objected strenuously to this trend. When, for example, the Jewish community of Fez in North Africa abandoned the practice, Rabbi Judah ibn Kureish rose to the defense of the Targum:

By your abandoning the Targum you liken yourselves to the foolish men of your community who consider the Targum superfluous and maintain that the people should rather understand the Hebrew language. But you must realize that your elders before you never pushed the Targum aside, and your ancestors in Babylon, Egypt, Africa, and Andalusia [Moslem Spain] never considered it superfluous. [60]

Rabbi Samuel Ha-Nagid, taking cognizance of those who had written to Rabbi Hai, rose to the defense of Spanish Jewry:

There are some rabbis who warn us here in Spain against discontinuing the use of the Targum, as is evident from the action of those who have addressed a question to Rabbi Hai Gaon, stating that Spain is a land in which the Torah has been disseminated since the earliest times, from the time of the Exile till this day, and therefore the abandonment of the Targum smacks of the Karaite heresy; furthermore, that Karaism has never existed here except in certain villages near to Edom [i.e., Christian Spain and France], which are suspected of nurturing this heresy in secret, and in which our early leaders have striven to stamp out this heresy by imposing the punishment of lashes. In view of all this, why therefore should the Targum be abandoned now? . . .

Our present customs came about in this way: The people would gather in the synagogues on the Sabbaths and set aside fixed periods of time for study until about two hours after sunrise. An inquiry was sent to the heads of the academies, who permitted them to delay the recitation of the Shema even after sunrise for the sake of spreading the Torah. After their studies they would hold the morning services, and then they would seat themselves and each one privately would go over the Portion of the Week twice and the Targum once. Then there would be the public reading of the Portion of the Week and its Targum translation, followed by the Prophetic Lesson and its Targum translation. They would then wait until toward sunset. This became quite burdensome for the people. Therefore they compromised—they would go over the Portion of the Week twice and the Targum only once in private. This has been our practice since then, except on those Sabbaths when there is a bridegroom present, and on Festivals when the Targum for the Prophetic Lesson is read publicly in order to add to the festivity of the occasion.[61]

The writings of the time also provide us with much information about the importance the Jews of Spain attached to Jewish learning. From a very interesting responsum of Rabbi Isaac Alfasi (1013–1103), we learn of mature men hiring teachers to instruct them.[62] It reads as follows:

Reuben lived in eastern France with his wife and children—a great distance from Spain. He left France for Spain and visited many communities. When he came to preach in a certain community, five of the leading Jewish people pleaded with him to bring his family there and settle among them and to be their instructor. After much persuasion he agreed to this. These five pledged themselves to pay him twenty-four gold coins a year for a three-year period, in return for which he was to give them instruction in Halakhah, Mishnah, Bible and the Weekly Portion, and any other subjects they might desire. . . . Some of them said, Let's start with the study of the Mishnah; others with the Talmud, until they all agreed to begin with the study of the tractate Berakhot. This they studied from Sunday through Wednesday; on Thursday they studied Bible; and on Friday they went over the Portion of the Week. After a while, one of the group became dissatisfied because he couldn't keep up with the studies, and he requested that they proceed at a slower pace. The others refused, and he therefore refused to pay his share of the tutor's expense.[63]

Nor was this an isolated case, for Rabbi Abraham ibn Daud, in his *Sefer ha-Kabbalah,* tells us that in the years 1045–55 a famous Jewish scholar came to Córdoba from France, and a Cordoban Jew by the name of R. Isaac ben Albaliyah "did well by him, provided all his needs, and learned from him." [64]

The Hebrew poets of the Golden Age in Spain wrote poems extolling the virtues of learning. The statesman-poet Samuel Ha-Nagid of the eleventh century stated:

> He who has toiled and bought for himself books,
> But his heart is empty of what they contain—
> Is like a lame man, who engraved on a wall
> The figure of a foot, and tried in vain to stand![65]

In another poem he urges the importance of getting an early start in one's studies:

> Learning's robe the good disciple decks,
> And youthful study sweet increase bestows;
> But he who in his age would wisdom gain
> Dies ere he wisdom's savor tastes.[66]

Again he writes in praise of books:

> The wise of heart forsakes the ease of pleasure,
> In reading books he finds tranquility;
> All men have faults, thine eyes can see them,
> The wise-heart's failing is—forgetfulness!
>
> Consult a man of sense and well-beloved,
> Put not thy trust in thine own device;
> For if thou turnest to thy heart's desire,

Desire will hide from thee the right;
Is it a yearned-for end? Thy heart
Doth make thy lust seem fair before thee![67]

The greatest poet of the Middle Ages, Judah Ha-Levi (1086–1146), sings the praises of learning in these words:

How shall I fear man, when a soul is mine
Whose whelps can dismay lions?
Why fret about poverty, when in her is wisdom
From whose hills I may hew jewels?
If I hunger, lo! her dainty fruits;
If I thirst, I find her streams!
Sit I desolate, when her harp
Charms me with her melodies?
Why seek a friend to hold converse,
And lose her cunning accents?
My harp, my lyre, are at her pen's point,
Her scrolls are my garden and paradise![68]

Rabbi Moses ibn Ezra (1060–1139), the Hebrew poet and liturgist, coined a Hebrew aphorism: "If you will not endure the labors of learning, you will suffer the burdens of folly." [69]

Rabbi Jonah Gerondi, writing in the early thirteenth century, states:[70]

It is a man's duty to engage in the study of Torah every day . . . for our sages have said: "The study of Torah is above everything else," [71] and in the Sifri it is stated: "Even as the reward for the study of Torah is greater than for any other mitzvot, so is the punishment for the neglect of Torah study greater than for any other averot." [72] We know that in the days of the first Temple, the Holy One, blessed be He, overlooked Israel's idolatry, incest, and bloodshed, but he did not overlook the sin of neglecting the study of the Torah, as it is said in Scripture: "Who is the wise man that he may understand this? And who is he to whom the mouth of the Lord hath spoken that he may declare it? Wherefore is the land perished . . .? And the Lord saith: Because they have forsaken my Law" [Jer. 9:11–12].
When people leave their work or their business and go home or

place themselves on streetcorners or sit in idleness or while away the
time in empty conversation, the evil they do is great and their transgression is heavy indeed, because they are putting the Torah to shame.
He who is able to engage in the study of Torah and does not do so,
despises the word of God. For this reason, everyone is duty-bound to
set aside one place in his home in which he should keep a collection
of books on Jewish law, the Book of Psalms, the Book of Prayers, so
that when he becomes free from his business concerns he can go there
to study or to read.

They who walk in the counsel of the wicked are those who occupy
themselves with the vanities of this world. I have seen with my own
eyes that many of the parnasim [communal leaders] in this land, to
whom God has given wealth and honor, who could devote time to
Torah study for fully half the day, yet they do not do so. They exchange
the books of the Torah for the ledgers of business, and they content
themselves with the little they learned in their youth.

"Thus shalt thou say to the House of Jacob, and tell the Children of
Israel" [Exod. 19:13]. When the Torah was given, Moses was commanded to address "the House of Jacob" first, and this refers to the
women. Why was he commanded to address the women first? Because
they send their children to study the Torah, they care for them tenderly
when they return home from school, they draw the hearts of the little
ones to love the Torah, and they watch over them so they will not
neglect their studies. . . . We therefore see that the women exercise a
great influence for the study of Torah and for the righteous life. Similarly, women of piety can also influence their husbands and rescue
them from too much preoccupation with business affairs, and they can
also remind their husbands when they are tired or forgetful to give a
portion of their time to study of the Torah. It is therefore the duty of
the women to remind their husbands to open a book and to study
Torah.

Rabbi Aaron Ha-Levi of Barcelona, writing at the end of the thirteenth
century in his Sefer ha-Hinnukh ("The Book of Education"), declares:

One of the mitzvot [positive commandments], which is the very foundation upon which all the others rest, is the commandment to study the
Torah. Only by the study of the Torah can a man understand the other
mitzvot so that he may observe them. For this very reason have our

sages of blessed memory instituted the practice of reading a portion of the Torah at public assemblies in the synagogue. By this means the hearts of the people will be aroused to turn to the Torah and to the observances week by week.[73]

Rabbi Israel ibn Al-Nakawa, who lived in Toledo and met his death there during the massacre of 1391,[74] produced a monumental work called *Menorat ha-Maor* ("The Book of Illumination"). It was not until 1929 that this book was rescued from oblivion by the late Dr. Hyman G. Enelow, who edited and published it from the only surviving manuscript, written in the fifteenth century. Of the book's twenty chapters, the fifth, entitled "On Fixed Hours of Study," offers much material for our interest, and in the passages that follow we shall summarize its contents in detail.

At the outset, Al-Nakawa points to the positive character of Jewish life, which requires not mere abstention from frivolous pastimes but rather devotion to spiritual and intellectual pursuits. Hence, the study of all branches of the Torah—Bible, Mishnah, Talmud—is obligatory for every Jew. This he derives from the rabbinic interpretations of the opening verse of the Book of Psalms: "Happy is the man who hath not walked in the counsel of the wicked, nor stood in the way of sinners, nor sat in the seat of the scornful, but his delight is in the law of the Lord; and in His law doth he meditate day and night." We read in the Talmud:[75] "Happy is the man who hath not walked," that is, to the theaters and circuses of idolators; "nor stood in the way of sinners," that is, he does not attend contests of wild beasts; "nor sat in the seat of the scornful," that is, he is not a spectator at hippodromes.[76] And lest one say, "Since I do not go to theaters or circuses, or attend contests of wild animals, or sit in at hippodromes, I will go and indulge in sleep," Scripture continues: "His delight is in the law of the Lord; and in His law doth he meditate day and night." Said Rabbi Tanhum ben Hanilai: "One should divide one's years of study into three, and devote one-third of them to Scripture, one-third to Mishnah, and one-third to Talmud."[77]

The chief distinction of the Jewish people, Al-Nakawa continues, is that they are the people of the Torah. They accepted the Torah while other nations rejected it.[78] Because the Jewish people cherishes the Torah so dearly,[79] they are possessed of angelic qualities, they are protected from perils, they are shielded from evil impulses,[80] and they merit wearing the crown which is superior to all others; namely, the crown of the Torah.[81] It is no wonder, then, that the sages of Israel have always regarded the Torah as the light, the joy, the healing, the shield, and the tree of life,[82] for which the Jew must be prepared not only to sacrifice his money but even his very life.[83]

In fact, Al-Nakawa maintains, the Torah can best be possessed through self-denial and sacrifice. That is why the Torah was first revealed in the desert: "to teach you that no man can acquire the Torah unless he renounces all ownership and makes himself as free as the desert. . . . Raba expounded the biblical verse, 'It [the Torah] is not in heaven . . . neither is it beyond the sea' [Deut. 30:12], to mean: 'It is not to be found among merchants or dealers.' "[84] The reward of such sacrifice is great in the hereafter, for when "a man dies neither silver nor gold accompany him, but only Torah and good works";[85] and we are also taught that "when a man is led in for judgment in the next world, he is asked: 'What were your deeds like? Did you fix times for learning? Did you infer the unknown from the known? Did you engage in the dialectics of wisdom? Did you deal faithfully?' "[86]

Sacrifices for the Torah also bring rich rewards in this world. They bring healing to the spirit, for we read: "He who takes the Torah to heart, there is averted from his mind all thoughts of conquest by the sword or thoughts that lead to folly, to adultery, to evil inclinations, to vain things, and to mundane affairs."[87] They also insure the survival of the Jewish people, for a wicked government succeeds in its evil decrees against the Jewish people only when Israel casts the words of the Torah to the ground. We also read, in the midrashic comment[88] on the biblical verse, "The voice is the voice of Jacob, but the hands are the hands of Esau" [Gen. 27:22], that when Jacob is unsteady in his voice, the hands of Esau have dominion; but when Jacob's voice chirps, the hands of Esau are powerless. By the word *chirps* is meant occupation with study and prayer. The patriarch Isaac said to Esau: "If you see your brother, Jacob, casting off the yoke of the Torah, you can decree apostasy on him and you will rule over him."[89] Therefore the Torah is precious, and he who learns it succeeds in this world and prospers in the next.[90]

Al-Nakawa maintains that the Torah should be studied during the day and reviewed again at night. He lays special emphasis on the value of study at night, quoting the talmudic sage Resh Lakish to the effect that "he who occupies himself with the Torah at night has a garland of grace drawn over him by the Holy One."[91] He then quotes several beautiful narratives from the Zohar illustrating the view of the Jewish mystics that nocturnal study is especially acceptable to God. Such study also has a practical advantage since it endures longer than study pursued in the daytime.[92]

Our author admonishes that "while one should always study the Torah, he should at the same time acquire an occupation from which he should earn his livelihood, so that he should not have to burden others for his support nor derive worldly gain from the crown of the Torah." To have an occupation is to be freed from many vices, temptations, and sins. The virtues of labor are extolled, and examples are cited of great Jewish personalities of biblical and rabbinic times who combined the study of Torah with an occupation.[93]

While having an occupation is extremely important, it must not be permitted to crowd the Torah out of one's life. One should follow the principle laid down by Shammai—to set aside fixed periods of time for study and devote the remaining time to one's occupation. True, this requires sacrifice and self-denial. But the pious men of former generations lived in this manner, and they derived supreme happiness from it. The best way to study is to acquire a master from whom to learn and companions with whom to learn. Group study is productive of the best results, for it sharpens the intellect, fires the enthusiasm, leaves more lasting impressions, and causes the Divine Presence to dwell in their midst. "Therefore," urges Al-Nakawa, "every man should attach himself to a teacher who will instruct him in the Torah. If not a teacher then let him acquire a fellow-learner or a pupil, even if the pupil knows less. From such joint study they will find mutual benefit and stimulation."

Thus did a talmudic sage teach us[94] when explaining the reason for comparing the Torah to a tree, as it is written: "It is a tree of life to those that lay hold of it." He said: "Just as a small tree can serve as kindling to a large tree, so lesser scholars can kindle the minds of greater scholars. This is in agreement with what has been said: 'I have learned much from my teachers, and from my colleagues more than from my teachers, but from my disciples more than from them all.' " The quest for a teacher must be accompanied by a readiness to spend one's material wealth and endure the discomforts of traveling great distances. To go from city to city and from country to country in pursuit of Jewish knowledge is especially meritorious, as illustrated by this talmudic passage:[95]

It was taught in the school of Rabbi Anan: What is the exposition of the biblical text, "Ye that ride on white asses, yet that sit on rich cloths, and ye that walk by the way, tell of it" [Judg. 5:10]? "Ye that ride on asses" refers to the learned men who travel from town to town and from province to province to study the Torah. "White" means that they clarify it like the brightness of the noonday. "That sit on rich cloths" means that they give true judgment for the sake of the truth. "That walk" refers to the students of Scripture. "By the way" refers to the students of the Mishnah. "Tell of it" refers to the students of the Talmud, all of whose talk consists of words of Torah.[96]

While one should not spare himself the trouble of travel in search of a teacher, yet it is advisable to have a fixed place for the study of Torah, so as not to be studying in one place one day and in another the next.[97]

Everyone has the capability for Jewish study. This is illustrated by the legend in which Elijah relates the following experience:[98]

One day, as I was walking along the way, a man met me and he began to mock me. I said to him: "My son, what will you answer your Father in Heaven on the Day of Judgment?" He replied: "I have an answer." I inquired of him what it was and he said: "I will say that I have neither knowledge nor understanding for I was not so endowed by Heaven." I then asked him: "What is your occupation?" to which he replied: "I am a fisherman." I then remonstrated: "Who taught you to take flax, to spin it, and to weave from it nets with which to catch the fish from the sea? Do you mean to say that for these tasks you are endowed with knowledge and understanding, while for the words of the Torah, of which Scripture says: 'The word is very nigh unto thee, in thy mouth, and in thy heart, that thou mayest do it [Deut. 30:14],' you are not endowed with knowledge and understanding?" Whereupon he groaned with remorse and raised his voice in weeping. I then consoled him, saying: "It is ever thus that those who draw away from the Torah, their own deeds testify against them, as the Prophet Isaiah said: 'They that spread nets upon the waters shall languish. Moreover they that work in combed flax, and they that weave cotton, shall be ashamed' [Isa. 19:8–9]."

The Mishnah and the Talmud are the best subjects of study, for they combine the Oral Law, the Written Law, and their commentaries. Even the accomplished student must not think he has achieved the end of all knowledge. On the contrary, if he studied today, he should go over it again and then once more on the morrow, because with every repetition he will discover something new which had not occurred to him before. So we have been taught: "Turn it [the Torah] and turn it over again, for everything is in it, and contemplate it, and wax gray and old over it, for thou canst have no better rule than this." [99] The words 'Turn it' mean that one should revert to the Torah time and again so as to understand its deepest interpretations, for in so doing one obtains new insights and additional wisdom. The words "wax gray and old over it" teach us that one should never say: "I have already studied in my youth and have covered the subject from all sides, of what value is it to me to study some more." On the contrary, study in your years of maturity, even if you did study in youth; all the more so if you did not study in your youth, for it is said in Scripture [Eccles. 11:6]: "In the morning," that is, in the morning of your life, "sow thy seed, and in the evening," that is, in advancing years, "withhold not thine hand." The words "contemplate it and stir not from it" mean that you should not exchange the study of the Torah for another occupation, for the Bible tells us [Josh. 1:8]: "This book of the Law shall not depart out of thy mouth, but thou shalt meditate therein day and night." This implies studying in youth as well as in old age, for what you can comprehend in maturity, you cannot grasp in youth. When the learner matures his wisdom increases, as the Psalmist says: "They shall still bring forth fruit in old age, they shall be full of sap and richness [Ps. 92:15]." A talmudic sage, Rabbi Simon ben Akashya, expressed similar views: "When the ignorant grow old, their understanding deteriorates, but when the learned grow old, their judgment ripens." [100] Important as the study of Torah is, it must nevertheless be combined with right conduct. Only in this way does the learner earn the love of God and of his fellowman and win others to emulate his example. Thus he serves as an instrument by means of which both God and the Torah are exalted. So the Talmud teaches,[101] in explaining the biblical verse, "And thou shalt love the Lord thy God" [Deut. 6:5]:

This means that the Name of Heaven is beloved because of you. If someone studies Scripture and Mishnah, and attends on the disciples of the wise, is honest in business, and speaks pleasantly to persons, what do people then say concerning him? "Happy the father who taught him Torah, happy the teacher who taught him Torah, woe unto people who have not studied the Torah; for this man has studied the Torah—look how fine his ways are, how righteous his deeds!" Of him does Scripture say: "And He said unto me: 'Thou art my servant, Israel, in whom I will be glorified' [Isa. 49:3]." But if someone studies Scripture and Mishnah, attends on the disciples of the wise, but is dishonest in business and discourteous in his relations with people, what do people say about him? "Woe unto him who studied the Torah, woe unto his father who taught him Torah; woe unto his teacher who taught him Torah! This man studied the Torah: Look, how corrupt are his deeds, how ugly his ways; of him Scripture says: 'In that men said of them: These are the people of the Lord, and are gone forth out of His land' [Ezek. 36:20]." [102]

One of the main reasons for studying Torah, our author declares, is to rise above the earthiness and grossness of life in order to know our Creator. The gross person counts for nothing and cannot be considered among the civilized. What is more, he hates learned men, he does not follow their example, and he does not pursue the path of good conduct. So we are told in the talmudic exposition of the verse in Isaiah 66:5, "Hear the word of the Lord, ye that tremble at his word"—this refers to scholars; "your brethren" to students of Mishnah; "that hate you" to the students of Scripture; "that cast you out" to the ignorant. [103] Al-Nakawa adds that the hatred of the ignorant for those who are learned in the Torah is greater than the hatred of the Gentile nations for Israel. After citing the many passages that show the low esteem in which the ignorant are held in Jewish law and Jewish life, he recounts the famous story of Rabbi Judah the Prince, as recorded in the Talmud:

Rabbi once opened his storehouse of food in a year of scarcity, proclaiming: "Let those enter who have studied the Scripture, or the Mishnah, or the Gemara, or the Halakhah or the Aggadah; there is no admission however for the ignorant." Rabbi Jonathan ben Amram pushed his way in and said: "Master, give me food." He said to him: "My son, have you learnt the Scripture?" He replied: "No." "Have you learnt the Mishnah?" "No." "If so," he said, "then how can I give you food?" He said to him: 'Feed me as the dog and the raven are fed." So he gave him some food. After he went away, Rabbi's conscience smote him and he said: "Woe is me that I have given my bread to a man without learning!" Rabbi Simeon the son of Rabbi ventured to say to him: "Perhaps it is Jonathan ben Amram, your pupil, who all his life has made it a principle not to derive material benefit from the honor paid to the Torah." Inquiries were made and it was found that it was so; whereupon Rabbi said: "All may now enter." [104]

Al-Nakawa concludes that every Jew should absorb the words of instruction of the sages as the thirsty man or the parched earth drink in water. It is not enough merely to study. It must be followed by practice. More is expected by way of practice from the learned than from the unlearned. This is emphasized in the parable of the king who engaged two laborers to work in his garden.[105] One planted trees and pruned them, while the other planted but did not prune. Upon whom did the king vent his displeasure? Surely not upon the farmer who both planted and pruned. So too, God metes out severer punishment to him who studies and does not practice than to him who has not studied at all. This is in consonance with the dictum of Rabbi Akiba, who taught that study should lead to practice.[106] This combination of learning and doing is the true glory of Israel.[107]

Next our author turns to the importance of teaching others. After one has fulfilled the duty of studying for oneself, it becomes his duty to teach others. "Every man who knows Torah," declares Al-Nakawa, "must impart it to others—even to those for whom he may have a personal dislike." He who teaches another, say our sages, is as if he had created and formed him. Thus we read of Abraham, "and the souls which they had made in Haran" (Gen. 12:5). Could Abraham create them? All human beings put together could not create a tiny gnat, how then could Abraham create them? What Scripture means by these words is that Abraham taught them and brought them under the wings of the Divine Presence, therefore it is as though he had fashioned them.[108] Similarly did an old master teach[109] that he who teaches his neighbor the Torah, Scripture ascribes it to him as if he had begotten him, as it says: "Now, these are the generations of Aaron and Moses" (Num. 3:1), while further on it is written: "These are the names of the sons of Aaron" (Num. 3:2), thus teaching thee that Aaron begot and Moses taught them, hence they are called by his name. Before imparting instruction, however, the teacher should look into the prospective student's conduct, character, and mental capacities. The most important quality is good character. Should the applicant be errant in his ethical conduct, every effort must be made to return him to the right path before giving him instruction. The teacher himself must be beyond reproach. No matter how great his learning, if his conduct is questionable, people need not listen to him until he returns to the good path. In this wise, do the sages interpret the verse in Malachi: "For the priest's lips should keep knowledge, and they should seek the law at his mouth; for he is the messenger of the Lord of Hosts" (Mal. 2:7). This means that if the teacher is like an angel of the Lord of Hosts, they should seek the law at his mouth, but if not, they should not seek the law at his mouth.[109]

Al-Nakawa then develops a system of pedagogics in which he sets forth the best methods of teaching. The teacher and his disciples should all be seated, the students facing their instructor in semicircular rows. The teacher must possess patience and be ready to expound the lesson again and again. The student must not be bashful and must not hesitate to ask questions. If, however, the students show a little laziness, it is proper for the teacher to become impatient and angry. Certain regulations should be observed governing the relations between pupil and teacher. A pupil should not put a question to his master immediately upon his entrance into the house of study, nor should two questions be posed at the same time, nor should the questions deal with any subject not being studied currently. This is to be done in order not to cause embarrassment to the teacher. He, however, may ask "catch questions," and may examine his pupils on subjects not being studied currently, in order to sharpen their mental powers and stimulate their interest. Study in private and in an audible voice is an aid to memory. There should be no sleeping or slumbering nor idle conversation in the house of study, for its sanctity exceeds even that of the house of worship. Every respect must be shown to one's own teacher as indeed to all men of learning.[110]

Describing the spiritual benefits accruing from each, Al-Nakawa summarizes the five steps of Torah study. First, he who studies Torah, learns from it how to observe the mitzvot and will therefore inherit the joys of life in this world and in the life of the world to come, as it is written in Proverbs: "Keep my commandments and live, and my teaching as the apple of thine eye" (Prov. 7:2). It is further stated in Scripture: "This book of the law shall not depart out of thy mouth, but thou shalt meditate therein day and night, that thou mayest observe to do according to all that is written therein; for then thou shalt make thy ways prosperous, and then thou shalt have good success" (Josh. 1:8). This means thou shalt be prosperous in this world and thou shalt have success in the next world. Similarly do the biblical words "that is thy life and the length of thy days" (Deut. 30:20) refer to thy life in this world and the length of thy days in the world to come.

Second, he who studies Torah and couples with it an occupation from which he earns a livelihood, thus placing his neck under the double yoke of study and labor, will save himself from the snares of sin, for he will have no time to sin. So are we taught in the Mishnah: "an excellent thing is the study of Torah combined with some worldly occupation, for the labor demanded by both makes sin to be forgotten." [111] So too does Scripture teach, for the words in the Psalms (128:1–2), "Happy is everyone that feareth the Lord, that walketh in His ways," mean in the ways of the Torah; "when thou eatest the labour of thy hands," imply that thou shalt have an occupation from which to draw a livelihood; "happy shalt thou be and it shall be well with thee" means thou shalt be happy in this world and it shall be well with thee in the world to come.

Third, he who studies Torah, knows the punishment resulting from transgressions and will avoid them. Thereby he will escape death at the hands of a civil court in this world and of condemnation to Gehenna by a heavenly court in the world to come. In this wise are we instructed in the Mishnah: "An empty-headed man cannot be a sin-fearing man," [112] and so too does Scripture teach us: "Unless Thy law had been my delight, I should then have perished in mine affliction" (Ps. 119:92). This means I would perish in this world. Again the Psalmist states: "I will never forget Thy precepts, for with them Thou hast quickened me" (Ps. 119:93). This applies to the quickening of life in the world to come.

Fourth, he who studies Torah attains the very highest rung of moral perfection in that he achieves communion with his Creator. When a man is engaged in the study of Torah, his soul becomes pure and whole, cleansed of sin and cleared of transgression. In this wise he becomes attached to his Maker and achieves the noblest form of human existence. So is it stated in Scripture: "Who shall ascend into the mountain of the Lord? And who shall stand in His holy place? He that hath clean hands and a pure heart; who hath not taken my name in vain and hath not sworn deceitfully. He shall receive a blessing from the Lord and righteousness from the God of his salvation" (Ps. 24:3–5).

Fifth, when a man studies Torah, he not only achieves merit for himself, but he is also the cause of bringing merit to others, for when people honor him they will also follow his example. So are we taught in the Mishnah: "Whosoever causes the multitude to be righteous, through him no sin shall be brought about. . . . Moses was righteous and he made the multitude righteous." [113]

Our author brings the chapter to a close with a paean of praise for the excellence of the Torah and the spiritual blessings it bestows upon those who devote themselves to it. Throughout this summation he uses the phrase *gedolah Torah*—"great is the Torah"—as a ringing refrain. Great is the Torah because it guards him who studies it from all harm. Great is the Torah because it is more precious than all the treasure in the world. All other valuables depreciate with age, but with the words of Torah the opposite is true, since they become more precious with age. Great is the Torah because it cannot be lost in barter, not even when it is exchanged for other words of Torah. When two men are engaged in business and one says to the other: "Let us exchange our merchandise," it follows that what is in the possession of one is lost to the other. This is not the case with words of Torah. For when two scholars meet and one is studying a certain tractate, and they say to one another: "Let us exchange our possessions," it follows that each scholar is enriched two-fold. Great is the Torah because it bestows holiness. Great is the Torah because it rescues Israel from the hands of its enemies and enables the Jew to survive. Great is the Torah because it leads to the ways of peace. For example, if a man has a litigation with another and if they accept the decree of the court, then peace is established between them. This bears out the truth of the biblical phrase: "Thou hast established equity" (Ps. 99.4). Or, if a man is on the road and he sees the donkey of his enemy fallen under his burden, and in obedience to the biblical injunction, "If thou see the ass of him that hateth thee lying under his burden, thou shalt forbear to pass by him; thou shalt surely release it with him" (Exod. 23:5), he does come to the assistance of the animal. Then his enemy will surely say to himself: "All along I have been thinking ill of that man and yet he has come to my aid." These two men will cease in their enmity and they will become friends. Thus the Torah caused the establishment of peace between man and his fellow. Thus, in truth, all the paths of the Torah are peace, and "great peace have they that love Thy law" (Ps. 119:165).

Toward the end of the fourteenth century, Rabbi Isaac ben Moses, known as Profiat Duran, a famous Spanish rabbi who in his youth had to live as a Marrano, formulated a set of fourteen rules as a regimen for study and an aid to memory.[114] Here are some of them:

1. One should study under an acknowledged master and in the company of worthy fellow-learners.

2. One should study from books written by renowned scholars in Israel—especially those books that are distinguished by their clarity and brevity.

3. One should concentrate upon his studies and review them with their commentaries.

4. One should keep notes on his studies.

5. One should study in one volume at a time so as not to jump from one book to another.

6. One should study from beautiful books and manuscripts in places of study that are pleasing and attractive.

7. One should study in an audible manner with verbal utterance, so that he can hear his own voice.

8. One should study with melody and song, for it adds to the desire and pleasure of study. . . .

12. One should study with peace of mind and slow deliberation, for there is no profit in hasty study. . . .

14. One should fix a definite time for study. . . . Each Jew must set aside a specific period for study during which he should turn away from business matters and should not think of anything else but his studies so that what he learns should reach his mind and heart. . . . The best time for such study is at night, for then one is free from worldly matters. A sage was once asked why it was that he derived more benefit from his studies than did others, and he replied because he spent his money on oil [for lighting the lamps at night] while they spent theirs on wine.

Because the collective conscience of the Jewish communities of Spain reflected the teachings of their great religious leaders, many communal regulations provided for Jewish study among adults. In the year 1432, Rabbi Abraham Benvenisti convened the Jewish communities of Castile in the city of Valladolid. Among the takkanot adopted at this convocation is the following:

We ordain that every Jewish community of forty families must engage a *marbitz Torah* ["dispenser of Torah," this was the title given to the rabbis in Spain] who should teach Talmud, laws, and Aggadah. The community must support him in a respectable manner . . . out of public funds so that he should not be in need and should not be compelled to go to individuals for funds. We further ordain that every rabbi should maintain a yeshivah to teach all who want to come to him for instruction.[115]

It would be appropriate to close this survey of the views of Spanish Jewry by quoting the last of the great Jewish scholars and statesmen of that era, Rabbi Isaac Abravanel (1437–1509). In his commentary on the Ethics of the Fathers, Abravanel offers the following terse admonition: "A man should first study and then speak." [116]

(7) THE LIGHT OF LEARNING IN PALESTINE AND THE NEAR EAST

The love of learning that characterized the Jews of Europe is also apparent in the Jewish communities of Palestine and the Near East. From a letter written by a disciple of Rabbi Isaac Luria, the kabbalist Rabbi Solomon (Shlomel) Meinsterl of Moravia, who came to Safed in 1603, we glean much of interest concerning the spread of Jewish learning.

I arrived in peace in the holy city of Safed during the Intermediate Days of the Festival of Sukkot in the year 1603. Safed is a city mighty unto the Lord and is filled with wisdom. It has nearly three hundred great scholars, eighteen talmudic colleges [yeshivot], twenty-one synagogues, and a large bet midrash [house of learning] with four hundred children and grown-up boys. In each of the synagogues, the congregations assemble immediately after the morning and evening services, dividing themselves into five or six groups, and seat themselves before eminent rabbis. Each groups spends some time in study before leaving the synagogue. One group studies the Rambam daily [the author is probably referring to Maimonides' great code, the *Mishneh Torah*]; another the *Ein Yaakov;* a third the tractate Berakhot of the Talmud; a fourth a chapter of the Mishnah with its commentaries; a fifth devotes itself to the study of halakhah, i.e., the Talmud with the commentaries of Rashi and Tosafot; a sixth group studies the Zohar; and still another the Bible. In this manner, no Jew in Safed sets out upon his daily work or business without having set aside a fixed time for study and without having learned something. So it is too in the evening-time, after the evening prayers. On the Sabbath, the whole population goes to hear the sermons of the rabbis.[117]

The writings of three of the most important figures of sixteenth-century Safed—Rabbi Moses Cordovero, Rabbi Abraham Golanti, and Rabbi Abraham Halevi—throw much light on the cultural life of that community. Each of these men composed a list of moral precepts and usages to be observed by his disciples, and, no doubt, by the community at large as well. Among the thirty-six rules that Cordovero formulated, no less than five deal specifically with Jewish study: "to engage daily in the study of Bible, Mishnah, Talmud, Kabbalah, Codes"; "to study the whole Talmud three times within a twelve-month period"; "to study Mishnah every Friday night"; "to learn by heart at least two chapters of Mishnah each week"; "to review each week all the Mishnah one had previously learned." [118] Rabbi Abraham Golanti, in his list of twenty-six regulations, includes: "to set aside daily, morning and evening, a time for the study of Torah, and one shall not retire for the night without having attended to this duty." [119] Rabbi Abraham Halevi informs us "that many teachers travel around the countryside to instruct women and children in the Prayer Book," and "many students study all through Friday night." [120]

In the city of Damascus, we are told by one Rabbi Moses of Italy, a Jewish traveler in the early part of the sixteenth century, "There are about five hundred heads of households, there are three synagogues built with great beauty and splendor. In each of them, a rabbi teaches the congregation something of the writings of Maimonides every morning after the services." [121]

In the large city of Smyrna, Jewish cultural life flourished among all elements of the population. One of the leading rabbis of the community in the nineteenth century, Rabbi Hayyim Palagg (1788–1869), has left us a fascinating description of the remarkable devotion to Jewish learning among the laboring classes of Smyrna.

In the city of Smyrna, as in other communities of the land, there exist many labor guilds and trade guilds. It is the duty of the head of each of these guilds to investigate and make certain that every member knows at least the Psalms in the early part of the daily morning prayers. In the event a member does not know these Psalms, he is obligated to hire a teacher to instruct him verse by verse. In the Wool Workers Guild there are more advanced requirements, for there is in force a haskamah [communal agreement] since the days of a former spiritual leader, Rabbi Isaac Mayo, to the effect that no one shall be admitted to guild membership unless he knows all of the morning, afternoon, and evening prayers. One cannot even be admitted to apprenticeship unless he meets that minimum requirement. This requirement had been permitted to lapse until the scribe of the guild, Rabbi Isaac Hazan, informed me of it. Thereupon, I girded my loins, and I prevailed upon them to allocate funds from the treasury in order to hire a teacher to instruct those members who did not know the prayers, and I further decreed that henceforth, in accordance with the aforementioned agreement, no one would be admitted to membership unless he knew all the daily prayers. It is most fitting that this shall be the rule in all the guilds.

The rabbi of Smyrna then reveals to us what transpired in the synagogues and homes of the community.

In most of the synagogues in our city, the practice is prevalent from olden times to conduct a study session every morning after the services when scholarly men seat themselves around tables and learn Torah. Each congregation has a sum of money, either from its treasury or from private donations, to maintain this work. This custom was first introduced by my grandfather, Rabbi Joseph Hazan, in his own congregation, the Neveh Shalom synagogue, and from there this practice spread to the other synagogues. . . . It is now my hope to establish study circles in the homes of many individuals. Would that they might do this as intensely as possible—at least to hold one session of a half-day per week when four or five men might band themselves together. They might study from a tractate of the Talmud with the commentaries of Rashi and Tosafot, or the expositions of Rabbi Elijah Mizrahi on the Torah, or the *Tosafot Yom Tov* [on the Mishnah] or the *Yad* of the Rambam, or the *Turim* and the *Bet Yoseph* in codes. Thank Heaven, that in our city there are many talmudic colleges [yeshivot], houses filled with libraries of Jewish books, in which scholars sit daily in the lap of halakhic studies. There is hardly a street in which such a yeshivah is not to be found filled with books and learners. But, alas, there are also many people who could establish a study group in their homes and do not do so. One should, however, judge them leniently, for such a project involves considerable expenses. Books have to be bought, a stipend may have to be paid a teacher, the cost of maintaining the house may be increased with people coming and going. It is also possible that these people live in very small quarters. Nonetheless, it should be possible for more people to have study groups in their homes, if meetings would be held for only a half-day each week. It would be most appropriate to inaugurate such a practice.

Reverting to the guilds, Rabbi Palagi tells us:

In former times, some guilds maintained their own synagogues, which were called by the name of that guild. In these synagogues, there were study groups which met daily after the morning services and on Sabbaths. [This was also the practice in most of the Jewish communities of Poland and Lithuania.] The rabbi of the congregation would teach them the Bible, the Midrash Rabbah related to the sidrah of that week, and also the books of ethics and the Zohar. In this wise, when one walked through most streets or neighborhoods on the Sabbaths, one could hear the voice of the Torah.[122]

Even in far-off Persia, in the region of Kurdistan and in the city of Mosul, Jewish learning flourished. In the early sixteenth century, a certain Rabbi Jacob ben Yehudi Mizrahi conducted an academy in Kurdistan. After a while he moved to Mosul and carried on his teaching work there. We are told that he was assisted in his labors by his very learned wife, who herself was the daughter of a famous scholar. After her husband, Rabbi Jacob, died, she maintained the academy until her son, Samuel, was old enough to take over its leadership. In the meanwhile she wrote to the Jewish communities of Kurdistan asking for aid. From her letter, it becomes evident that she possessed great learning.[123]

This bird's-eye view of Jewish devotion to learning during the Middle Ages is ample testimony to the fact that the Jew lived in an aura of intellectual and spiritual light amidst the encircling darkness of ignorance and persecution.

CHAPTER

VIII

THE COUNSEL OF FATHERS
TO THEIR SONS

(1) ETHICAL WILLS

The admonition concerning the value of lifelong learning which the great religious teachers imparted to their communities, they most certainly communicated also to their immediate families and to their own children. We have ample evidence of this fact from that unique branch of Jewish literature known as ethical wills. The practice of writing ethical wills—testamentary directions for the religious guidance of children—is as old as Jewish history, tracing its origin back to the patriach Abraham. It is of Abraham that God says: "I have known him to the end that he may command his children and his household after him, that they may keep the way of the Lord" (Gen. 18:19). This text has inspired many a Jewish parent, throughout history, to leave moral exhortations for his children's guidance. The subjects dealt with in these ethical wills are as varied as the total human experience, but almost without exception, the authors counsel their sons concerning the importance of continuous study.

(2) THE TESTAMENT OF RABBI JUDAH IBN TIBBON

In his justly famous testament, entitled "A Father's Admonition," Rabbi Judah ibn Tibbon (1120–1190) addresses his son, Samuel, who was destined to achieve renown as the translator of Maimonides' *Guide to the Perplexed,* in these words:

My son! Make thy books thy companions, let thy cases and shelves be thy pleasure-grounds and gardens. Bask in their paradise, gather their

117

fruit, pluck their roses, take their spices and their myrrh. If thy soul be satiate and weary, change from garden to garden, from furrow to furrow, from prospect to prospect. Then will thy desire renew itself, and thy soul be filled with delight![1]

Further on the father continues:

My son! Devote thy mind to thy children as I did to thee; be tender to them as I was tender; instruct them as I instructed; keep them as I kept thee! Try to teach them Torah as I have tried, and as I did unto thee do thou unto them!

Examine thy Hebrew books at every new moon, the Arabic volumes once in two months, and the bound codices once every quarter. Arrange thy library in fair order, so as to avoid wearying thyself in searching for the book thou needest. Always know the case and chest where the book should be. A good plan would be to set in each compartment a written list of the books therein contained. If, then, thou art looking for a book, thou canst see from the list the exact shelf it occupies without disarranging all the books in the search for one. Examine the loose leaves in the volumes and bundles, and preserve them. These fragments contain very important matters which I collected and copied out. Do not destroy any writing or letter of all that I have left. And cast thine eye frequently over the Catalogue so as to remember what books are in thy library.

Never intermit thy regular readings with thy teacher, study in the college of thy master on certain evenings before sitting down to read with the young. Whatever thou hast learned from me or from thy teachers, impart it again regularly to worthy pupils, so that thou mayest retain it, for by teaching it to others thou wilt know it by heart, and their questions will compel thee to precision, and remove any doubts from thine own mind. . . .[2]

Rabbi Judah ibn Tibbon brings his testament to a close with the following fervent plea written in verse form:

> Obey my mandate, heed thou my advice,
> And make, my son, the Law thy heart's desire!
> Incline to wisdom an attentive ear,
> Pursue the right, be faithful to the true!

Then Wisdom shall enthrone thee mid the great,
And fame become the meed of loyalty!
Serve but thy God with undivided love,
With dainties shall thy soul be satisfied!
To keep His Law hold ready hand and heart,
Heart to remember, hand as firm to do!
For lo, His word a lamp, His Law a light,
A refuge sure in storm and darkest wrath! [3]

(3) THE TESTAMENT OF AN AVERAGE JEW

We now come upon the curiously interesting testament of Solomon ben Isaac, a Spanish Jew of the fourteenth or fifteenth century, whom Dr. Solomon Schechter characterizes as "an average Jew of the Middle Ages." [4] It consists of two parts. The first contains the rules of self-taxation the author imposed on himself and recommends to his children. The second offers moral guidance to his children.

These are the regulations which I, Solomon, son of the holy Rabbi Isaac, the son of Zadok, of blessed memory, have drawn up for myself:
—That so long as I enjoy good health, am free from constraint, and think of it, I shall not eat on any day before I have studied one page of the Talmud or one of its commentaries. Should I transgress this rule intentionally, I must not drink wine on that day, or I shall pay half a ducat to charity. Again, that I shall read every week the Pentateuchal Lesson twice in the Hebrew text, and once in the Aramaic version. Should I intentionally omit completing the Lesson as above, then I must pay two ducats to charity. . . .[5]

And this is the text of the Testament which I, the aforesaid Solomon, have drawn up for my children, may God preserve them! That each of them shall pray thrice daily, and strive to utter his prayers with devotion. Again, that prayers shall be said in the Bet Hamidrash or in the Synagogue together with the congregation. Again, that each shall apply all his power to maintain the synagogues and houses of study and the endowments which our fathers, and I also, have built and established. Let each endeavor to imitate them to the end that good work shall never cease from among them.

Again, that each shall always have in his house a chair on which a volume or two of the Talmud, or any other talmudical work, shall rest;

so that he can always open a book when he comes home. Let him read what he can, making it a duty to read in any book he likes at least four lines before taking his meal. Again that he shall not omit to read every week the Pentateuchal Lesson twice in the Hebrew text and once in the Aramaic version.[6]

Each of them shall have the obligation to train his children to the study of the Torah, and to strive that one shall devote his whole life to the study thereof. All his children and household shall be directed in the right way and in the service of the Creator. And it shall be the duty of his brothers to support the one who makes the Torah his life work, to invest his moneys, making provision that he and his family may live respectably.[7]

(4) THE TESTAMENT OF ONE FAMILY THROUGH FOUR GENERATIONS

We now come upon a remarkable "tetralogy" of testaments, written by members of one of the most illustrious Jewish families of the Middle Ages over a period of approximately one hundred and fifty years. The first of these wills, only recently discovered and first published in 1964,[8] is by Rabbi Yehiel ben Uri, who was born in Germany in the year 1210. The second was written by his son, Rabbi Asher ben Yehiel (1250–1328), who was known as the "Rosh" from the initials of the words Rabbenu Asher. The Rosh settled in Toledo, Spain, after being exiled from Germany; and by his compendia on the Talmud he became the towering Jewish personality of his age. The third and fourth wills were written by his two sons, Rabbi Judah ben Asher (1270–1349), who succeeded his father as rabbi of Toledo, and his younger brother, Rabbi Jacob ben Asher (d. 1340), who wrote the famous code of Jewish laws called the Turim. Here, then we have practically four generations—a father, his son, and his two grandsons—each counseling those who come after him, and all emphasizing the centrality of lifelong study.

We turn first to the testament of Rabbi Yehiel, which the author himself entitled "A Letter on Engaging in the Study of Torah," the greater part of which is here quoted:[9]

In accordance with my best judgment, I shall write something concerning several matters which deal with learning. The prime quality in the learning process is industry. In the final analysis, a man cannot sit over his book all the time. He has to eat, to sleep, and to attend to business affairs. Therefore he who is industrious will be quick to return to his book. He will not be deterred by such thoughts as "the day is yet long," "there is still much of the year before me." It is for this reason that our sages have counseled us: "Say not, when I have leisure I will study; perchance thou wilt have no leisure." [10] Nor shall anyone say to himself: "It is already evening, and should I turn to the book now, I'll only have to rise from it soon to attend to my prayers," for it is better to sit down over the book and learn even if only for one hour than to be doing anything else in the world. So does Scripture teach us: "He that turneth away his ear from hearing the law, even his prayer is an abomination" [Prov. 28:9], and also, "The law of thy mouth is better unto me than thousands of gold and silver" [Ps. 119:72]. So too did the Holy One, blessed be He, say: "Better is it to Me the one day that thou sittest and engagest in learning than the thousand burnt offerings which thy son Solomon is destined to sacrifice before Me on the altar." [11]

The opposite of industry is laziness. It is laziness which deprives man of everything. When he sleeps and is lazy to get up, or when he is outdoors and is lazy to go indoors, he will not only fail to learn anything new but he will forget the old. All his previous labors shall have been in vain. So did King Solomon declare: "I went by the field of the slothful . . . and lo, it was all grown over with thistles, the face thereof was covered with nettles" [Prov. 24:30–31]. This is a fitting description of the man who engages in study but is too lazy to pursue it with zeal and with constancy. He is in truth like a field planted with wheat which produces thorns. King Solomon and the sages have warned us many times against laziness. Our sages have declared that the divine Presence cannot abide with one who is lazy.[12] Judah ben Tema said: "Be strong as a leopard, light as an eagle, fleet as a hart and strong as a lion to do the will of thy Father who is in heaven." [13] Rabbi Phineas ben Jair said: "Heedfulness leads to industriousness, and industriousness leads to cleanliness, and cleanliness leads to purity, and purity leads to abstinence, and abstinence leads to holiness, and holiness leads to humility, and humility leads to the shunning of sin, and the shunning of sin leads to saintliness, and saintliness leads to the gift of the Holy Spirit, and the Holy Spirit leads to the resurrection of the dead." [14] Note well, therefore, the great value of the quality of industry since it brings many virtues and rewards in its wake. Woe, then, to the lazy person who deprives himself of all these benefits. On this account, a man should be most industrious to pursue the book, to rise early and to stay up late in the study of the Torah, and to labor in it. One must also bear in mind the principle that when one engages in the study of the Torah, he should not engage in other matters since learning demands the attentiveness of the whole heart. If one does otherwise, he is bound to forget what has been learned before and is not going to benefit from what he is learning now. When a student, however, learns, reviews, and remembers what he learned, he will, with a rejoicing heart and a satisfied soul, want to continue to learn. For this reason, turn aside from worldly occupations and busy yourself in the study of the Torah; don't devote time to other things for they will prevent you from learning. So did a talmudic sage declare: "If one is a scholar, he is not a robber; if a robber, he is not a scholar," [15] and Hillel declared: "A man who is engaged overmuch in business cannot grow wise." [16] Our sages have interpreted the biblical verse "It is not in heaven neither is it beyond the sea" [Deut. 30:12] to mean that "it is not found among the arrogant nor is it found among merchants or dealers," [17] but it is found among those who dwell in the tents of Torah.[18] Therefore, one should heed the exhortation of our sages: "Lessen thy toil for worldly goods and be busy in the Torah," [19] and "Turn it and turn it over again, for everything is in it, and contemplate it and wax gray and old over it, and stir not from it, for thou canst have no better rule than this," [20] and no more valuable occupation than this.

Besides the virtues of industry and zeal, one should be abstemious in his habits of life. He who is to engage in the study of the Torah must not drink wine or indulge in rich foods or banquets. He should be content with "a morsel of bread and with water by measure," [21] because from over-indulgence in food and drink a man becomes sleepy and lazy. In addition, he habituates himself to frivolity and emptiness. He becomes a spendthrift and may end up without having funds for his barest necessities. In such poverty, he will surely not be able to pursue learning. For this reason, our sages have urged extreme moderation and they interpreted the biblical phrase "black as a raven" [Song of Sol. 5:11] to refer to those who for the sake of the Torah endure deprivation, for "they blacken their faces like a raven." [22]

The quality of constancy is also needed in the learning process, for study is different from any other occupation. In the case of any other

skill, once a man acquires it, even after many years he will not forget
it. But this is not the case with learning. If a man does not learn constantly, he will forget what he has learned. Even if he reviews a hundred
times, but should he turn his mind away from his studies, he is bound
to forget. Furthermore, plain logic will tell you that no other occupation requires so much of a man's heart. Once a man has learned an
occupation, he continues in it by rote. How different it is with acquiring knowledge. Your heart must always be in it. You must give
your whole self over to it constantly, otherwise you forget. Well have
our sages spoken when they observed that were it not for the fact that
a man forgets what he has learned, he would study the Torah just
once and be idle the rest of his life—and "idleness leads to stupefac-
tion," [23] which in turn leads to sin. It is no wonder then that Divine
Providence has ordained forgetfulness so as to motivate men to constancy in Torah study.[24] As a result, a man is led to the achievement
of merit and good deeds, for by his studies, he becomes familiar with
the punishment meted out for transgressions and with the rewards
given for the performance of mitzvot. On the other hand, abstention
from study leads to sin and brings man to the grave. Again, therefore,
a man must be industrious and constant in his studies day and night,
even when he walks by the way and when he lies down on his bed.
If he can't study by heart, let him go over in his mind what he remembers from what he has studied. In this way can he fulfill the
biblical injunction, "thou shalt meditate therein day and night" [Josh.
1:8]. The Bible uses the word *meditate* and not *utter* to teach us that
meditation is an attribute of the heart. For this reason Scripture states:
"When thou liest down and when thou risest up," and also "when
thou walkest by the way" [Deut. 6:7]. It is by such virtues that our
talmudic sages improved themselves. One Jewish teacher informs us:
"I have not walked four ells without Torah," [25] and we know of others
who constantly committed traditions to memory, or reflected upon what
they had learned.

Be well advised, therefore, to turn your whole heart and your mind
at all times and at every hour to the Torah, and you will find true life
and glory therein. You will merit many rewards in this life, since from
the study of the Torah, one acquires many qualities, such as wisdom,
reverence, good manners, humility, modesty, good deeds, and the
protection of the Divine Providence. So are we taught in the Ethics of
the Fathers: "Rabbi Meir said: 'Whosoever labors in the Torah for its

own sake merits many things.' " [26] Happy is he who follows this teaching of Rabbi Meir. May God grant that our hearts be turned to His Torah to meditate upon it day and night, and may we live to merit God's bounty and blessing in this world and in the world to come. Amen.

The second will of the "tetralogy," the work of Rabbi Asher ben Yehiel, is known as the "Rule for Health of the Soul." [27] One of the prescriptions for moral health reads as follows: "Before meals and before retiring to rest, regularly read the Torah, and derive from its pages topics for table talk." [28]

It is to the testaments of the Rosh's two sons that we must turn for fuller treatment of the subject. Rabbi Judah, writing at considerable length, advised as follows:

Make it your firm custom to study the Torah at fixed times, probe deeply into its contents and endeavor to communicate daily a portion of the rabbinic law to others; for to accomplish this you will be compelled to make your own knowledge precise, moreover by the exposition orally it will be fixed in your memories. Always repeat, if possible going back to the beginning of the tractate. Our sages of blessed memory have said (with regard to perfect service): "He who repeats his chapter a hundred times cannot be compared to him who repeats it a hundred and one times." [29] Read ye, therefore, every rule [halakah] 101 times, and appoint hours for studying Halakah from the codifiers every day, and also strive to read a tractate with Rashi's commentary. In fine, you must consider yourselves as laborers hired by the day to do the work of God, as it is said in the Talmud: "We are day laborers." [30] Much more is this the case with you, for all that you possess comes from the congregation and the trust fund. This support is given to you for the purpose of your studies, so that ye are indeed daily hirelings. See to it that ye do your tasks faithfully, and faithful is your employer to pay your wage, [31] nay your reward is already with you, for he has paid it in advance.

Think not in your heart that the Torah is an inheritance from your fathers, and needs no personal effort to win it. The matter is not so. If ye toil not therein, yet shall not acquire, and more than ordinary will be your punishment, in that ye forsake your family tradition. So we read in tractate Nedarim. [32] Why do not learned fathers invariably beget learned children? R. Joseph answered: So that people shall not say,

Your Torah is inherited from your fathers. R. Sheshet said: Because they call men "asses." Rab said: To prevent them assuming an overbearing attitude towards the congregation. Rabina said: Because they become careless with regard to the benediction before study. For your part, avoid all these things.

Also appoint regular periods for studying the Bible with grammar and commentary. As in my childhood I did not so study it—for in Germany they had not the custom—I have not been able to teach it here. Read weekly the Pentateuchal lesson with Rashi and other commentaries. Also make yourselves familiar with homilies and midrashim; this will make you more effective in public preaching, and to bring men back from iniquity. Our Sages said: He who wishes to become saintly should fulfil the words of the Fathers.[33] So, I, after making my confession, accustomed myself to read a chapter of the tractate Abot every day. Do ye the same at table, before Grace after meals, read a chapter daily till you know the whole tractate by heart. This practice will habituate and attract you to saintliness.

Discourse of matters of Torah at your meals, then will ye be as those who eat at the table of the Omnipresent.[34] Read regularly in the Duties of the Heart and in the Book of the Upright, and the Epistle on Repentance of Rabbenu Jonah, and similar books. Set your hearts on that which you read therein with devout intent to apply the lesson in your life. When you read, do so audibly.[35] And reason with yourselves a fortiori after this manner: If you had to speak before a king of flesh and blood, how carefully you would clear your hearts of all other thoughts. Your whole endeavor would be to word your speech acceptably, and you would think of nothing else. How much more should this be your method before the King of kings, blessed and sanctified be His Name![36]

The youngest of Rabbi Yehiel's grandsons, Rabbi Jacob ben Asher, counseled his son as follows:

Study the Law for its true end—for thyself, to know the right and to avoid the wrong; for others, to teach the men of thy generation, seeing that (for our sins!) the Law becomes ever more forgotten. Be a diligent student all thy days.

Ever turn thine eyes on thy superior in wisdom, and realize that the path to learning has no end. Nay, a man may even lose in a day or

in an hour much that he has acquired, if he suffer himself to relax into
worldly ambitions. Probe long and deep into the authorities to reach
clear decisions of law in matters necessary to the world, but spend not
overmuch time or thought in needless casuistry. The aim of most of
those who so act is to win a reputation for skill in puzzling scholars.
After reading a tractate of the Talmud, prepare a synopsis of all the
results, and of intricate discussions write a general summary. The main
heads will thus always be available, and easily found on a future
occasion. Follow this plan, and thou wilt be able to express thyself
with lucidity, and to retain what thou hast learnt. When studying the
Talmud read it aloud, do not mumble it; for its words are "life to
them that proclaim them, and health to all their flesh" [Prov. 4:22].[37]

(5) A "TRILOGY" OF TESTAMENTS

From Spain we turn to Central and Eastern Europe, where we come
upon the noteworthy Hurwitz family, which originated in Prague and
whose members were influential religious teachers and kabbalists throughout Europe and Palestine. Three successive generations of the Hurwitz
family during the sixteenth and seventeenth centuries have left us their
ethical wills: the grandfather, Abraham; his son, Jacob; and his grandson,
Shabtai.

The Hurwitz "trilogy" begins with the testament of Rabbi Abraham,
who counseled his son in these words:

Accustom yourselves to rise even in the summer time a little before
sunrise or at sunrise . . . and so too in the winter to study. You shall
always have with you at the Synagogue services a book from which to
study, such as the *Turim* or the Mishnah, so that when the hazzan
chants the Kaddish, or the Kedusha, or Ana or Hodu or Piyyutim, or
other passages in the prayers which the cantors are wont to prolong by
their chanting, you can look into the book and engage in silent study,
for it is not permitted to study aloud and to utter words for it is forbidden to do so during the prayers.[38]

Now the proper times for the fixed study of Torah, twice daily, are
these: (1) In the morning, before breakfast, immediately after leaving
synagogue. Nothing must be allowed to interfere with this practice, so
that you may fulfill the text: "They go from strength to strength"
[Ps. 84:8], from house of prayer to house of learning. At all events,

never leave home, even on necessary business, before studying a passage, or even a single rule or sentence if the matter be very pressing. (2) At night, immediately after evening service in the synagogue, before the evening meal, and again before retiring to rest. It is good to study early in the evening, before supper, either the whole or the greater part of the set portion, for eating makes one drowsy, and in that condition one is unable to learn. Do not trust to your power to rise before dawn, and to read your appointed portion then. As likely as not your sleep will be too strong for you. Night, say our sages often, was made for no other purpose than study.... So I command you to study every night before going to bed. Even in the short summer nights read a little before retiring, to fulfill the injunction, "Thou shalt meditate therein day and night" [Josh. 1:1], and fall asleep straight from filling your mind with the Torah. (And, let your reading be audible, and with a chant.) King David said: "Thy statutes have been my song" [Ps. 119:54], i.e., he read the Torah as a melodious song. I have often had to blame you for your habit of reading silently.[39]

The son of Rabbi Abraham, Rabbi Jacob Hurwitz, wrote his testament in the form of a commentary to his father's work. After urging his children to read Rabbi Abraham's will frequently, he adds: "Have always in your hand the well-known books on Reverence and Repentance, which draw mankind to the service of our Maker, and humble the unruly heart. Therefore meditate on such books continually, and read a definite section in them every day."[40]

The grandson, Rabbi Shabthai, goes into greater detail on the subject of study, and he also has a special word of counsel for his daughters and daughters-in-law.

With regard to academic study, read what my father has written at the end of his remarks on "The Oral Law." There he gives directions for reading Talmud and Tosafot, and how also to arrive at new thoughts. I should add that where the Tosafot raise objections to Rashi, it is a proper thing to reconcile the two, for this is the truly admirable type of ingenuity. For helping you to this desirable result, the works of Alfasi and R. Nissim and all the commentaries around the Alfasi are a fine specific and you will be able to do wonders with Rashi and Tosafot! Then, when you have filled yourselves brim-full of the Talmud and Codes, study, I bid you, the Cabbala, for without it the Fear of

God is impossible. He who reverentially learns the Cabbala, will see his soul in the Realm of Emanation. To gain this knowledge read through *The Dew-fall* and *The Garden* [by S. B. A. Hurwitz and Moses Cordovero, respectively]. . . . Moreover, my daughters and daughters-in-law, habituate yourselves to read the Pentateuch in German, and also the book called *A Good Heart* [a Judeo-German moralistic work by Isaac ben Eliakim of Posen].[41]

(6) TWO FAMILY LETTERS

From the city of Prague, in the early part of the seventeenth century, two family letters have been preserved. The writers of these letters were persons of no special renown, but the admonitions they offer to their younger generation urge the importance of Jewish learning. The first is the letter of a father, Israel Hamerschlag, to his married son, Hanoch. He urges Hanoch to come home and devote himself to the study of Torah, telling him that he did not bring him up to give his whole life over to money-making. After complaining that the son hardly ever writes to his parents, the father continues:

You must not make the excuse that you are studying so assiduously that you do not want to miss so much, and that you are, therefore, unable to write. For I know very well that this is not true. This, however, may be true: that you have no time because of your business. If I had known this, and if your father-in-law had given me his whole fortune, I would not have given you to him. Your father-in-law told me quite a different story at the wedding: that he would study with you (so intensively) that you would be able to hold your own even with a Morenu in barely two years. Instead you have studied making-money night and day (I have not educated you for money-making) and I am afraid that the Lord, may He be praised, may punish you for neglecting the study of Torah.

Therefore, my dear son, I am writing you here my firm will and opinion that you must do nothing else than come here for learning. You have time enough for trading, for I shall not permit you to go on with speculations. And I will provide you the best teacher of whom I can get hold in Prague. For people learn in my house, thanks to God, more than they learn in all Prague with any head of a family. I have engaged a teacher for my son-in-law Isaac, namely the Rabbi Noah, and Rabbi

Meier Gensel and Rabbi Meier Jokels and Aaron, my brother's son, are studying day and night. I hope, therefore, that you will learn here more than there. And you will not need to use up your own capital, as I am able to provide you full board, thanks to God. I hope, therefore, that you will obey me; imagine that you have gone once again to Poland in order to study there. You will not lose, as you still can become a merchant as your father-in-law intends. I did not expect that, after the wedding, you would not devote yourself to studies for some years. Otherwise I would not have made such great sacrifices for you. . . .

May it be the will of the Lord that you come hither for one or two years for learning. I cannot write you enough how much the Lord, may He be praised, has delighted me with my son-in-law Isaac, how he is learning day and night, and how steadfast he is. May the Lord, may He be praised, let him enjoy many years, Amen! And if you were here, he would be a great help to you.[42]

At about the same time, another Jew of Prague, David Ulmo, wrote his grandson, Salman, who lived in Vienna:

Only see to it that thou mayest study unceasingly, and be at peace with everybody, and be obedient to thy teacher and thy mother, and offer thy prayers with great devotion, and study diligently and repeat, and write sometimes if thou hast leisure . . .[43]

(7) TWO UNUSUAL TESTAMENTS

In the city of Prague, in the latter part of the seventeenth century, there lived two eminent rabbis and kabbalists, Rabbi Jonah Landsofer (1678–1712) and his friend, Rabbi Moses Hasid. On one occasion the chief rabbi of Prague sent them to Vienna to engage in a disputation with the followers of Shabbetai Zevi.[44] These two eminent rabbis both wrote unusual testaments.

We quote first from the work of Rabbi Jonah Landsofer, who presents plans of study for the unlearned as well as the learned. Among the latter he distinguishes several categories: the general learner, "who dwells in the tents of the Torah"; the talmid hakham ("disciple of the wise"), or scholar; the baal Torah ("master of the Torah"), who is an accomplished student but is not yet qualified to decide legal cases; and the yodea sefer, who is "familiar with the Jewish book" but is not quite a *lamdan,* a very learned man. For each of these categories he presents a separate curriculum.

Beginning with an admonition to his children, Rabbi Landsofer writes:

> Do not sit down to your meals before you have studied something from the Torah, no matter how little. He who is unlearned and not capable of study should read the books written in German, and he should not be ashamed. Should you, however, be of those who dwell in the tents of the Torah and be disciples of the wise, you must not permit the words of the Torah to be absent from your lips. Study the Bible—the Pentateuch, the Prophets, and the Hagiographa. You must realize in advance that the study of the Prophets and the Hagiographa may prove difficult, for there are many verses in the Later Prophets and especially in the Minor Prophets whose meaning it is hard to grasp. . . . Study the Scriptures so that you shall complete your studies at Simhat Torah.
>
> The order of study for one who is a talmid hakham shall be thus: —The study of the Bible as mentioned above. The entire Mishnah with many of the tractates to be learned by heart. The Gemara—each student according to his abilities—to be studied daily and no less than five pages. If one cannot complete the minimum of the daytime, he should do so at night. There should be no limit to the study of the *Shulhan Arukh*—the more the better. Happy is he who can manage also to study the *Four Turim* once each year with the *Bet Yoseph* commentary.

Our author lays great emphasis on the study of the *Turim* and the *Bet Yosef* as a way of knowing the sources for each Jewish law; but he gives preference over these authorities to the compendia of Jewish law by Rabbi Asher. He urges the student to make notes and outlines of what he has studied, and he decries the current vogue in talmudic casuistry.

He then continues:

> This is the way the baal Torah shall study: He shall fix most of his studies upon the Mishnah with the commentary of Rabbi Bertinoro. If he is able to study more he should make note of the comments in the *Tosefot Yom Tov,* which will clarify certain laws of special interest. If

he has the merit of thorough knowledge in the Mishnah, he should Talmud with diligence, and at all events he must not keep from his lips study the study of the *Shulhan Arukh* or the Commentary of Rabbi Mordecai Jaffe, called the *Levush,* or the *Orah Hayyim* with the commentary of some later scholar; also the study of *Yoreh Deah* with a commentary of a later scholar.

This is the regimen of study for a man who is not a lamdan but is a yodea sefer. He should see to it that he study and know the 613 commandments. He should study one of the existing manuals on these commandments and shall be expert in them. He shall also attend study sessions of those who study Mishnah, Bible, Midrash, and *Shulhan Arukh.* If he is not able to achieve such measure of knowledge, he should at least study the books printed in German, such as the *Ha-Maggid* [first printed in Prague, 1576] on the Bible, the book *Lev Tov* [by Rabbi Isaac ben Eliakim], and books similar to it. He should also attend lectures of those who teach Jewish laws and customs and all his actions shall be guided by the words and teachings of scholars.[45]

Rabbi Moses Hasid, the townsman of Rabbi Jonah Landsofer, left a most interesting testament in which he devotes considerable space to the question of lifelong learning:

The study of the Torah must be regular. Over and over again repeat what you learn. It must be like a table always set before thee; at this meal be not sparing; your teeth must be always ready to masticate the words of the Torah, as the millstone is ready to grind the grain.[46]

After this general admonition, he continues with these specifications:

With regard to learning, see to it that you study *Tur Orah Hayyim* diligently and review what you studied three or four times. . . . Study also the later commentaries diligently. . . . In the *Shulhan Arukh,* you go over the laws and the different *Simanim* [sections of the book] and then review it by heart. The same method should be followed in the study of the *Tur Yoreh Deah,* the *Even-ha-Ezer,* and the *Hoshen Mishpat.*

Devote an hour and a half daily to books of morals, to study of the Bible with commentaries, and to the midrashim. It is good to study each book two or three times and then to turn to another book.

I will give you counsel in the method of Torah study. Estimate for yourself how much time you have each day and each night for purposes of study. Make up your mind to cover five or six pages of the Talmud each hour, so that if you have ten hours for study you will cover fifty to sixty pages. . . . You should follow this method also in the study of Midrash, Bible, and ethical books. So, for example, a page in the *Tur* should be reckoned as being equal to four pages in the Talmud, a chapter of the Mishnah should be reckoned as one page in the Talmud; four pages of the *Shulhan Arukh* with the annotations of Rabbi Moses Ravkash should be equivalent to eight pages of the Talmud. On Sabbaths and festivals and also on the Eve of Sabbaths and festivals you should learn half.

Don't permit your evil inclination to tell you "you are on the road and it is therefore impossible to study." For there are many who devote time to study while they are stopping at inns. How good it is therefore to prepare "food for the way" before setting out on a journey. Take with you a volume of the Talmud with its commentaries or the Bible with Rashi and other commentaries. You will then be able to look into these books even when you are riding in the wagon.

Businessmen who cannot set aside fixed hours for study nevertheless can manage to learn some *Shulhan Arukh* and Mishnayot, depending upon their understanding and the time at their disposal. If they cannot study these books then they certainly can study the books printed in Yiddish-German, such as *Lev Tov* and *Brant Spiegel,* and they should not be embarrassed to study from these books because the more learned may ridicule them for it.[47]

(8) THE TESTAMENT OF THE GAON OF VILNA

The great religious leaders of Eastern Europe in the eighteenth and nineteenth centuries were at one with the spiritual giants of earlier centuries in urging the importance of Jewish study. The towering figure of world Jewry in the eighteenth century, Elijah Gaon of Vilna (1720–1797), wrote a will while he was on a journey to Palestine. For reasons not quite known, he did not complete his pilgrimage. While he tarried at Königsberg he composed this letter to his family. Addressing his wife on the education of their children, he wrote:

Among my books is the Book of Proverbs in German; for the Lord's sake let them read it every day, as it is the chief of moral works. They should also read Ecclesiastes constantly, in your presence; for this book exposes the vanity of temporal concerns. But the end must not be a mere perusal of these books, for man does not thus gain incentive. Many a man reads moral words without rousing himself to moral works. Partly because they merely read, partly because they fail to understand—this renders the reading fruitless. This is shown in the parable of one who sows without ploughing the soil, so that the wind snatches the seed and satisfies the birds.[48] Because he cannot restrain himself or make himself a fence, he is like one who sows without a fence, and the pigs consume it and tread it down. Sometimes one grows on stone, the stony heart into which no seed enters at all, and it is necessary to strike the stone until it is split. Therefore I have bidden you to strike your children if they refuse to obey you. "Train up a child in the way he should go, and even when he is old he will not depart from it" [Prov. 22:6]. This is the great rule! I include in all this exhortation my son-in-law, who must follow the course of reading which I have prescribed. . . . Accustom your children to the study of the Chapters of the Fathers, and in the Abot of Rabbi Nathan and the tractate Derek Erez, for good manners (the subject of the last-named) are precedent to the Torah. Show the utmost honor to your aged mother-in-law, and treat all men with mannerliness, with amiability and respect.[49]

(9) THE TESTAMENT OF RABBI JACOB OF LISSA

The famous talmudist and halakhist Rabbi Jacob of Lissa (d. 1832) left these words of counsel to his children:

You shall have a fixed period of study daily for the Bible and the Mishnah. Even though our sages tell us that "the Babylonian Talmud contains them all," [50] yet these same sages were filled with knowledge of the Bible and Mishnah. . . . Even though you don't see me doing this now, yet in my youth I did do it! Now in my old age, time does not permit me to do what is in my heart.

Set for yourselves a simple goal: To study no less than one page of the Talmud in consecutive order. You should also study daily a page or column of the *Shulhan Arukh, Orah Hayyim.* You shall also set aside time every Sabbath to study the *Zohar.* No matter what you learn you shall review it immediately, for it is impossible to remember something you learn only once.[51]

CHAPTER

IX

JEWISH LAW AND JEWISH LEARNING

The ideals and customs of a people inevitably shape themselves into legal enactments and ultimately into codes of law. What is at first the desired way of life finally becomes the required pattern. Once this transformation of custom into law is achieved, it serves to standardize and perpetuate the ideals that inspired it. Law is both the mirror and the molder of society.

(1) JEWISH LAW: THE MOLDER OF JEWISH LIFE

This is particularly true of the interaction between the ideals of Jewish life and the halakhah, which is the embodiment of Jewish law. Professor Louis Ginzberg, in his essay "Jewish Thought as Reflected in the Halacha," states: "Laws which govern the daily life of man must be such as suit and express his wishes, being in harmony with his feelings and fitted to satisfy his religious ideals and ethical aspirations. It is only in the Halacha that we find the mind and character of the Jewish people exactly and adequately expressed." [1]

One of the best examples of the way the halakhah concretizes Jewish idealism and transforms it into a regimen of conduct is to be noted in the manner in which the famous codes of Jewish law treat the ideals of Jewish learning.

135

(2) THE "LAWS CONCERNING THE STUDY OF TORAH" BY MAIMONIDES IN THE MISHNEH TORAH

The first great compendium of Jewish jurisprudence was the *Mishneh Torah,* popularly called the *Yad Hazakah* ("Strong Hand"), by Moses Maimonides, completed in the year 1180. Maimonides designed his code to be "a compendium of all the oral law, ordinances, customs and decrees from the days of Moses, our master, to the close of the Talmud, including the interpretations of the Geonim since that time." This monumental code opens, significantly, with the *sefer ha-Mada,* the "Book of Knowledge," which contains the oft-quoted *Hilkhot Talmud Torah,* the "Laws Concerning the Study of Torah." These in turn are subdivided into chapters and sections dealing with the affirmative precepts (*mitzvot Aseh*) to study the Torah and to honor its teachers as well as those versed in it. The following passages from the *Hilkhot Talmud Torah* are all relevant to our theme of lifelong learning among Jews.[2]

The Obligation for Life-long Learning

Every Israelite is under an obligation to study Torah, whether he is poor or rich, in sound health or ailing, in the vigour of youth or very old and feeble. Even a man so poor that he is maintained by charity or goes begging from door to door, as also a man with a wife and children to support, are under the obligation to set aside a definite period during the day and at night for the study of the Torah, as it is said "But thou shalt meditate therein day and night" (Josh. 1:8).

Among the great sages of Israel, some were hewers of wood, some, drawers of water, while others were blind. Nevertheless, they devoted themselves by day and by night to the study of the Torah. They are included among the transmitters of the tradition in the direct line from Moses.

Until what period in life ought one to study Torah? Until the day of one's death, as it is said, "And lest they (the precepts) depart from thy heart all the days of thy life" (Deut. 4:9). Whenever one ceases to study, one forgets. [1. 8–10]

What to Study

The time allotted to study should be divided into three parts. A third should be devoted to the Written Law; a third to the Oral Law; and the last third should be spent in reflection, deducing conclusions from premises, developing implications of statements, comparing dicta, studying the hermeneutical principles by which the Torah is interpreted, till one knows the essence of these principles, and how to deduce what is permitted and what is forbidden from what one has learnt traditionally. This is termed Talmud.

For example, if one is an artisan who works at his trade three hours daily and devotes nine hours to the study of the Torah, he should spend three of these nine hours in the study of the Written Law, three in the study of the Oral Law, and the remaining three in reflecting on how to deduce one rule from another. The words of the Prophets are comprised in the Written Law, while their exposition falls within the category of the Oral Law. The subjects styled Pardes (Esoteric Studies), are included in Talmud. This plan applies to the period when one begins learning. But after one has become proficient and no longer needs to learn the Written Law, or continually be occupied with the Oral Law, he should, at fixed times, read the Written Law and the traditional dicta, so as not to forget any of the rules of the Torah, and should devote all his days exclusively to the study of Talmud, according to his breadth of mind and maturity of intellect. [1. 11–12]

Education of Women

A woman who studies Torah will be recompensed, but not in the same measure as a man, for study was not imposed on her as a duty, and one who performs a meritorious act which is not obligatory will not receive the same reward as one upon whom it is incumbent and who fulfills it as a duty, but only a lesser reward. And notwithstanding that she is recompensed, yet the Sages have warned us that a man shall not teach his daughter Torah, as the majority of women have not a mind adequate for its study but, because of their limitations, will turn the words of the Torah into trivialities. The sages said "He who teaches his daughter Torah—it is as if he taught her wantonness." This stricture refers only to instruction in the Oral Law. With regard to the Written Law, he ought not to teach it to her; but if he has done so, it is not regarded as teaching her wantonness. [1.13]

The Crown of the Torah—Its Claim to Priority

With three crowns was Israel crowned—with the crown of the Torah, with the crown of the priesthood and with the crown of sovereignty.

he has The crown of the priesthood was bestowed upon Aaron, as it is
said, "And it shall be unto him and unto his seed after him, the covenant
of an everlasting priesthood" (Num. 25:13). The crown of sovereignty
was conferred upon David, as it is said, "His seed shall endure forever, and his throne as the sun before Me" (Ps. 89:37). The crown
of the Torah, however, is for all Israel, as it is said, "Moses commanded
us a law, an inheritance of the congregation of Jacob" (Deut. 33:4).
Whoever desires it can win it. Do not suppose that the other two
crowns are greater than the crown of the Torah, for it is said, "By me,
kings reign and princes decree justice. By me, princes rule" (Prov.
8:15–16). Hence the inference, that the crown of the Torah is greater
than the other two crowns.

The sages said, "A bastard who is a scholar takes precedence of an
ignorant High Priest; for it is said, 'More precious it is than rubies'
(Prov. 3:15), that is (more to be honoured is the scholar) than the
High Priest who enters the innermost sanctuary. (A play upon the
word *Peninim* [rubies] taken as *Lifny v'lifnim* [High Priest who entered
the Holy of Holies on the Day of Atonement])."

Of all precepts, none is equal in importance to the study of the
Torah. Nay, study of the Torah is equal to them all, for study leads
to practice. Hence, study always takes precedence of practice.

If the opportunity of fulfilling a specific precept would interrupt the
study of the Torah and the precept can be performed by others, one
should not intermit study. Otherwise, the precept should be performed
and then the study be resumed.

At the Judgment hereafter, a man will first be called to account in
regard to his fulfillment of the duty of study and afterwards concerning
his other activities. Hence, the sages said, "A person should always
occupy himself with the Torah, whether for its own sake or for other
reasons. For study of the Torah, even when pursued from interested
motives, will lead to study for its own sake." [3.1–5]

Learning Before Riches

He whose heart prompts him to fulfill this duty properly, and to be
crowned with the crown of the Torah, must not allow his mind to be
diverted to other objects. He must not aim at acquiring Torah as well
as riches and honour at the same time. "This is the way for the study
of the Torah. A morsel of bread with salt thou must eat, and water
by measure thou must drink; thou must sleep upon the ground and live

a life of hardship, the while thou toilest in the Torah" (Ethics of the Fathers 6:4). "It is not incumbent upon thee to complete the task; but neither art thou free to neglect it" (ibid. 2:21). "And if thou hast studied much Torah, thou hast earned much reward. The recompense will be proportionate to the pains" (ibid. 5:26) (The numbering of the paragraphs in the Ethics of the Fathers in the editions of the Mishna and in the editions of the liturgy does not always correspond.)

Possibly you may say: When I shall have accumulated money, I shall resume my studies; when I shall have provided for my needs and have leisure from my affairs, I shall resume my studies. Should such a thought enter your mind, you will never win the crown of the Torah. "Rather make the study of the Torah your fixed occupation" (ibid. 1:15) and let your secular affairs engage you casually, and do not say: "When I shall have leisure, I shall study; perhaps you may never have leisure" (ibid. 2:5).

In the Torah it is written, "It is not in heaven . . . neither is it beyond the sea" (Deut. 30:12–13). "It is not in heaven," this means that the Torah is not to be found with the arrogant; "nor beyond the seas," that is, it is not found among those who cross the ocean. Hence, our sages said, "Nor can one who is engaged overmuch in business grow wise" (Ethics of the Fathers 2:6). They have also exhorted us: "Engage little in business and occupy thyself with the Torah" (ibid. 4:12). [3.6–8]

Study Requires Humility and the Simple Life

The words of the Torah have been compared to water, as it is said, "O every one that thirsteth, come ye for water" (Isa. 55:1); this teaches us that just as water does not accumulate on a slope but flows away, while in a depression it stays, so the Words of the Torah are not to be found in the arrogant or haughty but only in him who is contrite and lowly in spirit, who sits in the dust at the feet of the wise and banishes from his heart lusts and temporal delights; works a little daily, just enough to provide for his needs, if he would otherwise have nothing to eat, and devotes the rest of the day and night to the study of the Torah.

One, however, who makes up his mind to study Torah and not work but live on charity, profanes the name of God, brings the Torah into contempt, extinguishes the light of religion, brings evil upon himself and deprives himself of life hereafter, for it is forbidden to derive any temporal advantage from the words of the Torah. The sages said, "Whoever derives a profit for himself from the words of the Torah is helping on his own destruction" (Ethics of the Fathers 4:17). They have further charged us, "Make not of them a crown wherewith to aggrandise thyself, nor a spade wherewith to dig" (ibid. 4:7). They likewise exhorted us, "Love work, hate lordship" (ibid. 1:10). "All study of the Torah, not conjoined with work, must, in the end, be futile, and become a cause of sin" (ibid. 2:2). The end of such a person will be that he will rob his fellow-creatures.

It indicates a high degree of excellence in a man to maintain himself by the labour of his hands. And this was the normal practice of the early saints. Thus, one secures all honour and happiness here and hereafter, as it is said, "When thou eatest of the labour of thine hands, happy shalt thou be, and it shall be well with thee" (Ps. 128:2). Happy shalt thou be in this world, and it shall be well with thee in the world to come, which is altogether good.

The words of the Torah do not abide with one who studies listlessly, nor with those who learn amidst luxury, and high living, but only with one who mortifies himself for the sake of the Torah, constantly enduring physical discomfort, and not permitting sleep to his eyes nor slumber to his eyelids. "This is the law, when a man dieth in a tent" (Num. 19:14). The sages explained the text metaphorically thus: "The Torah only abides with him who mortifies himself in the tents of the wise." And so Solomon, in his wisdom, said, "If thou faint in the day of adversity, thy strength is small indeed" (Prov. 24:10). He also said, "Also my wisdom stood unto me" (Eccles. 2:9). This is explained by our wise men thus, "The wisdom that I learnt in wrath, (Play upon the word 'aph'. אף, meaning 'also' and 'wrath'.)—this has remained with me." The sages said, "There is a solemn covenant that anyone who toils at his studies in the Synagogue, where it was customary to study privately, will not quickly forget." He who toils privately in learning, will become wise, as it is said, "With the lowly (literally, the reserved) is wisdom" (Prov. 11:2). If one recites aloud while studying, what he learns will remain with him. But he who reads silently soon forgets. [3.9–12]

Methods of Study

While it is a duty to study by day and by night, most of one's knowledge is acquired at night. Accordingly, when one aspires to win the crown of the Torah, he should be especially heedful of all his nights and not waste a single one of them in sleep, eating, drinking, idle talk and so forth, but devote all of them to study of the Torah and words of wisdom. The sages said, "That sound of the Torah has worth, which is heard by night, as it is said, 'Arise, cry out in the night' (Lam. 2:19): and whoever occupies himself with the study of the Torah at night— a mark of spiritual grace distinguishes him by day, as it is said, 'By day the Lord will command His lovingkindness, and in the night His song shall be with me, even a prayer unto the God of my life' (Ps. 42:9). A house wherein the words of the Torah are not heard at night will be consumed by fire, as it is said, 'All darkness is laid up for his treasures; a fire not blown by man shall consume him' (Job 20:26). 'Because he hath despised the word of the Lord' (Num. 15:31)—this refers to one who has utterly neglected (the study of) the words of the Torah." And, so too, one who is able to occupy himself with the Torah and does not do so, or who had read Scripture and learnt Mishnah and gave them up for worldly inanities, and abandoned and completely renounced this study, is included in the condemnation, "Because he hath despised the Word of the Lord." The sages said, "Whoever neglects the Torah because of wealth, will, at last be forced to neglect it owing to poverty. And whoever fulfills the Torah in poverty, will ultimately fulfill it amidst wealth" (Ethics of the Fathers 4:11, with order of sentences reversed). And this is explicitly set forth in the Torah, as it is said, "Because thou didst not serve the Lord thy God with joyfulness and with gladness of heart, by reason of the abundance of all things, therefore shalt thou serve thine enemy" (Deut. 28:47–48). It is also said "That He might afflict thee ... to do thee good at thy latter end ..." (Deut. 8:16). [3.13]

Who Shall Be Taught

Torah should only be taught to a worthy pupil whose conduct is exemplary or whose disposition is simple. One, however, who walks in a way that is not good should first be reclaimed, trained in the right way and tested (as to his sincerity); then he is admitted into the Beth Hamidrash (College) and given instruction. The sages say: "To teach a pupil who is unworthy is like casting a stone to Mercury (the idol), as it is said, "As one puts a stone in a sling, so is he that giveth honour to a fool" (The stone does not stay long in the sling; it is soon shot out, so honour given to a fool does not stay long with him.) (Prov.

26:8). There is no honour but the Torah, as it is said, "The wise shall inherit honour" (Prov. 3:35). So too, if a teacher does not walk in the right way—even if he is a great scholar and all the people are in need of him—instruction is not to be received from him till he reforms; as it is said, "For the priest's lips shall keep knowledge, and they shall seek the law from his mouth, for he is the messenger of the Lord of Hosts" (Mal. 2:7). Our sages applied this text thus: "If the teacher is like an angel of the Lord of Hosts, they may seek the Law from his mouth. But if he is not, then they shall not seek the Law from his mouth." [4.1]

Master and Disciple—Principles of Pedagogy

How is instruction to be imparted? The teacher is seated in the schoolroom facing the class, with the pupils around him like a crown, so that they can all see him and hear his words. The teacher is not to sit on a stool while his pupils are seated on the floor. Either all sit on the floor, or all on stools. Formerly the teacher used to be seated, while the pupils stood. But before the destruction of the Second Temple, it already had become the universal custom that pupils, while being taught, should be seated.

If it was his custom to teach the pupils personally, he may do so. If, however, he taught through a Meturgeman (an interpreter), the latter stands between him and his pupils. The teacher addresses the interpreter, who declaims what he has just heard to all the pupils. And when they put questions to the interpreter, he asks the teacher. The teacher replies to the interpreter who addresses the answer to the one who put the question. The teacher should not raise his voice above the interpreter's voice. Nor should the latter raise his voice above that of the teacher, when he addresses a question to him. The interpreter may not detract aught from the teacher's words, nor add to them nor vary them—unless he is the teacher's father or instructor. In addressing the interpreter, the teacher uses the introductory formula: "Thus my revered preceptor said to me" or "Thus my revered father said to me." But when the interpreter repeats the words to the listener, he recites them in the name of the sage quoted, and mentions the name if he were the teacher's father or teacher, and says, "Thus said our Master so-and-so" (naming him). He does so, even if the teacher abstained from naming the sage on the ground that it is forbidden to mention one's teacher or father by name.

If the teacher taught and his pupils did not understand, he should not be angry with them or fall into a rage, but should repeat the lesson again and again till they have grasped the full meaning of the Halacha (rule) he is expounding. So also, the pupil should not say, "I understand" when he has not understood, but should ask again and again. And if the master is angry with him and storms at him, he should say, "Master, it is Torah. I need to learn, and my intellectual capacities are deficient."

A disciple should not feel ashamed before his fellow-students who grasp the lesson after hearing it once or twice, while he needs to hear it several times before he knows it. For if this makes him feel ashamed, he will go through college without having learnt anything. The ancient sages accordingly said: "A bashful man cannot learn, nor a passionate man teach" (Ethics of the Fathers 2:6). These observations only apply when the students' lack of understanding is due to the difficulty of the subject or to their mental deficiency. But if the teacher clearly sees that they are negligent and indolent in their study of the Torah and that this is the cause of their failure to understand, it is his duty to scold them and shame them with words of reproach, and so stimulate them to be keen. And in this regard, the sages said, "Arouse awe in the pupils." It is thus improper for a teacher to indulge in frivolity before his pupils, or to jest in their presence, or eat and drink with them—so that the fear of him be upon them, and they will thus learn from him quickly.

Questions are not to be put to the teacher immediately on his entering the school, but only after his mind is composed. Nor should a pupil put a question as soon as he has come in, but only after he himself is composed and rested. Two pupils are not to put questions at one time. The teacher is not to be questioned on a topic not pertaining to the lesson, but only on the subject that is being treated, so as not to embarrass him. The teacher, however, should set "pitfalls" before his pupils, both in his questions and in what he does in their presence, in order to sharpen their wits, and ascertain whether they remember what he had taught them or do not remember it. Needless to add, that he has the right to question them on a subject other than that on which they are at the moment engaged, in order to stimulate them to be diligent in study.

No questions should be asked standing, nor answers given standing; nor should they be addressed by any one from an elevation, or from a distance, or when one is behind the elders. The teacher may only be questioned on the topic that is being studied. The questions are to be put in a respectful manner. One should not ask concerning more than three Halachoth (rules) in the topic.

Two individuals put questions. One of these questions is germane to the subject under discussion, while the other is not. Heed is given to the question that is germane. One question refers to a legal rule, the other to exegesis; the former receives attention. One question is exegetical; the other homiletical; the former is taken up. One question is homiletical; the other appertains to an inference a fortiori; the latter is answered. One question refers to an a fortiori inference, the other to an inference from similarity of phrases; the former is dealt with. Questions are put by two persons, one of whom is a graduated scholar, the other a disciple; attention is paid to the scholar. One of them is a disciple, the other is unlettered; heed is given to the disciple. Where both are graduated scholars, disciples or unlettered, and the questions of both concern two legal rules, or two responses, or two practical issues, the interpreter may in these cases give the preference to either.

No one should sleep in the Beth Hamidrash (House of Study). If a student dozes there, his knowledge becomes a thing of shreds. Thus Solomon, in his wisdom, said, "And drowsiness shall clothe one in rags" (Prov. 23:21). No conversation may be held in the House of Study, except in reference to the words of the Torah. Even if one sneezes there, the others do not wish him "good health." Needless to add, other topics must not be discussed. The sanctity of a Beth Hamidrash is greater than that of synagogues. [4.2–9]

The Honor and Respect Due to Teachers

Just as a person is commanded to honour and revere his father, so is he under an obligation to honour and revere his teacher, even to a greater extent than his father; for his father gave him life in this world, while his teacher who instructs him in wisdom, secures for him life in the world to come. If he sees an article that his father had lost and another article that his teacher had lost, the teacher's property should be recovered first, and then the father's. If his father and his teacher are loaded with burdens, he should first relieve his teacher and then his father. If his father and teacher are in captivity, he should first ransom his father. But, if his father is a scholar, even though not of the same rank as his teacher, he should first recover his father's lost property and then his teacher's. There is no honour higher than that which is due to the teacher; no reverence profounder than that which should be paid him. The sages said, "Reverence for thy teacher shall be like the fear of Heaven" (Ethics of the Fathers 4:15). They further said, "Whoever distrusts the authority of his teacher—it is as if he disputes with the Shechinah!; as it is said, 'When they strove against the Lord' (Num. 26:9). Whoever starts a quarrel with his teacher, it is as if he started a quarrel with the Shechinah; as it is said, 'Where the children of Israel strove with the Lord, and He was sanctified in them' (Num. 20:13). And whoever cherishes resentment against his teacher—it is as if he cherishes resentment against the Lord, as it is said, 'Your murmurings are not against us, but against the Lord' (Exod. 16:8). Whoever harbours doubts about his teacher—it is as if he harbours doubts about the Shechinah; as it is said, 'And the people spoke against God and against Moses' (Num. 21:3)."

Who is to be regarded as disputing his teacher's authority? One who sets up a college, holds sessions, discourses and instructs without his teacher's permission, during the latter's lifetime, and even if he be a resident in another country. To give decisions in his teacher's presence is forbidden at all times. Whoever gives a decision in his teacher's presence is deserving of death.

If there was a distance of twelve mils (A mil, Hebrew mile, is 2,000 cubits.) between him and his teacher and a question was put to him concerning a rule of practice, he may give the answer; and, to save a man from doing what is forbidden, he may give a decision even in his teacher's presence. For instance, if he sees one committing a violation of the Law, because that person did not know that it is prohibited, or out of sheer wickedness, it is his duty to check the wrongdoer and say to him, "This is forbidden." He should do so, even in the presence of his master, and even if the latter has not given him permission. For to save God's name from being profaned, we forego the honour due to the teacher. This, however, is only permitted casually. But to assume the function of a decisionist and give decisions regularly to all enquirers, even if he and his teacher live at opposite ends of the earth, is forbidden to a disciple, during his teacher's lifetime, unless he has his teacher's permission. Nor even after his teacher's death, may any disciple regularly give decisions, unless he has attained a standard of knowledge qualifying him to do so.

A disciple who is not thus qualified and nevertheless gives decisions is "wicked, foolish and of an arrogant spirit" (Ethics of the Fathers 4:9). And of him it is said, "For she hath cast down many wounded" (Prov. 7:26). On the other hand, a sage, who is qualified and refrains from rendering decisions and withholds knowledge of the Torah, puts stumbling blocks before the blind. Of him it is said, "Even the mighty are all slain" (Prov. 7:26). The students of small minds who have acquired an insufficient knowledge of the Torah, and yet seek to aggrandise themselves before the ignorant and among their townsmen by impertinently putting themselves forward and presuming to judge and render decisions in Israel—these are the ones who multiply strife, devastate the world, quench the light of the Torah and spoil the vineyard of the Lord of hosts. Of such, Solomon, in his wisdom, said, "Seize for us the foxes, the little foxes that spoil the vineyard" (Song of Songs 2:15).

A disciple is forbidden to call his teacher by his name, even when the latter is not present. This rule only applies if the name is unusual, so that anyone hearing it knows who is meant. In his presence, the pupil must never mention his teacher's name, even if he desires to call another person who bears the same name; the same is the rule with his father's name. In referring to them even after their death, he should use a descriptive title, ("my honoured father," or "my honoured teacher"). A disciple may not greet his teacher or return his greeting in the same manner as people are wont to greet their companions and return their greetings. But he should bow to his teacher and address him with reverence and deference, "Peace be unto thee, my teacher." If the teacher greeted him first, he should respond, "Peace to thee, my teacher and master."

So too, he should not remove his phylacteries in his teacher's presence, nor recline in his presence, but should sit respectfully, as one sits before a king. He should not recite his prayers, while standing in front of his teacher, or behind him, or at his side; needless to add, that he must not step (backward or forward) side by side with the teacher, but should stand at a distance in the rear, not, however, exactly behind his teacher, and then he can offer up his devotions. He must not go with his teacher into the same bathroom. He must not sit in his teacher's seat. When his teacher and a colleague dispute with one another, he must not, in his teacher's presence, interpose his opinion as to who is right. He must not contradict his teacher's statements. He may not sit down in his teacher's presence, till he is told "be seated," nor stand up, till he is told to stand up, or till he obtains permission to stand up. And when he quits, he must not turn his back, but should retire with his face to his teacher.

It is his duty to rise before his teacher, from the moment he sees him at a distance (and keep standing), till he disappears from view and is no longer visible; then the disciple may resume his seat. It is a person's duty to visit his teacher on the festivals.

Courtesy must not be shown to a pupil in the teacher's presence, unless the teacher himself is wont to show courtesy to that pupil. The various offices that a slave performs for his master, a pupil performs for his teacher. If, however, he is in a place where he is unknown, and has no phylacteries with him (only worn by free Israelites), and fears that people will say that he is a slave, he does not help his teacher to put on or remove his shoes. Whoever refuses his pupil's services, withholds kindness from him and removes from him the fear of Heaven. (Suggested by the exhortation in the Ethics of the Fathers, "Let reverence for thy teacher be as the fear of Heaven.") A pupil who neglects any of the courtesies due to his master causes the Shechinah to depart from Israel.

If a pupil saw his teacher violating the ordinances of the Torah, he should say to him, "Our master, thus and thus, hast thou taught us." Whenever a pupil recites a dictum in his teacher's presence, he should say, "Thus, our master, hast thou taught us." He should never quote a dictum that he has not heard from his teacher, without giving the authority for it. When his teacher dies, he rends all the garments he wears till he bares his breast. These rents he never sews up. These rules only apply to the chief teacher from whom one has learnt most of what he knows. But his relation to one from whom he did not acquire most of his knowledge is that of a junior to a senior fellow student. Towards such a senior student (who was at the same time his teacher), the disciple is not required to observe all the above-mentioned points of courtesy. But the junior has to stand up before him, and, on his demise, has to rend his garments, just as he does for a deceased relative for whom he mourns. Even if one learnt from a person one thing only, be it great or small, one has to stand up before that person and rend one's garments at his demise.

No scholar who possesses good manners will speak before his superior in knowledge, even if he has learnt nothing from him.

If one's chief teacher desires to excuse all his pupils or any one of them from all or any of these observances, he may do so. But even then, the disciple must show courtesy to him, even at the moment when he explicitly dispenses with it. [5.1–11]

Courtesy to Be Shown to Pupils

As pupils are bound to honour their teacher, so a teacher ought to show courtesy and friendliness to his pupils. The sages said, "Let the honour of thy disciples be as dear to thee as thine own" (Ethics of the Fathers 4:15). A man should take an interest in his pupils and love them, for they are his spiritual children who will bring him happiness in this world and in the world hereafter.

Disciples increase the teacher's wisdom and broaden his mind. The sages said, "Much wisdom I learnt from my teachers, more from my colleagues; from my pupils, most of all." Even as a small piece of wood kindles a large log, so a pupil of small attainments sharpens the mind of his teacher, so that by his questions, he elicits glorious wisdom. [5.12–13]

Reverence Due to All Men of Learning

It is a duty to honour every scholar, even if he is not one's teacher, as it is said, "Thou shalt rise up before the hoary head, and honour the face of the old man" (Lev. 19.32). The word "Zaken" (rendered "old man") refers to one who has acquired wisdom. When ought people to rise up before him? At the moment that he has approached within four cubits (and they should keep standing), till he has passed out of sight.

This courtesy is not to be observed in a bath-house nor in a latrine, for it is said, "Thou shalt rise up and honour" (Lev. 19:32); the courtesy of rising must be such as to express honour. Labourers, at the time when they are working, need not rise up before scholars, as it is said, "Thou shalt rise up and honour"; even as the "honouring" enjoined does not involve a monetary loss, so the courtesy of rising before the scholar is only required when it does not involve a monetary loss. And whence do we know that one should not shut one's eyes when a scholar passes, so as not to see him and thus evade the obligation of standing up before him? It is inferred from the text, "And thou shalt fear thy God" (Lev. 19:32); wherever the fulfillment of a duty is left to the conscience, the exhortation is added, "Thou shalt fear thy God."

It is improper for a sage to put the people to inconvenience by deliberately passing before them, so that they should have to stand up before him. He should use a short route and endeavour to avoid notice so that they should not be troubled to stand up. The sages were wont to use circuitous and exterior paths, where they were not likely to meet those who might recognize them, so as not to trouble them.

The same rule applies to riding as to walking. As it is a duty to rise up before the sage when he walks, so this courtesy should be shown when he rides by.

Where three are walking on a road, the teacher should be in the middle, the senior (of his disciples) at his right, the junior on his left.

On seeing a Chacham (a sage or religious authority), one does not rise till he has approached within four cubits; and as soon as he has passed, one resumes one's seat.

When a Chacham enters, each person stands up as he approaches him within four cubits, and then resumes his seat, and so does the next one till the Chacham has reached his place and is seated.

A pupil, in regular attendance, may only rise before his teacher in the morning and in the evening, so that the honour paid to the teacher shall not be more than that shown to God.

One rises up before an old man, advanced in years, even if he is not a sage. Even a learned man who is young rises up before an old man of advanced age. He is not obliged, however, to rise to his full height but need only rise himself sufficiently to indicate courtesy. Even a gentile who is aged should be shown courtesy in speech; and one should extend a hand to support him, as it is said, "Thou shalt rise up before the hoary head," without qualification.

Scholars do not go out to take part with the rest of the community in building, digging or similar work for the state, so as not to lose the respect of the common people. Nor are they assessed for the cost of building the walls, repairing the gates, paying the watchmen's wages, etc., or making a gift to the king. Nor are they obliged to pay a tax, jointly or severally levied upon the inhabitants of a city, as it is said, "Yea, though they hire (Joseph Caro in his Keseph Mishnah, explains this verse thus 'If they all study Torah [play upon Yitnu, which means in Aramaic, they study], God will gather them; if only a few do so, they will be diminished') among the nations, now will I gather them up, and they begin to be diminished by reason of the burden of kings and princes" (Hos. 8:10). So too, if a scholar has goods for sale, he is to be given the opportunity of disposing of them first; and no one else in the market is to be permitted to sell, till the scholar has first sold his stock. Similarly, if he has a cause pending and he is standing among a large number of suitors, his cause is taken first, and (during the hearing) he is seated.

It is exceedingly iniquitous to contemn sages or hate them. Jerusalem was only destroyed when its scholars were treated with contumely, as it is said, "But they mocked the messengers of God and despised His words, and scoffed at His prophets" (II Chron. 36:16); this means that they "despised those who taught His words." So too, the text "And if ye shall abhor My statutes" (Lev. 26:15) means "if ye abhor the teachers of My statutes." Whoever contemns the sages will have no portion in the world to come, and is included in the censure "For the word of the Lord hath he despised" (Num. 15:31). [6.1–11]

In the second book of the *Mishneh Torah,* which Maimonides titled *Sefer Ahavah,* "Book of Love," we find the *Hilkhot Tefillah,* the group of laws concerning prayer. In these, the great medieval codifier lays down several principles concerning the relative sanctity of the house of worship and the house of study.

The Supremacy of the Beth Hamidrash (The House of Study)

The House of Study is greater than the House of Worship. Many great scholars, even though they lived in communities which had many Houses of Worship, would nevertheless hold services of public worship in the places where they studied the Torah. [8.3]

It is permitted to convert a House of Worship into a House of Study, but it is forbidden to turn a House of Study into a House of Worship for the sanctity of the former is greater than that of the latter, for the rule is to ascend in the scale of holiness and not to descend. Thus, if the people of a community sell their House of Worship, they must purchase for that money a Holy Ark; if they sold a Holy Ark, they must purchase for that money mantles or a container for a Torah Scroll; if they sold mantles or a container for the Torah Scroll, they must purchase for that money a set of the Chumash; if they sold a set of the Chumash they must acquire for that money a Torah Scroll. If, however, they sold a Torah Scroll they cannot acquire for that money anything else but another Torah Scroll since there is nothing more sacred than a Sefer Torah. [11.14]

(3) THE LAWS FOR ADULT LEARNING BY JOSEPH KARO IN THE SHULHAN ARUKH

The code of Maimonides served as the basis for subsequent codes, of which there were many. But the highest peak in Jewish legal literature was reached four hundred years after Maimonides issued his *Mishneh Torah,* with the publication in 1567 of the *Shulhan Arukh* by Joseph Karo. It is the greatest and most authoritative of all codes of Jewish law, and popular recognition has made it the standard codification of Jewish teachings and traditional practices. As might be expected, the *Shulhan Arukh* contains a good many legal formulations dealing with education generally and also with adult education. This is particularly true of the second of the four books of the code, entitled, appropriately enough, *Yoreh Deah* ("Teaching Knowledge"), in which most of the material on education is found. There are also a few references to our subject in the first book, *Orah Hayyim* ("The Way of Life"), and in the fourth book, the *Hoshen Mishpat* ("Breastplate of Justice").

The vitality of Jewish jurisprudence is to be noted in the fact that even the *Shulhan Arukh* was not allowed to petrify the growth of Jewish law and custom. For, no sooner did its text appear than it became the basis for further interpretations and commentaries. Some of these soon achieved such an authoritative character that they were included as annotations to the printed text in every edition of the *Shulhan Arukh*. In the following translation, in addition to the main text, some of the more relevant of these comments are included as notes printed in smaller type.[3] We begin with some passages from *Yoreh Deah.*

OBLIGATIONS FOR ADULT EDUCATION

246, 1. The duty of studying the Torah rests upon every Jew, whether he be rich or poor, whether he be in sound health or an invalid, whether he be young or very old. Even the beggar who goes from door to door, and even a married man with a large family, must appoint some fixed time for study, both by day and by night, as it is said, "And thou shalt meditate thereon both by day and by night." (Josh. 1:8).

If he be very pressed for time and has read only the Shema both morning and evening, this suffices to fulfill the command, "My words which I have put in thy mouth shall not depart out of thy mouth, nor out of the mouth of thy seed, nor out of the mouth of thy seed's seed" (Isa. 59:21).

One who has given some decision of Jewish law without being paid therefor, or who has taught children without pay, can reckon this as fulfilling the command of fixed daily study. But if these actions are done for pay, they cannot be reckoned as satisfying the command for fixed daily study.

One who cannot learn because he is totally ignorant, or because of the distraction of his occupation, must make it possible for others to learn.

Then it is reckoned to him as if he himself is studying. A man may make an agreement that another man should occupy himself with the study of Torah on condition that the former supplies the latter with his means of livelihood; they then share the reward. But if the former is already engaged in the study of Torah, he may not sell his obligation of study for money.

246, 2. Let a man first study Torah and then marry; for if he marry first, he will not be able to study Torah once the millstones are around his neck. But if it get to be impossible for him to study without a wife because his imagination and his desire overmaster him, then let him marry first.

246, 3. Until when must one study? Until the day of one's death, as it is said, "Lest these words depart from thy heart all the days of thy life" (Deut. 4:9). So long as one is not busying himself with the Torah, he is forgetting it.

CONTENT OF ADULT STUDY

246, 4. One must divide the time he devotes to learning into three parts: one-third for the Bible, one-third for the Mishnah and one-third for the Talmud. The study of the Bible includes all the twenty-four books; that of the Mishnah includes the oral Law and the explanations of the written Law; and the study of the Talmud comprehends a deep understanding of the whole Torah, its development, deductions and analogies, the principles by which it can be expounded, an appreciation of the basis of the commandments, the basis for prohibitions and sanctions, and all similar traditional learning. How can this division of time be arranged? If he be an artisan, working three hours at his trade and nine hours at Torah, let him devote three hours of the nine to the Bible, three hours to the Mishnah and three hours to the Talmud.

This should be the division of time in the early period of his study. But when he becomes more skilled in the Bible, and he does not need to study Bible and Mishnah so frequently, then let him study these at regular intervals so as not to forget anything of these fundamentals of learning, and let him devote all the rest of his time to the Talmud, so far as the breadth of his understanding and his power of concentration will allow.

Some say that through the study of the Babylonian Talmud, which is made up of Bible, Mishnah and Gemara, one fulfils his obligation towards all three divisions of study.

A man should study only Bible, Mishnah, Gemara and the legal literature which goes with them, for in this way he may attain both this world and the world to come, which he cannot do through the study of other branches of learning. But he is fully allowed to study other subjects, except if they be heretical. This study of other branches of learning is called by the Rabbis "Walking in Paradise." But a man should not "walk in Paradise" until he has partaken to the full (literally, "filled his stomach with the meat and wine") of a deep knowledge of Jewish learning and ritual.

Nor should he study Kabbala (the mystic philosophy of Judaism) until he is forty years of age. For this study one needs special sanctity, purity, zeal and godliness. Most of those who presume to enter into this branch of knowledge before their due time come to untimely grief through it.

PAYMENT FOR ADULT TEACHING

246, 5. In places where it is customary, one may teach the Torah for remuneration; but it is forbidden to teach Mishnah and Talmud for pay. However, if a man cannot find anyone to teach him free, he may pay for instruction. Although he may have been compelled to pay for his instruction, he must not say, just as I have learned and paid for my learning, so will I teach for pay; he must be willing to teach others free. Since it is nowadays the custom to pay for teaching, the teacher may receive payment if he have no other means of livelihood. Even if he has means, he is allowed to take payment for his teaching in lieu of the business opportunities and other opportunities of earning money which he renounces for teaching.

All later authorities allow the teacher to receive payment for teaching.

EDUCATION OF WOMEN

246, 6. A woman who has studied Torah is meritorious, but not in the same measure as a man, because she does so at will not in response to a command. Although through study of the Torah she attains a reward, the Rabbis directed that a man should not teach Torah to his daughter, because most women have not a mind adapted to such instruction, and they would be apt to lose a sense of proportion on account of their deficient understanding. The Rabbis further said that anyone who teaches his daughter Torah is as if he is teaching her folly. When they said this, they referred to the difficulties of the oral Law; but in the case of the Bible, although the father need not teach his daughter, if he has taught her, it is not as though he taught her folly.

In any case, a woman must learn the laws affecting women.
She is not bound to teach her son Torah; but if she helps her son or her husband, enabling them to study Torah, she shares the reward with them.

MORAL CHARACTER OF THE STUDENT

246, 7. We should not go on trying to teach Torah to a student who is unworthy (with reference to Prov. 26:8). We must first try to change his disposition, put him on the right path, examine him, then bring him again to the House of Learning and teach him.

MORAL CHARACTER OF THE TEACHER

246, 8. Even though a teacher be very learned and all the people have need of him, if he does not walk in the right path, we may not go to him for instruction until he changes his ways (with reference to Mal. 2:7: "For the priest's lips should keep knowledge, and they should keep the law [Torah] at his mouth, *when* he is the messenger of the Lord of hosts").

CLASSROOM FORMALITIES

246, 9. What was the manner of instruction? The teacher would sit at the head of the room and the students would seat themselves before him, grouped around him in a semicircle, so that they all could see him and hear his words. The teacher should not sit on a chair while his students sit on the floor. Either he and they must sit on the floor, or all must sit on chairs.

Some explain that this ruling applies only to senior students who have reached the grade of ordination.

246, 10. When students have failed to understand what the teacher has been teaching, he should not be angry with them, but he should go over the whole matter again, time after time, until they understand thoroughly. The student should not say, "I understand" if he has not understood; but he should ask, if necessary again and again. Then if the teacher becomes angry, let the student say, "Master, we are studying Torah and I must learn it, though my understanding is slow."

246, 11. A student should not feel ashamed because a fellow student has mastered the subject at issue at once, or almost at once, while he has not grasped it after many explanations. For if he feel ashamed on this account, the result will be that he will enter and leave the House of Learning without having learned anything. Therefore the Rabbis said that the shamefaced cannot become learned, nor can the quick tempered be teachers.

What has just been said applies to the case where the students do not understand because the matter which they are studying is profound, or because their capacity is limited; but if the teacher knows that they are treating the study of Torah carelessly and in an offhand way, and on this account they do not understand, then it is his duty to show anger and to shame them with his words in order to spur them on. This is what the Rabbis meant when they said, "Scatter gall on your students." For this reason, also, the teacher may not indulge in frivolity in the presence of his students, nor play in their presence, nor eat and drink with them, so that he may preserve his dignity and the respect they owe him, and they may learn the more quickly.

246, 12. One may not ask questions of the teacher the moment he enters the House of Learning, before he has had time to settle down. Nor should a student ask a question immediately on his own entry, before he has had time to settle down. In order not to embarrass the teacher, two should not ask questions at the same time, nor should questions be asked except in connection with the subject of study. The teacher may mislead his students through catch questions or through other means, in order to sharpen their wits and to test whether they

remember what they learn. It is hardly necessary to add that in order
to stimulate them he may ask them questions about some subject other
than that which they are studying at the time.

246, 13. One should not ask a question while standing, nor should
one answer standing, nor from a height, nor from a distance, nor from
behind the teacher.

Some say that a question of ritual law must be asked standing.

The question must be to the point, and must be asked in earnest.
One should not ask more than three questions on the one subject.

246, 14. When two questions are asked at the same time, one being
to the point and the other not so, preference is given to the question
to the point. If of two questions, one has practical bearing and the
other is only theoretical, preference is given to the question with practical bearing. Of two questions, one of which refers to a point of law
and the other to a point of interpretation, preference is given to the
question referring to a point of law. Of two questions, one referring
to interpretation and the other to Aggadah, preference is given to the
question about the point of interpretation. Of two questions, one
dealing with Aggadah and the other with a deduction *a fortiori,* the
preference is given to the question about the deduction *a fortiori.* Of
two questions, one concerning a deduction *a fortiori* and the other an
inference from similarity of phrases, preference is given to the one
concerned with the deduction *a fortiori.*

246, 15. When there are two questioners, one of whom is a scholar
and the other a student, precedence is given to the more learned questioner. Similarly, between a student and an ignorant man, precedence
is given to the student. If both questioners are of equal standing,
whether scholars or students or ignorant men, and both have asked
questions of a like category, whether it be a question of law or any
other type of question, then the teacher may answer first whichever one
he chooses.

A learned bastard takes precedence over an ignorant priest.

CONDUCT IN THE HOUSE OF LEARNING

246, 16. One may not sleep in the House of Learning. Anyone who
slumbers in the House of Learning will find his knowledge grow ragged,

as it is said, "Drowsiness shall clothe a man with rags" (Prov. 23:21).

246, 17. Conversation should not be carried on in the House of Learning on any matter other than the study of the Torah. Even when one sneezes, his fellow students should not say to him, "Good health."

But nowadays this is permitted.

The sanctity of the House of Learning is greater even than that of the synagogue.

IMPORTANCE OF ADULT STUDY

246, 18. The study of Torah is regarded as equivalent to performing all the commands (because study leads to practice). When, therefore, one has before him the choice of carrying out a commandment or of studying Torah, if the command may be carried out by others for him, he should not interrupt his studies. Otherwise, he must fulfill the commandment and afterwards return to his studies.

246, 19. When a man is judged in the divine judgment, he is first judged according to the way in which he has devoted himself to the study of the Torah, and afterwards he is judged according to his acts.

246, 20. Let a man always devote himself to Torah, even though he does it not for its own sake, because in the end he will come to study it for its own sake.

This refers to cases such as when a man studies in order that he shall be the recipient of honor. But if he studies the Torah in order to criticize and attack it, it were better for him that he had never been born.

LEARNING VERSUS TEMPORAL INTERESTS

246, 21. Knowledge of the Torah will not abide with one who comes to it carelessly, or light-heartedly, or while eating or drinking. It will remain only with the one who is willing to suppress himself utterly and afflict himself unceasingly for its sake, and who will not give sleep to his eyes nor slumber to his eyelids (Prov. 6:4. The Rabbis graphically describe the acquisition of knowledge of the Torah as calling for a regimen of bread with salt, water drunk by measure, sleeping on the ground and a life of painful toil.)

Let not a man think to devote himself to the study of the Torah and at the same time to the acquisition of riches and honor; for one who lets this thought enter into his heart will never attain to the crown of the Law. (Three crowns were granted to Israel: the crown of the priesthood, to which only Aaron and his seed attained; the crown of royalty, to which David and his house attained, and the greatest crown of all, the crown of the Torah, which is free for all Israel.) To be successful in his study he must make it a fixed duty, and must make his occupation an occasional thing, minimizing his attention to business and making his main occupation the study of the Torah. He must abjure temporal pleasures. He must devote so much time to his daily work as is necessary for his support, if he have not otherwise the wherewithal to live, and the rest of the day and part of the night he should give up to the study of Torah.

It is a great virtue for a man to support himself by the work of his hands, as it is said, "When thou eatest the labor of thy hands, happy shalt thou be, and it shall be well with thee." (Ps. 128:2) Anyone who thinks of devoting himself to the Torah to the exclusion of all other work, while being supported by charity, is profaning the name of God and bringing the Torah into contempt. For it is forbidden to reap any material advantage from the Torah, and all study of the Torah which is not coupled with work leads to sin and robbery of one's fellowmen.

All this applies to a healthy man who, by spending some time at his craft or business, can support himself. But an old or a sickly man may derive benefit from his study of the Torah and be supported in it. Some say that even a man in full health may do the same, and therefore the custom has grown up everywhere for the Rabbi to be allowed a stipend from the community, in order to avoid his being obliged to engage in other work, and thus publicly bringing the Torah into contempt in the eyes of the masses. Only a Rabbi who has need of this income, and not one who is rich, may take advantage of this. But some allow even further for the Rabbi and his students to accept their needs from those who contribute to the support of students of the Torah, in order to allow them to devote themselves to study in comfort. Yet in any case, one who is able to support himself adequately by the work of his hands, and also to give up time to study, is living on the plane of piety. Such ability is a gift of God, to which not every man attains. For it is not possible for every man to give up time to study of the Torah and become proficient in it while supporting himself by other means.

Though it be granted that a Rabbi may receive compensation from the community, or a fixed income for his needs, he may not receive gifts from individuals. When, therefore, it is said that every one who brings a gift to the Rabbi is as if he were bringing the offering of first fruits, this applies only to small gifts, such as people are accustomed to give to an honored man, even though he be not learned. But some authorities allow the Rabbi to receive more substantial gifts; and the Rabbinical head of a

Talmudic College or of a Jewish Court may receive gifts without limit, for he is like a ruler. The latter must be very careful not to accept anything in the way of a gift from any litigant.

A Rabbi must keep himself far from the great shame of those few who run after money and ask for gifts. For they bring the Torah and those who study it into reproach. If even the priests were not allowed to ask for the portions which were theirs by law, how much the less may Rabbis ask for gifts. Such conduct is a great sin, "and the just shall live by his faith" (Hab. 2:4). A Rabbi may take a small part of something on which he is asked to give a ritual decision when this is necessary to make his decision clear. But he is prohibited from taking as a gift any considerable portion of some object which he has declared as ritually permissible.

He who uses the crown of the Torah for his own purposes will perish. But where the need exists, a young Rabbi may make himself known in a place where he is not known.

PLACE OF STUDY

246, 22. It is a tradition established as firmly as a covenant that everyone who learns the Torah in a synagogue will not quickly forget it. Everyone who labors at his study in privacy will become learned, as it is said, "Wisdom is with the modest" (Prov. 11:2). He who studies audibly will retain what he learns; but he who studies without giving voice to the words he studies will quickly forget.

LEARNING'S EXCLUSIVE CLAIMS

246, 23. He who wishes to attain to the crown of the Torah must be careful not to lose a single one of his evenings in sleeping, or eating, or drinking, or conversation, or similar ways of passing the time; but he must give them all up to the study of the Torah.

For the greater part of what a man learns, he learns at night.
One should begin night study from the fifteenth of Ab.
One who does not add to his knowledge is all the while diminishing it.

246, 24. A household in which the study of the Torah is not heard at night will be consumed by fire.

246, 25. One who is able to devote himself to the Torah and who does not do so, or one who has studied and has then turned aside to the frivolities of life, or who has neglected his learning and cast it aside, is one to whom apply these words, "For he has despised the word of the Lord and broken His commandment" (Num. 15:31).

It is forbidden to waste one's time in worldly conversation.

246, 26. He who gives up his study of the Torah because he is rich will in the end have to give it up on account of poverty (Avot 4:11); while he who persists in the study of the Torah in poverty, will in the end continue it in wealth (Avot 4:11).

It is forbidden to study Torah in filthy places.

When one finishes the study of a complete section of the Talmud, it is a religious duty to have some general rejoicing and enjoy a repast, called a feast of religious obligation.

Learning and the Fifth Commandment

240, 13. In case of a conflict of duties, studying the Torah takes precedence over the duty of honoring parents.

This is so, however, only if the son has to choose between leaving the city for study and staying in the city for his parents' sake; but if he remains in the city, he must first minister to his parents, and then turn to his study.

240, 15. If a father bids his son break one of the laws of the Torah, whether it be an affirmative or a negative precept, the son must not harken to him. (Lev. 19:3: Ye shall venerate every man, his mother and his father, *and* ye shall keep my sabbaths.)

240, 25. If a student of the Torah wishes to go to some other town where he is sure that his studies will be more effective because of a superior teacher there, though his father would prevent him through fear of the Gentiles in that town, the son need not in this matter harken to his father.

242, 1. One must show his Rabbi more honor and respect than he accords even his father.

EXEMPTIONS FOR STUDENTS AND SCHOLARS

243, 1. Rabbinical scholars are not wont to go out with the rest of the people to take part in building or digging operations for the city, and in similar work which would lower their dignity in the eyes of the people. Since they are free from such obligations, they do not have to hire substitutes to take their place.

243, 2. This is the case only if the call is for individual service. But if all the rest of the people are serving or hiring substitutes, Rabbinical scholars must do their share or hire others to take their place, and they must make their contributions towards a public work that is needed for the well-being of the community. But in the case of any work connected with guarding the city, such as repairing the walls or its towers, or the pay of the watchmen, scholars are not obliged to give their share, because they do not need protection. Their Torah protects them.

Similarly, scholars are free from having to pay any kind of tax or impost, whether it be a tax placed on the citizens as a whole, or on individuals, and whether it be a fixed tax or not. The other citizens must pay these taxes for them, even if the taxes were imposed on the individual.

All this applies only if the scholar is a professional Rabbinical scholar; otherwise, he must do his share with the others. He is regarded as a professional Rabbinical scholar if he is only slightly engaged in some business occupation that suffices to keep him with the necessities of life without his making money, and every hour that he can spare from this business he devotes regularly to study of the Torah.

There are some places where it is customary and others where it is not customary to free the professional Rabbinical scholar from the payment of taxes.

243, 3. A scholar who disregards the commands of the law, and who is not God-fearing, is reckoned as the least of the members of the community.

242, 14. A scholar who is qualified to teach the law and does not do so is guilty of withholding Torah and of putting stumbling blocks in the path of the community.

HONOR DUE THE SCHOLAR

243, 6. It is a great sin to treat a scholar with contempt, or to hate him. Anyone who treats the learned with contempt has no share in the world to come, and to him apply the words, "For the word of the Lord he has despised" (Num. 15:31).

244, 1. It is a positive command (Lev. 19:32) to stand up before any scholar even though he be only a young man. Even though the scholar be not one's own teacher, one must stand up before him, if he be the superior in knowledge.

Similarly it is a positive command to rise up before the hoary head, that is, a man of seventy years.

This applies to an old man though he be not learned, so long as he is not of bad character.

244, 2. From what moment must one stand up before the learned or the aged? From the time when they come within a distance of four cubits until they have passed by. This holds whether they are riding or on foot.

244, 3. When the scholar is approaching within the four cubits it is forbidden to shut one's eyes so as not to have to rise up before him.

244, 5. Artisans while engaged in their work are not obliged to stand before a scholar. If they are in the employ of someone else and wish to act strictly by rising up before the scholar, they are not free to do so.

244, 6. A scholar should not make himself troublesome to the people by purposely passing before them and making them rise before him. Let him go to his destination by the shortest way, so that he will not make many people stand. If he is able to go by a roundabout way so as to avoid passing many people, it is meritorious for him to do so.

This apparently applied only in Talmudic times when it was the custom to sit on the ground; but in principle it applies wherever it is troublesome to make the people rise. It therefore hardly has application where people are seated on chairs or benches.

244, 7. A scholar who is only a young man should rise up before a very old man, not necessarily to his full height, but sufficiently to show him honor. A venerable Gentile should be addressed with fitting honor and one should extend him a helping hand.

244, 8. Two scholars or two old men do not have to rise the one before the other, but each must show the other respect.

Even the teacher must show some honor to his pupil.

242, 33. The honor of the student should be as dear to the teacher as his own honor.

244, 11. Even while engaged in the study of the Torah, one must stand up before a scholar.

244, 12. A scholar, even if he be the outstanding figure of his generation, should stand before a man noted for his good deeds.

244, 15. When the president of the Sanhedrin enters the House of Learning, all those present rise up and do not seat themselves again until he says to them: "Be seated." When the head of the religious court enters the House of Learning, those present form two lines for him to pass between them until he is seated. When the Rabbi enters, those whom he approaches within four cubits stand before him until he reaches his place.

244, 18. In the religious court or in the House of Learning, learning is considered the determining factor. Therefore when there come together a great scholar who is young, and an aged man who has some learning, the young man is given the seat of honor and the privilege of having the first word. But at a wedding or social gathering, age is given the preference, and the old man is given the seat of honor.

If the scholar is a great scholar, and the elderly man is not very old, scholarship is accorded prior consideration; whereas if the old man is very old, while the scholar is not an outstanding scholar, old age is given the chief consideration so long as the old man has some claims to learning. But if the old man is not very old, and the scholar is not profoundly learned, greater consideration is given to old age.

A FATHER MUST LEARN FIRST

245, 2. If a father must himself study and also have his son instructed, and if he cannot afford to do both, then if the two have an equal capacity for learning, the father takes precedence over the son. But if the son is more intelligent and understanding than the father and has a better capacity for learning, it is the son who takes precedence. In this latter case, the father must not completely give up his own study but must study part of the time himself.

CHARITY AND EDUCATION

249, 16. There is some authority for holding that giving to the synagogue is a more important duty than giving in charity; but the charity of supporting poor boys in the study of the Torah or of giving to the needy sick is more important than the maintenance of a synagogue.

253, 11. A needy scholar should be given aid in a manner befitting his dignity. If he is unwilling to accept direct aid, he should be supplied with goods which have been bought cheaply, so that he can resell them profitably. But if he understands business, he should be given a loan to set him up in business.

259, 2. Charity funds which have been given for a synagogue or a cemetery may be diverted by the community for the needs of a House of Learning or a school, even against the will of the donors. But the funds of a school may not be diverted to the use of a synagogue.

This is so only when the trustees of the charity funds fear that the needs of the school will not be met. But where the community supports the school adequately, and if, when school funds are diverted to the synagogue, the community will make up the difference for the school, such a transfer is allowable, even in a place where ordinarily it is forbidden to change the use made of contributed funds.

If no immediate use can be made of funds contributed for a specific purpose, the donor cannot retract his gift. For example: when a plot of land has been given as a site for a House of Learning and the House of Learning cannot be built at the time, the gift must stand until such time as the House of Learning can be built. All this has application only where there is no definite local custom in the matter. . . . But where there is a definite local custom, it must be followed either way, for it is presumed that the gift is made by the donor and accepted by the community subject to the local custom governing the right of transferring charity gifts.

The theme of learning is also treated in the *Orah Hayyim.*

EARLY MORNING STUDIES

155, 1. When one leaves the synagogue at the close of the daily morning service, one should proceed to the House of Learning. One should fix a regular time for study, and that time must be unchangeable even at great personal sacrifice.

One who is too ignorant to study Torah with the others should nevertheless attend the House of Learning and thus get the reward of his attendance. Or he should take a seat apart and study a little of what he can, and thus have enter into his heart a spirit of conduct infused by veneration.

155, 2. One may eat a light breakfast before going to the House of Learning in the morning if one is accustomed to do so, and it is advisable so to accustom oneself (in order to preserve one's health for the service of the Creator).

THE PENTATEUCH, THE BASIS OF JEWISH LEARNING

285, 1. Although by regular weekly attendance at synagogue throughout the year, one hears the reading of the whole Pentateuch, one must nevertheless read for himself every week the portion from the Pentateuch for the week, twice in the Hebrew text and once in the Targum. (The ancient Aramaic translation of the Bible.) Even verses which consist only of names should be read also in the Targum.

285, 2. It is allowable to substitute the commentary of Rashi (The acrostic name of Rabbi Solomon, son of Isaac, of Troyes, 1040–1105 c.e., the author of the most popular commentary on the Bible and on the Talmud) for the reading of the Targum; but the pious will read both the Targum and Rashi's commentary. (The mystics prefer the Targum; others prefer to study Rashi's commentary.)

One who is unable to read Rashi's commentary should read a paraphrase of the weekly Pentateuchal portion in the vernacular, such as the Tseenah Ureenah (A Judaeo-German paraphrase, dating from approximately 1600 c.e. This paraphrase was especially popular among women) so that he gets to understand the content of the portion.

285, 6. Professional teachers of children who during the week have studied with the children the weekly Hebrew portion from the Pentateuch do not have to read it over twice more and once in the Targum.

307, 17. On Sabbaths and festivals it is forbidden to study anything but Torah, though some allow serious reading, such as of medical works, or the use of astronomical instruments.

The Statute Book of the Ashkenazic community in Amsterdam printed in the year 1737. Among its 102 regulations are those which prescribe programs for Jewish learning. This copy, which is in the possession of the author, bears the signature of the charity warden under an official declaration that copies without such signature are forgeries and their possessors are liable to a fine of ten guilders. There is also a copy of this volume in the Library of the YIVO Institute for Jewish Research. (See page 170.)

מודעה רבה

דש התקנות ביפר ניט פאר דיא רעכֿטי מוז' מורגיכעלֿי
תקנות אקהֿל יל"ו וועגרין גֿעהֿוטין זיין מֿן לֿם דיא דיא זעלֿבֿגֿי
סֿפֿרי התקנות ווֿאו דא מונטר חֿתֿיֿאֿת הקלֿין הגֿבֿמֿ
לֿדֿקֿה יל"ו מֿין ־סֿטֿין ווֿערט' ובֿמֿק הֿאֿלֿם יֿאֿלֿם מֿיֿכֿר הֿמֿבֿן זֿעֿוֿט
סֿפֿר תקנות ווֿאו חֿתֿיֿאֿה הֿג"ל ניט מֿין טֿטֿיט הֿוֿא אֿזֿוֿק' לֿוֿז' מֿוֿם
גֿיֿוֿטֿין ׃ מֿוֿל' דֿער זֿעֿוֿבֿיֿגֿר טֿמֿאֿלֿם מֿלֿוֿ כֿאֿו הֿקֿוֿה מֿאֿכֿו אֿוֿזֿן
קֿנֿס גֿעֿבֿן וֿלֿדֿקֿה עֿטֿרֿה זֿהֿוֿלֿבֿׁים בֿטֿבֿיֿוֿ כֿוֿ סֿפֿר ׃ מֿוֿל' דֿער מֿן
בֿרֿעֿנֿגֿר זֿמֿוֿ הֿמֿבֿן מֿהֿנֿה הֿגֿוֿנֿה אֿקֿהֿל יל"ו וֿהֿכֿוֿ כֿפֿי הֿעֿנֿין

CHAPTER

X

THE JEWISH COMMUNITY
AND JEWISH LEARNING

It is one thing to enact laws; it is another to gain compliance. National governments set up law-enforcement machinery and a penal system in order to insure obedience to the law. In the Jewish community, however, adherence to formulated codes and legal decisions was almost entirely voluntary. This is especially to be noted in the manner in which the self-governing Jewish communities went about the task of implementing the requirements of the law in relation to the obligation of lifelong learning. Through the instrumentality of the takkanah, or communal ordinance— promulgated either at provincial synods composed of representatives of a number of Jewish communities in one area, or at local kahal meetings held in each individual community—provision was made for bringing into life what was provided for by law. An examination of some of the takkanot that have come down to us, spanning many lands and many centuries, gives glorious evidence of the singular devotion of Jewish communities to Jewish learning.

(1) THE COMMUNAL ORDINANCES OF
THIRTEENTH CENTURY GERMAN JEWRY

If we survey the communal ordinances in chronological order, we come first upon the Takkanot Shum, enacted in the years 1220–23 by the synods of German Jewry residing in the Rhine provinces, more especially the communities of Speyer, Worms, and Mayence. These Jewish communities held frequent provincial assemblies, usually in the city of Ma-

167

yence. Among the leading personalities were Rabbi Elazar ben Yehudah of Worms, the author of the book *Rokeah;* Rabbi Eliezer ben Yoel Halevi, known as the Rabiah; and Rabbi Simhah ben Shmuel of Speyer. One of the ordinances deals with the obligation of study; it has come down to us in two versions:

> One who is unable to devote himself to the study of the Talmud should study half a page if possible or Midrash or Scripture or part of the weekly portion every day. (As it is stated at the end of Mishnah Minahot: He who can do much, and he who can only do little are alike.) Each should study daily unless prevented by an emergency.

> Every man shall set aside a definite time for study; if he is unable to study Talmud, he shall read Scripture, the weekly portion, or the Midrash according to his ability. He who does much and he who does little are alike, provided that he is not prevented by an emergency.[1]

(2) THE COMMUNAL ORDINANCES OF FIFTEENTH CENTURY SPANISH JEWRY

Turning to Spanish Jewry two centuries later, we come upon the synod of Castilian Jews held in Valladolid in 1432. It was convened by Abraham Benveniste, the rabbi of the court, with the approval of the reigning monarch, King Juan II, under whose rule Jewish life flourished in Spain. The synod met for ten days in the great synagogue of Valladolid, at the end of which it promulgated a far-reaching takkanah whose purpose it was, as stated in the preamble, "to deal with certain definite subjects and other matters, which are for the service of the Creator, the glory of the holy Torah, the service of the King, and the success and welfare of the communities."[2] Two of these regulations deal with the spread of learning among the adults of the various communities represented:

> A community having forty families or more shall be obliged to endeavor so far as possible to maintain among themselves a Rabbi who will teach them Halakot and Aggadot. The community must maintain him reasonably. His salary shall be paid from the income of the tax on meat and wine and the income from the Hakdesh, if there is any, or from the Talmud Torah Fund, so that he should not have to beg his livelihood from any of the leaders of the community, so that he

may reprove them and guide them in all things which pertain to the service of the Creator, blessed be He. Moreover, we ordain that each Rabbi maintain a Talmudical Academy where those desirous of learning may study the Halakah. He shall lecture at such hours as the Rabbis are wont to lecture.[3]

(3) THE COMMUNAL ORDINANCES OF SEVENTEENTH CENTURY CENTRAL EUROPEAN JEWRY

Moving to Central Europe, to Bohemia, to the city of Prague at the beginning of the seventeenth century, we come upon a remarkable communal ordinance enacted by this historic Jewish community, which at the time had some ten thousand Jewish inhabitants. This takkanah was composed by the famous rabbi and preacher of Prague, Rabbi Solomon Ephraim Luntschitz, and was agreed upon at the meeting of the rabbinic and lay leaders of the community in the month of Tishri in the year 1611. It shows the deep sense of obligation this famous Jewish community felt for the spread of Jewish learning among the adult population.

With regard to learning, we ordain as follows: Every Jew is obligated to study by himself at least one hour each day. Should he be unable, due to lack of knowledge to do so, he shall arrange to study with an instructor. Should he not be able to manage this, then he shall read some of the good books, dealing with the teachings of Judaism, in the Judaeo-German language. He, however, who is able to study must set aside daily a fixed period of time from his worldly occupation in order to study the Torah.[4]

About a generation later, in the year 1641, the Jewish community of Worms issued a set of takkanot, one of which declared that "each Jewish householder is obligated to set aside a definite time each day for study. The people should associate themselves into groups for purposes of study and each group should select a learned man who should instruct them in the book they have chosen to study.[5]

At about the same time, in the year 1650, in the city of Gaya, there was held the famous session of the Moravian Council, which represented more than a score of Jewish communities in Moravia and met with fair regularity every three years down to 1748. This council adopted the remarkable set of statutes that has come down in Jewish history as "The

311 Takkanot." [6] The first seventeen of these statutes deal with the study of the Torah. After ordaining that every Jewish community with more than thirty resident heads of families must maintain and support a rabbi, a yeshivah, and a certain minimum number of yeshivah students, and after making provision for instruction of the children, it was further ordained

> that every small community that maintains a teacher, or any community that has two or three or more members who have received rabbinic ordination and are scholars, and how much more so those communities that maintain a rabbi but have no yeshivah, they are especially obliged to set aside fixed periods of time for the study of the Torah every day in the bet ha-midrash. The head of the community is duty-bound to give special supervision to this activity under penalty of a strong fine and under the general direction of the district rabbi.[7]

(4) THE COMMUNAL ORDINANCES OF ASHKENAZIC JEWS IN EIGHTEENTH CENTURY AMSTERDAM

A notable example of the collective concern for the maintenance of Jewish learning among the grown-ups of the community is to be found in the takkanot of the Ashkenazic Jews of Amsterdam, printed in the year 1737. It was only some fifty or sixty years earlier that Ashkenazic Jews, coming from countries in Middle Europe, began to seek refuge in that friendly Dutch city. The newcomers soon established a very strong and highly centralized Jewish communal life of their own, apart and separate from the rather aloof and distant Sephardic Jews who already resided in Amsterdam. In the first third of the eighteenth century, the Ashkenazic community was rising to its full strength; when its own statutes were promulgated in a printed volume in 1737, the following rules were set down for the maintenance of the anticipated house of study:

> When the community will resolve to establish a bet ha-midrash, it shall be required that studies be carried on in it constantly and certainly no less than four hours daily, namely a minimum of two hours before midnight and a minimum of two hours after midnight. The rabbi of the community and none other shall also serve as the head of the academy. Only he shall be in charge, and he shall determine the program and method of study. All matters pertaining to the bet ha-midrash

and all affairs of administration shall, however, be governed by the lay officials, namely the parnassim and the gabbaim for charity. If possible, ten scholars shall be hired to be constantly at their studies in the bet ha-midrash. No one who is a visitor or a temporary resident in the city can be engaged for pay to be among those scholars. Only he can be hired as one of these scholars who has acquired the status of a permanent resident of the community in accordance with the stipulated regulations and with the approval of the majority of the communal officials, and who has also paid the required sum of 100 reichstalers in full.[8]

(5) THE COMMUNAL ORDINANCES OF EIGHTEENTH CENTURY LITHUANIAN JEWRY

Official communal support of Jewish learning is also to be noted in the statutes of the famous Lithuanian Council, which represented many Russian Jewish communities. At its session in the year 1761, held in the city of Slutsk, the council ordained that "in every bet ha-midrash there should be studied daily at least one chapter of the Mishnah. It is the duty of the gabbaim of each bet ha-midrash to see to it that this practice should be enforced." [9]

In this survey, spanning some five hundred years, from the thirteenth to the eighteenth centuries, and covering Jewish communities in lands from Eastern and Central, Western and Southern Europe, we see the same communal concern that was expressed in the opening statement of the takkanot of the Castilian Jews: "The first of our decisions and the beginning of our Takkanot has for its object the maintenance of students for our Torah." [10]

The Statute Book of the Hevrah
Kedoshah Agudat Bahurim of
Amsterdam, 1790. (See page 190.)
*Courtesy of YIVO Institute for
Jewish Research.*

The Statute Book of the Hevrah
Kaddisha Gemilut Hasadim of the
Ashkenazic community in Amsterdam printed in 1776 which
contains regulations for Jewish
learning. It is in the possession of
the author. (See page 186.)

CHAPTER

XI

HOLY BROTHERHOODS AND THEIR PROGRAMS FOR JEWISH STUDY

The requirement of constant study, founded in Jewish law and reinforced by communal ordinance, penetrated every organized form of Jewish group life. This is most especially shown by a study of the hevrah, or holy brotherhood.

In every Jewish community in past ages, the hevrah—a duly constituted society for the promotion of certain specific occupational, charitable, religious, or educational purposes—was the most significant unit of voluntary association. Hevrot were found wherever there were Jews, each of these confraternities bearing the appellation "kaddisha," for each such group was a sacred society or holy brotherhood.

From olden times down to our own day, the most commonly accepted meaning of the term *hevrah kaddisha* referred to the communal burial society or burial fraternity. This was so because the burial society performed the most holy of tasks, namely, ministering to the spiritual needs of the dying and attending to the burial of the dead, which is the highest type of love—*hesed shel emet*—inasmuch as the dead cannot return the love shown them.

However, there were holy brotherhoods of all kinds, as is indicated by their very names. Thus, to pick almost at random, one might mention the Holy Brotherhood of Tailors, the Holy Brotherhood of Woodchoppers,[1] the Holy Brotherhood for the Study of Torah, the Holy Brotherhood for Dowering the Bride, the Holy Brotherhood for Visiting the Sick, and the Holy Brotherhood for Lovingkindness.

173

(1) THE ORIGINS OF THE HOLY BROTHERHOODS

How the holy brotherhoods originated is hard to tell. Much has been written on this subject by many scholars, and various theories have been advanced.[2] Since the Talmud refers to a *kehilla kadisha* in Jerusalem,[3] there is every likelihood that the holy brotherhoods of later centuries had their prototype in talmudic times. It is also very likely that similar types of associations existed in Palestine and Babylon before 500 C.E. These early communal fraternities took the form of burial associations and possibly also of sick-care societies.

We are on more certain ground when we come to Spain in the thirteenth century. "It is only here," writes Dr. Jacob R. Marcus,

> that for the first time we find evidence of Jewish Brotherhoods in the fully developed traditional pattern which still exists today. Rabbi Solomon ben Adreth of Barcelona (1235–1310) mentions these societies in his Responsa.[4] Throughout the 14th and 15th centuries there appeared in that country a series of societies, hevrot, confradias, confratrias, confrarias, which busied themselves with burial of the dead, education of the poor, dowering of orphan brides, support of the poor, and visiting and providing for the sick.[5]

It was not until the sixteenth century, according to available historical records, that this Jewish societal form made its appearance in Italy and later in the German lands, due in large measure to the influence of the Spanish Jews who settled in those countries after the Expulsion in 1492. The oldest known such society was in Prague in 1564. In the German lands, very possibly, the structure and scope of these Jewish socio-religious agencies were influenced by the prevalent Christian religious and craft guilds, but we must note that there were many dissimilarities, reflecting the special character of the Jew and Judaism.[6]

It was also in the sixteenth century, and more noticeably in the seventeenth, that holy brotherhoods emerged in the life of Polish and Lithuanian Jewry. Their greatest development came in the eighteenth century, and many were centered in the Jewish proletariat. The Jewish working classes formed hevrot in accordance with their various occupations. Since most societies also established their own places of worship, it is noteworthy that in Vilna there were nearly one hundred small synagogues named for the occupations of their members. Thus there were the conventicles, or klausen, of the bakers, the carpenters, the tailors, the leather-workers, the shoemakers, the weavers, the glaziers, the bookbinders, and the tinsmiths.

(2) THE FUNCTIONS OF THE HOLY BROTHERHOODS

The holy brotherhoods came into being mainly to serve the economic and religious needs of their members.[7] Christian workingmen had their craft guilds, and Jewish workingmen found it necessary to organize similar societies for their own economic protection and betterment as well as for mutual aid. Jews were excluded from the Christian craft guilds, and if an exception was made, special taxes had to be paid for the privilege of membership. Besides, the Christian guilds were related to the Church and were involved in many of the observances and festivals of Christianity. Quite naturally, the Jewish member did not feel quite comfortable in such an environment. In addition, the surviving records show that Jewish members of Christian guilds were so discriminated against that their livelihood was endangered.[8] It was quite natural, therefore, for the Jewish workingman to establish hevrot in order to safeguard his economic security. Rules and regulations were set up concerning the training of apprentices, the admission of qualified members, the elimination of unfair competition, the prevention of workingmen from other cities taking away work opportunities from members of the local community, and also to assist members with food, clothing, shelter, and medicine when needed.[9]

(3) THE EMPHASIS ON PRAYER AND STUDY

Along with caring for the economic welfare of their members, the holy brotherhoods also gave total attention to their religious needs. The first religious duty of the Jew is prayer. The societies, therefore, required their members to engage in daily prayer and to be in regular attendance at the appointed place of worship. Thus, in the very first paragraph of the Ordinances in the City of Tchortkov, we find this regulation:

It is written in Scripture: "The beginning of wisdom is the fear of the Lord" [Ps. 111:10]. We have therefore obligated ourselves to worship God with reverence, with joy and with trembling so that it is forbidden for any workingman to begin his daily work until he first goes to the prayer services of the synagogue or the minyan of his affiliation. This must be especially adhered to on Mondays and Thursdays when the Torah is read. God forbid that anyone should begin his daily work until the services are ended. Anyone who violates this regulation will be required to pay a fine of one guilder to charity. So, too, when the shamash knocks upon the doors of the workrooms for the time of the Minhah—[the afternoon prayers], we are obligated to stop in our work and go to the places of worship. In the keeping of this regulation, God will reward us by blessing the work of our hands.

The holy brotherhoods in Tchortkov further required that on Friday afternoons there should be stoppage of all labor in time to prepare for the Sabbath; and that on Hol ha-Moed, the weekdays of the festival seasons, no work should be done except by special permission. The Ordinances of the City of Sokolov require that during the Reading of the Torah, all the members must remain standing to listen attentively to each word and if anyone engages in idle conversation he shall be fined three gedolim (groschen—there were thirty gedolim in a guilder).[10] As is already evident, each of these societies had its own place of worship— most often a rented room in the larger synagogue or in some home. If a society could not afford its own place of worship, it endeavored at least to present a Sefer Torah (Scroll of the Law) or a menorah to the synagogue.[11]

If prayer was important, then surely study was equally important. Therefore a predominant characteristic of the holy brotherhoods, regardless of type, was the emphasis on Jewish learning. No matter what the central function of the society might have been—whether to render some kind of charitable service or to unify specific occupational groups around a common purpose—no matter how diverse their programs, they all provided in their ordinances for the study of Torah. The preambles of the constitutions of all the holy brotherhoods reveal the deep religious roots from which they stemmed. Many of them refer to the well-known maxim of Simon the Just (ca. 300 or 200 B.C.E.), quoted in the Ethics of the Fathers: "The world is founded on three pillars: Torah—religious instruction; Avodah—the worship of God through prayer; and Gemilut Hasadim—the performance of deeds of lovingkindness." [12] The typical Jewish holy brotherhood attempted, therefore, to have a well-rounded program, busying itself not only with its own prescribed function and with prayer, but also with study. All of them—almost without exception—saw to it that the pillar of religious study should stand firm in their total activities.

A variety of methods were employed to further the study of Torah. All the brotherhoods, without exception, made arrangements to study Mishnah on behalf of the dead for the first week or month of mourning, or even for the first twelve months.[13] It would be well to cite a number of illustrations of this prevalent practice. The minute-book of the Hevrah Kaddisha of the Moravian town of Triesch (1687–1828) provides that Mishnah be studied at least for the first seven days of mourning.[14] In the minute-book of the Hevrah Kaddisha of Altona in Germany (1827), there is a regulation that when a member dies, all the members are obliged to worship and study in the house of mourning for thirty days.[15] The Benevolent Society of Pursuers of Righteousness in Frankfurt, as the preamble to their statute-book of 1786 indicates, derived their name from the verse in Proverbs (21:21): "He that followeth after righteousness and mercy findeth life, prosperity, and honor." Their major charitable activity was the distribution of kindling wood in the winter and their regulations had an unusual provision in this regard: when a member of the society died, the two overseers of the society were to hire eight men of the poor families in the community, who directly after the burial repaired to the house of mourning in order to be part of the minyan and to attend the period of study; they also attended every morning and evening during the seven days of shivah; and further attended the shiur—the study session of a portion of the Mishnah or the Talmud—every evening for the full thirty-day period of mourning. The hired men each received one guilder for being in attendance during the thirty days. The two overseers were required to be present at these services in order to supervise the minyan and the study session.[16]

Turning from the German lands to the Jewish community of Amsterdam, we find the Holy Brotherhood of the Glory of Young Men (Unmarried). In its statutes of 1778, this society requires that

> if a member is sitting shivah, the gabbai shall give to that member one reichstaler from the treasury, and the members are obliged to form a minyan both morning and evening and also on the Sabbath for purposes of prayer and study. He who absents himself from any one service shall pay a fine of one-half basch [bank schilling]. A member may purchase his release from this obligation by the payment of three basch. All the members, and of course the rabbi and sexton of the society, are required to escort the mourner to the synagogue and back to his home on the Sabbath during shivah. Failure to do this will impose a fine of one basch upon members and two basch upon the gabaim.[17]

We also come upon the Hevrah Kaddisha Talmud Torah, which offered instruction for the children of the community in several schools and employed a large staff consisting of a rabbi, a sexton, and a number of teachers, making full provision for Jewish study during periods of mourning. In its statute-book, revised and printed in 1804 in Amsterdam, the following regulations occur:

> For every member who becomes a mourner, the society must provide a minyan in his home both morning and evening. The following must be present: the sexton and one of the teachers of the youngest children and six additional men who shall be designated and paid for this purpose. The teacher shall conduct the daily shiur. On the Sabbath of the week of mourning, the regular period of study before minhah prescribed for the entire membership, shall be held in that home instead of in the synagogue. The society shall also provide a minyan, only for the evening services, through the entire thirty days of mourning, and on all these Sabbaths the study period shall likewise be held in the home.[18]

> A mourner who wishes that study be conducted in his home for an entire year shall pay the sum of twenty-five gulden.[19]

Similar practices were in vogue in the Jewish communities of Eastern Europe. The pinkasim—minute-books—of the Society of Tailors in Bialystok, dating from the middle of the nineteenth century, although their use dates back to an earlier period, contain this provision:

> Should any of the members die, the officers and the gabbaim are obliged to send a minyan from the membership to the home of the deceased to recite the Psalms from the time of death to the time when the body is removed from the home. Afterwards the society must send at least twelve of its members to daily services in the house of mourning for a period of thirty days. Furthermore, should the deceased not have sons and therefore not have anyone to say Kaddish, the reader of the society is required to recite the Kaddish.[20]

Similarly, the pinkas of the Society of Zeritz requires that in addition to supplying a minyan of worshippers at the house of mourning, they would also bring the Scroll of the Law and volumes of the Mishnah for study.[21]

The holy brotherhoods did not limit their instructional programs to times of mourning. This might be described as their minimal effort, for they did a great deal more in the furtherance of Torah study. Most of the brotherhoods made regular provision for systematic daily or weekly instruction on either elementary or advanced levels. All branches of Jewish study were represented in these programs: Bible, Mishnah, Gemara, Midrash, and so on. The more learned studied the Talmud (Mishnah and Gemara), the less learned studied the Portion of the Week with the commentary of Rashi (humash and Rashi), or Midrash, while those not capable of concentrated study would gather to chant the Psalms.[22] Practically all the brotherhoods had their own designated instructor, either a lay scholar or a rabbi. He it was who conducted the prescribed periods of study either before or after the daily or Sabbath services. It was likewise frequently his duty, on stated occasions, to preach on moral or ethical themes. In many societies this rabbi received an annual stipend for his instructional and spiritual ministrations.

(4) HOLY BROTHERHOODS AROUND THE WORLD

It will prove very illuminating to turn from generalizations to case studies. These will enable us to see the inner workings of the holy brotherhoods in their endeavors to hold firmly to the pillar of Torah in various European communities through the centuries.

Italy and Central Europe

The oldest record of any such society goes back to Venice in the year 1611. It is especially important and interesting since the society concerned, the Hevrah Kenessiah le-Shem Shamayim ("Brotherhood for the Sake of Heaven"),[23] was unknown until recently. The pinkas (minute-book) of this society, a beautifully bound leather volume, faithfully records the history of the society from 1611 to 1843, a period of 232 years.[24] The society's first statutes, drawn up in 1611, contain a number of regulations pertaining to Jewish study. The statutes were revised in 1612, and it is from the revised version that the following quotations are taken.

The parnasim [the chief elected lay officials] shall have the power to order each member to come each day to study in a place designated for that purpose and at a specified time. In the wintertime the study session shall be held at night, and in the summertime (from the beginning of the month of Iyar to the end of the month of Elul), during the afternoon after the children are dismissed from the Talmud Torah in the ghetto. The parnasim are not exempt from this rule. As soon as the rabbi enters, the study period begins. A member who does not come before the close of the session shall be fined two soldi. Neither the parnasim nor the rabbi have the right to exempt anyone from attendance. . . .[25]

The parnasim who shall be serving during the months of Nisan and Tishri shall, fifteen days before the end of these months, find a place, agreeable to the rabbi, for purposes of study. Each parnas shall be obliged to attend the study sessions, on penalty of one-half ducat for each absence. . . .[26]

All books purchased by the parnasim for the society shall be suitably inscribed. This is to be done no later than three days after the purchase of the book, under penalty of four ducats for each failure to do so. The parnasim shall make an inventory of the library each Rosh Hodesh, and enter into the pinkas the fact that on such and such a day so many volumes belonged to the society. Failure to make such a monthly inventory shall bring the penalty of a fine of five soldi. . . .[27]

The rabbi shall have the power to instruct us, and shall have equal power with the parnasim to issue orders in all matters that seem right to him, as long as they are not contrary to the statutes. None of our members shall protest his decisions under penalty of one-quarter of a ducat. . . .[28]

In the month of Adar, it shall be the duty of the parnasim, fifteen days before Purim, to collect from every member—themselves included—two lira for the purpose of purchasing a gift for the rabbi as a token of love and esteem. The parnasim have the power to compel those who refuse to give. Should there not be sufficient funds, they can assess the membership, without further authorization, for an additional ducat. . . .[29]

Each and every member of the society is obliged to come to study each day—both summer and winter—as explained in a previous regulation—under penalty of a fine of two soldi for each absence. . . .[30]

All the members are required to come to study at a special assembly on the eve of the Fifteenth of Shevat [Tu bi-Shevat] under penalty of four ducats. Each member shall contribute whatever the parnasim assess—not exceeding one lira per member—to buy fruit so as to recite the appropriate blessings for this festive occasion [this custom is not found in any other society]. . . .[31]

The parnas must come daily, at the proper hour, to open the place of study and to arrange the books as per instruction of the rabbi or the parnasim. Failure to do so will impose a fine of four soldi.[32]

In the lands of Central Europe, the earliest record to date of holy brotherhoods with activities of a religious and cultural character is to be found in Prague. The statutes of three Jewish guilds of Prague have so far been published: The Barbers' Guild (1688), the Tailors' Guild (1690), and the Shoemakers' Guild (1730). In addition to regulations and policies pertaining to internal organization, apprenticeships, journeymen, hours of work, competition, workmanship, and relations to workers outside of Prague, the statutes impose certain religious duties on their memberships:

> Journeymen and apprentices were required to attend the morning services, particularly on Mondays and Thursdays. On Fridays and the eve of holidays, work stopped in the shops at 1 P.M. in the winter and at 3 P.M. in the summer. Masters, journeymen, and apprentices all left the shops in order to prepare for the coming of the Sabbath or holiday. No work was permitted on the intermediate days of Passover and Sukkot. Members of the shoemakers' guild were requested to attend Sabbath lectures on Jewish law held by a rabbinical scholar engaged for that purpose by the guild. Absentees had to deliver half a pound of candles to the school for needy children which was maintained in the ghetto. In the tailors' guild even the journeymen and the apprentices were required to attend Sabbath lectures, absentees furnished candles to the synagogue.[33]

Austria and Germany

In Vienna, in the year 1763, a group of young people founded a society called the Hevrah Kaddisha shel Bahurei Hemed be-Vina ("Holy Society of Choice Young Men of Vienna"). Its purposes were as follows:

1. To conduct lectures on halakah and aggadah every Saturday instead of spending the day in amusement.

2. To support the poor in a manner not humiliating to them.

3. To provide for poor brides.

4. To clothe the needy.

5. To visit the sick, provide them with medical treatment, pray for their

restoration to health, and, in case of death, to arrange for the recital of the Kaddish by a relative, or an orphan from a neighboring community.

The young founders of the society hoped by their example to encourage the older generation to engage in similar work. Every member undertook to devote some time daily to the study of the Talmud, privately or with a teacher. In view of the fact that communal worship was prohibited in Vienna, it was arranged that on every eve of Rosh Hodesh (New Moon), six members would take their turn in fasting. Offerings were made for the building of a synagogue, for the poor in Palestine, for the redemption of captives from pirates, and so on. When a member became ill, ten of his associates read the Psalms in his behalf daily and studied a chapter of the Mishnah. As in other cases, anyone who was unable to perform his duties contributed money to the treasury of the organization or provided a substitute for himself.[34]

In Vienna, the Burial Society, in the latter half of the eighteenth century, had an elaborate plan for talmudic studies. The rabbi of the town would open each academic semester with special talmudic lectures in which he would display his dialectic skill and then urge his audience to study regularly by themselves. The rabbi himself lectured each week for the more advanced students, who were asked to prepare assigned lessons. All these lectures were open to the public.[35]

The Burial Fraternity in Horn, a town in southern Austria, in its statutes of 1784, ordained "to engage a teacher who shall instruct us in the weekly Prophetic Lesson. Every member is required to attend the study session of the society to be held every Sabbath throughout the year at 4 P.M. in the summer months and at 3 P.M. in the winter months. On Shavuot and Hoshana Rabbah the study session shall be limited to members only." [36]

The Benevolent Society of the Pursuers of Righteousness in Frankfurt, issued a statute-book in 1786. The very first ordinance states:

It is our firm and unanimous decision that every Sunday evening after the services, the officers and overseers together with the two sextons [shamashim] shall come to the study hall [lernzimmer] of the Old Synagogue [Altschul] in order to be in attendance at the study session to be conducted by the rabbi of the society in the text prescribed for study. He who absents himself without good excuse shall pay a fine of two kreutzer. The money from these fines shall be deposited in the Small Box to help defray the expenses of the Society Feast on the Sabbath of Hanukkah. These fines are to be paid at the bi-monthly financial meeting of the overseers. . . .[37]

On Shavuot and on Hoshana Rabbah, the officers, the overseers, and the members, as well as the rabbi and two sextons, shall gather in the evening at the meeting place of the society in the Old Synagogue in order to learn together. Tardiness shall be fined by eighteen pfennigs. If one of the overseers has been a member of another society for a longer period of time than in our society, he may go to the other society. To defray the costs of these study sessions, the overseers are permitted to take from the treasury two and one-half gulden for each occasion, to be spent as follows: two gulden for coffee and cake, and one-half gulden for the waitress in the study hall.

The salary of the rabbi of our society shall be ten taler per annum. In return for which his duties shall be as follows: He shall conduct a study session every Sunday evening after services in the meeting room of the society in the Old Synagogue. When, God forbid, in the case of the death of one of our members, he shall attend the services in the house of mourning both morning and evening so that immediately thereafter he shall conduct the study period. He shall also teach on the evenings of Shavuot and Hoshana Rabbah in the meeting room of the society. He shall pay a fine of eighteen pfennig for being late. He shall receive a half-measure of wood more than the other officials.

Each year on the Sabbath of Hanukkah, the officers and overseers are obliged to attend the services in the meeting room of the society in the Old Synagogue both morning and afternoon. All monies collected from fines all year shall be allocated for the Society Banquet.

The overseers may take five gulden from the treasury to cover the cost of a feast in connection with the celebration of a siyyum. At such occasions, the officers with the consent of the members, may draw money from the treasury to present to the rabbi a gift following his lecture. Should no feast be held in connection with a siyyum, no gift need be presented to the rabbi.[38]

In Hannover, in the late eighteenth century, the local Burial and Sick-Care Society conducted studies daily. The Bible was read with the traditional commentaries, together with the laws of the standard legal code, the *Shulhan Arukh,* particularly the volume *Orah Hayyim,* which deals with the prayers and blessings. The rabbi of the society also recommended ethical books for reading by the members. Daily studies in Hannover were held after the evening services in a special study hall belonging to the society.[39]

The Burial Society of Altona records in its statutes of 1827 that "All members must assemble every Sabbath at an hour to be announced by the shammash in the home of the gabbai to listen to instruction from the maggid and to recite the Minhah prayers. Those who are late will be subject to a fine." In addition, under penalty of a fine, all members were required to assemble on the nights of Shavuot and Hoshana Rabbah to study in the home of the gabbai, wherever he might be living—either in Altona or in Hamburg.[40]

In the year 1860, the Verein Holcha Tom was founded in the town of Kempen in the province of Posen. In the preamble to its pinkas, which has entries till the year 1888, we are told that this society was started with forty-four members, and that its name and purpose are expressed in the words of the psalmist: "Happy are they that are upright in the way, who walk in the law of the Lord" (Ps. 119:1). The members affirm their intent to devote themselves to the three pillars of Torah, prayer, and deeds of lovingkindness. They are required to come daily for worship and study. They are to attend at the house of mourning of a deceased member. Once each year they must distribute potatoes or other produce to the poor (perhaps the members were farmers). They were also to assist their own members when in need. The society was to meet each year on the fourth day of Hol ha-Moed Pesah in order to ballot for three gabbaim, one treasurer, and five trustees. Each member was to pay his annual dues of six pagim (an abbreviation for perutah gedolah—a large coin worth eighteen groschen) before being allowed to cast his ballot.[41]

Western Europe

In Western Europe, in the city of Saragossa in Spain, we come upon one of the oldest holy brotherhoods on record. It is the Jewish Shoemakers' Guild of that city, to which King Pedro IV of Aragon issued a charter on March 15, 1336. This remarkable document is still in existence, and has been translated from the Latin-Spanish original into English. Some of the articles in the charter deal with matters of religion, learning, and welfare.

Care of ailing members was an important concern. Guild wardens were required to visit their sick twice a week, on Mondays and Thursdays. Members destitute as the result of illness received two dineros daily from the guild treasury. On Saturdays, it was the duty of every member to visit ailing members. When a member died, the entire guild remained with the body until burial, conducting religious services in the house of the deceased. Eight days after burial, a service was held in the synagogue and a sermon was preached in praise of the deceased. Guild members absent from this service were fined a dinero. The guild helped members celebrate such family events as a wedding, a *brit mila*, etc. Personal offenses were punished by fines, as well as by exclusion from the *cofradia* for one month, which bespeaks the high sense of honor of the Spanish Jews. Members gathered twice yearly to listen to a reading of the guild articles—"so that everyone may know how to conduct himself."

Also in Spain, in the seaport city of Barcelona, there existed Jewish butchers', dyers', and sailors' guilds. These guilds enjoyed autonomy, which was supported by the rabbinic authorities.

Rabbi Solomon ibn Adret (1235–1310) was for many years the spiritual leader of the community in Barcelona. He took an active interest in guild matters. Asked for his opinion on the legality of the guild regulations of the Jewish butchers, dyers and sailors, he declared:

"If these guilds pass a rule concerning their trades, it is binding upon the individual tradesman as are the laws of the Torah, for every trade organization is a city unto itself and does not require the consent of the outer community for its enactments. . . . The members of a guild are as autonomous in their own affairs as are the citizens of the city. Therefore, each group or community is permitted to conduct its affairs and to prescribe fines and punishments which may not be found in the laws of the Torah. This is the practice of all the holy congregations and no one has ever questioned its legality."

This statement is remarkable for the complete backing it gives to the regulatory practices of the guilds, whose enactments Rabbi Solomon ibn Adret likens to the laws of the Torah.[42]

Turning to Amsterdam in Holland toward the end of the eighteenth century, we come upon a flourishing Ashkenazic community. Until a little over a century before, the Jewish community of Amsterdam had consisted almost entirely of Spanish-Portuguese Jews. Beginning with the second half of the seventeenth century, Ashkenazic Jews, coming from countries in Middle Europe, began to seek refuge in that friendly Dutch city, and after a while they established a strong Jewish communal life of their own, apart and separate from the rather aloof and distant earlier Jewish settlers. We have the records—two in print and two in manuscript —of four holy brotherhoods of varying scope and purpose—yet all of them have this in common, that they provide and require devotion to Jewish study. In 1776, the Hevrah Kaddisha Gemilut Hassadim ("Holy Brotherhood for Deeds of Lovingkindness," that is, the burial society), printed its statutes, which contain fifty-nine provisions. The first three, dealing with the obligations, time, place, and manner of study incumbent upon the members, read as follows:

Every weekday (with the exception of the day preceding the Sabbath, the holidays, and Rosh Hodesh) all the members must assemble half an hour after the Minhah and Maariv service in the new synagogue of the society in order to study under the tutorship of the rabbi for at least three-quarters of an hour. Failure to attend shall be subject to a fine of one-quarter of a bank schilling.

Every Sabbath, from the first of Nisan to Tishri, except on those Sabbaths when the required Scripture Lesson is read from two Torah Scrolls (and hence makes the service a little longer), all the members are obliged to assemble in the great synagogue in order to listen to the word of God. For failure to attend, a fine of one bank schilling shall be imposed. Each member shall occupy his assigned seat as drawn by lot. Failure to do so shall draw a fine of one schilling.

On the first night of Shavuot and on the night of Hoshana Rabbah, all members shall, as is the custom, occupy themselves with the study of Torah—at least for most of the night.

During all times of study—whether on weekways, Sabbaths, Shavuot, or Hoshana Rabbah—it shall be forbidden to eat or drink in the place of study. It is especially forbidden to smoke or to conduct oneself in a spirit of levity either by word or deed. He who violates these regulations on a weekday shall be fined one schilling, and on the other occasions a half-schilling.

The signatures of the officers of the society and the officers of the Ashkenazic community are appended to the statutes, along with the approval of the famous Rabbi Saul of the Amsterdam Ashkenazic community.[43]

In 1804, the Hevrah Kaddisha Talmud Torah ("Holy Brotherhood for Talmud Torah") of Amsterdam revised its by-laws and printed them with the approval of the Ashkenazic community. Those eligible for membership in this society were "married men, single men, married women, and widows, whether they live in our community or are temporary residents." The minimum weekly dues was two bank schillings for men and one and one-half bank schillings for women (by-law 18). The society conducted a number of schools for the children of the community, with a staff of teachers and an elected official who supervised the educational program (by-law 19). The curriculum consisted of three subjects: Hebrew reading, Prayer Book, and Humash. The period of instruction was "one hour after the morning service till midday; then from 1:30 to 5:30 during the summer months and from 1:30 to 3:30 in the winter months. The Humash pupils were to study till 5:30 even in the winter months (by-law 21). Classes were limited to thirty pupils, and preference was given to local residents in filling the registration quota (by-law 25). Pupils who completed the elementary program could be advanced to the next higher school, the Hevrah Kaddisha Lomdei Torah ("Holy Brotherhood of Students of the Torah"). A bonus of six gulden was given each teacher who advanced at least six pupils to this higher school (by-law 22).

As is evident from the above, this society was dedicated to providing Jewish education for the children of the community. Nevertheless, it did not neglect to provide Torah for its grown-up members. The very first of its fifty-nine ordinances states:

The beginning and end of all life is the fear of the Lord. We therefore set aside a fixed time for the study of Torah every single Sabbath afternoon one hour before Minhah.

They further ordain that:

The rabbi of the society (the present rabbi being R. Elijah Leverden) shall be duty-bound to conduct this period of study. His annual salary shall be sixty florins. He shall receive an additional 7:10 florins for holding a siyyum upon the completion of the study of the Early Prophets and a similar amount for the Later Prophets. [by-law 19]

Members of the society who would like the privilege of having this
Sabbath-afternoon study session conducted in their homes shall pay the
sum of twenty-five florins annually. [by-law 20]

Of exceptional interest are the manuscript statute-books of two brotherhoods composed entirely of young unmarried men. In 1778 the Hevrah
Kaddisha Tiferet Bahurim ("Holy Brotherhood of the Glory of Young
Men") was organized in Amsterdam. It was a mutual benefit and philanthropic society whose purpose, as indicated in its full name, was to be
"Pursuers of Peace and the Dowering of the Bride." Its statute-book was
written in 1783.[44] These are the regulations providing Jewish study for
its membership:

Concerning the Rabbi of the Society

The members of the society have elected R. Meir the Bookseller to
be the rabbi of the society. He must teach for one hour every Saturday
before Minhah. He must come to the house of study designated for
this purpose by the gabbaim, and he must not object to the place of
study. Should the rabbi be prevented from coming, he must obtain a
substitute. On the eve of Shavuot and Hoshana Rabbah he must teach
from the Zohar. The rabbi's salary shall be eight reichstalers a year
beginning from Rosh Hodesh Sivan 1778. He is not to ask for an
increase until after the first wedding to be held among the members
of the society. [This was because each member, when he got married,
was required to pay a certain percentage of the bride's dowry into the
treasury.] After that, the gabbaim and the four trustees and the treasurer will have the authority to give him an increase without the consent of the rest of the members. The rabbi can request payment of his
salary each quarter, but he is not to be paid in advance. . . .

*Concerning the Prohibition of Unseemly Conduct during the Time of
Study*

No member is permitted to engage in unseemly conversation during
the time of study. All the more so is he forbidden to speak ill of the
gabbaim, the trustees, the treasurer, or any of the members. No one is
permitted to come to the study group in improper attire, even on the
nights of Shavuot and Hoshana Rabbah. The officers of the society
are empowered to fine anyone who violates this regulation as much as
they see fit up to one-half a reichstaler.

Concerning Attendance at Study on the Sabbath

The two gabbaim must be present during the study period every Sabbath. Should he be absent, he must pay a fine of three bank schillings. Should any member absent himself, he must pay a fine for each absence of one bank schilling. An exception is made in the case of the exemptees [*freileuten;* see next regulation]. Present members of the society who belonged to another society prior to the formation of ours, and who attend the study period of the former society, which meets at the same time as ours, are also exempt. These two categories are exempted from coming, except when the officers call a special meeting, absence from which is punishable by a fine. All—even the *freileuten*—must attend. A member who is sixty years old or over is not obliged to come to the regular Sabbath afternoon study period, but he must attend the special meeting. Likewise, doctors and barbers are not required to attend except the above-mentioned special meetings.

Concerning the Exemptees [Freileuten]

All the members, except the two gabbaim, have the privilege of purchasing half-year exemptions from the obligation to attend the study period on Sabbath afternoons, upon the payment of one-quarter of a reichstaler. If such payment is made, he is exempt from attending all study sessions, even those held during the shivah period in the house of mourning, but he is obliged to make the donation for the nights of Shavuot and Hoshana Rabbah. No one can purchase such exemption except during the following four stated times: the first days of the months of Tishri, Tevet, Nisan, and Tammuz, and never for more than a half-year period. . . .

Concerning the Rules for the Eves of Shavuot and Hoshana Rabbah

On the nights of Shavuot and Hoshana Rabbah, all the members are required to come to study at the house designated for that purpose. A member who absents himself shall pay a fine of one schilling, and the gabbaim shall be fined double. Each member is obliged to make a donation for these nights of at least one schilling, and the donation of the gabbaim shall be double. In addition, the gabbaim shall make a gift to the rabbi and the sexton. It is optional for the members to make such a gift. He who had joined another society before joining ours is exempt from attending on these two nights, but not from making the donation. On the night of Hoshana Rabbah, the privilege of chanting each of the five books of Psalms shall be auctioned off, and similarly the privilege of holding the session at his home, the latter privilege to be sold for a two-year period.[44]

In 1790, in Amsterdam, seven young men organized the Hevrah Kedoshah Agudat Bahurim ("Holy Brotherhood of the Fraternity of Young Men"). That same year they wrote down their statutes in twenty-six paragraphs in a well-bound volume with a beautifully executed front-page in ink scrollwork. On the last pages appears the red seal of approval and signatures of the officials of the Ashkenazic community of Amsterdam.

Four of the twenty-six enactments make provision for Jewish learning. They are as follows:

On Learning Every Sabbath

Every member is required to come to learn every Sabbath at 1:30 in the afternoon. If he is late and comes in the middle of learning, he shall pay a fine of one-half a bank schilling. No disturbances are permitted before, during, or after study, subject to a fine by the gabbaim of one-half a reichstaler. Full respect shall be shown to the gabbaim in order to maintain the unity of the society. No one shall come without a coat, or with improper attire. No one shall chew tobacco. If one wishes to be excused from coming to learn, he shall have to pay three bank schillings every quarter.

On Learning on Shavuot and Hoshana Rabbah

On the nights of Shavuot and Hoshana Rabbah, all must come to learn and must maintain perfect decorum in a spirit of holiness and purity. No one shall, God forbid, conduct himself at study with annoyance or use vile language. Those who violate this regulation, and those who come late, shall be subject to fine by the gabbaim. Those who are frivolous-minded, or who are fish merchants, are excused from attending on Hoshana Rabbah but not on Shavuot.

On Selling the Privilege for Learning in One's House

Before Passover, a sale shall be held for the privilege of having the learning in his home for the ensuing year. It shall be conducted as follows: Beginning three Sabbaths before Passover, the shamash announces the impending sale. On the third Sabbath, the one who buys this privilege must soon thereafter make payment of half the purchase price before the study periods begin at his home. He must make the remaining half of the payment before the year is up. If one who purchased this privilege regrets his action, or later finds that his residence is not suitable, he must pay a fine, and the privilege is put up for sale again. One who lives in a bad or disreputable neighborhood, or who maintains a house of amusement or a gambling house, or who does not have a separate and adequate room for study, does not have the right to purchase this privilege. Neither is one permitted to purchase this privilege for a nonmember. The purchaser must give a written guarantee that he will return the books belonging to the society. . . .

When a Member Becomes a Bridegroom

When a member becomes engaged, he contributes one-half a reichstaler to the society, half of which is paid out at the engagement and the other half before the wedding. Such a member is excused from coming to learn on the Sabbaths before and after the engagement and also on the Sabbath before the wedding and on three Sabbaths after the wedding.

As an appendix to the statute-book there appear a number of amendments made twenty-one years after the society was founded. One of them reaffirms the rule that every member must attend the Sabbath afternoon study session, but removes the penalty of a fine for those whose occupation keeps them up late at night, namely for "musicians, fish and meat merchants, and bakers." [45]

Eastern Europe

To round out this series of case studies, we turn to Eastern Europe. The earliest reference to societal requirements for Jewish learning goes back to the year 1628 in Lithuania, where we find the following ordinance: "Everyone who belongs to a hevrah must set aside fixed times for daily study." [46]

Next we come upon the Hevrah Kaddisha Shivah Keruim ("Holy Brotherhood of the Seven Summoned Men") in Minsk, Russia. Its minute-books begin in 1763 and continue to 1823, but it is apparent from the records that the society was in existence long before the first entries were made. The society's distinctive name, which centers around the number seven, is derived from several facts. First, it goes back to the talmudic tradition of the *shivah tuvei ha-ir,* the "seven leaders of the community." Second, the members were required to worship every Sabbath in their private conventicle within the synagogue edifice so that each Sabbath seven different members could be honored by being called to the Torah. Third, applicants for membership were admitted only on the recommendation of no less than seven members. Such rather exclusive societies had good reason for their position of self-importance because they were second in influence only to the official Jewish community—the Kahal itself. The standards for admission to membership were very high. According to the revised statutes of 1780:

> No one shall be admitted into this society unless he is known as a communal leader or is able to learn the Mishnah. After his entrance fee shall have been determined by the officers—in no case is it to be less than three rubles—his name shall not be inscribed as a member until after a probation period of thirty days, during which time he must come to the bet ha-midrash every day and lead in the learning of a chapter of the Mishnah. If he is prevented from coming on certain days during this probationary period, he must continue in attendance until the full thirty days are completed. Unless this requirement is complied with, his membership application is null and void. . . .
>
> He who is accepted to membership must attend the Sabbath morning services in the private conventicle of the society and must bring his own Humash with him. On the first Sabbath of his attendance, he is obliged to play host and provide brandy and pancakes for Kiddush after the services.

The number of members at one time was fifty-one and at a later date rose to sixty-six. Since the society placed a high premium on the Jewish learning of its members, it was natural that it should possess a considerable library. In 1763 the kahal decided to allow this society an annual subvention of two hundred Polish gulden for the purchase of books. By 1770 this decision had not yet been implemented, and the gabbaim of the society summoned the leaders of the Jewish community to the Jewish court—the bet din—which reaffirmed the original pledge and ordered the communal leaders to pay out this sum on a weekly basis from the income of the *Korobke* tax. One of the statutes deals with the library:

All the books in the bet ha-midrash, whether they be old or new, shall be recorded and catalogued in the pinkas. At the end of each month, when one gabbai turns over his duties to the next, he shall count the books and check against the catalogue. Books not recorded shall be recorded and books missing shall likewise be recorded. The gabbai should see to it that the shamash should count and check the books at least once each week, preferably on Friday.

Each year a Simhat Torah celebration was held, and one of the statutes requires that:

The gabbai shall spend money for this event for the purchase of brandy and cake but not more than eight gulden. He shall also purchase honey.[47]

Another Russian Jewish community, the one in Odessa, had a most interesting hevrah, called Halvoas Chen. It was a Hebrew Free Loan Society. In its pinkas for the year 1837, one of the ordinances states:

Every member must come to daily services morning and evening. On Saturdays, right after the Sabbath nap, they shall assemble for the recitation of the Psalms.

Some of the other ordinances deal with such matters as: if a member lost money in a business venture, the society shall try to lend him funds to reestablish himself; it is forbidden to embarrass anyone who has made a loan from the society; if a member buys a new garment he shall pay forty kopeks into the treasury; if, however, the garment is of cloth from China, he shall pay eighty kopeks; and if made from silk he shall pay one ruble and twenty kopeks; if a member marries off a child he shall pay one ruble at the time of the writing of the Tenaim and one-half a ruble at the time of the wedding; at the time of Yahrzeit, a member shall pay forty kopeks; all debts to the society must be paid by Shavuot; if a Jew comes to Odessa from another city and wants to join this society, he must enter into the pinkas not only his own name but also the names of his wife and his father and mother so that in the event of his death, his wife shall not remain an agunah; the annual elections shall be held during the weekdays of the Sukkot festival at which time there shall also be held the annual feast.[48]

Turning from Russia to Poland, we find in the town of Nashelsk a hevrah of tailors in whose pinkas, dating from the years 1753–78, there is the ordinance that every Sabbath the members "must come to the bet ha-midrash to the learning period and not spend the afternoon strolling around in idle conversation which leads to gossip, quarrels and transgressions. Whoever does not attend the learning session will be fined one guilder." Some of the other regulations deal with economic matters, but of special interest is the one forbidding the members to quarrel with the gabbai in the synagogue over the kind of aliyah they are assigned at the Sabbath services.[49]

In the small town of Kurnik, situated in the eastern part of the province of Posen, there existed a Tailors' Guild. Its 150-page minute-book tells the story of the guild from 1754 to 1820.[50] During that period Kurnik had a general population of 1,347 and a Jewish population of 336 persons. The minute-book offers a detailed account of all the economic, social, and religious aspects which this organization developed as a semiautonomous unit under the general communal government of local Jewry.

While the economic motive was predominant, the guild also had a strong religious and cultural character. In the year 1764 it unanimously adopted the following resolution to strengthen the organization by providing spiritual guidance and leadership.

> Whereas we are facing an evil condition and the very foundation of our Guild is threatened, and, whereas, this is caused by the fact that we have no guide who can point the way either in spiritual matters or in wordly affairs, therefore, it was unanimously voted in public assembly that we invite the Rabbi of our community to be also the spiritual leader of the Guild, and that we assemble as a group, every Sabbath to hear his teaching and preaching, which will inspire our hearts.

The Kurnik tailors' guild has been studied in depth by Michael Zarchin, who writes:

> In pursuance of this resolution the Rabbi was officially engaged as the spiritual leader of the guild at an annual salary of twelve florin and three groschen, and it became compulsory for every member of the guild to attend his weekly ethical discourses and furthermore to bring before him all grievances in matters of litigation among the members of the guild and he, in association with one of its lay leaders, was to judge their altercations.
>
> The guild also requested and received special religious privileges from the communal administration. This is well illustrated by the fact that the tailors of Kurnik were allowed to conduct the reading of the

Torah separately in a special place assigned to them in the synagogue building, provided they had a *minyan* in addition to the reader. For this privilege the guild contributed four reichstaler every year to the committee on charity which was under the auspices of the Kehillah. The scroll was kept either by the parnas of the guild, or else in the synagogue, and was taken out for special occasions as agreed upon, namely, on Sabbaths and holidays. Incidentally we learn that the reader of the Torah of this *minyan* received as remuneration for his services from the guild four reichstaler per year and at least one florin extra for the holidays.[51]

In the town of Wloclavek there existed the Holy Brotherhood for the Dowering of the Bride. According to its pinkas, it was founded in 1844 and the record of the election of its officers continues down to 1887. On the first page there is a statement by the rabbi of the community extolling the members for their deeds of charity connected with providing dowries for poor brides. He commends the formation of this society by its twenty founders and urges that peace and harmony shall prevail. If this will be the case at the end of the first year, he will then give his final approval. The society flourished, and the minute-book reveals that on Shavuot, 1886, the rabbi began to study the Portion of the Week with the members every Sabbath afternoon.[52]

Jerusalem

We conclude our survey in the Holy City of Jerusalem. In the year 1874, we find, there was founded a hevrah called Poalei Zedek ("Workers of Righteousness"). As the name implies, it consisted of workingmen in a variety of occupations, such as carpenters, shoemakers, blacksmiths, painters, and tombstone engravers. Its pinkas, which comprises twenty paragraphs, deals with a variety of matters, such as mutual aid in times of joy and sorrow, aid to newcomers to Jerusalem from the lands of exile, and the payment of initiation fees. But most interesting for our purpose are the six paragraphs concerning Torah study:

Each member is required to set aside time for daily study, especially so on the Sabbath. The workmen must get off from work every day for at least two hours so they will have time for learning. Each member must come daily for morning and evening services. When a member reaches the age of sixty, efforts should be made so that he stop working in order to devote the rest of his days in the study of Torah.[53]

CHAPTER

XII

HEVROT FOR JEWISH LEARNING

The crown of Jewish societal life was the hevrah organized solely for purposes of *lehrnen*—learning and the pursuit of Jewish study. The Jewish occupational and charitable holy brotherhoods had their counterparts in the Christian guilds, but there are no parallels in any other religious culture to the holy brotherhoods for Jewish learning.

(1) THE UNIQUENESS AND VARIETY OF THE ASSOCIATIONS FOR LEARNING

The hevrot for learning are unique, and represent a most distinctive aspect of Jewish religious life. Judaism, unlike other religions, did not have a separate learned caste. Every Jew was required to learn, in fulfillment of the biblical injunction, "And all thy children shall be taught of the Lord" (Isa. 54:13), and this was accomplished through forming hevrot devoted to learning and setting aside fixed times for sacred study.

The subjects studied ranged through the full expanse of biblical and rabbinical literature, and there were many types of hevrot for learning, each concentrating on a separate field of knowledge. The most learned elements in the community belonged to the Hevrah Shas, the association for Talmud study (Shas is a Hebrew acronym for *Shishah Sedarim,* the "Six Orders," or main divisions, of the Talmud). Those with only limited talmudic training belonged to the Hevrah Mishnayot, the association for studying the Mishnah. In addition there were societies devoted to Bible study—usually the Weekly Portion and the commentaries; codes—usually

197

the *Hayyei Adam;* and the ethical books—usually the *Ein Yaakov* or the *Alsheikh.* For the relatively unlettered masses, there were always a great many associations for chanting the Psalms.

(2) THE HISTORY OF THE HEVROT

At what point in Jewish history these associations originated, it is hard to tell. We do know that already in talmudic times, the people were urged to form groups for purposes of study: "Form yourselves into bands to study the Torah, for the Torah is not acquired except in groups." [1]

The first definite post-talmudic reference to such learning activities is found in the writings of Natronai, who was the gaon of Sura in Babylonia from the years 853 to 856. In one of his responsa, he states:

> Jews come early to the synagogue on Sabbaths and Festivals to learn. This custom goes back to the first Babylonian exile. . . . On Sabbaths especially, Jews come very early in order to recite the Shema like the pious men of old at the time of sunrise, and remain late after the services in order to partake in the learning and explanations of the Weekly Portion. [2]

This custom continued right into the Middle Ages, and many sources from the twelfth through the fourteenth centuries bear out this fact. In Northern France, we learn from one of the Tosafists, the usual practice appears to have been, that after the morning service the Jews attended to their daily occupations until midday, then returned to the synagogue for organized study. [3] We are afforded glimpses of regular courses of study for adults in some of the responsa, for when a difficulty arose it was referred to a higher authority. Thus Rabbi Solomon of Dreux writes to Rabbenu Tam (1100– 71): "Thy servant was engaged with his colleagues in the study of the Tractate Yebamoth and this week the following difficulty was encountered . . . ," while another Tosafist writes that "when we were studying Leviticus . . . we taught this in the college." [4] The same practices prevailed in Spain in the thirteenth and fourteenth centuries. In the responsa of Rabbi Solomon ben Adret (Rashba) of Barcelona (1235–1350), we learn that the bet ha-midrash was frequented by laymen and merchants who, in the evenings and during seasons of leisure, would be there poring over sacred biblical and rabbinical writings. [5] An older contemporary of the Rashba, Rabbi Nissim Gerondi, writing in his responsa in 1350, enumerates the following five societies in the city of Perpignan: "for the study of the Law, for visiting the sick, for providing light in the synagogue, for relief to the poor and for burials." [6] So, too, in North Africa in the fourteenth century, for we learn from the responsa of Rabbi Simeon ben Zemah Duran (the Rashbaz) that, "adjoining the synagogue there was a House of Learning—a Bet Hamidrash—where adults would repair in the evenings or other leisure hours for the purpose of study. Study circles, the members of whom were known as Maskilim—the Intelligenzia—were formed at which the works of Maimonides were read and studied." [7]

If we are desirous of knowing exactly when a certain type of hevrah came into existence, we are fortunate when it comes to the Hevrah Mishnayot. Its founder was the famous Rabbi Judah Loeb of Prague, popularly known as the Maharal, who died in the year 1609. He was opposed to the prevailing tendency in his time to rely exclusively on the codes and to neglect the study of the Jewish legal sources, particularly the Mishnah, which he regarded as the major source for the halakhah. In the sixth chapter of *Sefer Derekh Hayyim,* his commentary on the Ethics of the Fathers, he severely criticizes the program of Jewish learning in his day:

> The sages of old, the tannaim, the amoraim, and the geonim, followed the accepted order of studies. They began with the Bible, continued with the Mishnah, and after that with the Talmud. The present generation, however, begins with the Talmud. They start the education of six- and seven-year-old boys with the Talmud and afterwards they turn to the Mishnah. Even then, they use the Mishnah not for purposes of systematic study, but only for purposes of reference.

Acting on these convictions, the Maharal ordained that all the congregations under his influence should establish hevrot for the study of the Mishnah. This fact is fully recorded by his great disciple, Rabbi Yom-Tov Lipmann Heller, in the introduction to his classic commentary on the Mishnah, the *Tosafot Yom Tov,* first published in the years 1614–17:

> Our great teacher and master, Rabbi Judah Loeb, the son of Bezalel of blessed memory . . . directed that people shall turn once again to the Mishnah. As a result, many societies and many groups were formed . . . that occupy themselves daily with the study of a chapter of the Mishnah and upon its completion begin anew the study of the Mishnah. This is

indeed the Lord's doing and has become an established rule which is not violated. This practice prevails not only in Prague, where it was first instituted by Rabbi Judah, but also in other communities near and far that have taken upon themselves the perpetuation of this custom.[8]

It would seem, then, that the original purpose of the Maharal was to correct the curriculum of study so that the Mishnah would be given its rightful place and be studied as a source for the halakhah. In this respect, he did not succeed.[9] Yet his efforts did bring about the formation of hevrot for Mishnah study. This great achievement is further attested to by the great preacher, Rabbi Ephraim Luntschitz, who toward the end of his life—he died in 1619—became the rabbi of Prague. In his book *Amude Shes,* he writes:

I have seen the great good which has come from the study of the Mishnah—a practice established by Rabbi Judah Loeb of blessed memory here in Prague in all the congregations to study in groups one chapter of the Mishnah after services. As a result, even those men who because they lack the knowledge to study Talmud, or because of lack of time, they at least learn daily a chapter of the Mishnah. I am therefore determined to strengthen and perpetuate this practice with all my might, especially since there has been published the commentary of *Tosefot Yom Tov* on the Mishnah. This practice has been followed in every city and in every community.[10]

(3) HEVROT IN MANY LANDS

The Ottoman Empire

Many sources, from every period of Jewish history and from many of the lands in which Jews were settled, speak of the prevalence of associations for Jewish study. If we turn to the Ottoman Empire, Rabbi Samuel de Medina (the Rashdam) tells us that in sixteenth-century Turkey "each congregation had its own Beth Hamidrash whose members and strangers spend a few hours in study," and that "the Beth Hamidrash is frequented by laymen and merchants who in the evenings and during periods of leisure are found poring over religious texts." [11] At about the same time, at the very beginning of the seventeenth century, a Moravian Jew by the name of Shlomo Shlomiel ben Hagim wrote a letter from Safed dated July 1607, in which he states:

And thus I came to the Holy Land, to Safed, may it be rebuilt, in upper Galilee, on the intermediate day of the Feast of Tabernacles 5363 [1603] in peace. I found here a holy community, even a big city before God, a city full of salvation. In all the houses of prayer the whole community assembles immediately after the evening and morning prayer, in five or six groups in each house of prayer. Each group studies before leaving the house of prayer: one of them studies Maimonides seriatim, another Ein Jacob, the third a section of Berakot, a fourth one section of the Mishnah with commentary, a fifth a Halakah with Rashi and Tosafot, and the others study the Zohar or the Bible only. In this way nobody can be found in the community who begins his daily occupation in the morning without having learned something of our teaching. And the same is done by the whole of Israel in the evening after the evening prayer.[12]

The German Countries

We now turn to the German countries. Writing in the mid-seventeenth century, Rabbi Sheftel Hurwitz, the son of Rabbi Isaiah Hurwitz, the author of the *Shenei Luhot ha-Brit,* tells us:

. . . when I was rabbi and head of the academy in Frankfurt, the custom prevailed for people to gather at midday, flock by flock, group by group, society by society. Each group had a scholar at its head who instructed them. After the period of study, a Kaddish de Rabbanan was recited and a donation was made to the treasury. From these funds festive occasions were arranged. Happy is the eye that hath seen these things, and happy is the generation in which mature and renowned men hearken to the humble. In each place and in each community—whether large or small—this practice prevailed.[13]

In the communal ordinances of Worms from 1641, we find the provision that "each Jew is obligated to set aside a time each day for study. They should form different associations and each group should select a learned man who should instruct them in the book they have chosen for study." [14] About one hundred years later, Rabbi Isaac Wezler of Celle in Germany, in his Yiddish-Deitch book *Liebes-Brief*—so titled because of the love of the author for his Jewish brethren—written in 1749 and describing the Jewish life of his time, records the fact that "one must not forget the old custom prevailing in Frankfurt a.M. in which Jewish laymen who were not able to study in their youth, affiliate themselves with some association." [15] He further adds:

> . . . there is also that class of learners who when they are married do not give the Torah a get [bill of divorcement] simultaneously with giving their wives a ketubah [marriage contract]. No! They set aside fixed periods of time for study even after marriage. They study a page of Gemara every day privately or in some communities there exist Hevrot Shas—societies to learn the Talmud, or Shas Kupah—a Talmud circle with which they affiliate and thus study a page of the Talmud daily in groups. [16]

In the city of Vienna in the year 1835, Rabbi Lazar Horwitz established a Hevrah Shas,[17] and in Cologne a similar hevrah was formed in 1861.[18]

Italy

The same conditions are found in Italy during the sixteenth and seventeenth centuries. Azariah da Rossi describes the associations for Torah study during the period of the Italian Renaissance at the end of the sixteenth century. While the main purpose of these societies was Jewish study, they also were formed to elevate the moral life of their members, requiring them to forego taking oaths "in the name of God," playing cards, and having recourse to Gentile courts.[19] In seventeenth-century Venice, every synagogue had attached to it voluntary associations for the purpose of study, to which the greatest scholars of the period would regularly expound the classical Jewish texts. Wealthy enthusiasts would establish regular courses of instruction in their own houses, engaging some well-known savant to teach. One of these amateur academies, set up by the wealthy Calonymus Belgrade, held its meetings in a garden, under the open skies. No evening passed on which a class was not held; and study was reckoned an integral part of the sabbatical delights.[20]

In seventeenth-century Rome, eleven societies were engaged in promoting educational and religious aims. One met for daily devotions and study, another for the same purposes on Sabbaths, a third for night prayers on the eves of the seventh day of Passover, the first day of the Feast of Pentecost, and the seventh day of Tabernacles. There were two societies for providing the necessary minyan (quorum) of ten adult males at the memorial services held daily in the private houses of mourners, and another society supplied the minyan in the evenings.[21]

Eastern Europe

In more recent times, the Hevrot found their maximum growth in the lands of Eastern Europe. In the city of Minsk, in the year 1801, "the houses of study were filled with groups studying during the days and during the nights." [22] In 1802 there was a Hevrah of the Chanters of the Psalms[23] and also a Hevrah Mishnayot,[24] and in 1805 a Hevrah Mishmorim, whose purpose it was to study in the early hours after the earliest service.[25] In the pinkas of the Bible Society of Gombin in Poland, which covers a hundred-year period from 1792 to 1892, mention is made of a Hevrah Tehillim,[26] a Hevrah Mishnayot,[27] and a Hevrah *Ein Yaakov*.[28] In the city of Lemberg (modern Lvov), there was a holy brotherhood by the name of Anshe Maamad; it was the duty of the members to study daily in the synagogue, and—as expounded in the takkanot of the society—not only to study themselves but to teach others. Thus the society's constitution states:

> They must also give instruction, without reward, to the *baale-batim* [the Jewish householders] who are occupied with their trade or business by day, in the evenings or Saturdays and holidays. These learners should be divided into groups and they should be instructed in the Written and Oral Torah, in Aggadah, Midrash, Codes, and Laws, especially those pertaining to the holy days and festivals, also the books of ethics and morals.[29]

Coming closer to our own time, Professor Chaim Tchernowitz speaks of the many societies in Poland,[30] while Samuel Winter, in his study, "Minute Books of Societies," states: "To this day [1938] there still exist in practically every Polish town several societies such as Hevrah Shas, Mishnayot, *Hayyei Adam*, Mikra, Tanakh, Tehillim, and others similar to them." [31]

In tracing the story of the Jewish community of Vilna, Israel Cohen describes the unique institution of the klausen, which were rooms or houses in the nature of conventicles, primarily used for the study of rabbinic literature, and also serving as houses of prayer:

> These "klausen" were a characteristic feature of Jewish life in Eastern and Central Europe. Their membership was generally based on some common interest—social, religious, or economic—and in Vilna alone they were developed to such an extent that there are now [i.e., before

World War II] over a hundred, and most of them connected with various trades.[32]

The author continues by giving us a closer view of the klausen:

The Klaus, which is (or, after the devastating effects of the second World War, one must say "was") a characteristic institution of most Jewish communities in Eastern Europe, probably reached its highest efflorescence in Vilna. It was a combination of house of prayer and house of study, in which all the time not needed for prayer was devoted to the study of the Talmud or other rabbinical literature. Only in a minority of cases were the students men training for the vocation of rabbi; for the most part they were students for love of the sacred lore, to which they applied themselves with remarkable zeal and concentration. Many of them were engaged in business or manual trades during the day and were thus able to "learn," as the expression went, only in the evening; others, who were supported by some charitable society, pored over the talmudical tomes day and night. Some studied under the guidance of a teacher or *Rosh Yeshibah* (principal of the academy); others studied in couples, in the interest of mutual help in the un-ravelling of knotty passages; and others again ploughed their lonely furrow. Most of them, at night, used candles to illumine the island of text surrounded by a sea of commentaries; and some even slept in the Klaus on a hard bench, from which they rose at dawn, eager to resume, with renewed zest, where they had left off the previous midnight.

In Vilna, at the time of the annexation by Soviet Russia, there were over a hundred Klausen, many of which belonged to the members of a particular trade. Thus, there were separate Klausen for the bakers of white bread and for the bakers of brown bread, for glaziers and wood-choppers, for drapery sellers and skin-dealers, for shopkeepers and shop assistants, for tailors and cap-makers, butchers and fishmongers, furriers and skin-dressers, carters and candlestick-makers, window-cleaners and water-drawers, painters and sign-writers, musicians and bookbinders, saddlers and embroiderers. Each Klaus had its wardens and various societies for the study of particular subjects, and there was a separate teacher (*Rebbe*) for each subject, e.g., the Scriptures, the Talmud, the Mishna, the Midrash, the *Shulhan Arukh,* and so forth. Each Klaus also had its preachers, who discoursed on the Sabbath evening in the winter or the Sabbath morning in the summer; and some supported three or four teachers, each of whom was a specialist in his subject. In many of them there was a collection box, by means of which large sums were obtained.

Concluding his description of this aspect of East European Jewish life, Cohen says:

The devotion to Jewish religious lore was not confined to the Rabbi or the professional student, but was shared by the merchant and the artisan, who when their daily work was over, would cheerfully wend their way to the Beth Hamidrash or the klaus, to become immersed in a page of the Talmud, a chapter of the Mishna, or a portion of some other volume on the multifarious laws and customs of Israel. Cloistered within their houses of learning, where their wits were inevitably sharpened for the battles of life, they found some solace for the sorrows of the struggle and strife without.[33]

Another writer, Rabbi Daniel Sternfeld, had founded a yeshivah in Brodshim (Bohorodczany), Galicia, in 1905. While bemoaning the low state of learning in his new community, he extols the high level of Jewish study in Russia, from whence he had come.

There in Russia, how good and how pleasant it was to enter the bet ha-midrash. Around the tables there always sat young and old, rich and poor, the scholarly and the less-learned, engaged in Torah study. How delightful it was even to pass by a bet ha-midrash and to hearken to the sweet voices—veritably, the voice was the voice of Jacob—bursting forth from the indoors, ascending heavenward and captivating the hearts. Not long ago, there was founded in the city of Bialystok a Mishmar Society in the bet ha-midrash of Rabbi Yechiel Neches of blessed memory, and each night two minyanim sit down to learn till the morning hours. This society grows in members from day to day. In Russia, generally, one can find many tailors, cobblers, blacksmiths, butchers, chimney-sweeps, and drawers-of-water who have a thorough knowledge of the Talmud and are God-fearing men.[34]

A most illuminating and inspiring example of the practice of lifelong learning among the Jewish masses of Eastern European Jewry is the Association for the Study of the Mishnah at the Woodcutters' Synagogue in Berdichev. The city of Berdichev, in the Ukraine, once had a Jewish population of over fifty thousand and boasted seventy houses of worship. It also had a large Jewish artisan class that maintained its own houses of worship according to occupation. It is not surprising that there was a woodcutters' group large enough to maintain its own synagogue. Other callings must have been proportionately represented in the community. What is amazing and fills the heart with pride is that these woodcutters, among the lowest in the social and economic hierarchy of the community, formed an association not for the recital of the Psalms or the study of the Pentateuch, as was customary among the less learned groups, but for the study of the Mishnah, which requires considerable educational background and attainment.[35]

What will probably stand out as the classic modern instance of the way Jews set aside fixed times for group study, even under the worst, most hazardous circumstances, is found in the diary of a German intelligence officer who was stationed in Warsaw during World War I.

This diarist records that his office learned that something very mysterious was going on in the Jewish section. It was said that coachmen would come one after another without passengers and disappear mysteriously into a certain courtyard. The writer continues that he went to investigate for himself and arriving at the place in question with two detectives, stood and watched. It was true. Coachman after coachman was driving in with no passengers in his cab. All of them disappeared into a courtyard into which the scholarly writer followed. He finally came into one of the upper stories of the building. There he opened the door and saw two long tables, surrounded by coachmen who were sitting in their high hats, bent over books, and listening attentively to a man who was expounding something. The officer realized at once that there could be no question about a plot being fomented against the government. Nevertheless, he stood, dazed. He reports that he remained motionless, observing the occupants of the room without being able to comprehend what was going on. Finally he motioned to one of the listeners, for until then no one had even taken notice of the intruders. Utilizing his imperfect knowledge of Yiddish, the officer asked the Jew, "What is this?" "Why, this is a synagogue," the Jew replied. The officer repeated his question, "What is this?" "Why, they are sitting and studying the Law." The officer asked, "Is today Yom Kippur, a Holy day?" "No," the Jew said, "this is what we do every day." "You mean to say that every day you come here and listen to a lecture on the Law?" "Why, certainly," the Jew said. "After a hard day's work?" "Yes, that is what we do." The officer was convinced, and he concludes his account by saying, "It is amazing. It is unthinkable. It is inconceivable that German drivers should come every day to the University and listen to lectures on law!" The officer, of course, could only have realized dimly, if at all, what the Torah had meant to the Jews through the ages; how, like a lone beacon, it alone had relieved some very gloomy pages of Jewish history, and how the Jew clung to it and found comfort in it.[36]

"Pinkas Min Ha-Havurah Maggidei Tehillim Ugmilut Hasadim",
Kiev, 1895. This is a beautifully bound large volume written in
different colored inks with Hebrew letters similar to the letters of
a Sefer Torah. (See page 210).
*Courtesy of the Photographic Archive of The Jewish Theological
Seminary of America. Frank J. Darmstaedter.*

CHAPTER

XIII

THE HEVROT FOR JEWISH
LEARNING SEEN THROUGH
THEIR MINUTE-BOOKS

We now turn to a detailed investigation of quite a number of hevrot
for Jewish learning. The story of these associations, in all its richness and
societal significance, is revealed through an examination of their pinkasim,
or minute-books. Every hevrah kept a pinkas. Usually these books are
beautifully written volumes; some are handsomely bound, with specially
designed title pages and other adornments, often in color. Their great
value, however, lies not in their outer appearance but in their contents.
The pinkasim of most hevrot contain a statement of aims and purposes,
as well as the society's takkanot, or constitution and by-laws. In addition,
many pinkasim contain regulations pertaining to the election of officers,
admission of new members, obligations of members, sources of societal
income, fellowship benefits, disciplinary rules, the society's annual banquet,
and new rules as they are adopted, as well as the minutes of regular and
special meetings, descriptions of special events and celebrations, and various lists of officers and members. From all this we are able to describe
the structure—and in many cases the history—of the hevrot under consideration, often with fascinating side-glimpses at intimate details of their
day-to-day operations.

We shall have opportunity in this chapter to examine some thirty
pinkasim. Some of them are still extant in their original manuscript form,
and a number of these are here presented for the first time.[1] Others have
been previously studied, and their contents noted and described in printed

209

books and articles.[2] To facilitate our presentation, we have grouped all these documents into seven categories based on their contents and following an ascending scale of advancement in Jewish learning.

1. Hevrot for the Recital of Psalms

2. Hevrot for the Study of the Bible

3. Hevrot for the Study of the Bible and Related Literature

4. Hevrot for the Study of Codes

5. Hevrot for the Study of Moral and Ethical Literature

6. Hevrot for the Study of Mishnah

7. Hevrot for the Study of Talmud

(1) HEVROT FOR THE RECITAL OF PSALMS

Havurah Maggidei Tehillim u-Gmilut Hassadim of Kiev

As indicated by its name, the Chanters of Psalms and Doers of Deeds of Lovingkindness of Kiev, founded in 1895 with a roster of sixty-seven members, had a twofold purpose: religious fulfillment and mutual help. The first of these is elaborated in the preamble to the society's pinkas:[3]

> Upon those who are able to study the Torah by themselves and upon those who are less learned, there rests the duty to chant the Psalms every day. But because of preoccupation and the burden of finding a livelihood for the support of one's household, there is alas no time even to recite several Psalms. King David has said: "I am a companion of all them that fear Thee" [Ps. 119:62]. It is therefore helpful and necessary to perform this task in friendly company. For this reason, we who live here have bestirred ourselves to become associated for this great mitzvah and have organized the Holy Society called "Maggidei Tehillim." When the day of rest, the Holy Sabbath, comes we shall assemble in the bet ha-midrash in the winter before sunrise and in the summer at the noon hour, to recite the whole Book of Psalms in congregation assembled, from beginning to end, and to conduct ourselves in accordance with the ordinances contained in this pinkas. They form a statute that shall not be violated, and each man shall help his neighbor to say: "Be strong, be strong, and we shall all be strong!"

The list of takkanot—ordinances—follows:

1. The men of this holy society have agreed that each one is obligated to arise at dawn every Sabbath and holiday to come to the bet ha-midrash of the Lubavitch Hasidim to recite Tehillim in public with devotion and pleasantness. He who is not away on a journey, and has refrained from coming, shall be fined. He is to pay three kopecks to the treasury of the society for each time he is absent.

2. Each member must pay weekly dues [referred to as *wocher*] totaling ten kopecks per month. The money shall be turned over to the treasurer.

3. Members who do not pay their weekly dues or fines for the period of a year, shall take no part in the elections and cannot be elected to any office.

4. A member who has not attended the bet ha-midrash to recite the Psalms at least twelve times during the year, even if he has paid his fine, cannot take part in the elections and cannot be elected to any office.

5. All the members of the society shall assemble annually on the second day of Hol Hamoed Sukkot in the bet ha-midrash Luba-vitch and shall hold elections for three selectmen [*borerim*]. They shall have the power to appoint three trustees [*gabbaim*], a trea-surer, an auditor, and a recording secretary. The names of these officials shall be inscribed in the pinkas.

6. The selectmen must not delay their appointments beyond Hoshana Rabbah. On that day they are obliged to turn this pinkas over to the newly appointed trustees, together with the money and all the financial records. Should the elected selectmen fail to do this by Hoshana Rabbah, then the former officials shall retain their posts and these names shall also be written in this pinkas.

7. It is the duty of the trustees to supervise with an open eye and to diligently collect each week both the weekly dues and the fines —and to turn the money over to the treasurer once each month. It is the duty of the supervisor to write down each Saturday night the name of those who did not come that Sabbath morning to recite Tehillim and to give that name to the trustees.

8. New members who wish to join the society may do so on two occasions during the year. Once at the time of the annual elections, when the outgoing selectmen and trustees can admit anyone they see fit, and the second time on the fifth of Hanukkah, when all the members get together for a party and festive celebration. No one can be admitted without an initiation fee.

9. New members are not elected to full membership until after one year has elapsed from the time of their application and until after the initiation fee has been paid. After that they are full-fledged members.

10. Should a member get married, or should he marry off a son or a daughter, he is obliged to donate one ruble to the treasury, and for the engagement, a half-ruble. If a son or daughter should be born to any of the members, a donation of eighteen kopeks must be made.

11. The society shall come to the financial assistance of its members who are in need and shall also extend loans from the treasury. When "God will expand the boundaries" of those who had received loans, they are obliged to return the money to the treasury.

12. There is no limit to the amount of the loan, depending on the size of the treasury and the judgment of the trustees.

13. Should one of the members become sick, it is the duty of the trustees and the members to visit him and see if he needs money for medicines and for the maintenance of his family. If he is in need, the trustees must help from the funds of the society as much as possible.

14. If a member is dangerously sick, the society must foregather in the bet ha-midrash to recite Tehillim and other prayers—without any financial reward. If one of the members cannot come, he should hire someone to take his place.

15. If a member should die, the society must assemble in the house of mourning to chant the Psalms and to accompany the deceased to his eternal resting place—"for this is the end of man."

16. During the shivah, the members of the society are obliged to worship in the home of the deceased and to recite five Psalms

each day after the services. The day of the deceased member's death shall be inscribed in the pinkas, and if he died without children, then the society shall observe the Yahrzeit and recite the Kaddish.

17. Should the trustees and the heads of the society wish to purchase something for the use of the society, or to institute a new regulation, they must record such fact in the pinkas and sign thereunto. They can then execute their decision. No member of the society shall protest such action on the part of the officers. He who stirs up controversy over such matters shall be severely fined, and it shall be recorded in the pinkas. In extreme cases such recalcitrant members can be expelled.

18. On the second day of Shavuot, which is the Yahrzeit of King David, the author of the Psalms, the society shall kindle a twenty-four-hour candle in the bet ha-midrash so that during the time of the recitation of the Psalms, the lights may shine forth. May his [King David's] merit stand us in good stead to hasten our redemption speedily and in our day. Amen.

Then are listed the names of sixty-seven members of the society.

For the years from 1899 to 1916 there are separate pages setting forth the results of the annual elections. These pages too are beautifully done in the manner of a scribe. Each page lists the officials.

Psalm Readers of Belostok

A very touching example of the way the masses of the people, who were not sufficiently educated for advanced Jewish studies, were happy to have an opportunity at least to chant the Psalms, is indicated in the preamble to the minute-book of the Psalm Readers Association of Belostok:[4]

We, the undersigned, are not learned. We do not understand the Torah ourselves nor can we afford to support students of the Torah. Indeed, for lack of time, we are unable to chant the Psalms every day. We therefore take upon ourselves, under oath, the responsibility of gathering as a body in the synagogue at least on Saturdays, Holidays, on the Eve of the New Month and public fasts, for the purpose of completing the reading of the Book of Psalms from beginning to end. It shall be chanted quietly and slowly. One shall chant a verse, and everybody shall repeat after him.

At a later time, it seems, this society set higher standards for itself, for its members attempted not merely to chant the Psalms but also to study them. They employed a teacher "who was to expound the Psalms with the Rashi commentary and to supplement this exposition with moral exhortations."

Hevrah Tehillim of Izbitza

The pinkas of the Psalm Society of Izbitza, which is near Brisk (Brest) in Russia, covers a period of 125 years (1821–1926).[5] It begins with a letter of endorsement by the rabbi and the communal leaders (the *tuvei ha-ir*):

We hereby grant permission for the organization of this new association and this document shall have the force of a communal ordinance.

One of the conditions contained in this letter required

that the association shall be under the supervision of the rabbi. He shall draw up for them their takkanot [by-laws]. Without the rabbi of the community, no one shall raise hand or foot in matters small and large.

This condition was strictly adhered to, for we note that in working out the takkanot the members consulted the rabbi. The founders declare that:

whereas all the members might not be of one opinion and this may lead to dissension, it was therefore decided to turn to the rabbi, who will select three men for the trustees [*Kesherim*] and they, together with him, shall draw up the takkanot.

We also learn from this pinkas that because of the rabbi's unavailability due to illness, no new trustees could be selected in the year 1829 and the former officials carried over into the new term.

The takkanot of the society specify its program as follows:

1. Every weekday morning, before the services, to recite the group of Psalms prescribed for that day. This is to be done in a slow, digni-

fied manner, chanting the Psalms verse by verse. The precentor shall chant a verse; the congregation shall wait till he finishes and then respond with the verse that follows.

2. On the anniversary of the founding of the society, which occurs on the eve of the month of Elul and on the night of Yom Kippur and also on the night of the Seventh Day of Adar, which is the anniversary of the death of Moses, the entire Book of Psalms shall be chanted.

3. On the anniversary day of the founding of the society (on the day preceding the month of Elul), all the members are required to fast till noon, to recite the prescribed prayers for Yom Kippur Katan [Day of Atonement Minor], to listen to a sermon by the rabbi, and participate at night in the anniversary banquet. At this public feast the three trustees, whose names had been drawn from the urn on the fifteenth of Av previous, shall designate who the gabbaim shall be for the ensuing year.

The remaining takkanot for the governance of the association are as follows:

4. If a member took sick, there should be recited for him after the daily set of Psalms had been chanted, the "Special Prayer for the Sick" and preceding this prayer there should also be chanted those verses from Psalm 119 whose first letters spell out the Hebrew name of the sick member.

5. On the seventh of Adar—the Yahrzeit of Moses—there is to be made a wax candle to be kindled in the synagogue.

6. If a member died, a special Prayer for the Soul of the Departed was recited after the set of Psalms for the day.

From the above it is apparent that the aims of the Izbitza Society were largely religious. That is why the dues were so small—only three groschen per week. And when a member was sick, the only benefit he received was a prayer. Obviously the members of this society were economically better circumstanced since they did not require material assistance from the society. (The sixth takkanah makes reference to the fact that the members were merchants.)

Many items of cultural interest are reflected in the pinkas of this society. Thus we learn that because of the Revolution in November 1831, the society did not hold elections that year. Also, that a certain Reb Abraham, the physician, was accepted into membership without paying the required entrance fee and without having to serve his preliminary apprenticeship. In return for these special considerations, Reb Abraham pledged to give free medical care to the membership. Also, that a certain Reb Samuel enrolled his child as a member and agreed to pay dues of three gedolim per week until the boy would reach his eighteenth birthday, when he would pay his own dues. The father also pledged that at his son's Bar Mitzvah he would treat the society to wine and cake. It may be that this child was sickly and this act on the part of the father was a kind of "charm" to insure the child's health and life. In the pinkas, the name of the child is framed in black. Apparently he died. It is further noted that a certain member fell into ill-repute. Although it was later ascertained that the facts were not as rumored, the society felt it was a disgrace to have this man continued as a member. It was, however, decided that he be fined the sum of 136 gulden as a penance and permitted to remain. The man complied with this decision.

Hevrah Tehillim of Brisk

How different, and how much more elaborate, is the complexion of a similar society in a neighboring community. The takkanot in the pinkas of the Psalm Society of Brisk (Brest)[6] cover a period of sixty-two years (1850–1912). The first four provisions deal primarily with religious functions.

1. Every morning before dawn to recite 18 chapters of Psalms and to complete the remaining chapters on Sabbath afternoon.

2. Every day between Mincha and Maariv to study one chapter of Psalms and every Sabbath to learn the Pentateuch under the instruction of a Rabbi. From this it is obvious that these members were of the working class since they did not have time for the full set of Psalms prescribed for each day and since the Psalms they did recite were said before dawn. Also their learning was not advanced since they had to study Chumash with a Rabbi.

3. Every year on the Monday of Parshat Shemot (i.e., when the first

Portion of the Book of Exodus was read) all the members shall fast all day, recite all the Psalms in the Psalter, the Preacher shall deliver a sermon of an exhortatory character, and after the fast, a banquet shall be held.

4. On the 2nd day of Shevuos (the Yahrzeit of King David, the author of the Psalms) all members must come to the synagogue, kindle 150 candles to correspond to the 150 Psalms. The chanting of the Psalms shall be led by a suitable person to be selected by the gabbaim who shall intone the Psalms sweetly, verse by verse. Afterwards, the Rabbi should select one of the Psalms for special study and for pointing out the greatness of King David.

But in addition to the takkanot dealing with religious functions, this pinkas contains many regulations that deal with economic and social aspects of the life of the members. For example:

8. If a member has litigation with another member or with a Jew not a member, he must go to a Jewish court and obey its decision. If he violates this rule he shall be expelled. If the other party refuses to go to Jewish court, the matter should be turned over to Gabbaim. The Society has charge of the just conduct of its members.

One of the regulations required that all litigations between members of the society must be brought before the rabbi of the society or settled in consultation with the gabbaim.

9. If a member is guilty of unworthy conduct, after due investigation he shall be expelled and lose all his privileges. Such member relinquishes all claims against the society. The society has charge of the moral behavior of its members.

10. If a member gets seriously sick so as to be in need of *Mishmorim* (i.e., watchers who sit up with the sick and who chant appropriate prayers), the Gabbaim must see to it that one of the members shall be on duty till midnight and another member from midnight till the morning. He who is assigned and cannot serve must provide a substitute and pay him for it. A member who refuses to serve, shall be "cited" in the Pinkas recording his act of dis-

obedience. The Society concerns itself with the sick-care of its members.

11. If a member should, God forbid, die, the procedure shall be as follows: All members must go to the funeral and also to services in the home of the deceased and say Tehillim during the Week of Shiva, except on Sabbaths during that week. The Society takes care of all religious rites due to a departed member. . . .

22. None of our members—whether a workman or a merchant—shall enter into competition with a fellow-member or to encroach upon his livelihood. He who violates this rule shall be fined in accordance with the decision of the Gabbaim and the Kesherim and he must return the money that he profited as a result of his misdeed. The Society protects its members from dishonest competition. . . .

24. Because of the widespread sinful practice of card-playing which in addition to being condemned by our Sages when they declared: "he who gambles with cards is disqualified to serve as witness," and which also leads to quarrels between the players, often between husband and wife, we have therefore decided to keep away from this evil. If any of our members shall go contrary to our decision this shall be his judgment: At the first offense he shall be fined twice 18 *Gedolim;* for the second offense he shall be fined 18 *Pagim* (The Hebrew letters *peh* and *gimmel* are the initial letters for the Hebrew words *Perutah Gedolah.* This was a large coin which equalled six Polish *Groschen.* These coins were popularly called *Pagim*); and for the third offense he shall be expelled. The Society forbids the playing of cards.

The weekly dues in the Hevrah Tehillim of Brisk were three groschen per week. A member who was in arrears for four weeks did not get an aliyah. But there were also other payments in order to cover the expenses of the social functions of the society, such as:

1. When a member made a circumcision feast—eighteen gedolim

2. When a member had a daughter—nine gedolim

3. When a member married off a son or a daughter—eighteen gedolim

4. When a member made a garment for himself or for his wife—eighteen half-groschen

5. When a member made a garment for a child—eighteen half-
groschen

The method of selecting gabbaim in the Hevrah Tehillim of Brisk was
not quite the same as in the Hevrah Tehillim of Izbitza. The drawing of
names from the urn took place annually on the eve of Hoshana Rabbah.
The first six names drawn were the kesherim, and they in turn selected
two gabbaim. The six kesherim and the two gabbaim conducted the affairs
of the society. They also had the right to admit new members. (In Izbitza
new members were admitted only by majority vote of all members.) The
new members had to pay an entrance fee of twice eighteen gedolim. If
they wanted part ownership in the Sefer Torah, they had to pay eighteen
gulden. These fees had to be paid out within the first year of membership.
During the first year the new member was an apprentice—or probationer.
The son of a member pays only eighteen gedolim entrance fee. A member
could also enroll his minor son and pay for him eighteen groschen as
entrance fee and one groschen per week as weekly dues. The hevrah
received one groschen per week from each member. A general meeting
was called for important occasions. With the approval of the majority, the
same kesherim and gabbaim could continue in office without a general
election.

One of the interesting sidelights in this pinkas is an entry forbidding
members to work or trade on the intermediate days of the festivals.[7]

Hevrah Tehillim of Liubranets

The Psalm Society of Liubranets, whose pinkas[8] covers a period of
sixty-six years (1843–1909), was in the nature of a workmen's guild since
it consisted entirely of tailors. New members were accepted only with the
majority consent of the members. The new member had to pay an entrance
fee and serve as an apprentice for three years, and at the end of this
period he had to treat the society to a small feast. Only then was he considered a full-fledged member with the right to vote and make decisions.
A new member was referred to as *Einkaufer*. At the end of the proba-
tionary period he was called *Auskaufer*. The period of being an apprentice
or probationer was often shortened.

The weekly dues were a minimum of four groschen. If a member did
not pay eight weeks in a row, a general meeting was called to decide on
the case. If a male child was born, the father had to pay eight groschen
into the treasury. If a member married off a child, he paid twice eight

groschen. Members had to worship in the synagogue of the society. On the night after Sukkot the annual election of kesherim was held. The latter then selected the gabbaim. The kesherim could not name themselves as gabbaim. New members had to be elected by majority vote. A new member had to pay the entrance fee in advance and be in the service of the society for several years—both items to be decided on by the society. Each new member had to give a minimum of two Polish gulden to the rabbi.

Each year, on the fifteenth of Shevat, in a year when a Sefer Torah was to be written for the society, all members gathered. The rabbi preached (and was paid five gulden for it). Then a banquet was held.

Every three years, on Hoshana Rabbah, six kesherim were chosen who in turn chose two gabbaim. These two gabbaim had complete charge. Neither could act without the other. In case there were no funds in the treasury, neither gabbai could advance more than twenty gulden out of his own pocket. By majority vote the two gabbaim could continue in office. The gabbaim, with the consent of the rabbi and several members, could admit new members. A new member paid an entrance fee of twice eighteen gulden, which could be paid in installments. He had to serve for a year as a probationer. If the entrance fee was paid in only two installments, he did not have to serve as a probationer.

The pinkas of this society reveals that the general cultural level of its membership was quite low. Most of the entries are not in Hebrew but in Yiddish, and there are many gross misspellings of Hebrew words. Nor were the affairs of the group always peaceful. An entry speaks of the expulsion of the gabbai rishon (the first trustee) only one month after his election because he had insulted the rabbi. At a later date, he apologized to the entire membership and to the rabbi, paid a fine, and was readmitted. An interesting and brotherly touch to the story was the decision on the part of the membership never to reproach the trustee for his misdeed.

Hevrah Maggidei Tehillim of Kovno

The pinkas of the Chanters of Psalms of Kovno, founded in 1790 by the workingmen of the community, contains the takkanot with twenty-six ordinances.[9] These set forth the purposes of the society together with other regulations. The major requirement stated that "During the summer, all the members must assemble in the Beth Hamidrash every Saturday at 2 o'clock in the afternoon to recite the Book of Psalms. During the winter, they shall gather three hours before daybreak in order "to tell forth in the morning God's lovingkindness and His truth" (Ps. 92:3). New members did not require the vote of the entire membership. Application for membership was made to an admissions committee, and a minimum of eight votes of this committee was required for favorable action. Dues were paid weekly. The Society Feast took place annually on the second day of Shavuot. It was quite modest in character. Immediately following the religious services on that day, the gabbai would distribute brandy and cake to all the members. That evening the members would stay up all night in order to chant the entire Psalter in honor of King David. Unforeseen expenditures required the approval of the entire society, and the officers were obliged to call a special meeting for this purpose.

Upon the demise of a member, from the time of death to the time of burial, the society conducted services and chanted Psalms in a corner of the house. The gabbai was empowered to take eighteen coins from the treasury, and a similar amount from the money of the deceased, and give this sum to charity as the body was being removed from the house in order to fulfill the command "righteousness goeth before him." If the deceased was poor, the Gabbai was to take the additional sum also from the society's treasury.

Hevrah Maggidei Tehillim ve-Ner Tamid of Lodz

The Psalms and Perpetual Light Society of Lodz,[10] founded in 1820, had the twofold purpose of reciting Psalms and of tending to the lights in the synagogue. Each day, before the morning service, the group of Psalms prescribed for that day were chanted, while on Saturdays, after the morning service, the entire Book of Psalms was chanted. New members had to serve an apprenticeship of three years. Elections were held on the first of Heshvan, and three electors were chosen. The weekly dues were three groschen and the annual banquet was held on the Monday during the week of sidrah Shemot (when the first section of the Book of Exodus was read).

Hevrah Tehillim of Gombin

The Psalm Society of Gombin, a city near Plotzk in Poland, was founded in 1794. Its pinkas[11] contains an introduction by its spiritual leader, Rabbi Moshe Lichtenstein. Ten years later, we come upon an entry telling us that the members had to elect a new leader, Rabbi Yehuda Leib Muravnik, whom they called from the neighboring town of Shepsk. The minutes then continue:

> Since we want him to come to Gombin to be our rabbi, and since among his duties he will be conducting a regular shiur [study session] every Sabbath afternoon in our synagogue, therefore each and every member of this society shall obligate himself to give to the treasurer each month the sum of six gedolim of Polish money. The treasurer shall pay to the rabbi the sum of six gulden. This sum shall be in addition to what the kehillah and the other societies shall be paying him in order that he shall live and teach among us in dignity.

(2) HEVROT FOR THE STUDY OF THE BIBLE

Hevrah Mikra of Gombin

Also in the city of Gombin, there existed for a full century a Society for the Study of Bible. The two pinkasim of this hevrah are preserved in the library of the Jewish Theological Seminary,[12] and they tell its history in great detail from the time of its founding in 1792 to the day of the last entry in 1892.

What is most remarkable about this hevrah is the fact that in eighteenth-century Poland there should even be founded a society for Bible study. Such a society is a rare phenomenon for that time and place because the whole region was thoroughly steeped in the talmudic tradition and was given over wholly to talmudic studies. The forty-four charter members of this organization therefore found it necessary to include in the preamble of the charter the many reasons impelling them to bring the new society into existence. This preamble offers an inspiring presentation of the values and benefits to be obtained from the study of the entire Bible, that is, the Pentateuch, the Prophets, and the Hagiographa. One of the most beautiful passages in this part of the preamble reads as follows:

> It is written in Massekhet Soferim that the Bible is likened to water, the Mishnah to wine, and the Gemara to spiced wine. Surely, the world is in need of water, and of wine and spiced wine. A rich man can benefit himself from all three. But one can get along without wine and without spiced wine. But it is impossible to live without water. So is it impossible to live without the Torah, which is symbolized by water. Furthermore, water is needed for wine and for spiced wine, for without

water no liquor can be made. So, too, the basic study for us must be the Torah.[13]

The preamble continues with a lament on the neglect of the study of the Written Law—the Bible—and the overemphasis on studying only the Oral Law—the Talmud—appealing to the rabbis of the time in these words:

In truth, much depends on the recognized scholars among the populace for them to set the example. If the people will see that the learned Jews set aside time in study groups for the study of the twenty-four books of the Bible, then they will not consider it unbecoming to do likewise. But if the learned men abstain from studying Scripture because it is beneath their dignity, then the masses of the people will be adversely influenced. For in the final analysis, the conduct of the people is like the conduct of their leaders.[14]

The document concludes with these words of noble self-dedication:

For all the above reasons, our hearts are lifted up in high resolve. We, the undersigned, have agreed that, with God's help, we herewith establish the Hevrah Mikra to study the Torah, the Prophets, and the Writings. We shall do so daily toward evening and in their proper order. May this our action be pleasing in the sight of Heaven and may the graciousness of the Lord, our God, be upon us, and may He establish the work of our hands. Amen.[15]

The two pinkasim give ample evidence that throughout the century of the hevrah's existence, the members adhered fervently and faithfully to the high resolves stated in the preamble. There are records of the annual siyyum ha-gadol—the Great Feast celebrating the completion of the study of all the twenty-four books of the Bible—and also of the frequent holding of a siyyum ha-katan—the Small Feast marking the completion of the study of a major division of the Bible, such as the Early Prophets and the Later Prophets.

The two pinkasim also contain lists of the members. At times the membership was as high as sixty-nine. Between 1840 and 1892, there were 128 members.[16] There is a record of the admission of the members. Each new member had to pay an admission fee to be paid out over several years and was also obliged to pay weekly dues. He also had to present a full set, or part of a set, of the twenty-four books of the Bible, and in addition had to treat the members to cake and brandy. A rare exception to these requirements for admission of new members was made on the twenty-eighth day of Heshvan in the year 1855. Let the minutes of the meeting for that day tell their own story:

> There came before us the respected Reb Zeev Yehuda, who requested of us, the kesherim [electors], and also of us, the members, to grant him admission into our society. Instead of the regular admission fees and weekly dues, he volunteered to serve the members of the society by going to the homes of the members all the days of his life, on every Sabbath afternoon to wake them from their Sabbath nap before the Minhah service; also by calling the members together for important occasions such as the annual meetings at which the elections are held, special meetings, and festive assemblies at which cake and brandy are served. As a reward for all these services to be performed so generously and voluntarily by said Reb Zeev Yehuda, we are admitting him as a member to our society.[17]

Hevrah Mikra of Brisk and Liubranets

The cities of Brisk and Liubranets, both in Poland, each had a Bible Society. In the pinkas of the Hevrah Mikra of Brisk we are told: "All the members held a special assembly in order to repair the breach after all the destruction and to revive the society and to renew our ordinances." It is further stated: "Our Hevrah shall be under the guidance of the rabbi of the community, and no one shall dare to do anything without his authority." In a similar vein we find in the pinkas of the Hevrah Mikra of Liubranets: "Lo, because of the oppressiveness of the times, many days have passed since we were met to choose a worthy man to teach us Torah every Sabbath day, and as a result our society had disbanded. We are therefore assembled now to re-establish our Bible Society." [18]

The Koidanovo Bible Society

The members of the Bible Society of Koidanovo were most earnest in their desire to cover the study of the entire Bible. We read in the very first paragraph of their ordinances:

The Association, as a group, shall study in the morning a portion of the Pentateuch, and in the evening the twenty-four books of the Bible, in their order, without the omission of even a day. All members present in the synagogue shall join the group while the lesson is in progress. It is desirable that those members who are not present in the synagogue shall study the lesson at home.

The earnestness of this group is further evidenced by the following later entry:

As soon as, by divine grace, we are able to purchase sets of *Ein Yaakov* we shall, after the morning lesson in the Pentateuch, study also a lesson in that book.

The care of the society library was of concern to its membership, for the by-laws provide that

it is incumbent upon the supervisors to care for the books that are in the synagogue and to see to it that they are always in their proper places. They shall examine all the books at least twice each year to determine whether or not they are in good condition. If a book is in need of repair, the warden of the month shall be informed about it, and he shall arrange with the treasurer to have the repairs made.

It was also ordered that "no book shall be withdrawn from the synagogue premises except to take it to the bindery, or to the society's place of prayer and study, or for consultation by the court."

The entrance fee for new members was four silver rubles, and the weekly dues were twenty-five groschen. The annual election was held during the Intermediate Days of Passover, at which time the following officers were chosen: three to five electors, three wardens, one treasurer, four auditors, four supervisors, and two guardians. The annual Society Banquet took place on Shabbat Bereshit.[19]

The Lodz Bible Society

The Bible Society in Lodz, which was founded in 1836, employed a teacher to instruct the members in the Portion of the Week on Saturdays and in other parts of the Bible on weekdays. Its annual elections were held on the Intermediate Days of Passover, at which time there were chosen two wardens and one auditor. The weekly dues were three groschen, and the Society Banquet was held on Simhat Torah.[20]

(3) HEVROT FOR THE STUDY OF BIBLE AND RELATED SUBJECTS

Hevrah Lomdei Torah of Kovno

Some associations did not limit their studies to the Bible. They combined with it the study of Midrash and often added other texts as well. An outstanding illustration of such an association is the Hevrah Lomdei Torah of Kovno (modern Kaunas, in Lithuania),[21] which was founded in 1833. The very name "Students of the Torah" is indicative of the wider scope of studies. The society's statement of purpose is beautifully expressive of the members' desires. It reads:

> It is widely known in Judah and Israel that the study of our Torah is supremely holy and that it is the source of our life and indeed of the life of the universe. . . . We have therefore decided to associate with one another in one group to study every Sabbath the weekly Portion of the Pentateuch with the commentaries of Rashi and of the Midrash. In addition we shall study every weekday afternoon between Minhah and Maariv or after Maariv, a lesson in Aggadah. And since it is not study alone which is of prime importance but doing is of prime importance, we shall also add to the study of Aggadah, a lesson in *Hayyei Adam* so that we may be instructed in the way we shall go, and in the deeds we shall perform.
>
> As evidence of our earnestness we have further decided to expend money from our purses and to tax ourselves for an entrance fee and for weekly dues so that we shall have funds wherewith to purchase books and to employ a teacher who shall instruct us daily. So it shall be that on Sabbaths, on festivals, and on weekdays, our membership shall come to hearken to the word of God in our own bet ha-midrash from the mouth of our own rabbi.

That this association was blessed with success is indicated by the fact that one of the eminent rabbis of Kovno, Rabbi Mendele the son of Zeev Wolf, wrote into the pinkas of the society that it attracted so many people and served its purpose so well that it was ordained in 1837—only four years after its founding—that no new society of a similar character should be organized.

Four of the ordinances in the pinkas of this society deal with such organizational items as the election and admission of new members, the schedule of study, and the duties of the rabbi. After the passage of some years it apparently became necessary to strengthen the organization as well as the zeal of its members, so a unique plan was devised:

Whereas our society was formed so that people shall not be dispersed among the hills and go wandering on the street-corners like sheep without a shepherd, thereby going about in emptiness without the yoke of the Torah upon them; and whereas we have elected a rabbi who shall be our teacher and give us regular and systematic instruction between Minhah and Maariv each day, and in the afternoons each Sabbath, and whereas we have now taken note of the fact that the rabbi sits and conducts the lessons at the appointed times, but alas very few members of our association are in attendance, nor do they say to themselves, "I will go to the bet ha-midrash, I will listen to the words of the Torah, I will hearken to the instruction of our rabbi." Instead, our members each go their own way, and our rabbi sits and learns by himself. . . . It was therefore resolved with the unanimous consent of all that from now on we shall divide our membership into five teams [degalim—"troupes"]. Each weekday another team shall be required to be in full attendance during the study period. The order of attendance shall be drawn by lot. If a member of a team does not attend as required due to the lack of time or for another reason, he shall pay a fine of three Polish gedolim. If his absence is due to his being away from the city or because of some unavoidable reason, he is excused from paying the fine.

At the same time that the above reorganization plan was introduced, it also became necessary to raise the weekly dues from two to three Polish gedolim because "the expenses of the society now come to five gulden per week in addition to other expenses, such as the purchase of books and the like." If a member did not comply with this new system of dues by the time of the next annual election, he would be denied the right to vote.

Other Bible-study Societies

In Zhagory there was an association of students of the Bible and

Aggadah, and in Lodz a society originally organized for the study of the Bible subsequently turned to the study of the Midrash.[22]

(4) HEVROT FOR THE STUDY OF CODES

Hevrah Hayyei Adam of Izbitsa

Since Judaism is a way of life prescribed by laws, it was quite natural that many societies should be formed to study the popular codifications of Jewish law, the best-known and most authentic of which is the *Hayyei Adam* by the Lithuanian codifier, Rabbi Abraham Danzig.

An example of such a society is to be found in the Hevrah *Hayyei Adam* of Izbitsa, whose pinkas describes its activities for a period of thirty-eight years from its founding in 1867 down to 1905.[23] The ordinances of this society are typical of many others:

1. Members must come to the rabbi to study at the times fixed.

2. If a member absents himself intentionally, he is to be fined eighteen groschen.

3. During the Reading of the Torah conversation is forbidden.

4. No member is to complain or grumble against the gabbai who distributes the aliyot.

5. Each year, on the Monday of the sidrah Shemot, the annual banquet is to be held. The rabbi is to preach and is to be paid extra for it.

6. Each year, on the fifteenth day of Av, the electors shall be chosen, and they in turn select the gabbaim. The electors can name themselves as the gabbaim.

7. If a member quarrels with a gabbai, he is obliged to pay a fine of twice eighteen groschen.

8. No quarrels are allowed among the members. Anyone who violates this rule is to pay a fine. If a member quarrels with the gabbai, he is to pay a fine of thrice eighteen groschen. If a member quarrels with the rabbi, he is to be fined four times eighteen groschen.

9. The salary of the shamash is to be twenty gulden per year.

(5) HEVROT FOR THE STUDY OF MORAL AND ETHICAL LITERATURE

Many preferred to study some great text expounding the moral and ethical precepts of Judaism. The names of such associations reflect the text selected; for example, Midrash Society, *Ein Yaakov* Society, *Menorat ha-Maor* Society, *Alsheikh* Society, or a general name like Aggadta.

The Alsheikh Society of Grodna

In Grodna there was a society for the study of the *Alsheikh,* a very popular homiletical commentary on the Bible by Rabbi Moses Alsheikh, who lived in Safed in the sixteenth century. Its minutes state that:

The entire membership shall assemble on each Saturday, holiday and intermediary days of the holidays in the house of prayer and shall study as one group the lesson in Alsheikh until the hour for the afternoon prayer arrives. Anyone who separates himself from the group shall be regarded as absent. Only in case a scholar is delivering a lecture in the synagogue, or in case of an accident, is one exempt from studying the Alsheikh. At the conclusion of the study period one of the members is to recite the Kaddish.

That the membership of this society came from the lower economic elements is evidenced by the fact that the weekly dues were only one groschen.[24]

The Hevrah Aggadata of Bosk

In the middle of the nineteenth century in the city of Bosk, Russia, where about a generation or two later, Rabbi Isaac Kook was the spiritual leader before he settled in Palestine, there existed a society for the study of the Aggadah. In its pinkas we come upon a description of the society banquet held to celebrate the completion of the text which had been studied. It was a siyyum, or feast of completion. From this record, we can see how great was the joy of our fathers when they reached such an important milestone in their religious-cultural pursuits. Let their words speak for themselves:

On Tuesday, the fifth of Nisan, 1843, there was held a great feast by the Hevrah Aggadta. It was both a feast and a festival, and we rejoiced that God has aided us to study and to complete the Aggadta. May God further help us to study and to teach, to observe and to do. We celebrated for two whole days. On Tuesday we finished the Aggadta, and we made a party and a festive day. We invited 123 guests, not counting the musicians and the fifteen beadles. Four different and elaborate courses were served. The food was so plentiful that it was left over on the plates. If a man had not eaten in three days, he had more than enough to eat. The musicians were stationed in the women's gallery of the synagogue. Our joy was exceedingly great. Wine poured like water —some pouring it into their throats and others on the floor. On Wednesday we began anew the study of the Aggadta, and we obligated ourselves to study the *Ein Yaakov*. On that day too we made a great feast. The people made merry with trumpets and violins until, it seemed, the earth would split with the noise. The people who stood outside envied us our joy and our *simhah shel mitzvah*.[25]

The Musar Movement and the Educational Role of Preachers

Around the same time the preceding document was written, there sprang up the so-called Musar movement, which emphasized the practical application of the moral teachings of Judaism. Founded by Rabbi Israel Salanter in Vilna in 1840, and focusing on the study of the ethical and moralistic texts of Judaism, the Musar movement was, in effect, an adult Jewish education program. Salanter succeeded in establishing special Musar conventicles throughout the Jewish world of Eastern Europe.[26] These studied such classic texts as Bahya ibn Pakuda's *Hovot ha-Levavot* ("The Duties of the Heart"), Moses Hayyim Luzzatto's *Mesillat Yesharim* ("The Way of the Righteous"), and other moralist literature of the medieval and subsequent periods.[27]

In this connection, it is important to speak of the labors of the maggidim —itinerant preachers—in the popular education of the Jewish masses. Tracing their origin to talmudic times, the maggidim began to reach their highest influence from the sixteenth century on down to our own times. The title of maggid mesharim ("preacher of righteousness") probably dates from the sixteenth century, and it has been notably associated with some of the greatest maggidim of the eighteenth and nineteenth centuries. Among the most famous of these was Rabbi Jacob Kranz, known as the Dubner Maggid, who died in 1804. He was famous for his use of parables, fables, and incidents of daily life, and therefore Moses Mendelssohn named Kranz the "Jewish Aesop." The most celebrated maggid during the nineteenth century was Moses Isaac ben Noah Darshan (1828–1900), the Kelmer Maggid. He was known as a "Musar maggid" and a "terror maggid," because he preached moral and religious conduct as a safeguard against the terrible punishments of the Day of Judgment. The Kelmer Maggid preached to crowded synagogues for over fifty years in almost every city of Russian Poland. Other popular Jewish teachers and preachers were more philosophical in character, and with the rise of the Zionist movement some of them became known as "nationalistic" or "Zionistic" maggidim. The most famous of these was Zevi Hirsch Masliansky, whose major activity was in New York City.[28]

There is an interesting parallel to be drawn between the labors of the Jewish maggidim and the Christian friars of the late Middle Ages. Scholars who trace the history of learning state that "the Friars—the Franciscans and Dominicans were skillfully trained as preachers—to go to hear a Friar preach was a recognized holiday attraction; their racy stories, direct moral appeal and emotional style gave them great power to move their hearers." [29] The impact of these popular preachers was so great that a historian of culture refers to their work as "almost a forerunner of the modern university lectures." [30] It is a pity that during certain eras these friars used their talents for inciting the populace against Jews and Judaism.

The Zohar Study Society in Padua, Italy, and its "Rules for the House of Study"

One of the most unique study groups in many a century was founded by Moses Hayyim Luzzatto (1707–47), the famed author of the *Mesillat Yesharim,* when he was still a young man in his native city of Padua, Italy. All his life Luzzatto was a student of Jewish mysticism, and in his youth he established a group primarily for the study of the Zohar but also as an aid to the saintly life, aimed at "the restoration of the Divine Presence and . . . of all Israel." He and the members of his group drew up "Rules for the House of Study." The following is the complete text of this most fascinating religious document of eighteenth-century Italian Jewry:

With the help of God may we begin and prosper, amen.

These are the words of the covenant, the laws and ordinances and teachings, which the holy associates hereunto subscribing have taken upon themselves for the unification of the Holy One and the Divine Presence all acting as one, because "Jephthah in his generation is even as Samuel in his generation" [Talmud, R.H. 25b; that is to say, the comrades are to be considered equal regardless of intellectual status.] —to perform this service of God, which shall be reckoned to the account of all. The following are the obligations which they have accepted:

First, to prosecute in this House of Study a continuous uninterrupted study of the holy book of Zohar, each man his portion, one after another, daily, from the morning until the Evening Prayer, except for the Sabbaths, holy days, Purim, the Ninth of Av, the eve of the Ninth of Av, and except for the Friday afternoons, according to the condition which we have stipulated before God:

1. That this study shall not be reckoned a vow. That is to say, an omission shall not, God forbid, become a stumbling block to the comrades and be considered a default of a vow. But it shall be imposed upon them with all the power and stringency that mouth can utter and heart can feel.

2. That the study shall never be interrupted, and when one man takes the place of his comrade, he is to begin before his comrade has finished, so that the study shall never be interrupted.

3. If a comrade shall be absent on a journey, be it near or far, the remaining comrades shall complete his study, and it shall be reckoned to his account, as if he had studied with them.

4. This study shall not be performed for the purpose of receiving any reward, of whatever nature, not even, God forbid, in thought. But it is to be performed only for the purpose of the "restoration" of the Divine Presence, the "restoration" of all Israel, the people of the Lord, that they may bring joy to their Creator; this study shall entail no reward but the merit of doing more such deeds for the purpose of the unification of the Holy One and the Divine Presence and the "restoration" of all Israel.

5. If (God forbid!) it should happen that the study is interrupted in any manner, either through duress or error or forgetfulness, may such interruption produce no evil impression whatsoever, either on earth or on high. The object of the comrades in prosecuting this study is solely perfection, and not any iniquity whatsoever.

6. The general teachings of our teacher and master, Rabbi Moses Hayyim, which he teaches in the House of Study at noontime daily, may be reckoned as part of this study.

7. Each of the comrades may upon occasion honor one who does not belong to the holy brotherhood by allowing him to study in his place and at his hour; and it shall be considered as if it was one of the holy members doing the reading.

8. The comrades have also undertaken to combine day and night in this study.

9. This study may not be undertaken for the individual perfection of any one of the comrades, nor even in atonement for a sin; its sole meaning is the "restoration" of the Divine Presence, and the "restoration" of all Israel.

10. No one of the comrades shall be assigned any fixed hours for this study, but each shall study as his heart dictates, whenever he is able.

Those who have concluded this sure covenant subscribe hereunto: [signed] Israel Hezekiah Trevis, Isaac Marini, Yekutiel of Vilna, Jacob Israel Forte, Solomon Dina, Michael Terni, Jacob Hayyim Castel Franco.

The following regulations are subjoined to the above, that the new comrades may serve God in truth and with a whole heart. The comrades have taken the following upon themselves:

1. They will perform their service before God in truth, with humility and perfect love, with no expectation of reward for themselves, but only for the sake of the "restoration" of the Divine Presence, and the "restoration" of all Israel. Any reward due them for their fulfillment of the commandments and their good deeds they offer up as a gift to all Israel, to show their love of the holy Presence, and to bring joy to their Creator.

2. The comrades have all united to serve their Creator as one man with a simple and a pure service; when any comrade fulfills any commandment, it shall be considered as fulfilled by all the comrades for the sake of the perfection of the holy Presence. But any

sin or fault committed by any single comrade shall not be reckoned to the community at large. For the community has been formed to share perfection, not iniquity.

3. The comrades have taken upon themselves to love one another, and to treat one another kind-heartedly and with brotherly love, and to accept remonstrances from one another with great love, without anger or hate, but in a loving spirit and in a peaceful manner, so that they may be accepted before the Lord.

4. The comrades have undertaken to keep all the words of the Holy Book [the Zohar], which they have learned, a sealed secret, and to reveal nothing except with the permission of the master.

5. They shall all endeavor to come to the study of the Zohar every day at whatever hour they find it possible.

6. They are all under obligation to be present, unless detained by an accident, at the holy House of Study every Sabbath after the After-noon Prayer for instruction by their master, may his light shine.

7. They shall make themselves resolute to perform their service before the Lord, and to pay heed neither to the jesting nor to the laughter of others.

8. The newly consecrated comrades have undertaken to leave the room without objections, in the event that the holy comrades who subscribed to the original regulations find it necessary to transact any business the nature of which cannot be revealed to others in the House of Study.

9. If any person wishes to join their company afterwards, all condi-tions hitherto obtaining among them shall apply to him as well.

10. The comrades shall guard their mouths and tongues from evil speech, and transact their affairs and fill their needs with all respect and reverence for the holy Presence. Far be it from them to treat lightly any stringent law or usage in Israel. But they will add ob-servance to observance in their wish to remain pure before the Lord God of Israel.

The following are the signatures wherewith they subscribe to these regulations: [signed] Isaiah ben Joseph, Isaiah ben Abraham, Mordecai ben Rephael, Solomon ben Samuel, Moses ben Michael, Abraham ben Jacob, Isaac Hayyim ben Jacob, Isaac Katz, Simeon ben Jacob Vita, Mordecai ben Benzion.

These are the statutes of this holy House of Study:

The comrades have taken it upon themselves to speak nothing but what concerns the Torah at the holy table of study of their master, Rabbi Moses Hayyim. Nor shall they linger in conversation in other houses of study, when the hour of study approaches, but they shall seat themselves at the table with reverence and awe. And Rabbi Israel, son of Rabbi Michael, one of the comrades who has been chosen for this special duty, is to raise his voice and announce: "Give glory to the Lord God of Israel!" Immediately the holy comrades are to bow their heads, and no further word is to escape their lips. They are required to break off their conversation and to remain silent in great awe. If the comrades engage in unnecessary talk, even if it is not the hour of study and they are not at the study table, Rabbi Yekutiel has the right to motion to Rabbi Israel, and Rabbi Israel shall say, "Give glory to the Lord God of Israel!" Then everyone is immediately required to fall silent. If quarrels should break out among the comrades (God forbid) even outside the House of Study, Rabbi Israel can bring any comrade to silence by saying to him, "Give glory to the Lord God of Israel!"— and the comrade must become silent. The other statutes dealing with silence are indeed written in the book of the covenant to which the comrades have subscribed with their own hands.

In their pursuit of saintly living the comrades have taken it upon themselves not to utter any idle word whatsoever anywhere in the whole House of Study. And they have further taken the following upon themselves:

Whenever any comrade shall come into this House of Study, his head should be bowed and he should give greeting with the words, "Let the glory of the Lord endure forever!" Then those sitting in the House of Study will reply, "Blessed be the name of the Lord from this time forth and forever!"

Whenever any comrade leaves the House of Study, he must go backwards, saying, "Praised be the Lord out of Zion!"

When the master Rabbi Moses Hayyim shall enter the House of Study, he shall say, "May the Lord our God be with us!" Then those sitting in the House of Study shall reply, "May the Lord give strength unto his people!"

When the master Rabbi Moses Hayyim shall seat himself at his table, he shall say, "The Lord is high above all nations," and the comrades shall reply, "Who is like unto the Lord our God, that dwelleth so high, that looketh down so low upon the heavens and the earth?" Then Rabbi Israel shall say, "Give glory to the Lord God of Israel!" and the comrades shall immediately bow their heads and fall silent, prepared to study before the holy Presence in fear and trembling and awe. Then Rabbi Yekutiel shall say to all the holy comrades, "Apply your minds!"

The comrades have also taken it upon themselves not to raise their voices in the holy House of Study in the course of their studies, even where they may, except for Talmudic dissertation. They have also taken it upon themselves to do nothing in the House of Study without the permission of their master, Rabbi Moses Hayyim, may his light shine.

Furthermore, all the holy comrades, both of the first company and of the second, have agreed to guard themselves closely against speaking any falsehoods, and to make it their endeavor to allow only truth to pass their lips, forever. Consequently, when one comrade shall say to another, "Speak the truth!"—it shall be considered the most binding oath possible.

The comrades have further taken it upon themselves that one of the comrades shall daily recite, first the Ten Commandments and then the Six Hundred and Thirteen Precepts, and then Psalm 119 from verse 9, "Wherewithal shall a young man keep his way pure," until the end of the section.

They have further taken it upon themselves to read all through the Bible, and some comrades all through the Mishnah, every month.

They have further taken it upon themselves to tithe their days before the Lord in fasting. Every tenth day shall be holy, and one of the comrades shall fast on that day. The comrades are all to fast in rotation.

Further they have taken it upon themselves to perform absolution of all reproaches and absolution of all ill will every month.

The comrades have further added to the regulation concerning the daily study of the holy Zohar the provision that they shall study all day until the sixth hour of the night, with the exception of the nights from the close of the Day of Atonement until after the Feast of Booths, and the nights of the fourteenth and the fifteenth of Adar, and also the nights from the day of preparation for the Passover festival until after the festival, and the nights from the day of preparation for the Feast of Weeks until after the festival. Nor are they to study during the nights preceding and following the fast days of the Seventeenth of Tammuz, the Ninth of Av, and the Day of Atonement. But if the requirements of the hour dictate the necessity of study, the decision is to lie in the hands of the master, Rabbi Moses Hayyim.

That which the comrades have taken upon themselves is for the purpose of perfection only, and not for any iniquity whatsoever. The comrade who sins shall bear his own guilt, and the collective holiness shall not suffer. And the comrades have subjoined that they shall not neglect the study of the Zohar even during the hour of general instruction by Rabbi Moses Hayyim.

The Lord has helped them to this point; may he nevermore forsake them, until the Messiah shall come whose coming is proper, unto whom "shall the gathering of the people be" [Gen. 49:10], as it is written, "For then will I turn to the people a pure language, that they may all call upon the name of the Lord, to serve Him with one consent" [Zeph. 3:9]; "and the Lord shall be King over all the earth; in that day shall the Lord be One, and His name one" [Zech. 14:9].[31]

(6) HEVROT FOR THE STUDY OF MISHNAH

The more learned members of the community belonged to societies that studied the Mishnah. We shall examine the workings of three such associations as revealed in their own minute-books.

Hevrah Mishnayot of Grodna

The records of this society state:

1. The lesson shall be studied regularly, on weekdays immediately following the morning services and on Saturdays and Holidays during the hour preceding the afternoon services. Even in winter when the days are short, classes shall be held before the afternoon services.

2. If a chapter is difficult and intricate, requiring much mental speculation, it is permissible to divide it into several lessons, provided it meets with the approval of the majority of the members.

3. A fine shall be imposed upon those who interrupt the studies with idle chatter.

4. Those finishing the reading of the chapter before the others shall nevertheless remain until the Kaddish is recited or else shall pay a fine of 1 gross Polen.

The annual elections were held during the Intermediate Days of Passover, at which time the following officials were chosen: five electors, four wardens, two treasurers, two auditors, and four supervisors. The weekly dues were only one-half a gross Polen (Polish groschen).[32]

Hevrah Mishnayot of Shchuchin

Among its ordinances this association has the following provisions:

1. One chapter of the Mishnah is to be studied in a group, at a table in the synagogue, on weekdays, excluding Saturdays and Holidays; and two chapters on the Eve of the New Month, as well as during public fasts and during the Ten Days of Repentance.

2. During the nights of Pentecost and Hoshana Rabba the entire Holy Mishnah Society shall study together all the night through. The wardens shall decide what to study. Absentees shall be fined 18 gross Polen.

3. During the nights of Public Fast Days, members named in alphabetical order shall keep watch in groups of two, before midnight and after midnight. Exemption from this duty may be obtained by sending a substitute or by paying a fine of 18 gross Polen.

4. If a member is in town and does not attend the stated study sessions, he is to be fined 1 gross Polen for each absence unless he has an adequate reason. If a member is away from town much of the time and is unable to attend his weekly dues shall be 3 gross Polen instead of the regular dues which were 1 gross Polen.

The entrance fee to the society was eighteen zlotys. The annual election was held at the same time as the siyum feast, and the following officials were designated: three electors, three wardens, one treasurer, two auditors. The weekly dues were one Polish groschen. The society provided a study session for the entire seven days of mourning in the home of its members. It also had special days for itself in the synagogue on the Sabbath when the Weekly Portion was Yitro.

One of the by-laws of this hevrah, dealing with the procedure to be followed after a member's death, is worth noting:

> May the Lord, blessed be He, fulfill the days of every one of our brethren. After his days will have been fulfilled the entire association shall betake itself to the house of the demised and there pray for his soul, study six chapters of the Mishna and recite Kaddish de Rabbanan (a special rabbinic version) for his soul for a period of seven days after his death. During the year following, immediately after completing the study of the chapters selected to start with the letters of the name of the deceased, the entire Society shall say the appropriate prayer for the purity of his soul and shall end with reciting the Kaddish de Rabbanan.

To carry out this duty, the society was divided into units, or "troupes" (*degalim*), of a minimum of ten each, which performed their tasks in turn.[33]

Hevrah Mishnayot of Gombin

In the pinkas of the Hevrah Mishnayot of Gombin, we are told that the society was founded in 1794. In the opening pages of the pinkas, there is an introduction setting forth the merits attained through the study of the Mishnah, with passages quoted from Maimonides and other sources to show the benefits inherent in Mishnah study. The pinkas contains entries going back to the year 1867. We therefore have a most interesting record of this society, covering seventy-three years. It is apparent that the members all were regarded as men of considerable learning. In 1806, it was ordained that only those who were well versed in the Gemara and in the commentaries of the Tosafot could quality for membership. Through the years there are special entries boasting the names of great rabbis and scholars who were admitted as members. It is also to be noted that the members were quite well-to-do, because there were surplus funds in the treasury, which were invested, with the profits used to replenish the library. The society also used its surplus funds to invite all the learned poor of the community to its annual feast. This was the established practice. In 1839 an attempt was made to abolish it, but without success. The place and importance of this society were so secure that when, in 1840, an attempt

was made to start another Hevrah Mishnayot in Gombin, it was completely
foiled. Members were held to a strict discipline, and when one of them
spoke insultingly of the Hasidim of Ger, he was fined and had to make
a public apology.[34]

(7) HEVROT FOR THE STUDY OF TALMUD

The crown of all associations for study was the Hevrah Shas, which
devoted itself to the study of the Talmud. We shall have opportunity to
examine the minute-books of eleven such associations. They range in time
over a century and a half, beginning with the middle of the eighteenth
century and coming down to the twentieth century. They represent communities in Moravia, Russia, Poland, Palestine, and also America.

Hevrah Shas of Helishau

The pinkas of the Talmud Society of Helishau, Moravia, records the
fact that this association was organized on Monday, sixteen days in Sivan,
1759, by twenty-six men.

In the preamble to the takkanot the reasons for the organization of this
society are given. Because of the troublous times and the difficulty of
earning a livelihood, little time is being devoted to the study of the Written
Law and the Oral Law.

> Therefore in order that the Torah should not be forgotten from our
> mouths and from the mouths of our children, and in order that God
> should create in us a clean heart and a new spirit, we, whose names
> are signed below, have banded ourselves together, and we have de-
> termined to set aside fixed times for the study of Torah so that our
> souls may be nourished as we have been commanded by our sages.
> May God reveal to us the glory of His Torah, and may those who will
> attend be aided by Heaven. Thus our enactment will be established by
> these regulations which we write down for our society.
>
> This is the first decision we have agreed upon. It shall be the duty
> of all whose names are appended here to gather daily in a home to
> study with concentration one page of the Gemara with the commen-
> taries of Rashi, Tosefot, and the Maharsha. We have decided to begin
> with the tractate Berkahot. May God grant that even as we are inspired
> to begin the study of the Talmud, we shall be able faithfully to con-
> tinue until we complete the study of the Talmud.

The members shall assemble at midday, i.e., from the sixth hour to the seventh hour, and if the period of study continues longer, then a greater blessing will be ours. [Note: This was also the practice in Frankfurt, when they would stop their work at noon and go to the study sessions.]

The place of meeting shall be at the home of the gabbai. Each year a new gabbai shall be elected by lot. This first year the sessions shall be at the home of David Segal.

Each day another member shall recite the page. For this reason we have ordained that each member shall prepare the lesson daily most carefully with all its commentaries so that if he should be chosen by lot to lead in study that day he should not fall short in the requirements. If he is not fully prepared he shall pay a fine of three kreutzer to the treasury of the society. We have also ordained that any member who became negligent by not attending and his seat is vacant during the session, he shall pay a fine of one kreutzer. An exception will be made in the case of a member who is on a journey or is ill, in which case no fine will be exacted.

On Sabbaths and festivals the time of study will be three hours after midday so as not to disturb the Oneg Shabbat [Sabbath delight], since a nap on the Sabbath is a delight. On Erev Shabbat, when people are very busy, the time of study shall be in the morning immediately after the morning services in the synagogue.

These are the days when teachers shall take holiday—days on which there shall be no sessions: Erev Yom Kippur, Erev Tisha be-Av, Tisha be-Av, Purim, and the Fast of Esther.

We have also decided that during the winter months, when the nights are long and the days short, the time for study shall be at night after the evening service.

We have further ordained that if, God forbid, one of our members shall die, the place of study shall be at that member's home.

It has also been agreed that each year a new gabbai shall be chosen. According to his word all matters should be conducted. The treasury shall be in his keeping, and the sessions for study shall be at his home. We have also obligated ourselves to pay each week one kreutzer into the treasury, and the time of payment shall be each Erev Shabbat and at the latest at the end of the month. No one shall violate this regulation for our sages have written, "No one shall transgress" [Meg. 2a].

It shall be the duty of each gabbai, at the termination of his year in office, to arrange for a festive seudah out of the funds of the treasury.

God forbid that we should miss a single day of study. Even if most of the members are absent, and even if only one member is left in the city, he must repair to the meeting place to study the assigned lesson for that day.

We have further decided that if any one of the undersigned shall withdraw, he should be fined six edomim.

All the conditions above we have impressed upon ourselves with the greatest eagerness of spirit and without any coercion, but on the contrary with a perfect heart and with a willing soul and with a consenting mind.[35]

Hevrah Lomdei Shas of Kovno

The pinkas of the Learners of the Talmud Society of Kovno states that it was founded in 1824. The beautifully illuminated title page gives the purpose of its formation:

We the undersigned are brought together by bonds that will endure into an association for the work of righteousness and for the performance of a great mitzvah in which one will strengthen the other and say, "Be strong and be zealous in the Oral Law." We, the undersigned, as members of the Hevrah Lomdei Shas, shall study a page of the Gemara daily in the bet ha-midrash of our community immediately following the morning services so that we shall be going from strength to strength [i.e., from prayer to study]. We shall begin as soon as the Mishnah Association has completed its studies so that thereby we shall be ascending in holiness from the Mishnah to the Gemara.

We, the undersigned, further pledge ourselves to try with all our might to come for the morning services to the bet ha-midrash in which we hold our study sessions, thereby bringing further brotherliness into our camp. Let each one follow the lesson in accordance with the understanding which God has granted him, and let no one enter into lengthy arguments and dialectics [pilpulim] until after the required daily page has been studied, thereby avoiding any waste of time during the lesson. We obligate ourselves to pay weekly dues. The money shall be entrusted to a treasurer, and from it we shall purchase sets of the Talmud with commentaries. May God grant that even as we began the study of the Talmud on the day after this last Yom Kippur, so shall the Almighty enable us to complete it in its entirety. Dated the sixth day of Hanukkah, 1824, in Kovno.

There are twenty-four ordinances, of which the first thirteen were formulated at the time of organization, while the remaining number were adopted in subsequent years. Several of these ordinances are of special interest. The first deals with a self-imposed tax on clothing:

At a duly constituted meeting of our society, held on the eighth day of Tevet, 1827, it was unanimously decided that each member shall voluntarily contribute to the treasury the sum of one kopeck for every new large garment whose cost shall be one ruble or over. [A large garment was defined as an overcoat, a fur coat, or a hat.] This shall be in force through next Passover, and at that time this matter will be up for reconsideration.

In order to insure regularity of attendance, the following rule was adopted in 1827:

Whereas, according to ordinance #2 in our pinkas, a fine of one gross Polen is assessed against a member who fails to come daily to study the required page of the Talmud and to stay through the completion of the study period, and whereas this regulation is one by which the majority cannot abide because the fine is too great, therefore be it resolved that henceforth, if a member does not attend at least two times during the week right after the morning services, he shall be required to pay a fine of one half gross Polen.

However, this revision apparently did not satisfy the members either, for only six months later they repealed the revised ordinance and reverted to the original regulation.

The material well-being of the members must have been on the increase, because in 1829 the minimum entrance fee for new members was raised from three rubles to six rubles. In 1832 the fee was raised to nine rubles. An exception was made, however, in the case of any applicant for whom this sum was excessive, provided he was "a great scholar and a pious man." [36]

Hevrah Shas of Bialystok

In the city of Bialystok, a group of learned Jews had been meeting daily for nine years to study a page of the Talmud in the bet ha-midrash at the home of Reb Yechiel Dov Wilkowisky. On the sixteenth of Heshvan, 1865, they held a feast to celebrate a siyyum ha-gadol, marking the completion of the study of the entire Talmud. On that happy occasion they decided to formalize their association by founding a Hevrah Shas. They chose five electors, who in turn appointed the following officials: secretary and keeper of the pinkas, treasurer, two keepers of the takkanot, and an auditor. There were eighteen founders of this society, and every time a new member was admitted, his name and date of election were listed with the signatures of the officials.

The takkanot of the society are nineteen in number, written in the form of an acrostic of the Hebrew alphabet, beginning with Alef and continuing till Kaf. The Preamble states that "these ordinances shall serve to bind the membership into an enduring bond and to bend the shoulders of each of us to the yoke of the Torah day by day." The ordinances are as follows:

1. Upon us the founders, and upon those who will later be elected into our midst, thre is imposed the duty to study every single day one page of the Talmud with the commentary of Rashi following the order of the tractates of the Talmud. When, God willing, we shall complete the study of the Talmud, we begin again and continue till we finish again, and so on we shall always complete and begin over again the study of the Talmud. We are not to study the daily page on Erev Pesah and Erev Yom Kippur, as we have already been commanded by our sages to lessen one's studies because of the sacredness of the festivals.

2. We are to study the daily shiur in a group in the bet ha-midrash after the morning prayers both summer and winter without any change. He who will not be able to attend the study session shall continue with his studies in private so that he shall complete the tractate being studied in time for the siyyum in the bet ha-midrash. It is the duty of each member to be present at the siyyum.

3. He who absents himself even once a week, without cause, shall be fined at the discretion of the officials. If he continues in his absence for a month, and shows no interest, it is the duty of the officials to expel him from the society, and he cannot be readmitted.

4. We have agreed that at the conclusion of the study of a tractate,

at the siyyum, we shall eat sweets and drink wine, in order to increase the joy and to make a Seudah at the conclusion of the study of the tractate. When, God willing, we shall complete the study of all the tractates of the Talmud, we shall make a Great Feast [*seudah gedolah*] on the day of the siyyum. On the day when we begin anew, and also on the next day, shall the rejoicing continue.

5. We have agreed that the expenses for the celebration of each feast and of the Great Feast shall be borne out of the pockets of the members. The supervisor shall supervise these festivities, to see to it that they are conducted with the decorum suitable for such occasions.

6. The conduct of the elections shall follow the procedures prevalent in Israel and shall take place each year at the time of the siyyum. There shall be a suitable urn and five slips of paper, and the names that are drawn first from the urn shall be the electors. They shall have the authority to appoint the other officials required by the society. . . .

7. The electors must make their appointments on the day of the election, or at the latest on the morrow. They shall appoint the gabbaim and other officials, and shall inscribe their names in the pinkas. It is understood that the electors must not prolong making the appointments two days beyond.

8. The electors shall appoint three gabbaim who shall direct and guide the affairs of the society, and also three supervisors who shall act in the absence of the gabbaim.

9. There shall also be appointed a keeper of the pinkas, in whose keeping the pinkas shall be entrusted during his term of office. He shall also be the auditor, together with the supervisor, to render a financial report before the ballots are drawn and to keep the records in the pinkas.

10. All the officials together must plan and govern the affairs of the society. Should they desire to institute a new takkanah, they must augment their number with five members-at-large, and if agreeable to all, the new regulation shall be ordained. After that no member is permitted to violate the new regulation.

11. No new member shall have the right to express an opinion, to participate in the election, to stand for office, or to vote, for the first two years of his membership. After that he shall be fully accepted and inscribed in the pinkas, and shall have the privilege to voice an opinion and to vote.

12. He who wishes to be admitted into our society but, God forbid, does not have the money to pay the initiation fee, then if he comes to learn every day with regularity until they finish a whole tractate, it shall be within the power of the electors at that time, to admit him even without the payment of the initiation fee in order to increase and exalt the Torah.

13. Power is hereby granted by all the undersigned to punish those who violate these regulations, or who foment quarrels and disturb the peace, or, God forbid, cast aspersions on another member of the society, by the payment of a fine, or another punishment, or even removal from membership. This shall be at the discretion of the elected officials and any five members of the society when it affects a new member, and at the discretion of the elected officials and the majority of the members when it involves one of the charter members.

14. When one of our members dies, we take upon ourselves to hold services in the house of mourning for two weeks with a full quorum of ten from our own membership. During Sheloshim [the thirty days of mourning], our members will recite the Kaddish after the study periods; the Memorial Prayer will be chanted the first year each Sabbath, and the date of the Yahrzeit shall be inscribed in the pinkas as an everlasting remembrance. Memorial Prayers shall also be recited at each *siyyum ha-gadol*. It is the duty of the elected officials to enforce this regulation with the utmost care.

15. It is our duty to give every encouragement to anyone who wishes to study the fixed shiur with us day by day. Let him begin and finish the whole Shas with us and faithfully perform his obligations for daily study with us. Such a man we shall admit to our society at the completion of the study of the Shas without any initiation fee, even if he can afford to pay.

16. It is the duty of the supervisor to supervise and enforce all the words contained in this pinkas, as well as any new regulations

that may be enacted in the days to come for the common good. We, the undersigned, have resolved to be on guard and to strengthen our work. May God be our help so that we may learn, teach, and observe the words of our sacred Torah and the words of our sages. May we go up to Zion with song, and may we, whose beginnings are small, behold the increase of our latter end.

17. We hereby make it known that all the possessions of the society, whether money, books, or other items, belong exclusively to the entire corporate body, and no individual shall take anything for himself.

18. We have agreed that all the appointees whom the electors shall choose during the time of the election shall not have the right to decline and refuse to serve.[37]

Hevrah Shas of Zhagory

Among the noteworthy ordinances of this society are the following:

1. Members shall study each day one page of the Talmud with the commentary of the Tosafists.

2. A reader to be appointed by the electors shall learn the lesson [shiur] aloud.

3. No questions shall be asked during the lesson.

4. The times for study shall be: in winter, immediately after the evening services; in summer, during the hour following the after-noon services. . . .

11. The place of study shall be the first table situated on the south side of our synagogue. . . .

19. Those who cannot recite the lesson before the society shall not be admitted unless they pay double weekly dues.

The entrance fee of the society was fifteen rubles. Elections were held during the Intermediate Days of Passover, at which time the following officials were designated: three electors, two wardens, one treasurer, two auditors. The weekly dues were one gross Polen, and the annual society banquet was held at the time of the siyyum.[38]

Hevrah Shas of Grodna

The regulations of this society provided that the Talmud with its Rashi commentary should be studied during the winter in the evening and during the summer after the morning services. One of the ordinances tells us that:

Whereas in late years our association has shown signs of succumbing to the burdens of earning a livelihood, so that we are unable to assemble for the study of the Talmud regularly, we have decided to allot to each member of our Holy Society the task of completing for himself several pages of the Talmud, so that the entire Talmud may be completed by the Festival of Simhat Torah.

When this society acquired a set of Talmud, it was ordained that unless members paid their full dues they would forfeit their part ownership in the set. Nonmembers were prohibited from using the society's library.

The entrance fee for new members was three rubles. The annual elections were held between the third and fifth days of Sivan, at which time the following officers were chosen: five electors, three wardens, two treasurers, three auditors, four supervisors. The weekly dues were five groschen.[39]

Hevrah Lomdei Torah, Shas u-Mishnayot of Safed

In the preceding sections we discussed societies that studied Talmud and societies that studied Mishnah. Now we come upon an unusual group whose learning program focused upon both these massive bodies of Jewish lore, the Association of the Students of the Torah, Talmud, and Mishnah at the famous Ari Synagogue in Safed. The pinkas of this hevrah is in the Ari Synagogue.[40] From it we learn many interesting facts. The hevrah was founded in 1903; its purpose is described in a long, beautiful preamble, which concludes by expressing the firm resolve that the members will complete the study of the entire Talmud once each year, and in addition will complete the study of the Mishnah once each month or once each quarter of the year. Among the takkanot of this hevrah, the following are of special interest:

1. *The Order of Study*

There shall be a daily shiur in Talmud and Mishnah according to the following order:

a. The tractates of the Talmud shall be assigned each year to the members. Each is to study his tractate daily so that by the end of the year the members together can hold a siyyum to celebrate the study of the entire Talmud.

b. The Orders of the Mishnah shall likewise be assigned four times each year to the various members, each studying his assigned part daily. At the end of the quarter, all the members together shall have completed the study of the Six Orders of the Mishnah and shall hold a siyyum.

c. The dates for holding the siyyums shall be as follows: On the fifth day of Av, which is the Yahrzeit of the Ari, there shall be held the annual siyyum of the Talmud and also the first siyyum of the Mishnah. On the first day of Hanukkah there shall be the second siyyum of the Mishnah. On the seventh day of Adar, commemorating the death of Mosheh Rabbenu, the third siyyum of the Mishnah. On Lag ba-Omer, the thirty-third day of the counting of the Omer, in commemoration of Rabbi Simeon bar Yohai of Meron, there shall be held the fourth siyyum of the Mishnah.

d. Each siyyum shall be a convocation of all the members. At its conclusion the gabbai shall distribute the assignments for the next period of study.

2. *The Administration of the Hevrah*

a. The head of the hevrah shall be Rabbi Raphael, the *av bet din* [chief of the Jewish court] in Safed, and all shall be governed by his word.

b. If anyone wishes to become a member, he shall be interviewed by a committee of three, and they shall determine his qualifications and the amount of his entrance fee into membership.

c. The lay leader shall be the gabbai, who may serve for three years, and the election shall be held secretly at the annual siyyum.

d. The accounts shall be kept by the gabbaim of the synagogue, who shall enter into our pinkas, under their signatures, a semi-annual statement of our finances. If there is a surplus, it should be used for the repair of the books and the synagogues.

e. The gabbai shall record in the pinkas the study assignments given to each member.

3. *The Activities of the Hevrah*

a. All the members shall be bound together in one band and shall live with one another in fraternity and peace, each helping one another; and God forbid that our members shall harbor hatred one toward another.

b. On the Sabbaths when the Decalogue is read, a Mi Sheberakh prayer shall be made for our hevrah, for its leaders and members, invoking God's blessings upon them.

c. At the quarterly siyyum observance, if the members so decide, there shall also be held a *seudah shel mitzvah* [feast], the expenses to come out of the treasury and from taxing each member.

d. In addition to the entrance fee, each member shall pay quarterly dues.

e. If a member gets sick, he should be visited, and if he needs any financial aid, he should be helped from the treasury.

f. If a sick member is on his deathbed, the members shall attend him to recite the Viddui [Confessional], and a minyan shall stand by until the departure of his soul.

4. *Memorial for the Last Days*

Provisions are made for honoring and memorializing the dead by requiring the members to attend the funeral and at the house of mourning; to learn the Mishnah in memory of the departed for the first thirty days and also at the Yahrzeit. This shall be done for each member even if he left nothing in his will to the society. However, it is expected that if a member or his survivors can afford it, some funds should be willed to the society.

Hevrat Yeshivat Bar Yohai of Safed

Another unusual association, combining the twofold duties of study and prayer in its program, was the Hevrat Yeshivat Bar Yohai, founded in Safed in 1890. It was organized by 120 members who were devotees of the great rabbi of the second century, Rabbi Simeon bar Yohai, who was the reputed author of the basic kabbalistic work, the Zohar, and whose tomb in nearby Meron has been a place of pilgrimage for his disciples throughout the centuries. The story of this unusual society is printed in a book appropriately entitled *The Gates of Torah* [Study] *and Tefillah* [Prayer], and its purpose is more fully described in these words:

> We are to study the Zohar, the Shas, and the *Shulhan Arukh,* and we are to hold the siyyum [the feast of completion of these studies] each year in Meron at the tomb of our master, the Divine Tanna, Rabbi Simeon bar Yohai. In addition, we are to make a pilgrimage there each Erev Rosh Hodesh, on Rosh Hashanah and Yom Kippur, and also on other specified occasions, in order to pray there for the well-being of our members and of the whole House of Israel.

The society always had at least 120 members so that it could send a different minyan (prayer quorum of ten men) to learn and study at Meron each Rosh Hodesh. Every year, on the seventh of Adar, the birthday of Moses, the society met; at that time, each member was assigned a separate portion of the Zohar to study, and thus, when the siyyum was held in Meron on the Yahrzeit of bar Yohai, the members would have together studied the entire Zohar. What is most unusual is the fact that these students of the Kabbalah, who revered bar Yohai, were also students of the Halakhah and revered Rabbi Joseph Karo and his great work, the *Shulhan Arukh.* Every year, on the thirteenth of Nisan, they held a siyyum in the Rabbi Karo Synagogue and then went to visit his grave in the Safed cemetery. Similarly, they held an annual siyyum of the study of the Shas on the eighth day of Hanukkah.

The society's treasury paid the expenses of those who made the pilgrimages from Safed to Meron on the required occasions. Any guests who accompanied the members on the pilgrimage were treated to tea and sugar without charge. The society had three categories of membership, depending on the sum paid in annual dues: *haver temidi* (permanent member), *haver nikhbad* (honored member), and *haver meyased* (foundation member). Each category of membership had its prescribed benefits and privileges, both in life and after death.[41]

(8) HEVROT IN AMERICA

Since there were associations for learning in every land of Jewish habitation, this vital institution quite naturally found its way to America as the waves of Jewish immigration to the new land began to swell and grow.

We know little of any hevrot that may have been founded in the early days when the Sephardim were settling in this country. But beginning with the migration of German Jews in the 1840s such societies were founded, and with the great migration of Russian and East European Jews from the 1880s on, their number multiplied greatly. In 1841 several members of the Spanish-Portuguese congregation, Shearith Israel, in New York, started an adult school, the Hebrew Literary and Religious Library Association. Classes were held in Hebrew reading and translation and also in the laws and customs of Judaism. In 1846, Rabbi Max Lilienthal organized a Hevrah Shas in New York. In the 1850s Rabbi Abraham Joseph Ash gave shiurim—lectures on Talmud—in his Beth Hamidrash Synagogue, which later became the Beth Hamidrash Hagadol of New York. While New York City was the largest center of Jewish life, such societies sprung up in other American cities as well. In Rochester, New York, which became a center of the tailoring industry, there existed a Tailors' Hevrah for chanting the Psalms. In Chicago a Hevrah Mishnayot and a Hevrah Shas were established in 1894. In Philadelphia, as early as 1882, there were hevrahs for the study of Bible, Mishnah, Talmud, *Ein Yaakov,* and *Shulhan Arukh.*[42]

Fortunately, it has been possible to obtain the pinkasim of some of the hevrot in America, and we shall have an opportunity to learn from them how this Jewish tradition was carried forward from the Old World into the New World.

Hevrah Shas of Bnai Zion of Providence, Rhode Island

We turn first to the Jewish community of Providence, Rhode Island, where a Talmud society was established in the last quarter of the nineteenth century. From the pages of this society's pinkas, written in Hebrew, we learn the following important facts, as summarized by Mr. Bernard Segal, a local Jewish teacher and writer:[43]

1. The Chevrah (Society) Sons of Zion was organized in 1875 by 17 immigrants from Lithuania, nine of whom were married, and eight of whom were single.

2. This Society bought the land for a Jewish cemetery in Moshsuck the following year, and founded the Chevrah Kadisha, the Burial Society.

3. It was not until 1882 that the Society had a permanent house of worship for Sabbath and the holidays on Canal St. The "Shul" was in use until the Orms Street building was finished in 1892 at a cost of $23,500.

4. Mr. Salmen Feinberg served as the first spiritual guide of the Congregation, though he was not an ordained Rabbi, and he offered his services free.

5. The first official Rabbi was Reb Nathan Yehudah Rabinowitz, who came from a little town near Kovno (now Kaunas), Lithuania, in 1887.

6. Rabbi Rabinowitz and his relative, Reb Yosef Shoel Rabinowitz, organized the Chevrah Shas, a society for the study of the Talmud. Of this Reb Yosef it is said he was a fiery preacher and a man of deep convictions, as well as a brilliant scholar. He refused to make his learning a source of livelihood, and earned his meagre income by door-to-door peddling. His evenings were devoted to teaching and to studying with the members of the Chevrah Shas, without remuneration.

Noting that the hevrah's long list of regulations took up several pages in the pinkas, Mr. Segal selected several a being of particular interest:

1. Members are pledged to come to the synagogue and to study a page of the Talmud every day.

2. The members are to live together in friendship and in brotherhood.

3. Each member pays weekly dues of five cents.

4. When a member is sick, the Chevrah appoints two brethren to spend the night at his bedside. They are to arrive at the home of the sick member at 10:30 P.M. and remain with him until 5:30 in the morning.

5. Once a year the members of the Chevrah Shas hold their own Sabbath services at which every member is given an Aliah; that is, he is called up to the Reader's desk and a portion of the Torah is read for him.

Reb Yosef Shoel Rabinowitz, mentioned in the quotation from the pinkas, became a living legend in the Jewish community of Providence. In

1948, Mr. Segal wrote this beautiful memorial tribute after visiting the grave of Rabbi Rabinowitz:

A cemetery is a morbid place to visit on a bright Autumn day. And the day was a rare one when I stood at the headstone of a man I never knew. I stood and meditated on the mystery of life and death, and of the unseen threads that bind the living to the dead. Here lie the remains of Reb Joseph Saul Rabinowitz, a man I never knew; yet I am haunted by his name and by his deeds. As far as I could determine there are no descendants of his in Providence, and very few of our older citizens know of him. Only here on the head stone over his grave on Moshassuck cemetery, and on the pages of the Book of Records of the Sons of Zion Synagogue, is his name inscribed with reverence.

The headstone is a white thin slab, eroded considerably by the rains and the winds of fifty-five summers and winters on this old cemetery beside the Lonsdale Mills, in Smithfield. The letters will not remain legible much longer; grains of sand adhere to the finger tips on touching the stone. In two places the elements have bored holes through the slab. In all likelihood the monument will not be replaced when it crumbles all together.

Yet there was a time when hundreds came to listen to words of wisdom and learning from the lips of him who rests here.

I like to think of him as the pioneer in Adult Education in Providence, though Reb Yoseph Shoel would shudder at this appelation. He came to our city from a little town in Lithuania where the study of the Torah, of the Talmud and of the Mishnah was as common as breathing. And as essential, too, for a full, meaningful life. A lonely man was Reb Yoseph Shoel, and a poor man.

We are told that he peddled from house to house in the manner of all newcomers at the end of the last century. We are also told that he was not a well man. Think of him knocking on doors of strangers and asking in a strange tongue for something to sell or to buy. Think of him as suffering humiliation, drinking the bitter cup of ridicule. It was not uncommon in those days for youngsters, and also for not-so-young hoodlums to throw insults and even more tangible objects at Jew peddlers.

But then came eventide. Ah, the Minchah time at the Shul. Reb Yoseph Shoel the peddler raises his voice in chanting. Reb Yoseph Shoel praises his creator. And after the evening prayers, who is it

*sitting at the head of the long table reading from the large folios in clear
ringing accents? Is this the peddler Reb Yoseph Shoel? Yes, it is Reb
Yoseph, the teacher of Talmud, leading the Chevrah Shas, the Society
for the study of the Talmud which he organized.*

Every evening, summer and winter, they congregate, the members of
the Chevrah in Providence, to spend their leisure in the study of the
books written by Rabbis and scholars in Babylonia centuries before. It
is more than a class room. It is a club, a fellowship. Fellow members
are visited in sickness, helped in adversity, and remembered when they
pass on.

The Chevrah Shas of the congregation Sons of Zion erected a monument to the founder and teacher of the Society when he passed on. A
monument in stone and in words, which I, a stranger, came to visit
more than half a century later, and to decipher and to translate the
testimony to the man whom nobody remembers today. I feel a strong
kinship to this pioneer teacher, this planter of seeds of Jewish learning
in new virgin soil. And I repeat the words inscribed by an anonymous
man of letters on the thin slab of white sandy stone on Moshassuck
cemetery;

Even the stone cries out of a wall,
For Joseph is not. Alas he left the living.
He went back too soon, went back, went up to heaven,
But his spirit remains alive in our midst.
For his deeds, yea, all his achievements for his fellowmen cause him to
    be remembered.
From afar his feet carried him to sojourn here.
Whenever his brothers sought him in the House of God, they found
    him therein.
He taught the Law of the Lord. With his might he extended the Revela-
    tion of God.
Out of his great knowledge he preached morning and evening to his
    brothers.
Before confraternities he made Talmud and Mishnah as harmonious as
    twins of gazelle.
At the sound of his voice men gathered, and held council upon the
    foundation stone.
How great is his achievement, his glory, and his constancy.
His memory is a blessing, and very great is his reward.

He is the distinguished scholar, descendant of a noble family, scion of martyrs, our Master Joseph Saul son of Rabbi Hayyim Solomon Rabinowitz, whose memory is a blessing of the city of Krakinovo.
He went to his eternal rest on the Sixteenth of Mar-Heshvan, in 5654, Anno Mundi, in the reckoning of centuries.[44]

Hevrah Mishnayot and Ein Yaakov of the Synagogue Kesher Israel of Providence, Rhode Island

The Mishnah and *Ein Yaakov* Society of the Kesher Israel Synagogue in Providence was founded in 1907. Its large pinkas, with extremely beautiful decorations and Hebrew script, numbers some six hundred pages. The preamble and provisions are as follows:

With the help of God—The first day in the portion "And my soul shall live because of thee."
We the brotherhood . . . have gathered ourselves here in Providence. "In the multitude of people there is the king's glory." And all of us as one man took upon ourselves the yoke of the kingdom of heaven to delve in His perfect Torah day and night and we have organized a Chevra Mishnayes and Ain Yaacov amongst us to study every day in the evening and in the morning one chapter of Mishnayes and a few folios of Ain Yaacov and we pray to the God of Blessing and Praise to bless the work of our hands and that we may be worthy of seeing sons and grandsons engaging in Torah and Mitzvos for their own sake through our (efforts). And may our eyes see, when God returns, the captivity of our people and the coming of the Redeemer speedily in our days, Amen. So shall be His will.
These Are the Rules of the Chevra

1. The purpose of this Chevra and its goal is to study one chapter Mishnayes every morning and a few folios of Ain Yaacov every evening.

2. The members are obligated to live among themselves also in their private lives in peace, tranquility, brotherhood and friendliness.

3. If one of the members is visited after the visitation of all men, then there is an obligation on the members to accompany the body to his resting place and afterwards to come to his house and con-

sole his mourners, and the Gaboyim are required to send to his house, all during the Shiva, ten men from the Chevra to worship there in the morning and in the evening and to study Mishnayes and if God forbid he has no sons then the Chevra is required to appoint one of the Chevra in order to recite Kaddish the entire year, also the Yahrzeit shall be reordered in the record book and every year the Chevra is obligated to study in his honor Mishnayes on the day of the Yahrzeit.

4. The Sabbath of the Sidra of Naso is reserved as the Sabbath of our Chevra, then all the members shall assemble to worship together and each and every one shall be called to the Torah. And after a hundred years when members shall have passed away their souls should be remembered.

5. Every one of the Chevra takes upon himself the obligation to send 10 cents to the treasury of the Chevra each and every month. And as long as one is in arrears for one payment he shall have no right to take part in the elections.

6. The time of elections shall be once a year on the First Day of Shevat, and then they shall install for the entire year, two Gaboyim, a Treasurer, and a Secretary.

7. New members may be accepted every first day of a month. The new member is required to contribute to the Chevra's treasury on behalf of his appointment to the Chevra.

8. If God forbid, one of the members shall become ill, then there is a holy obligation on every one of the Chevra to visit him.

9. At all times of assembly the Chevra may institute new rules by a two-thirds majority of those assembled and according to the judgment of the members.

10. At important assemblies such as the election meeting or at the time of a Siyyum there is an obligation to read out loud before all of those assembled, all of the above rules.

11. Also all of the men whose hearts inspire them with wisdom to be inscribed on the record book of our Chevra.

These are the Rules of the Chevra

1. When one of the Chevra, God forbid, passes away, every member of the Chevra must go to worship in the house of the deceased the entire week in a minyan of people.

2. If one of the members cannot go to worship, for instance due to business, he will be required to pay $1.50 to hire someone to take his place. If not, the members are not obligated to go and worship in the house of the mourner after a hundred years. He will have to give $20.00 to the above Chevra (that is, if he wants the service of minyan after his demise.)

3. When a woman of the above Chevra passes away, God spare us, the heirs must give 10 dollars to Chevra, and if not, the members are not obligated to go there and worship and say Kaddish in the synagogue and at the cemetery.

In the hundreds of pages that follow, the pinkas contains all kinds of records, such as the names of the gabbaim, the names of the hundreds of members arranged alphabetically (first men, then women), and listings of memorials and Yahrzeit dates.[45]

The Beth Hamedrash Association of the Chizuk Amuno Congregation of Baltimore, Maryland

Also dating from the latter part of the nineteenth century is the society formed by members of the Chizuk Amuno Congregation in Baltimore, Maryland. In the minutes of the congregation it states:

It was on February 1, 1874, a little less than three years after the founding of the Chizuk Amuno Congregation which occurred on April 2, 1871, that there was formed within the Congregation the "Beth Hamedrasch Association." It melt in the Beth Hamedrash which was the ground floor of Exeter Hall and it drew up its Constitution which contained seven articles. Article No. 7 dealt with the Library and reads as follows:

"The Room of the Association shall be open to the public daily from 2 o'clock P.M. till Sundown and any member or visitor shall have free access to the books of the library but no books from the library shall be allowed to be taken away or home, unless by a member of the Association and not without having first asked the privilege thereof of the

Presiding Officer present, and of which a memorandum shall be kept by the Secretary but no member has a right to retain any book for a longer period than two weeks. Any book kept longer than two weeks shall subject the holder thereof to a fine of 25 cents per week, for each and every week for each book so retained."

The formal incorporation of the Beth Hamedrasch Association did not come until December 5, 1878, when the State of Maryland issued a "CERTIFICATE OF INCORPORATION." The following are quotations from this document:

"KNOW ALL MEN BY THESE PRESENTS, that we

Judah Rosewald	Henry W. Schneeberger
Philip Herzberg	Jonas Friedenwald
Henry S. Hartogensis	

hereby form a Corporation under the name of

"The Beth Hamedrasch Association of the City of Baltimore."

"We Do Further Certify, that the said Corporation so formed is a Corporation for Literary Purposes, under the General Laws of Maryland, Article 26 of the Code, and Supplements and Amendments thereto: That is to say, for encouraging and studying the Hebrew language and literature.

"We Do Further Certify, that the operations of the said Corporation are to be carried on in Baltimore City, Maryland, and that the principal office of the said Corporation will be located in Baltimore City, Maryland.

"We Do Further Certify, that the said Corporation has no capital stock, its funds being derived from fees, dues, contributions, etc."

"We Do Further Certify, that the said Corporation will be managed by six Directors:

Henry L. Cohen	President
Tobias Hartz	Vice-President
Jonas Friedenwald	Treasurer
Henry S. Hartogensis	Secretary
Dr. Henry W. Schneeberger, Hertz Oppenheimer	Electors[46]

Hevrah Mishnah of the Tifereth Israel Synagogue of Baltimore, Maryland

This hevrah, also in Baltimore, was founded in 1932; its takkanot contain the following regulations:

1. Every member is obligated to come to the study session daily. If he absents himself he shall pay a fine of 25 cents for each absence.

2. The name of the departed members shall be inserted on the Memorial Tablet. A chapter of the Mishna shall be studied in his memory for the entire first year after his departure and each Yahrzeit shall be kept thereafter.

3. On the Sunday after "Shabbos Bereshis" the annual elections shall be held for the ensuing year.

4. At this annual meeting new members may be admitted. The Admission Fee shall be three dollars or more according to his ability. Non-members of the congregation shall be charged one dollar more for membership.

5. Wives of members may become members and pay two dollars dues.

6. If members do not pay their dues for three months they shall be dropped from membership.[47]

CHAPTER

XIV

PICTURES OF JEWISH CULTURAL LIFE IN THE LAST CENTURY

From the writings of social historians and memoirists of our own time, there emerge a number of clear pictures of Jewish cultural life during the last one hundred years. While these sources are written in a variety of languages—Hebrew, Yiddish, German, English—and depict Jewish life in such diverse communities as Minsk and Vilna in Lithuania, Boisk in Latvia, Moscow in Russia, Mezerich in Moravia, and Jerusalem in the State of Israel, they nevertheless present a uniform pattern of Jewish experience. Its dominant characteristic is expressed in the word *lehrnen,* "to engage in learning." The late Maurice Samuel, noted author, lecturer, and translator, caught the precise meaning of *lehrnen* in his book, *In Praise of Yiddish:*

The Germanic *lernen* means both "to learn" and "to teach," and unless the context specifically points to a secular subject it implies only the sacred Jewish field. If one says of a man *er ken lernen,* "He knows (how) to learn" (itself an idiom for "He is a man of learning"), only the sacred books are implied, that is to say, all Jewish books ultimately related to Jewish thought on God and man. The question *ir hot amol gelernt?,* "Did you at one time learn?", means "Did you at one time attend a yeshiva (or receive equivalent instruction)?" If directed at secular subjects—and even general ethics would come under that heading—the Germanic *shtudirn* is in order, and the question would be *ir hot amol shtudirt?,* "Did you at one time study?", meaning, "Did you at one time attend a university?" One may, however, say *er lernt*

261

(*zikh*) *franteseyzish,* "He is learning French," as well as *er shtudirt frantseyzish,* but one cannot say *er shtudirt bobe metsiye* (a popular tractate of the Talmud).[1]

This preoccupation with learning was generally diffused among the populace and was usually centered either in a society for Jewish study in the synagogue or in a yeshivah.

(1) PICTURES PRESENTED BY CULTURAL HISTORIANS

We shall turn first to the Jewish communities of Eastern Europe. In a precise yet comprehensive portrait of the cultural life of Lithuanian Jewry, Dr. Max Grunwald, writing in German in 1925, says as follows:

"Learning" not for the sake of furthering the knowledge of worldly things, but because it is one's religious duty; "learning" not for professional training, but without practical goal—but only "to know" or "to be learned" because "he who learns, knows everything"; because "a Gemara head is fitted for everything"—this is the conception of learning among Jews.

Once the boys grow up, get married, become heads of families, and assume responsibilities for material needs, then learning first begins to assume a new role in their lives. One doesn't think of learning from a practical point of view, since each has his calling—tradesman, merchant, or worker. One studies in his spare hours; one learns in order to lift himself out of the daily world and to forget for a while the lowliness and weariness of daily life; one learns to fulfill God's will and for spiritual pleasure. Is there a higher delight than to learn? Where can one pour out his heart better than in a piece of Gemara, and where can the weariness of life be better forgotten than in learning? The Jews of Lithuania stand in daily strife. Day breaks and closes with deep anxiety: how to make a living and from what? But the end of the daily struggle is always in learning.

The cardinal point of the social life is the learning. When Jews come together they relate something about learning to one another—either about a *derashah* (sermon) or a "piece of Torah" heard in the synagogue from the preacher; or they talk about so and so who has gifted children, which implies that they learn well, or this one has a "good head," while the other is a *masmid* (diligent student). The many so-

cieties, the hevrot, in the city are organized for purposes of learning—
for Shas, *Hayyei Adam,* or Mishnayot. The workers' societies (guilds)
are also close to learning. Tailors, shoemakers, butchers, etc., have
their own associations and found their own synagogues because they
don't feel so much at home in the company of the more well-to-do
merchants and burghers. In the latter synagogues they could only
seldom aspire to get "the better aliyot." In their own bet ha-midrash
they feel at home—equals among equals—and their goal too was
learning. Each society had its rabbi. Between Minhah and Maariv he
held forth from the *Ein Yaakov;* Saturdays he expounded the Portion
of the Week, and from time to time delivered a sermon. Many societies
want more. They want to have students in their bet ha-midrash all the
time so that it will become a *makom shel Torah* (a place of Torah).
For this reason they bring *yeshivah bahurim* (yeshivah students) to
study in their bet ha-midrash. They provide "days" for them and maintain them with food and shelter.

The bet ha-midrash is open all day. Rabbi and yeshivah bahurim are
studying; others come too. The merchant comes too—drops his anxieties
to absorb a page of the Gemara. In the evening, at the end of a day's
work, the hum of voices becomes stronger in the bet ha-midrash; the
tired and discouraged come for afternoon and evening prayers and also
to study. At different tables the different societies gather—Shas, *Ein
Yaakov, Hayyei Adam,* etc. At some tables individual students sit and
"learn for themselves." On Saturdays, the hours after the afternoon
nap are best for learning. Rested, the atmosphere of the community
seems to be full of Jewishness; Sabbath rest disturbed only by melodies
of the chanting of Psalms and the sing-song of Talmud study. Out of
windows is heard the learning of Perek, or the sound of women in the
women's synagogue learning the *Tze'eneh u-Re-enah*—the blending
of disturbing melodies into a soulful sound.

The Yeshivah—From the yeshivah came forth many rabbis. But it
was not a rabbinical seminary. It was attended by all—by every type
of Jew. Everyone may and should come to learn. In the long history
of the yeshivot, no textbooks were written or methods developed. The
Talmud is open—let all come and learn it. Here Jews are educated
and molded. Here they sleep, eat, and learn. Mostly learn.[2]

In a Hebrew book published in 1901, Zevi Hirsch Halevi Kolk recalls the way of life in the generation just gone by. He presents us with an interesting picture of the material and moral life of Lithuanian Jewry in the latter half of the nineteenth century. In a section called "Bet ha-Midrash," "The House of Study," he writes:

> The bet ha-Midrash was the meeting place for the learners of the Torah. . . . Most of these houses of study were the cultural centers and the libraries for all who wanted to come and learn. Even the man whom God had blessed with wealth, and who had everything in his own home including many books, would prefer to go to the bet ha-Midrash to study. There no one would disturb him, and the temptation in his home to attend to worldly matters would be banished in the hum of many voices lost in study. There many books were spread open on the long tables. There the benches were filled with groups seated in study. Some learn Mishnah and some Gemara; others Aggadah, and some Bible or the books of ethics. From each group emanates the particular sing-song of the subject being studied. In other parts of the bet ha-Midrash young men, most of them so poor they have to "eat days," sit at the tables or stand leaning against the *shtender* and concentrate on their studies. Some of these young men form themselves into "night-watchers" so that throughout the night, as one of these groups leaves for a little sleep, another group enters to resume the learning. It is not only these young men who "stand in the House of the Lord in the nighttime," there are also older men who actually sit and live in the house of study all through the week and repair to their homes only for the Sabbath. Among these perpetual learners, are many well-to-do *baalei batim,* whose homes are filled with all that is good and who have soft and comfortable beds. They too often come and stay through the night in study. These men of prominence, together with the older men, serve as an example to the younger men. During the winter months, when the Sabbath sets in early on Friday afternoons and the Sabbath Eve was a long one, the bet ha-midrash was more than ever a place in which the Torah was exalted. Soon after the Sabbath Eve meal, people would take a short nap and then proceed to the house of study. The sexton had so arranged the lights that they burned all night. The tables would soon fill up and many had to stand. The sweet and holy chant of learning filled the air until the morning hour when it was time to recite the Shema. At these study tables, poor and rich sat shoulder to shoulder. Whoever would place his open book on the table

would acquire the right to that seat. The Torah cannot be defiled by pride and arrogance. In its presence all are humble. While at public worship, the rich man sits in his accustomed place of prominence up front, at the "Mizrah Wall," and no poor man would dare to move up and take his place near the rich man, yet at the study tables the rich man considers it an honor to sit with the poor man who is a fellow-learner and may excel him in learning. Through Torah study are the haughty humbled and the lowly exalted. Thus men of means and manual laborers would sit together united in the common pursuit of God's word.[3]

From another Hebrew source, by Rabbi Yaakov Lipschitz, we get a similar picture of the cultural life of Russian Jewry around the middle of the nineteenth century:

The houses of study and prayer, which were called klausen, were the gathering places for the general populace. In each of them there were men whose constant habit it was to arrive at four o'clock in the morning both winter and summer in order to study until the time for the morning prayers. . . . Among them were the "Pure in Mind" [nakiye ha-daat] who provided themselves with wax candles made so thin and long that they were about ten yards in length, and folded up in such a manner that the learner did not have to rekindle any candles or soil his hands with the fat. In the early hours of the morning more men would begin to arrive. Some would come one to two hours before the morning services and spend these hours in study. Only those who were day laborers would leave the klaus right after prayers. The rest would stay to learn either Mishnah, Gemara, or Ein Yaakov, and the general public for chanting the Psalms. The klaus would fill up with people again prior to the Minhah service. The interval between Minhah and Maariv was devoted by most of the people to study. Some of the elders would conduct groups in the study of the Bible with Rashi's commentary, or the Alsheikh. Young students who were already study-ing gemara would use this time to learn the Bible for they were con-sidered advanced enough not to require an instructor for Bible. Some would sit around to talk about the news of the day or about world events and the current wars. After Maariv and mostly in the wintertime, many would remain for an hour or two and join one of the several hevrot in the study of their special interest. . . .[4]

The various hevrot, such as the societies for the study of the Shas, the Mishnah, the Torah, or the Psalms, and also the various societies for charity, would each assemble at the respective homes of their gabbai on the late afternoons of Shemini Atzeret. After being treated to food and drink, they would form in processions and escort the gabbai with songs and dances to the synagogue to welcome the Simhat Torah festival and to rejoice in the Hakafot with the Scrolls of the Law. The celebration of the Hevrah Kadisha was the most elaborate. It was the most prominent and most prosperous of the societies, and the leading figures of the community would be invited to its observance. The gabbai, together with the rabbi, marched under a canopy in the procession to the synagogue to the accompaniment of waving flags and dancing feet. . . .[5]

It was the general practice for all elements in the community—the rich and the poor, the storekeepers and the artisans, as well as the working people—to attend public worship in the synagogue of their choice both morning and evening. Those possessed of greater leisure would remain for a period of learning after the morning services either in groups or privately. It was in the interval between Minhah and Maariv that the general populace would engage in study. The tables were crowded by the different hevrot. Some studied Bible; others *Ein Yaakov* or *Hayyei Adam* or *Menorat Hamaor,* or some other standard work on Jewish ethics. At times the studies were interrupted so that all could listen to a sermon by a magid—an itinerant preacher. From the fifteenth of Av, there began the season for study even after the Maariv service. This practice of studying at night would continue through the fall and winter up to Passover. The study tables were crowded with learners. The pious women obligated themselves to supply candles to all the synagogues. In some of these places of study, they would even arrange to keep the light of learning burning all through the night by arranging for several "watches." The first such group would learn from 9 P.M. to 1 A.M.; the second from 1 A.M. to 4 A.M. By that hour the members of the Anshei Maamad would arrive to carry on with their own program of study and prayers. . . .[6]

In order to keep the house of study supplied with books, the children were formed into clubs called *Pirhei Shoshanim* ["rose buds"]. These clubs were modeled after the hevrot of the grown-ups, the children electing their own officers and paying less than a kopek for dues each week. An adult would supervise each club. It was the practice of these young members to visit the home in which a new child was born in order to inscribe the name of the new-born into the pinkas of the club as a new "bud" on the Pirhei Shoshanim. Often the parents would make a donation to the club. In this way, the children would save enough money to buy a new set of the Talmud or the Rambam or the *Turim* for the bet ha-midrash. The presentation ceremony was elaborate. The new books would be carried by the children in a torchlight procession to the house of study, and there, in the midst of song and festivity, they were deposited in the book-cases. . . . It was therefore natural that each house of study was at the same time a library.[7]

The author summarizes:

The bet ha-midrash was thus the place of assembly for the learners and the house of prayer for all those who set aside a fixed time for study. It was a resting place for the weary and a refuge for the troubled. It was a shelter for the aged and poor and also a hospice for the wanderer. It was a house of life for those who were giving their lives to the study of the Torah.[8]

One of the most eminent Hebrew educators of our time, Professor Zevi Scharfstein, in his history of Jewish education, aptly depicts the European Jewish cultural scene of recent times:

The bet ha-midrash and the yeshivah were the higher institutions of Jewish learning. Young men studied in them until the time came for them to get married. In essence, however, the marital state and the responsibility for supporting a family did not constitute a bill of divorcement from one's studies. When a father sought a bridegroom for his eligible daughter, he would turn to the head of the yeshivah, describe the virtues of his daughter, detail his economic status and the number of years of support he could give to the prospective bridegroom. On the basis of such an interview the proper match was proposed. If there was no yeshivah in that town, the father would turn to a professional matchmaker—the shadchan—or to the local rabbi or a prominent communal figure. In every instance the request was made for a

young man who was a good "learner." In connection with the marriage
ceremony, the bridegroom would deliver a sermon to show his mastery
of Talmud and related subjects. After the marriage, the young husband
would settle down to further study, being supported by his father-in-law.
If the latter were well-to-do, he would even engage the best instructors
to learn with the young husband privately. If, however, the newlywed
were compelled to earn a livelihood, he would still manage during
leisure hours to go to the house of study morning or evening, to study
and to pray. Those whose economic level was lower and who became
artisans and laborers would likewise not discontinue their learning.
They would affiliate with one of the societies for study—either the
hevrah Mishnayot or the hevrah *Ein Yaakov* or the hevrah *Hayyei
Adam* and the like. They would attend daily to study or at times to
listen to a local or itinerant maggid. The study of the Torah was therefore the very curriculum of life.[9]

It is apparent from the above that parents were less concerned with
training their children to make a living than with training them to make
a Jewish life. Learning took precedence over worldly success. This was in
accord with ancient and modern Jewish teaching. Rabbi Meir taught:
"Give less attention to business affairs and devote yourself to Torah." [10]
Rabbi Judah ben Ilai said: "Whoever makes the study of the Torah primary and worldly affairs secondary, he will achieve prominence in this
world; while he who makes worldly affairs primary and Torah secondary,
he will achieve little in this world." [11] Rabbi Abraham Isaac ha-Cohen
Kook, the late Chief Rabbi of Israel, expressed the aim of Jewish education
in these words:

> The goal of Jewish education is to qualify man for his predestined role
> to lead the good and upright life. From earliest times, when, as the
> Bible tells us, our ancestor Abraham began "to call on the name of
> God," it has become our inheritance that the more deeply rooted there
> is in the heart of each man the habit of "calling upon the name of
> God," the more will the goodness and the uprightness of that man
> increase and the more will he be happy and a source of happiness to
> society. This historic Congregation of Israel has been chosen among
> all peoples to raise aloft this banner which proclaims that man's good-
> ness and uprightness is his supreme destiny and that the "calling on
> the name of God" is the most adequate discipline for the achievement

of this noble purpose. In order for this habit of calling on God's name to take deep root in the heart and soul of the individual and also of the entire nation, it becomes necessary to dedicate oneself to fixed programs of Jewish learning. This process must begin with earliest childhood when the child attends the Talmud Torah. . . . The preparation of man for the making of a living and for the battles of life are regarded among Jews as a secondary goal of Jewish education and not a primary one.[12]

The late Rabbi Simhah Asaf, after examining the vast source-material pertaining to Jewish education in all of post-biblical Jewish literature, concludes: "One single aim and one only did our people have for the education of their children, namely to make them whole Jews, knowing the Torah, fearing God, observing the commandments, and inculcating them with such a love of God that when called upon they would readily give up their lives for the sanctification of God's name."[13] This Jewish educational ideal of the ages was also the motivating power for the Jewries of many European lands in the last century.

(2) PICTURES PRESENTED BY MEMOIRISTS

From the writings of the cultural historians we turn to the more personal literary records of the writers of memoirs. These reminiscences paint beautiful word-pictures of the life lived by our parents and grandparents. Dr. Solomon Simon, in his autobiography, *My Jewish Roots,* recalls the days of his youth in his native town of Kalinkovitch near Minsk. Here are several excerpts:

Torah! Everybody talked about Torah. Psalms were Torah. Psalms were recited all the time. There was a special society of Psalm-Sayers. They were called "King David's Guards." Father was a Guardsman. On Sabbaths he got up at the crack of dawn, earlier even than Mother got up on weekdays to prepare the dough. "But no matter how early I get up," Father complained, "I never get there first. There are better Guards than I."

Before Shimon could walk he knew what Gemora meant, and Mishnayos, and Ein Yaakov, and Midrash. They were all Torah. Home was filled with reverence for it, though neither Father nor neighbor Zusie was a scholar. . . .[14]

In Azarich, Shimon was also much impressed by the Bes Midrash which was crowded every evening. The place remained brilliantly lighted till very late. In Shimon's home town, the synagogue was crowded only during the evening prayers, whereas in Azarich it truly came to life only after the evening prayers. Then nearly the entire male population came here to study, some in groups, others individually, and some young men remained all night. . . .[15]

But in an instant she changed her tone. "Benche," she now said gently, "you never realize how good I am to you. And what if I do shout sometimes, what of it? If my wishes for you were to happen to me, I'd be satisfied. What's bad if I send you to recite psalms? Last night you fell asleep at the table, so I woke you and told you to have another piece of chicken and another portion of tzimmes, because for six weeks you didn't have a hot meal. But don't forget that during these six weeks you were among Gentiles and you also didn't pray with a Minyan even once. So now I want you to have a taste of Psalms with the Society. Is that bad? The synagogue is cozy and bright and the chant of the Psalms warms the soul. Paradise, I suppose is wonderful, but a few Psalms here, I know, are not so bad either. I only wish that we women had a mitzvah like this to perform."

"A tongue!" father said admiringly. "You won't get lost in the hereafter either, with your tongue. You will give God such an argument that even He will have to concede that you're right. And then they will take you into the best salon, and I'm sure you'll drag me along with you."

Shimon heard Mother's laughter fluttering quietly in the air. "Stop it," she whispered, "It is time for your Psalms."

Father sighed: "A mehre I got! Sweet as sugar."

This was the only time Shimon ever heard words of tenderness exchanged between his parents.

The Sabbath afternoon which Shimon vividly recalls also involved the reciting of Psalms. The Psalm-Sayers Society included nearly all the artisans in town. On Saturdays they read the Book of Psalms three times. But while their morning and noon readings were done by the members of the Society solely, the late afternoon reading was joined by practically everybody in town. Psalm 119, which consists of one hundred and seventy-six verses was generally read when the sun had already set and dusk was gathering quickly.

Shimon was present only once during the morning recitation of the

Psalms, around noontime he was always in Heder; but he never missed the late Saturday afternoon readings which somehow became the summit of the Sabbath because of the intensity of the mood which they evoked.

Friday afternoons the town was in haste. As the hour of lighting the Sabbath candles approached, this haste to be rid of the weekday cares assumed a feverish quality. Saturday afternoons, after the traditional nap, the town surrendered to a mood of gentle melancholy. The Pirkei Avos and the Sabbath Minhah were said in tones that lacked the cheer of the morning. When the Zemiros were sung after the third traditional "Feast" of the day, the melancholy assumed a still more somber tone. The climax of the transition from Sabbath to weekday was reached in reciting the Psalms. Yoshe the Blind led the readings by common, unvoiced consent. He was reputed to know the Psalms by heart backward as well as forward. He would stand before the lectern, his blind eyes shut, enunciating each verse with great fervor, and the audience repeated after him. Most of the audience understood barely more than one out of ten words they recited; but they put their heart's longings into the melody to which they read the Psalms, and they made it express their sorrow at the departure of the day of spiritual and physical rest, and a plea to God to lighten the burden of their harsh lives, and an appeal to come to the rescue of the people of Israel, which was like a sheep beset by wolves. . . .[16]

"Just listen to what happened, Rabbi. I went into the Bes Midrash and there was Reb Mordecai Kroll sitting with the Talmud Society, and he turned to page six of Berakhos, and challenged them, 'It says here, these are the Tefillin of the Holy One. And what is written in them? "Who is like unto Thy people Israel, one nation in the world." To this Tosephes says: "That is why on the first day of Passover we read in the special prayers, the Tefillin added glory to His crown." And now, you Kalinkovitch scholars, who will tell me what is the question raised by Tosephes and what is the meaning of the answer?' "[17]

Another memoirist is the late Mr. Israel Matz, the well-known benefactor of Hebrew letters. Reminiscing about his young manhood in his native Lithuanian town of Kalvaria in the latter part of the nineteenth century, he writes as follows about the devotion to Jewish learning:

After maariv all the members of the Chevra Shas would seat themselves around a long table in the Beth Hamidrash and study together the daily page of Gemara. Thus they studied every night except Friday: point by point, systematically, page after page, chapter after chapter, tractate after tractate, until in seven years they ended the whole of Shas (the six divisions of the Talmud). In mighty satisfaction they celebrated the Siyum Hashas (the festival of completion) with much pomp and a huge banquet in which all balebatim (householders) of the city would participate, even those who never in their lives had studied a page of Gemara. To that banquet everyone would bring his own knife and fork and spoon. There was no dearth of potables either; and there was such merry-making as to keep in the memory until the next Siyum Hashas seven years hence.

Apart from the Chevra Shas there was a Chevra Mishnayis (for the study of the Mishna), for the not so scholarly. Often enough they found themselves in need of a rabbi to help them crawl through the chapter of Mishnayis after morning prayers.

There was also a Chevra Ayn Yankev, consisting of simple but decent Jews who would foregather in the Beth Hamidrash every Saturday evening after havdalah (the Sabbath exit prayer). Boruch Itzel, the Gemara-teacher, would read to them from the Ayn Yankev and immediately put it into Yiddish. To those sessions the men would repair with great eagerness—first because, after all, it is not becoming for any Jew to be altogether an amhaaretz (an ignoramus), and secondly, because they really drew great enjoyment from the beautiful tales in the Ayn Yankev which Reb Boruch Itzel with his gray beard and serene face, would so tenderly and luminously translate.[18]

The well-known Hebrew writer Daniel Persky reminisced about his native city of Minsk in an article in the Hebrew weekly *Hadoar*.[19] Describing "the synagogue only three houses from the home of my parents," a most unique institution known as "Reb Isser's Heder," he says:

Reb Isser could rightly be called in our terms, an educator of adults. He became known in Minsk and its environs as "The Workingman's Rabbi." He had a real genius for teaching the masses of the people and for disseminating Jewish learning among them. While still a young man, he began to gather about himself the common folk: manual laborers, tailors, shoemakers, blacksmiths, locksmiths, cokeburners, and the like. With their aid and with his actual participation, they built together the synagogue structure which later became known by his name. The Holy Ark which was placed in this synagogue was designed by Reb Isser and it took three years to carve it. Lovers of Jewish religious art would come from great distances to admire this Ark. This rabbi devoted all of his life and his energies to teach the Bible and the Talmud to the Jewish masses of Minsk. He transformed his synagogue into a heder— a school for adults. He would search out the grown-up people and learn with them in subjects ranging from the alphabet to the Gemara. As many as five hundred men from the working classes would sit before him for instruction. He would be on the bimah and learn a section of the Mishnah, which the students repeat in a loud chant that could be heard on the street. In the wintertime these sessions were held from two in the morning till eight in the morning, when the students had to go to work. In the summertime they learned for several hours before the morning service and also in the interval between Minha and Maariv. At the end of every seven or eight years, they would hold a siyyum to celebrate the completion of a tractate of the Mishnah or Talmud, to which the leading rabbis and communal heads were invited.

In this way, many people who were secularly illiterate became Jewishly cultured. They could even learn a page of the Gemara by themselves. Some who graduated from Reb Isser's Heder became scholars and men of learning. Many hundreds of Reb Isser's students, bearded and elderly men, loved and revered their master, who carried on his noble work for more than fifty years.

In concluding, Mr. Persky recalls that Reb Isser's synagogue was still standing when he visited Minsk in 1928.[20]

We get another interesting picture of Minsk at around the same period from the memoirs of the late Rabbi Yitzchak Nisenbaum, the famous preacher. In the winter of 1894, Rabbi Nisenbaum tells us, he decided to open a school for the young men of the city, many of whom were quite poorly educated. The school was located in the Bet ha-Midrash shel ha-Tzoviim, the Tanners' House of Study, and offered courses in Bible and Jewish history. Here is Rabbi Nisenbaum's description of the curriculum:

> ... the Portion of the Week, *Shulhan Arukh,* the Psalms, and Jewish history. Of course no one objected to my teaching the first two subjects. While there were some who might object to teaching the Prophets, they could not do so with the Psalms, for after all, many of them were part of the daily prayers. As for Jewish history, I managed to get that in by describing it as "Jewish history of the past." The sessions were held on Saturday nights from six to ten in the winter months, and on Saturday afternoons from one till Minhah time in the summer months. About a hundred attended this school.[21]

In the same volume, under the heading "A Quarrel Does Not Cancel the Study Session," Rabbi Nisenbaum recalls an incident of the days when he was in Babroisk. Two Jews had agreed to study a page of the Gemara together every morning in the bet ha-midrash. Something caused them to quarrel, and for a long time they were not on speaking terms. But during this entire period they did not interrupt their daily study sessions.[22]

The large Jewish community of Vilna deserves our special attention. In his book of memoirs, *Sefer ha-Zikhronot,* Eliezer Eliyahu Friedman tells of the flourishing Jewish cultural life he found in Vilna in the year 1880.

> Every evening at sundown the houses of study would become full of all kinds of people: Wagoners who had no time to take their horses and wagon home would leave them in the courtyard; porters still covered with the dust of flour or lime from the sacks they had carried all day; cobblers with their tanned hands; tailors with the needles still sticking in their garments; blacksmiths with their faces full of soot; carpenters and other artisans—all of them crowded the many houses of study, the klausen, and the synagogues which were to be found in the streets of Vilna. There they hearkened with love to the words of instruction in the Torah. After the day's toil, these men found strength and sustenance in the house of study.[23]

Friedman also speaks of the prevalence of hevrot—societies for study—singling out two of them because of their truly unusual character. The first was the Hevrat ha-Netz ha-Hamah—"The Society of the Rays of the Sun." Its members obligated themselves to climb to the hilltops outside Vilna every day before dawn in order to watch for the first rays of the sun, whereupon they would immediately constitute themselves into the necessary quorum for public worship and recite the Shema Yisrael. This they did in fulfillment of the verse in Scripture: "They shall fear Thee as long as the sun is upon them" (Ps. 72:5).

The second society was the Hevrat Shaalu Shalom Yerushalayim ("The Society for Seeking the Peace of Jerusalem"), whose purpose it was every year to send one of its members, chosen by lot, on a pilgrimage to Eretz Yisrael.[24] The most exceptional of these societies was the Asirei Kodesh ("The Holy Ten"). Its history went back some 250 years. At that time ten of the most gifted young scholars had been selected. Their material needs were provided for, and they gave themselves over entirely to learning. One of these ten became world-famous. He was Rabbi Shabbetai Cohen, the author of the *Shakh*—the commentary on the *Shulhan Arukh*. Through all the subsequent generations, ten such scholars were always studying in a curtained-off section of this society's klaus. The name of the society was derived from the verse in Leviticus 27:32, "The tenth shall be holy unto the Lord." [25]

The same author also recalls his visit to Kiev around 1896, at which time a group of merchants founded a new synagogue. Some of the leading personalities of the community worshipped at the Synagogue of the Merchants, and two hevrot were organized for the study of Shas and *Ein Yaakov*.[26]

One of the noted figures of Lithuanian Jewry was Rabbi Abraham Danzig, the author of the *Hayyei Adam*. In his book on Vilna, the historian S. I. Fin mentions that many *Hayyei Adam* societies were formed in Vilna and other Jewish communities after Rabbi Danzig's death in 1821.[27]

In his Yiddish article on the schools of Vilna, M. Shalit lists a number of well-known societies that functioned in that city at the beginning of the present century. The Society Tiferet Bahurim ("The Glory of Young Men") was chartered in 1907. Its aim was to attract young Jewish workers in particular, and the Jewish proletariat in general, to the knowledge and practice of Judaism. The number of students was about six hundred, and together with auditors reached as high as a thousand. Both young and middle-aged men were enrolled. The language of instruction was Yiddish, and the courses were given from 7:30 in the morning till 10 o'clock at night. In the morning courses were offered in Siddur and Mishnah. In the afternoon children who had already been taken out of the heder were given instruction in Humash with Rashi, Bible, and *Kitzur Shulhan Arukh.* The evening session was devoted to adults. In addition to the courses offered in the morning and afternoon sessions, there were courses in Jewish history, the meaning of prayer, and public speaking. On Sabbath and Festival afternoons there were informal sessions on the Haftarahs, *Ein Yaakov,* and Mishnah, and discourses by the rabbi. Before each of the Holy Days instruction was given in the laws and customs of the particular observance.

A similar society, the Zeirei Zion ("Youth of Zion") was founded in 1915. It sponsored an evening school for adults, and its aim was to afford young people of both sexes, whether they had learned Hebrew once and then forgotten it, or had never learned it, an opportunity to master the language and become familiar with some of its literature. The school attracted young people from the ages of eighteen to twenty-two, and the more than seven hundred enrollees were drawn from all classes of the community. The language of instruction was Hebrew whenever possible, and a tuition fee of two rubles a month was charged. Workers had to pay only one and one-half rubles, and free tuition was accorded to many. The sessions were held from six to eight in the evening during the winter, and from four to seven in the summer. The school was graded into four sections according to the students' level of Jewish knowledge. The curriculum included the Prophetic books and Hagiographa in addition to Hebrew grammar and composition, Jewish literature, and Jewish history.

A remarkable venture in adult Jewish education was the "People's University" of Vilna, which in December 1915 opened with festivities in the Hall of the Handworkers. Its purpose was to afford popular yet scholarly courses to the masses in a wide variety of fields, such as science, sociology, literature, and history. The sessions were held every evening except Friday, and twenty-one courses were offered, with the language of instruction being Yiddish, although some courses were given in Hebrew. This school attracted more than eighteen thousand students. Unfortunately, it was of short duration because the government ordered it to close its doors, as it did to many other similar institutions.[28]

Ben Zion Alfas, writing in 1941, recalls his years in Vilna:[29]

I liked particularly the Society of Workingmen [Hevrat Poalim], which the saintly Rabbi Hirsch had founded. This society transformed many workmen and clerks into learned and God-fearing Jews. The repute of this society was so great that the chief rabbi of Vilna, Rabbi Bezallel ha-Cohen, would come from time to time to listen to them learn portions of the *Hayyei Adam*. At times when the instructor, Rabbi Hirsch, was sick, I would conduct the study period.

The same author makes reference to the Society Tiferet Bachurim described above by M. Shalit:

This society had two instructors, and in the year 1924 they required another teacher and I was appointed to this position. I also was the teacher at that time of the Society Bahurei Hemed of the Mizrahi.

The famous Zionist leader and publicist Nahum Sokolow recalls a trip to Vilna in 1885 in these words:

Many workingmen were scholars and, on a tour which I made one Sabbath among the synagogues, I heard a carpenter teach the Mishna with commentaries of Maimonides, Bartenuro and Tosafot Yom Tov; and a blacksmith lecturing on the Torah Reading of the week with the commentary of the Baal Ha-akeda.[30]

In a memoir entitled "The City of Boisk and Its Rabbis," Rabbi Aryeh Zeev Rabiner speaks of the seven years from 1891—1903 when Rabbi Abraham I. Kook, later to become the first Chief Rabbi of Palestine, was rabbi in this Latvian town:

Rabbi Kook founded the "Hevrah Tiferet Bachurim—The Society of the Glory of Youth." Its members were young working men. He learned with them the Bible and the "Horeb" by Rabbi Samson Raphael Hirsch. This Society also acquired a sizeable library and the choice of books was made after consultation with the Rabbi. This group of young men were so devoted to their Rabbi that they were known in Boisk as "The Rabbi's Guards." They had their own orchestra and during the

Intermediate Week of Succos they would call at the home of their Rabbi in order to sing and to play for him.[31]

From Latvia we turn to Moravia and the memoirs of the famous Jewish scholar Isaac Hirsch Weiss, author of the monumental *Dor Dor ve-Dorshav*—and rabbi of the great Synagogue in Vienna. His book of memoirs, published in 1895 in connection with his eightieth birthday, records his youth in his native town of Mezerich, which was in Moravia (Mehren) near the Bohemian border. He says:

At that time there lived in Mezerich 150 Jewish heads of families. This was the number of officially permitted Jews, but in reality there must have been more. Among them there were several Jewish scholars, although I could hardly state that it was a city full of learned men. Nevertheless there were in existence many societies for Jewish study. There were two such societies for the study of the Talmud, tractate by tractate, and also two for the study of Mishnah. There were two more for the study of the Portion of the Week with the Rashi commentary, and there was also a society called Shiur Hevrah, whose members gathered every Sabbath afternoon in the summer months and they would get instruction from one of the books of ethics.[32]

Another memoirist, Yehezkel Kotick, published his reminiscences in Yiddish in 1922.[33] Recalling his days in Moscow, that far-away Russian city where the number of Jews was limited by government edict, he notes that he found six minyanim in the bet ha-midrash each morning. Many were there to learn from the hour of seven till noon. "It was especially impressive to come to the bet ha-midrash in the evening. In a city predominantly Christian, in which scores of church spires tower to the skies, sit tens of Jews studying in loud joyful voices."

Rabbi Jacob Mazeh, the chief rabbi of Moscow, in his memoirs tells of the formation of a new Hevrah Shas in the year 1901, although he recalls attending the study-sessions of a similar hevrah when he was a student in Moscow in the 1880s.[34]

It is interesting to turn to the writings of two Zionist leaders of our times who helped to found the State of Israel. The first of these is the late Rabbi Yehudah Leib Maimon. He recalls that:

Rabbi Hayim Zanser of Brody, who was a contemporary of Rabbi Yehezkel Landau, would sit all night and study. He kept two vessels of water on the table and placed one hand into one of them. If he fell asleep, the container of water would turn over and spill the water, which would wake him. He then put both hands into the second vessel and thus remained awake the rest of the night. He used to say: "Why do all the tractates of the Talmud begin with page 2 and not with page 1? In order to teach us that no matter how much you study you have not reached the first stage of Jewish learning." [35]

The second of these Zionist leaders is Zalman Shazar, the third president of the State of Israel. In his autobiography, *Morning Stars,* he writes of his youth in the town of Steibtz and speaks glowingly of the love of learning among the Jewish masses:

Yet these simple, unlearend people of Steibtz had the most profound reverence for learning and respect for the learned.

Though the yeshiva was in Mir, crumbs from its table nourished all the towns of the area. So the *Batei Midrash,* the houses of learning of Steibtz received many a young man on his way to or out of the yeshiva—some who had come from such a distance that they were too late for the opening of the term; others who had turned skeptic and been forced to leave the yeshiva; students soon to be ordained who wished to study by themselves for a year without interruption; youthful kabbalists in search of uncensored solitude. The artisans of the town took it upon themselves to find lodgings for the young men and "days" for them to eat regularly in various houses. There was no *Bet Midrash* in the town without students in it, and no synagogue where the sound of learning was not heard all day and even till the small hours of the night.

The Old and New Synagogues were the special province of the younger students, but the *prushim,* who had left their families in some far-off town, found their place in the hasidic *shtiebel.* Needing to send money home for the support of their wives, the *prushim* could not simply make do with the meals given them in private homes; they did some teaching besides—instruction in Gemorra to some respectable householder or some brilliant youngster who had no more to learn in the *heder* and had not yet reached the yeshiva but was studying by himself in a synagogue. The *parush* would stand behind him and guide him along the uncharted paths of the Talmud. Between afternoon and evening prayers you found a *parush* teaching a whole group of townsmen at the wooden table behind the stove in the *Bet Midrash*—one taught *Hayei Adam* in the Talmud Torah building, another *Ein Yaakov* in the *shtiebel*.

There was much studying in Steibtz. In the Old Synagogue a Gemorra lesson was led by the rabbi's young son-in-law, in the New Synagogue by Shlomo the *shochet*. In the artisans' *Bet Midrash* on Yurzdike, Iche Tanhums delighted his hearers by expounding chapters of the Bible in a sweetly sung melody and with the aid of sage and charming parables—to be sure, only on nights when Iche Tanhums was not engaged in reading from the Book of Job in the homes of mourners.

Aside from the yeshiva students and the *prushim,* for whom every hour of the day and night was a time for learning, not a few simple householders and artisans also set aside hours for study in the *Bet Midrash*. They would remain there after morning or evening prayers, entrenched at their *stenders,* each totally immersed in his book despite the bustling street outside and the worries of the market place and the river bank.

In the middle of the day Reb Shmuel Yehoshua, the shopkeeper, would come into the larger *Bet Midrash*. Though his shop was always full of customers, he could rely on his wife to manage the business. Opening a large Gemorra on the table behind the stove, he would try to recollect what he had learnt in Volozhin before his marriage.

And here was the blind Reb Abraham putting his soiled handkerchief on the open Gemorra he was studying from memory; he would beg one or another of the young men in the room to do him the kindness of looking up the commentary in *Ktzot ha-Hoshen* dealing with the page he had reached.

Then the tall Yoshe Frades would walk in. Shopkeeper though he was, he opened his volume of the Mishna and studied for a good full hour, reading in a loud voice. He simply disregarded the unkind comments to the effect that he was "working towards a eulogy." Let the critics rail—he would go on "studying like a bell," as they said in the town.[36]

Turning from Europe to the Holy Land, we come upon a fascinating book of memoirs published in 1941 by Ben Zion Alfas at the age of ninety.[37] In 1872, on his first visit to Palestine, he came to Jerusalem from Jaffa by donkey. After recounting how he was shown to the bet ha-midrash of Reb Yeshayah, where they learned Mishnayot after the morning service, he writes:

While I was in Jerusalem I attended a large public meeting at which an important issue was being discussed. I heard one after another say: "If Reb Nissan the Cobbler is not here we must not reach a decision." I began to wonder who this lowly cobbler could be, and finally I was shown to his house. Arriving there, I beheld a shoemaker's shop. A number of workmen were sitting at their cobbler's benches, and among them sat Reb Nissan, the owner, with an apron on his body, fixing a pair of shoes, and an open folio of the Talmud on his knees. I recognized at once that here was no ordinary man and that his workmen too were people of refinement. I came for a second visit and this time I saw only the workmen. I inquired for Reb Nissan, but they made no reply. As I sat waiting, I heard the chant of learning coming from a back room. I inquired whether it is permissible to go to the back room and I was told it was. When I entered there, I beheld Reb Nissan poring over the Talmud and lost in study. After a while he rose to greet me and requested me to be seated. I visited him often and became deeply attached to this man and came several times each week to study with him. . . . He would frequently stop his employees from their work to learn with them some Humash or *Hayyei Adam,* and he was wont to say: "Since I pay you a weekly wage, I have a right to use your time for whatever purpose I please." As I got to know him more I could not help but think that in Reb Nissan I had found reincarnation in miniature of Reb Yohanan ha-Sandlar [the cobbler] of talmudic times. He devoted one-half of each day to work and the other half to study. Nor was Reb Nissan unique in Jerusalem. I also met another man, who was a mattress-maker by occupation, who was the teacher of a Hebrew school in which he taught Bible and

Talmud daily without any monetary reward. I could not help but reflect that we Jews were fortunate to have such workingmen![38]

To conclude our survey of Jewish cultural life in the last century, we turn finally to America. Jewish learning in any organized form is not known during the period of the American Revolution or in the decades immediately thereafter, and it is not until the middle of the nineteenth century that we come upon the record of an established association for Jewish study:

> In the year 1841 several members of Shearith Israel started an adult school which they called "The Hebrew Literary and Religious Library Association." Classes were held in the reading and translation of Hebrew and in the laws and customs of the Jews. Simeon Abrahams, Montgomery Moses and Professor Isaac Nordheimer of New York University were on the staff. It is not known how long the school lasted.
>
> In 1846, Rabbi Max Lilienthal organized a Hevrah Shas (a Society for the study of the Talmud) at his Union of German Congregations. It is also said that a number of adults studied the Talmud in the late 1850s at the Beth Hamidrash Synagogue where Rabbi Ash Abraham gave shiurim (lectures). This synagogue is said to have had a library of talmudical, rabbinical and kabbalistic books.[39]

Isaac Leeser organized courses for adults at Mikveh Israel and later at Beth-El Emeth, both in Philadelphia. One of the most popular courses on the Bible was attended by as many as one hundred people. Sabato Morais likewise established a weekly study course.[40]

It was only after the beginning of the East European Jewish immigration that societies for Jewish learning came into being in this country. They rapidly increased in number. The Hevrah Shas of the Bnai Zion Congregation in Providence, Rhode Island, was founded in 1875. In 1882 the B'nai Abraham Congregation of Philadelphia had several hevrot for the study of *Ein Yaakov,* Bible, Psalms, *Shulhan Arukh,* and Talmud. Every seven years they held a siyyum to celebrate the completion of the study of the entire Talmud; three such observances were held in the twenty-one years following the founding of the hevrah. In 1894 a Hevrah Mishnayot and Shas was founded by the Mariampol Synagogue of Chicago. There is a record of a Tailors Tehillim Society in Rochester at about the same time.[41]

The Yiddish orator and preacher, Reverend Zevi Hirsch Masliansky, tells us in his memoirs that in the Orthodox synagogues of Cincinnati, at the end of the nineteenth century, he found several hevrot for Shas, Mishnayot, and Tehillim, and also a Hevrah *Hayyei Adam*. "Many Jews," he reports, "were sitting and learning at long tables and benches between Minhah and Maariv just as in Vilna or Berdichev."[42] In New England, around the same time, he writes, "The Boston lomdim and maskilim [the learned and cultured Jews] founded the Society Kerem Yisrael, which was an adornment to Boston Jewry. All its members were learned in Torah and would gather for lectures on Jewish history and for the discussion of Jewish problems."[43]

CHAPTER

XV

THE JEWISH LOVE FOR BOOKS

The Jewish love for books is evident in many of the laws and customs of the Jewish people.[1] It is not permissible for a book of Jewish religious content to lie on the ground; and if by accident a book is dropped to the floor, it is instantly picked up and given a kiss.[2] A Jewish book is not to be left open unless it is being read, nor is it to be held upside down.[3] It is not permitted to place a book of lesser sanctity on top of a book of higher holiness, so, for example, one must never put any book whatsoever on top of a Bible volume. If one says to another: "Please hand me this book," the book should be given with the right hand and not with the left hand.[4] If two men are walking together, the one who is carrying a book should be given the courtesy of entering and leaving a room first.[5] The late Rabbi Isaac Halevi Herzog, the first Chief Rabbi of the State of Israel, always carried a volume of the Tanakh in his hand whenever he walked through the streets of Jerusalem or any other city of the world, so that if people would respectfully rise as he passed by, the implication would be that they were not paying honor to him but to the book.[6] This feeling of reverence for the Jewish book has come down to our own day, as revealed in a contemporary autobiography:

... on Fridays, Mother would stand before the mirror fixing her hair for the Sabbath, but ... before removing her kerchief she would ask Simcha, the older son, to draw the curtain over the bookshelves. This was Simcha's assignment and, if he happened to be playing outside at the time, he would be called in. Simcha used to object and protested

285

against climbing to the shelves twice, first to shut the curtain and then
to open it again after Mother finished fixing her hair. Mother would
chide him: "Why do you argue, Simcha? You know that I can't stand
with bare head before the holy books." The argument would be renewed after she had finished, and sometimes it required a slap to add
conviction to her argument. "Do you think that we can leave books
covered? This is a Jewish home and the books must be seen."

While these disputes between Mother and Simcha raged, Simon
would . . . suck his thumb with great concentration, and wonder how
the sacred words on the pages inside the closed volumes could possibly
see Mother's hair. But he learned soon that the words were so holy
that they imparted some of their sanctity to the book covers. There
was ready proof of this: If a book fell to the ground, it was picked up
and its cover was reverently kissed.[7]

(1) REVERENCE FOR THE SEFER TORAH

These ingrained habits, which have become second nature for the Jew,
have very deep roots in the Jewish experience. It all started with the
profound reverence in which the Sefer Torah—the Scroll of the Law—has
been held throughout Jewish history. Special sanctity is attached to the
Sefer Torah. One must stand up while the Sefer Torah is being carried.[8]
If one drops a Sefer Torah, he is required to fast. If one sees a Sefer
Torah being torn or burned or desecrated in any other way, he must
tear his garments, as if in mourning, no less than two times; the first time
in sorrow for the torn parchment, and the second time for the desecrated
text.[9] Even a desecrated Scroll of the Law, or one too old and worn to
be permissible for use, must receive reverence and homage.[10] Not only
the scroll itself, but all its appurtenances, such as the holy ark, the Torah
mantels, the Torah pointers, the Torah crowns, and other ornaments, are
regarded as sacred and hence are to be dealt with reverently.[11] Maimonides summarizes these requirements admirably in these words:

> He who sits before a Sefer Torah must do so with solemnity, with rever-
> ence, and with awe, because he is the true witness before all mankind
> to the Covenant God made with His people Israel, as it is written in
> Scripture: "Take this book of the Law . . . that it may be there for a
> witness" [Deut. 31:26]. Our early sages have stated: "Whoso honors
> the Torah will himself be honored, but whoso dishonors the Torah will
> himself be dishonored" [Avot 4:8].[12]

Since the Torah Scroll was held to be so sacred, it was considered highly meritorious for every Jew, if at all possible, to make of himself a sofer—a scribe—so that he should by himself and for himself write a Sefer Torah. The Talmud states that it is a positive commandment for a Jew to do so, and "even if he inherited a Torah Scroll from his fathers, it is still a mitzvah to write his own Torah Scroll, as it is commanded in Scripture: 'Now therefore write ye this song for you' [Deut 31:19]." [13] The Talmud further states: "If one writes a Scroll of the Law with his own hands, it is ascribed to him as if he had received it directly from Mount Sinai." [14] It is further stated: "Even if one does no more than correct a scribal error of only one letter in the entire Sefer Torah, it is as if he had written the entire scroll." [15] The question is then raised: How is it possible to equate the importance of correcting merely one letter to writing an entire scroll? The answer given is: After all, you must remember that any scroll in which even one letter is missing or is superfluous is forbidden for synagogue use.[16] Of course if one was not capable of writing a scroll himself, it was also held highly meritorious to engage a qualified Sofer to do it for him. In recent centuries, the custom has grown up for the Sofer who completes the writing of a scroll to trace the final sentences of the Torah in outline only. At the subsequent festive celebration, or siyyum, each letter in those sentences is filled in by a different man, who thereby symbolically takes part in the writing of a sacred scroll.

If the act of writing a scroll was so highly prized, then it follows that the professional scribe—the Sofer—was greatly esteemed.[17] This is dramatically illustrated in the following talmudic tale: "Rabbi Meir said: When I came to study Torah with Rabbi Ishmael, he inquired of me: 'My son, what is your occupation?' I replied: 'A scribe'. He then said: 'My son, be sure to prize highly your occupation for it is a work of heaven.' " [18] The task of writing scrolls, and of making them available to others through sale, was so greatly valued that the talmudic teachers even excused the scribes from the fixed times of prayer and from the wearing of the phylacteries: "Scribes of books of the Law, their agents are free from the obligations of prayer and phylacteries and all the commandments mentioned in the Torah. This confirms the words of Rabbi Yose the Galilean, who laid down the rule: He who is occupied with the performance of a religious duty is at the time free from the fulfillment of other religious duties." [19]

With the beginning of the post-biblical period and the passing of the centuries, the initial love and reverence for the book par excellence, the

Bible, was also attached to the subsequent creations of Jewish literature, namely the Mishnah, the Talmud, the commentaries, the codes, the responsa, and the writings of the Jewish philosophers, poets, and moralists. In a broader sense these writings also became "Torah." Just as it was meritorious to write a Torah Scroll, so did it become meritorious, before the age of printing, to write manuscripts of any sacred book. And so, Rabbi Joseph Karo in the *Shulhan Arukh*, basing his view on the talmudic dictum that "it is a positive commandment for each Jew to write for himself a Sefer Torah," states that "in our time it is a positive commandment to write the Pentateuch, the Mishnah, the Gemara, and its commentaries." [20]

(2) LAMENTING THE LACK OF BOOKS

That there was great need for more manuscripts of all the sacred texts is abundantly evident from the way in which the great rabbis were constantly lamenting the lack of books and the shortage of even the most essential texts. Here are some illustrations of this situation: [21] Rabbenu Tam, the grandson of Rashi, and the leader of French Jewry in the twelfth century, in one of his responsa writes: "If you send me the parchment, I will be able to send you the answer." [22] Another French scholar, Rabbi Eliezer the Great, laments the fact that he could not study the tractate Avodah Zarah for the simple reason that there was none available to him. [23] Rabbi Meir of Rothenburg, the leading rabbi in Germany in the thirteenth century, complains about the shortage of books in one of his responsa. [24] Rabbi Israel Isserlein, the leading authority in fifteenth-century Austria, writes: "I cannot properly explain your question because I do not have this volume." [25] Rabbi Isaac ben Sheshet, the great legal authority of fourteenth-century Spanish Jewry, writes to his son-in-law as follows: "I do not have the Mishnah of Seder Zeraim, nor do I have a copy of the Jerusalem Talmud. I had to beg someone to look up the passage there and write me about it." [26] The famous Rabbi Jacob ibn Habib, who lived in Salonica in the early sixteenth century, and was the author of the popular anthology of aggadic literature, the *Ein Yaakov*, writing at the end of the tractate Zeraim tells us:

I have not heard of, nor seen, in this city, a single volume of the Jerusalem Talmud and its commentaries with the exception of the first tractate. For this reason I had made up my mind not to include in my work any selections from the Jerusalem Talmud. But many respected and revered friends urged me not to exclude the aggadic passages from the Jerusalem Talmud, and they advised me that a certain renowned Jewish scholar in this very city had in his possession a trustworthy manuscript containing, without commentaries, many of the Midrashim from the Babylonian Talmud and the Jerusalem Talmud. I went to this scholar and implored him to permit me to examine this volume. Only after doing so, did I first realize how really important and valuable was this material from the Jerusalem Talmud.

Rabbi Judah ibn Tibbon, the father of the famous translators living in Lunel in the south of France toward the end of the twelfth century, informs his sons in his will that "most of the students will wander from town to town in order to find a certain book, and they will look in vain because they won't find it." [27] In the yeshivah of Rabbi Israel Isserlein, students who had their own books would study from them in the daytime, while students without their own books, would borrow the books for study during the night. [28]

(3) THE MERIT OF LENDING BOOKS

With such scarcity of books, it became especially praiseworthy for those who did own precious volumes to lend them to others. There is a considerable literature on the subject of lending books. [29] To begin with, the Jewish sages of the Talmud interpreted the verse in the Psalms, "Happy are they that do righteousness at all times" (Ps. 106:3), to refer to those "who write books and lend them to others." [30] Rabbi Judah the Pious, who lived in Regensburg in the thirteenth century, taught that "those who lend books to students, their reward for it in the world to come will be as great as if they themselves had studied from these books. [31]

This matter of lending books is so crucial that it is dealt with quite extensively in the responsa literature, which reflects the daily concerns and problems of Jewish life. Thus the question arose: "Is the lending of books to be regarded only as mitzvah for the performance of which there is a reward, or is it actually a duty of such urgency that a Jew could and should be forced to comply with it?" The leading legal authorities gave different answers. The great codifier of the thirteenth century, Rabbi Asher ben Yehiel, held that lending books is a duty. Therefore the bet din, the Jewish tribunal, has the right to compel compliance because the one who does not lend his books is guilty of causing the cessation of Torah study in his community. Furthermore, anyone refusing to lend a needed volume could be fined ten gulden for each day of his refusal. However, the lender should be protected by requiring the borrower to leave a deposit for the book and also compelling him to pay for any damage to the book.[32] Rabbi Moses Isserles, the eminent Polish commentator on the *Shulhan Arukh* in the sixteenth century, concurs with the view of Rabbi Asher, and it was his own practice to forbid students to enter his yeshivah to hear his lectures if they refused to be lenders of books.[33] But there were also opposing opinions. Rabbi Meir of Rothenburg maintained: "It is not a duty to lend one's books, for they may be damaged or lost." [34] Rashi, the great commentator on the Bible and Talmud, likewise holds this view, stating that "certain books should neither be loaned nor rented because they may become damaged." [35]

But no matter what the legal authorities decided, there were some Jews who were very reluctant to lend their manuscripts and books. This is perfectly understandable, since books were scarce, costly, and much in demand, and there was always the danger of damage or loss. A Spanish rabbi of the fourteenth century, Rabbi Judah Companton, in his introduction to the Talmud, expresses himself very frankly on this subject:

> Of a truth, a man's wisdom goes only as far as his books go. Therefore, one should sell all he possesses and buy books; for, as the sages put it: "He who increases books increases wisdom."
>
> Rashi, of blessed memory, speaks to the same effect in interpreting the injunction of the rabbis: "Acquire thyself a companion." Some read, according to him: "Acquire thyself a book"; for a book is the best of all companions. If a man reads only borrowed books, he is thus in the category of those of whom the Bible speaks: "And thy life shall hang in doubt before thee" [Deut. 28:66].

In a similar vein, Rabbi Shabsai Sopher, writing in 1601, stated: "Because I have not been careful in the matter of lending books, I have suffered many losses. I have therefore taken a vow never to let a book out of my house without requiring that the borrower leave a deposit." [36]

In a manuscript volume found in the Hebrew University Library in Jerusalem, Rabbi Menachem Azariah of Fano wrote: "Now that I have finished writing this book, I have taken a vow, which I shall firmly adhere to, that no matter who it may be who will come to me to borrow this book, I will under no circumstances lend it to him." [37]

An unknown poet, who was obviously a lover of books, wrote a Hebrew quatrain which freely translated proclaims:

> Remove from me him
> Who would a book borrow;
> All he does is bring me sorrow
> Because my book is my beloved
> How can I share her with another? [38]

(4) LOVING CARE FOR BOOKS

With books so rare and precious, it became a special virtue to make them beautiful in appearance and to give them loving care. Rabbi Judah the Pious taught that "one must be careful about honoring his books; therefore he should make sure that even the binding should be elegant." [39] He bolsters his instruction by telling the story of a man who had a dream that his grave was desecrated because he had not properly bound his books. [40] He also counseled that the bookcase should be a handsome one. [41] Rabbi Judah ibn Tibbon admonished his son in these words: "Take particular care of thy books. Cover the bookcases with rugs of fine quality; and preserve them from damp and mice, and from all manner of injury, for thy books are thy good treasure." [42]

Similarly, the author of the book *Kav ve-Naki* stated that "because of the love of the Torah one's books should be beautifully bound." [43] The kabbalist Rabbi Benjamin Halevi, listing the ways Torah is acquired, says: "Study in books that are beautiful in script or print and handsome in appearance, for it will draw your eye and heart closer to the contents." [44] And Rabbi Akiba Eiger, who lived in the first half of the nineteenth century in Posen and was the leading talmudic authority of his time, wrote to his son Solomon: "I request you, my dear son, to see to it that a book should be printed on good paper, with clear black letters, for in my opinion the soul is inspired, the intellect stimulated, when one studies in a beautiful book." [45] Rabbi Eliezer Papo adds: "It is a duty to remove the dust from the books from time to time." [46] There is a tradition that Rabbi Shimon bar Zemah Duran (1361–1444), a leading rabbinic authority of North Africa, was one who loved, honored, and tenderly cared for his books. He would dust them daily with a silken cloth. As a reward, according to legend, no volume in his library ever suffered from deterioration or rotting away. Furthermore, any books written by Rabbi Duran even when they stood next to other volumes which were deteriorating, his books would never be affected.[47]

This love of books found its expression in organized Jewish life and in Jewish literature. Dr. Shimon Federbush, writing in 1965, reminisces about his boyhood in Galicia:

> In my native town, there existed a young men's club named Tikkun ve-Kinyan Sefarim—a club for the repair and purchase of books. Its members went from house to house every week to collect pennies for the purpose of repairing old books and purchasing new ones for the local bet ha-midrash. When they had sufficient funds to purchase a new set of Shas or the Rambam, they would arrange for a special celebration. The individual volumes of these sets would be distributed among the leading men of the town, who formed a procession and in a festive spirit proceeded to the bet ha-midrash and there danced around the bimah with the books in their hands before depositing them on the shelves of the bookcases.[48]

(5) THE COMMUNITY PROVIDES BOOKS

The admiration and need for books, coupled with the paucity of books, made it necessary for the organized Jewish community to provide them. As far back as the talmudic period, we come upon the injunction that "the people of the community shall compel one another to purchase the books of the Pentateuch and the Prophets."[49] This Jewish law, as prescribed in the *Shulhan Arukh, applied* to all sacred books of the post-biblical period down to our own time.[50]

In keeping with this tradition, the pinkas of Lithuanian Jewry for the year 1655 records that "when the leaders saw that the printers had ceased to print books because the sales had fallen down, thus causing a decline of Jewish study, they therefore decided to require the heads of each Jewish community in Lithuania to purchase a specified number of Gemara volumes and to use every method of compulsion to achieve compliance with this edict."[51]

This edict was promulgated after the terrible Chmielnicki persecutions of 1648, during which many Jewish communities were devastated. As a consequence of this tragedy, there was a grave decline in book purchases and book printing. Twenty years later it was necessary for the leaders of Lithuanian Jewry to return to this problem. They reinforced their earlier enactment by requiring the parnasim and rabbi of each community to hold themselves responsible for supplying the necessary books in their respective communities. The local communal leaders were also expected to encourage individuals to purchase books, to provide free books to poor students out of the communal treasury, and to designate one official in their community to supervise the purchase and distribution of books.[52]

There is a certain humorous flavor to the case recently discovered by Professor S. D. Goitein during his researches in the Cairo Genizah records, dating from the eleventh through the thirteenth centuries. A Jewess had left to the Jewish community a valuable cloth of siglaton, a highly cherished fabric. Musing about what to do with this piece of public property, the elders decided to let every member of the congregation each wear the precious garb for one Sabbath. A learned judge, whose decision was requested in the matter, denounced the idea; he decided instead to sell the siglaton and use the money received to buy a book for the synagogue library.[53]

(6) GREAT JEWISH LIBRARIES

The love of books, coupled with the obligation to make them available to the Jewish community, brought into existence great private libraries and even greater public libraries. The yearning of the Jewish book-collector is well expressed by Rabbi Menahem ben Yehudah in the rhymed introduction to his book *Beraita de Rabbi Eliezer and Midrash Agur* (Safed, 1587): "From the day I reached manhood and money came into my hand, I deprived myself of food and drink in order to pursue and to purchase books." [54]

Perhaps the first avid collector of Jewish books was the Jewish scholar of the sixteenth century, Rabbi Yosef Shelomo Delmodigo, who lived on the Greek island of Candia. He tells us: "I have often traveled hundreds of miles by land and by sea in order to search out, and buy, even a small volume." [55] A modern spiritual descendant of this rabbi was the late Rabbi Judah Leib Maimon, the first Minister of Religion in the State of Israel. He was a great book-collector and possessed one of the finest private libraries of the twentieth century. On the occasion of his eightieth birthday, his daughter wrote an appreciation of her eminent father in which she glories in his love of books.

My father's motto was the words of Rabbi Yosef Shelomo Delmodigo, who lived three hundred years ago and had written: "If I am not blessed with sons or with material possessions, I am fortunate in acquiring books. It has never happened that I should hear of a rare book anywhere in the world which I would desire and would not acquire." In my father's eyes, his library was something living and dynamic. It required constant attention and needed continuing beautification, enhancement, and completion. His library was always in a state of motion: books had to be repaired or bound, new and better editions had to be exchanged for old, books had to be rearranged, bookcases had to be added. Some of the books were present in every edition ever published, as, for example, the books of Rambam. In addition there were rare books, incunabula, and manuscripts. When guests came to the house—and they were numerous—mother would set up refreshments to honor them. But father would honor them by showing the delights on his shelves. He would stride into the library ahead of his guests, beaming all over, and the guests would follow him. He would stop at each bookcase, take out a volume here and there, handle it affectionately, and expound on its merits. In my father's library there were more than forty thousand books.[56]

The story of Jewish libraries is fascinating.[57] Here one can only mention some of the most famous treasuries of Jewish literature. Perhaps the very first great Jewish library was brought together by Rabbi David Oppenheim (1664–1736) of Prague. From his father and father-in-law, he inherited a substantial fortune. This enabled him to collect a large and marvelous library of Hebrew books and manuscripts; many books were specially printed for him on vellum or blue paper. This library, with its rare treasures, was acquired by the Bodleian Library of Oxford University in 1829, and there it rests as one of the Bodleian's chief glories to this day.[58] Rabbi Mathias Strashun (1817–85) collected a magnificent library in Vilna, as did the Hebrew bibliographer Heimann Joseph Michael (1792–1846) in Hamburg. Michael's collection is now in the British Museum in London, while the great book collection of the Austrian scholar Solomon Halberstam (1832–1900) is now in the library of the Jewish Theological

Seminary of America. Men of wealth also assembled famous libraries. Among these were the German Jewish banker Abraham Merzbacher (1812–85), whose collection, one of the largest private Jewish libraries in the world, later became part of the city library of Frankfurt on the Main; the German bibliographer Eliezer Rosenthal (1794–1868) of Hannover, whose library found its final home in the Amsterdam University Library; the Russian philanthropist Moses Friedland (1826–99), who for more than thirty years was general army contractor for the Russian government and built the famous Bibliotheca Friedlandiana, which he bequeathed to the Asiatic Museum of the Imperial University in St. Petersburg; and the Russian Jewish orientalist, scholar, and communal leader Baron David Gunzburg (1857–1910), whose library was one of the largest private collections in Europe. In the English-speaking countries, great Jewish libraries were brought together by Elkan Adler of London, and by Judge Mayer Sulzberger and Dr. A. S. W. Rosenbach of Philadelphia.

As already indicated, many of these private collections ultimately found their way into great public libraries. The collections of Solomon Halberstam, David Cassel, Moritz Steinschneider, Elkan Adler, and Mayer Sulzberger are the foundation of the vast accumulation of literary treasures housed in the library of the Jewish Theological Seminary in New York, the largest library of Judaica in the world. Some other important Jewish book collections are the libraries of the Yeshiva University and the YIVO Institute, both in New York; the Dropsie University in Philadelphia; and the Hebrew Union College in Cincinnati. One of the greatest Jewish libraries today is that of the Hebrew University in Jerusalem. The important Schocken Library, which is now part of the Jewish Theological Seminary library, is also located in Jerusalem.

(7) ENEMIES OF THE JEWISH BOOK

There is no people in the world whose history is so fully reflected in the history of its books as the Jewish people. The fate of the Jews also became the fate of their books. Whenever and wherever enemies and destroyers arose against the Jews, they also vented their destructive furies on the Jewish book.[59]

It became an axiom of the persecutors that in order to destroy the Jewish people one must begin by destroying the Jewish book. Even a rapid survey of this sad chapter in Jewish history will bear testimony to this tragic truth. Going as far back as the days of the Maccabees, we come upon Antiochus Ephiphanes, who offers us one of the first cases of book-burning in recorded history. We are told in the Apocrypha: "And they made Israel to hide themselves in every place of refuge which they had. . . . And they rent in pieces the books of the law which they found, and set them on fire." [60] The destruction of Jewish books by Antiochus is also referred to in the Mishnah, which tells us that among the five calamities that befell our people on the seventeenth day of Tammuz was the burning of the Sefer Torah.[61] In the days of the Hadrianic persecutions, the study of Torah was forbidden. The Talmud records the fate that befell Rabbi Hanina ben Teradyon, who was one of the Ten Holy Martyrs, in these touching words:

> The Roman soldiers found him sitting and occupying himself with the Torah, publicly gathering assemblies and keeping a Scroll of the Law in his bosom. Straightway they took hold of him, wrapped him in the Scroll of the Law, placed bundles of branches around him, and set them on fire. They then took tufts of wool, which they had soaked in water, and placed them over his heart, so that he should not expire quickly. His daughter exclaimed: "Father, that I should see you in this state!" He replied: "If it were I alone being burnt, it would have been a thing hard to bear; but now that I am burning together with the Scroll of the Law, He who will have regard for the plight of the Torah will also have regard for my plight." His disciples then called out: "Rabbi, what seest thou?" He answered them: "The parchments are being burnt, but the letters are soaring on high." [62]

The martyred Rabbi Hanina's words of comfort and courage tell us that the Jewish book may be destroyed, but its spirit and message are immortal and indestructible.

We Jews, above all peoples, venerate the memory of our martyrs. We shed tears for the Ten Holy Martyrs in the liturgy of Yom Kippur in the heart-breaking prayer Eleh Ezkero. Our martyrology is long and cruel. But even among our martyrs, the highest place is held by our books. If anything exceeds the brutality with which Jews were mistreated during the centuries, it is the brutality with which Jewish books were tracked down, condemned, burned, destroyed. In the Middle Ages the enemies of the Jewish people focused their fury on the books of the Talmud. The first public burning of the Talmud took place in Paris on the eve of the

Sabbath in June 1244, when twenty-four cartloads of Hebrew books were committed to the flames. This holocaust evoked bitter strains of lamentation in France and Germany. The elegy of Rabbi Meir of Rothenburg, who was present at the conflagration of the books, is chanted to this day on the Ninth of Av. Its opening lines, addressed to the burned books, are deeply moving: "O, ye who are seared in the flames, pray for the peace of thy mourners!"

Funeral pyres for books of the Talmud flamed all over Europe in those dark days. But the most horrible examples of such holocausts took place in Spain and Italy. The fiends of the Spanish Inquisition resorted first to the burning of books before deciding on the burning of Jews. The following eyewitness account has come down to us from Rabbi Abraham Sebag:

> Now while I was in Portugal, after having come thither with those expelled from Castile, it came into my mind to compose a commentary on the Five Scrolls, which I did. At that time, the anger of the Lord was kindled against my people in the Second Expulsion, from Portugal. I therefore abandoned all my books, and determined to take with me to Lisbon (the port of embarkation) only the commentary I had composed on the Pentateuch and the commentary on the Five Scrolls, and a commentary on the Ethics of the Fathers, and the work "Hibbur haKasef" that I had composed in my youth. When I arrived in Lisbon, certain Jews came and told me that a proclamation had been issued, that any person in whose possession a Hebrew book was found should be put to death. Forthwith I went and concealed them beneath a certain olive tree, verdant and fruitful, but in my eyes bitter as wormwood: and I called it the Tree of Weeping, for there I had buried all that I held most dear.[63]

The peak of Jewish book-burning in Italy took place in Rome on Rosh Hashanah of 1553. On this day of great solemnity in the Jewish religious calendar, the enemies of the Jewish people committed the tomes of the Talmud to the flames of the Campo dei Fiori. Here too an eyewitness account has come down to us through the words of Rabbi Judah Lerma in his book *Lehem Yehudah* (Sabionetta, 1554):

> This work of mine I published for the first time in Venice. Now on the New Year's Day of the year "For God hath dealt bitterly with me" (that is, 1553) the Curia of Rome issued an edict in all the countries

that owed it obedience and they burned the Talmud and all works allied thereto. In the month of Marheshvan, the Bitter Month, the edict was published in Venice, and they burned the Talmud and all like works on a Sabbath day, and among them were all the copies of my book which I had just printed, 1,500 volumes in all. Thus I lost everything that I had in Venice, and I did not have even so much as a single leaf either from the original or from the printed work as a remembrance. So I was forced to begin all over again and to write it from memory from the very commencement. After I had written three chapters anew, I found one single copy of the printed work in the hands of a non-Jew who had snatched it from the blaze, and I purchased it at a very high price; and I found that by the providence of God I had made the second copy more complete than the first.[64]

The burning of Jewish books and synagogues has ever been a prelude to attempts at destroying the Jewish people. This we have seen even in our own time in Germany and in Russia. Less than five months after Hitler became chancellor of Germany, on the eve of May 10, 1933, he ordered a great conflagration of more than twenty thousand Jewish books in the Square at Unter den Linden in front of the University of Berlin. Similar scenes were staged in all parts of Germany. Such barbaric sights had not been seen in Europe since the dark Middle Ages. These conflagrations of books were but a prelude to the burning of the synagogues on the infamous "Kristallnacht" on November 9, 1938. As the Nazi hordes swept through Europe, they carried out a systematic policy of pillage, robbery, confiscation, and destruction of Jewish books. Nor has the fate of the Jewish book been much better in Soviet Russia. While there have been no overt acts of destruction, yet a death sentence has been passed on the Jewish book since none may be printed and distributed. During the Stalin regime the purge of Jewish intellectuals, poets, and writers was accompanied by the purge of Jewish literary treasures. Indeed, the fate of the Jewish book is inexorably linked to the destiny of the Jewish people. We Jews are called the "people of the book" and also the "eternal people." In great measure we are an eternal people because we are the people of the book.

(8) THE JEWISH BOOK: BASTION OF JEWISH SURVIVAL

To the Jew, books were not, as they were for his neighbor, objects of veneration, of mystery, of distrust. Books were a sheer necessity of everyday life. Books were his "survival-kit," enabling him to stay alive as a Jew and to perpetuate the existence of the Jewish people and the Jewish religion. The psalmist expressed this truth beautifully when he sang: "Unless Thy law had been my delight; I should then have perished in mine affliction" (Ps. 119:92).

In a similar vein, Job, in the midst of his anguish, before he could make the affirmation, "But as for me I know that my redeemer liveth," had to have the solace of the written word:

Oh that my words were now written!
Oh that they were inscribed in a book!
That with an iron pen and lead
They were graven in the rock forever!
[Job 19:23–25]

The book became the Jew's "portable homeland"—to borrow a phrase from Heinrich Heine. In books the Jew found surcease from his sorrows and strength to survive. The truth of this is attested by many passages in Jewish literature. For example, the renowned Rabbi Joseph Teumin, in the introduction to his book *Peri Megadim,* quotes from a letter sent him by an anonymous Jew who signed himself only as "Levi the Poor Hebrew Teacher":

When I wake up during the long winter nights, and my wife weeps because there is no bread for the children, and my mind is filled with agonizing thoughts, it is then that I sit down to open a book and to learn. The book then becomes my city of refuge and my bastion of courage.[65]

Did not the great Hayyim Nahman Bialik ascribe Israel's strength to the same source when he wrote these lines:

And shoulds't thou wish to know the source
From which thy tortured brethren drew
In evil days their strength of soul?
. . . .
Then enter the House of God
The House of Study . . .
Perhaps thy eye may still behold . . .

The profile of some pallid face,
Upon an ancient folio bent.[66]

It is no wonder, then, that in all of Jewish literature, from early times down to modern times, the value of the Jewish book is highly extolled and the honor due it is constantly expressed. Rabbi Hai Gaon (938–1038) in his *Musar ha-Sekhel,* a rhymed ethical treatise consisting of counsel for guidance in life, offers the following characteristic admonition:

If children thou shouldst bear at length
    Reprove them, but with tender thought.
Purchase them books with all thy strength,
    And by skilled teachers have them taught.[67]

. . . .

To three possessions thou shouldst look:
Acquire a field, a friend, a book.[68]

The great Hebrew poet of medieval Spain, Judah Ha-Levi, spoke of his library as "my garden and my Paradise," [69] while the Spanish statesman, Rabbi Samuel ha-Nagid, wrote:

The wise of heart will abandon ease and pleasures
For in his library will he find his treasures.[70]

But the prince of medieval Jewish book-lovers was Judah ibn Tibbon, the great scholar, grammarian, and translator, who lived in the Provence in the thirteenth century. His will, in the form of last injunctions to his son, deals to a large degree with the treatment of his library.

I have honored thee by providing an extensive library for thy use, and have thus relieved thee of the necessity to borrow books. Most students must bustle about to seek books, often without finding them. But thou, thanks be to God, lendest and borrowest not. Of many books, indeed, thou ownest two or three copies. . . .

Never refuse to lend books to anyone who has not the means to purchase books for himself, but only act thus to those who can be trusted to return the volumes. Thou knowest what our sages said in the Talmud, on the text: "Wealth and riches are in his house; and his merit endureth forever" [Ps. 122:3]. But "Withhold not good from him to whom it is due" [Prov. 3:27], and take particular care of thy books.[71]

Similarly, about the year 1400, the grammarian, chronicler, and wit Profiat Duran gave this advice to the intelligent student in the introduction to his Hebrew grammar *Masseh Ephod*: Use works which are brief or systematic", he said. But he goes on with a really memorable piece of advice: "Use only books that are beautifully written, on good paper, and well and handsomely bound. Read in a pretty, well-furnished room, and let your eye rest on beautiful objects the while, so that you will be brought to love what you read." [72]

Rabbi David ibn Zimra, one of the leading Jewish scholars of the sixteenth century, Chief Rabbi of Egypt for forty years, author of more than three thousand responsa and many volumes on Halakhah and Kaballah, expressed the view, "that if one buys a new book, he should recite over it the benediction of the She-Heheyanu." [73] Perhaps this eminent rabbi was influenced in this judgment by the opinion in the Talmud that "for the study of Scripture or Midrash or Mishnah or Talmud, a benediction is required." One sage, Rabbi Hiyya bar Ashi, said: "Many times did I stand before Rab to repeat our section in the Sifra of the School of Rab, and he used first to wash his hands and say a blessing and then go over our section with us." [74]

In contemporary Jewish literature, the Jewish book has inspired great poets and writers: Bialik wrote an exalting poem called "Standing before the Book-Case," which opens with the rhapsodic words:

> Receive my greetings
> O, ancient tomes!
> Accept my kisses
> Ye shrivelled parchments![75]

The first Hebrew writer to receive the Nobel Prize for Literature, Samuel Joseph Agnon, extolls the Jewish book in all of his writings. In an essay of reminiscences, he glories in the remembrance of his grandfather's bookcase, and he writes repeatedly of the sanctity and saving power of the Jewish book.[76] In one of his famous stories, "In the Heart of the Seas," Agnon tells of a Rabbi Hananya who went on a hazardous journey by sea to the Land of Israel. A fierce storm broke out. The rabbi, naturally, was afraid, but then he saw someone sitting on a kerchief spread on the

deck, studying calmly from an open book. His fears vanished, for he knew
"that no tempest at sea would cause him to sink and no beast of the deep
could swallow him up." Agnon intended this to be a piece of literary
symbolism that the Jewish people will survive the brutal and wild storms
of life if only they hold fast to the book.[77]

The greatest Hebrew essayist of modern times, the philosopher of
Jewish nationalism Ahad Ha-Am, put it well: "Even if books just lie in
the corner, without anyone paying attention to them, they still have a
spiritual effect just by being in the house, for the simple reason that they
represent in physical and visible form the fact that sometime, somewhere,
a man's thoughts and ideas were concretized in print." [78]

One of the greatest Jewish saints of modern times was Rabbi Israel
Meir ha-Cohen of Radin, known, from the title of his famous book, as
the Hafetz Hayyim. He used a prayer of intercession for Israel, asking
for God's mercy on His people solely because they were the guardians of
the Jewish book:

Behold, O, Thou Master of the Universe, the honor which Thy people
Israel bestows upon Thee. Just look down from Heaven and see the
crowns with which they have crowned Thy Torah. Thou hast given to
Thy people a Torah small in size, yet see how many mighty towers they
have built upon it. Thy studied every word, every letter, every dot. All
of these they have adorned and illumined with ornaments as white as
pearls and bright as sapphires. Just consider the two Talmuds—the
Babylonian and the Jerusalem Talmuds; and then further chaplets of
grace without number: the Midrash, the Zohar, the Sifra, the Sifri, the
Mekhilta, the Tosefta, Alfas, Rambam, the Early Sages, and the Later
Sages! Consider also the circumstances under which these expansions
of the Torah were created: In the long and bitter Exile, between the
fire and the sword, under conditions beyond human endurance and yet,
they studied, and learned, and wrote. So, dear Master of the Universe,
why art Thou wrathful with Thy people Israel? Do you have any other
nation to compare with it? Therefore, how long, how long, dear Father
in Heaven wilt Thou allow Thy faithful people Israel to endure its
sorrows and sufferings?![79]

We will conclude this chapter on a humorous note with a story about
one of the famous Jewish scholars of this century, Professor Abraham
Berliner (1833–1915), who spent many years doing research at the

Vatican Library in Rome. A friend and colleague, Professor Abraham Epstein, often sat beside him in the reading room, both of them examining rare manuscripts. Professor Berliner came daily as soon as the library opened in the morning and stayed till it closed at night. Since he would not take time out even for lunch, he always brought a roll and an egg with him. Professor Epstein, on the other hand, would work only in the mornings, then would go for a stroll before having lunch. He often urged Professor Berliner to join him, but without success.

One day, however, Professor Epstein managed to persuade his colleague to come along for a stroll. Professor Berliner walked with head lowered and shoulders stooped as if he were peering into an ancient manuscript. Professor Epstein, however, walked erect with his head up, gazing at the blue skies above and at the green grounds of the Vatican Gardens with their beautiful flowers. He became ecstatic at the view and tried to get his stooped colleague to notice the beauties of nature, prodding him and exclaiming, in the words of the Psalmist, "How great are Thy works, O Lord! How manifold are Thy wonders!"

Finally, noticing his walking partner's ecstasy and enthusiasm, Professor Berliner inquired in astonishment: "Why are you so aroused?" Professor Epstein replied: "Look up at the heavens and see! Look around the gardens and behold! Are they not beautiful and inspiring?" Whereupon Professor Berliner did look up and around, and grudgingly said: "Yes, they are beautiful indeed. But these glorious expanses are not parchment scrolls." [80]

CHAPTER

XVI

INTO THE TWENTIETH CENTURY

The tradition of lifelong learning, which stretches back to the very beginning of Jewish history, has reached into the twentieth century. In our times, for contemporary reasons and using current techniques, adult Jewish learning has been playing a most vital role in the life of many Jewish communities around the world.

(1) IN GERMANY: BEFORE AND DURING THE NAZI ERA

The creative spirit and religious genius of Franz Rosenzweig revolutionized adult Jewish education in the modern world. His biographer, Dr. Nahum N. Glatzer, states: "Soon after Franz Rosenzweig saw his way clear to remain a Jew and to dedicate his life to the cause of Judaism, he realized the need for a radical reorganization of Jewish instruction on all levels and a re-thinking of Jewish scholarship in Western Europe" [1] While serving as a German soldier on the Balkan front in March 1917, Rosenzweig wrote down, on army postal cards, a kind of manifesto under the ringing title, "It Is Time!" (*Zeit ists!*). In this epistle on Jewish learning, the "Jewish philosopher of the trenches," as Rosenzweig is sometimes called, proposes that a synthesis of scholarship and education, as was so admirably achieved in classical Judaism, would provide a way for Central European Jewry to end its stagnation. Moreover, it would counteract the problem of assimilation and form the basis for a possible renascence of Jewish life. [2] Three years later, early in 1920, he pressed forward his ideas on the revitalization of Jewish learning in an essay entitled "Bildung und Kein Ende," which could be freely translated as "Education without Graduation." In this appeal for German Jewry to establish schools of never-ending Jewish learning, he laments the fact that "Jewish study and teaching, Jewish learning and education—they are dying out among us," [3] and hails the beginnings of "the 'Jewish adult education movement' . . . as the latest and perhaps most important movement among contemporary German Jews." [4]

In this essay, Rosenzweig laid the foundations of the *Freies Jüdisches Lehrhaus* (Free House of Jewish Studies) in Frankfurt on the Main. The word *Lehrhaus,* with its reference to the traditional bet ha-midrash, was chosen intentionally, for the institution he founded was to be a modernized bet ha-midrash. The word *free* indicated that registration was open to all without entrance examinations; it also conveyed the notion of free inquiry.[5] The Lehrhaus opened with a convocation on October 17, 1920. In the keynote address, "On the Old and the New Learning," Rosenzweig stated that while the old learning had its starting point in the Torah and was designed to lead into life, the new learning will lead from wherever we stand in life, back to the Torah. We cannot disregard what we are, or renounce what we have acquired, but we shall lead everything back to Judaism. This new learning will be a process from the periphery, where we stand, to Judaism, which we still feel to be the center despite our alienation. Our purpose is not apologetics, self-defense, but an attempt at clarification within ourselves.[6]

In addition to his own teaching, Rosenzweig assembled a great faculty composed of the leading Jewish scholars of the time. Among them, to mention only a few, were Dr. Nehemiah A. Nobel, the leading Conservative rabbi in Frankfurt; Dr. Nahum N. Glatzer, now a professor at Brandeis University; Dr. Ernest Simon, who played a major role in the Jewish renaissance in Germany and, from 1928, is a leading educator in Israel; S. Y. Agnon, the Hebrew writer, who at the close of his life, in the State of Israel, was the first Hebrew writer to win the Nobel Prize for Literature; Dr. Gershom Scholem, who later became a professor at the Hebrew University and the leading authority on Jewish mysticism; and, perhaps the most famous of all, Martin Buber, the great Jewish theologian.[7] In its fourth academic year (1922–23), the Lehrhaus reached its highest enrollment: eleven hundred adults out of a community of almost thirty thousand Jews, that is, four percent of the total Jewish population of Frankfurt. The underlying philosophy and programs of the

Frankfurt Lehrhaus served as an example for the establishment of similar institutions in other German cities. Rosenzweig headed the school until his early and tragic death in 1929, after which its activities diminished.

With the rise of Hitlerism and the subsequent degradation and persecution of Jews of Germany, something miraculous happened to the declining Lehrhaus. It experienced a new birth, a new efflorescence, whose purpose it became to offer Jewish adult education as a means of spiritual resistance against the Nazis. Martin Buber became the head of the Lehrhaus in 1933, and he was its guiding spirit till its forced closing in 1937. The historian of this final phase of the Lehrhaus is Professor Ernest Simon.[8] He tells us that Martin Buber foresaw the task before the Jews of Germany, admonishing the representative body of German Jewry (the Reichsvertretung der Deutschen Juden) to establish a cultural program that would help the Jews both in offering spiritual resistance as long as they could remain in Germany and also, ultimately, in emigrating to other lands. This thought Buber expressed succinctly and powerfully in these words: "Let no one ask for which country we wish to educate people. For Palestine if it may be so; for any foreign country if it must be so; for Germany if it can be so." The three auxiliary verbs used here, observes Dr. Simon, reveal a gradation of meanings which needs no commentary. "Palestine was the optimum; any other country of emigration a forced solution; continued life in Germany a conditional possibility. But the same thing applied to all three: There is one goal—one education."

Dr. Glatzer describes the blessings the Lehrhaus brought to the Jews of Germany before their total annihilation:

> The tragic situation in which German Jews—most of them unexpectedly—found themselves, evoked forces of heroic inner resistance. Many Jews reacted to the events in self-respect, even with pride. The degradation of the Jewish Name was answered by many by a more dedicated adherence to the name of Israel. . . . The mighty word of Martin Buber, who headed the *Lehrhaus* in those crucial years, was heard beyond the limits of the Frankfort community. He reminded the Jew of the Sinai covenant which established a community of faith that lives on against the judgment of those who carry the sword. In the new *Lehrhaus* the Jew received an orientation toward new ways of life in the land of Israel and in other parts of the world. But also, brought again into a living contact with the word of the Bible and the classical tradition of Israel, he learned to be a Jew.[9]

308   LIFELONG LEARNING AMONG JEWS

(2) IN THE UNITED STATES

The decade that saw the destruction of six million Jews in the Nazi Holocaust had a very shattering, sobering, and, at the same time, salutary effect on the American Jewish community. It helped to produce a kind of Jewish revival in America in the late 1930s and in the 1940s. It is no accident, therefore, that it was precisely during this period that an adult Jewish education movement began to emerge and develop in America.

The reasons for this are easy to recognize and describe. The adult education movement was a response to the conditions and needs of the times. In the first place, the death of Jews and Judaism in so many European lands stirred American Jews to the realization that destiny had marked them out, in the words of the Hebrew prophet Zechariah, as the "brand plucked from the fire" (Zech. 3:2). The American Jew began to sense that the perpetuation of the Jewish people and the Jewish religion was now in his trust. The American Jew responded, in part, by turning to Jewish learning as a means of self-perpetuation. Jewish study became a kind of weapon for survival. The synagogues, and whatever schools for adults were in existence at the time, served this need.

Secondly, Nazi propaganda had poured the poison of anti-Semitism into the bloodstream of America. The peak of anti-Semitic activity in all of American history was reached during and after the Hitler era, and it kept pouring calumny and shame on the Jew. The spread of anti-Semitism brought fear and panic into the lives of American Jewry. One of the undermining influences of anti-Semitism was the fact that many Jews were prone to adopt the anti-Semite's estimate of their own selves. To such Jews, being a Jew was a misfortune. Moreover, many Jews were weary of battling against a hostile world. They were on the verge of despair, of spiritual exhaustion. No wonder, then, that they were beset by doubts about the whole question of the worthwhileness of being Jews. During this period, the national Jewish organizations of America had been spending millions of dollars each year in anti-defamation work, telling the non-Jews what the Jew was not—namely, that the Jew was not what the Nazis said he was. However, many thoughtful American Jews began to realize that it is more important to familiarize the Jew with what he is than to tell the non-Jew what he is not. Let the Jew know himself. Let him reclaim his heritage. Let him return to Jewish books and Jewish sources. Thus, self-knowledge became a weapon against the self-deprecation and self-hate brought on by anti-Semitism. Here again these needs were served by the synagogues, by local boards of Jewish education and Hebrew colleges, and by some of the national Jewish organizations which centered around philosophies of Jewish survival.

Thirdly, in the early 1940s America was at war with the Nazis. The American Jew was going through a critical period of strain and sacrifice. He was very much distressed and disturbed, in need of spiritual sustenance so that he could live with courage and serve with strength. The concerns of the day were for peace of mind, strength of spirit, and faith for the future. These needs the American Jew shared with all his fellow-citizens. But destiny had placed two additional needs on the shoulders of the American Jew. The first of these was to prepare himself to become the rebuilder of most of the world's Jewish communities, which were then being systematically destroyed. He had to begin thinking in global terms and to develop an international-mindedness that would fit him for the vast roles of relief, rehabilitation, and reconstruction he was sure to play upon the world Jewish stage. Moreover, there was the realization that American Jewry was destined not only to be the rebuilder of other Jewish communities, but also to become the builder in America of the largest Jewish community of all of Jewish history. In response to these needs, occasioned by the war and its aftermath, American Jewry created programs of adult Jewish education centered largely in the synagogues and in the national Jewish organizations, such as the Joint Distribution Committee, the United Jewish Appeal, the American Jewish Committee, the American Jewish Congress, and the B'nai B'rith.

It will help us to understand the temper of the period if we make even a brief examination of a few of the words spoken and written by Jewish educators in those days. The author of this volume, in an address entitled "Objectives in Adult Jewish Education," delivered at the thirty-eighth national convention of the Rabbinical Assembly of America, held in June 1938, stated:

> Our first objective must be *to educate the whole Jew*. Jewish education must not be limited to childhood or adolescence; instead it must be life-long in duration. We Jews must provide and achieve in our synagogues a program of Jewish education which should be co-extensive with the whole life-span of the Jewish man and the Jewish woman. . . . Our second objective is *to make the Jew whole*. It can be said, that since the period of Emancipation, the major problem of Judaism in the modern world has been and ever must be to bring completeness,

wholeness to the Jewish mind and the Jewish spirit. . . . Our third objective, closely allied to the above aim, is *to make the Jew feel the worthwhileness of Jewish life.* . . . The real worthwhileness of Jewish living cannot be experienced merely by contributing to Jewish relief or by donating to Jewish charity, or by paying dues to philanthropic institutions or even by belonging to a synagogue. The feeling of being fortunate and prideful and grateful in one's Jewishness can only be achieved through Jewish knowledge. . . . Our fourth objective, which is closely allied to the above two, is *to give to the American Jew a sense of kinship and integration with the total Jewish community in America and at the same time with "Kelal Yisroel"—with the totality of the Jewish people of the world.* . . . If the objectives heretofore stated, emphasized more the ways in which Adult Jewish Education should and could be serviceable to the Jew, it is well to turn to yet another goal which should seek to make the Jew serviceable to the Jewish people. Thereafter, our fifth objective must be *to train and enlist the Jew to become an intelligent, responsible and active factor in the solution of Jewish problems.*[10]

In October 1940, on the occasion of the launching of the National Academy for Adult Jewish Studies, Dr. Louis Finkelstein, then the chancellor of the Jewish Theological Seminary of America, wrote as follows:

This Academy has been founded to perform a double function. A broad knowledge of historical Judaism will bring psychological reassurance to the Jew of today, by showing him the present crisis in its proper perspective. A study of the Bible, the Talmud, and medieval and modern Hebrew literature, will also indicate the manner in which Judaism, and indeed civilization, can be saved in periods of crisis.[11]

That same month, Professor Mordecai M. Kaplan, whose teachings and labors have enhanced and advanced Jewish life in America, wrote:

The illiterate Jew is his own worst enemy because he himself is to blame for the breakdown of his morale under the impact of anti-Semitism. Morale is courage in the face of danger. It presupposes an undivided mind of self-confident spirit. When the enemy succeeds in getting us to doubt ourselves, it is entirely our own weakness and not his strength that undermines our self-confidence. Our ignorance of the

Jewish tradition renders us susceptible to self-doubt which brings on inner strife and breaks down our resistance.

Let the Jew learn the inner meaning of the stories of the Patriarchs and of the recorded experiences of Israel in Egypt. Let him try to understand the towering spirit of Moses. Let him have a general view of the forces that molded Israel into a nation. Let him discern the unique traits that reveal themselves in the renascence of the Jewish people in the Maccabean revolt, in the rise of Christianity, in the rise of Rabbinism, in the endless migrations and in the repeated recoveries. He will then realize how, throughout all the years, the Jewish spirit grew in clearness of purpose and strength of resolve to carry on. It will then dawn on him why a people with such an exceptional career, scattered among so many nations, is chosen as a convenient scapegoat for the world. The Jew who knows the facts which give the lie to all the Pharaohs, the Hamans, the Apions, and the Hitlers, can never lose confidence in himself and in his cause. . . .

The Jew who cultivates the tradition of his people does not merely inform his mind. He gains for himself an ancestry; he acquires status; he satisfies the need to belong to a permanent kinship and to be a part of a spiritual organism. The Jew who can rise to his feet and before all the world acclaim, "Our God and the God of our fathers." [12]

Fourth, the tragedy of the Holocaust was followed by the joy of the establishment of the State of Israel in November of 1948. The effects on the American Jew were colossal. He was filled with pride in his Jewishness and with a deeper reaffirmation of his Jewish identity. Being Jewish became more beautiful than ever. The desire increased to be more involved in Jewish affairs on every level and to find greater satisfaction and self-fulfillment in Judaism. This naturally led to the need for more Jewish learning, especially in such fields as the history of Palestine, the place of Eretz Yisrael in the life of the Jewish people, and Hebrew language and literature. This need for adult Jewish education was again met by the synagogues, the local boards of Jewish education and local Hebrew colleges, the Jewish community centers, the B'nai B'rith and such national organizations as the Zionist Organization of America and the Hadassah. The birth of the State of Israel also lent additional impetus to the growth of departments of Judaic studies, or Mid-Eastern Studies, in many American colleges and universities.

Finally, coincidental with all the above, still another important factor contributed to the flourishing of adult Jewish education in the two decades of the 1930s and the 1940s. This was the rise and rapid spread of a popular social-cultural force throughout America called adult education. The term *adult education* first appears in the literature of American education no farther back than 1916. Ten more years had to elapse before there was sufficient warrant for the formal organization of the American Association for Adult Education. This took place in 1926. It was estimated by the 1940s that some sixty million American men and women were enrolled as students in one or another study program for adults, approximately one-third of the total population at that time. This tremendous general interest in adult education had a stimulating influence upon Jewish life. It helped to revitalize our own traditional devotion to learning and to bring about the adult Jewish education movement. Added to all this, the postwar period saw the rise of magnificent new synagogue buildings and of very large Jewish community centers which provided the most inviting physical facilities for all kinds of learning programs for adults. And also at the same time, many Jewish educators began to specialize in the art of teaching adults, thus providing the needed professional leadership.

All these factors combined—the historical, the social, and the psychological—have created an adult Jewish education movement of major proportions, which today plays an important part in the life of American Jewry.[13]

If Franz Rosenzweig was the mentor who taught German Jewry the importance of lifelong Jewish learning, the same task was performed for American Jewry by Professor Mordecai M. Kaplan. This creative thinker, who happily is still with us in the tenth decade of his life, was a prime mover in getting American Jews to establish the adult Jewish education movement. As far back as 1948, in *The Future of the American Jew,* he had a chapter entitled "How to Vitalize Adult Jewish Study," in which he wrote:

> Our main concern in popularizing adult Jewish study should be to make it relevant and vital to present realities. We cannot create a demand for Jewish knowledge unless we are prepared to help the Jew find some meaning in the events in which he plays a part, and to cope with the problems that beset him as a Jew. Some of us may be so conditioned as to find delight in learning anything that has to do with Jewish life, past or present, near or remote. But we should not forget

that most Jews are nowadays without any cultural Jewish background. They can be roused by a harangue on anti-Semitism. But if we expect them to devote some time each week to studies that have to do with normal Jewish living and thinking, they must be convinced that those studies will help them to make the most out of their own lives as human beings. . . .

In sum, if we expect adult Jewish study to avoid the Charybdis of boredom and the Scylla of short-lived faddism, it must be made relevant to the problem of overcoming the centrifugal tendencies in Jewish life which threaten to disintegrate Jewish solidarity, to vitiate the Jewish ethic and to minimize the worth of the Jewish religion. It must neither pontificate nor speak with the kind of authority which treats all alternative views as either non-existent, or as unworthy of consideration, nor must it speak with the aloofness of encyclopedic scholarship, which has not the least concern whether you take or leave what it has to offer. Jewish adult study must concern itself with Jewish literacy as a means to Jewish experience. It must, above all, get as many of the Jewish laity as possible to cope personally with the problem of Jewish survival and growth, for only then will that problem receive a satisfactory solution. Such is the hope that breathes in the ancient prophecy which reads: "And all Thy children shall be taught of the Lord; and great shall be the peace of Thy children." [14]

Dr. Kaplan kept hammering away at this theme through the years. Speaking in 1956 before the national convention of the United Synagogue of America, he declared:

If adult Jewish education is not to be merely a temporary fad but a lifelong pursuit, its purpose should be to provide an answer to the questions of why and how to live as American Jews and as citizens of the world. As Jews, we have to learn to understand and love our ancestral culture and religion. As American Jews, we have to contribute to the moral and spiritual life of our country. As citizens of the world, we have to be in a position to act intelligently on all matters that pertain to the well-being of mankind as a whole. [15]

The status of adult Jewish education in America in the middle 1970s is not easy to ascertain. No national survey has been taken since 1964, when the American Association for Jewish Education published "The

Adult Jewish Education Activities of the American Jewish Community: Highlights and Insights." [16] But enough is known to recognize adult Jewish education as a major activity in American Jewry.

The three major branches of Judaism all have programs of Jewish studies for adults for the synagogues affiliated with them. The National Academy for Adult Jewish Studies of the United Synagogue of America (Conservative) was founded in 1940. The Department of Continuing Education of the Union of American Hebrew Congregations (Reform) goes back to 1948. The Department of Adult Education of the Yeshiva University (Orthodox) was established in 1955. In many hundreds of congregations throughout the country, there are thriving and on-going schools for adults. Many of them are called Institutes of Jewish Studies for Adults. In these programs, tens and tens of thousands of Jewish adults devote some time each year to Jewish learning.

Alongside the synagogues in each community, adult Jewish education programs are also offered by the local boards of Jewish education and by the local Hebrew colleges, where such exist.

All the national Jewish organizations are deeply concerned with the dissemination of Jewish knowledge and Jewish information. The B'nai B'rith has done most effective work in this area by the publishing of many books and, in addition, its quarterly magazine, *Jewish Heritage*. In various degrees the same is true of the other national organizations, such as the Zionist Organization of America and its Theodor Herzl Institute; Hadassah and its local study groups; the National Council of Jewish Women and its local study programs; the National Jewish Welfare Board; the American Jewish Congress and the magazine it publishes, *Judaism;* the American Jewish Committee and its important magazines, *Commentary* and *Present Tense,* together with its wide range of pamphlet literature; the National Council of Young Israel with its own institutional programs. One must also note the creative work in the Jewish education of adults being done by the Brandeis Camp Institute in California. It is hoped that what has so far been achieved will mark only the beginning of a deepening, expanding, and enlarging adult Jewish education movement in America.

(3) IN THE STATE OF ISRAEL

Even prior to the birth of the State of Israel, there was great concern for the furtherance of Jewish learning among the masses of the people. This concern was powerfully voiced by none other than the poet laureate of the Jewish people, Hayyim Naḥman Bialik. In the winter of 1934, he spoke at the opening exercises of the extension courses for adults offered by the Hebrew University to the people of Tel Aviv. He began his address by turning to the social and cultural conditions then prevailing in the all-Jewish city of Tel Aviv. He lamented the fact that people were wasting their leisure time on frivolous purposes. He noted with dismay the abundance of movie theatres, amusement centers, and social clubs, and the existence of all kinds of institutes. There were institutes for dancing, institutes for physical culture, institutes for beauty culure, but, exclaimed Bialik, there were no institutes for Jewish culture! He concluded with the cry and the challenge: "Has not the time come to establish institutes for Jewish learning? Is it too soon to lay the foundations in this city for an institution of Torah?"

Bialik then proceeded to declare that such an institution for the Jewish education of adults must serve two goals:

The first must be to draw streams of Jewish knowledge from the heights of Mount Scopus [where the Hebrew University was situated] in order to have them flow down to the lowlands [where the masses of the people live]. We shall not build our Jewish national life here by having the stores of Jewish wisdom confined within the four walls of a university. Judaism has ever conceived of our Torah as belonging to everyone. The rabbis interpret the words of the Bible, *"Mi-midbar mattanah"* (Num. 21:18) as indicating that the Torah is a *mattanah,* a gift given in the *midbar,* in the wilderness. This is to teach us that just as the vast wilderness has no owners, so does the Torah have no owners. Everyone who but wishes, can possess the Torah. And here is the second goal: To revive among us the precious practice of setting aside fixed periods of time for Jewish study. With us Jews there is no such thing as the end of learning. No other nation in the world is subject to the biblical commandment "And thou shalt meditate upon it day and night" (Josh. 1:8). According to his ability, every Jew is duty-bound to devote part of each day to Torah.[17]

The State of Israel, since its founding in November 1948, has striven mightily and sacrificially to spread the light of Jewish learning to the old settlers and also to all the newcomers from the many lands of the Jewish dispersion. The Ministry of Education and Culture has a vast network of schools and programs for adults. Among the best known are the *ulpanim,* which are residential schools teaching basic Hebrew, mainly to new settlers belonging to the professions. This ministry also publishes a wide variety of magazines and textbooks especially directed to the abilities and interests of the adult population. Of course the Israel Defense Forces have a vast program of Jewish learning for all in the armed services.

In addition to the work of the government, there are also vital and large voluntary public agencies which provide exciting programs of lectures and study courses. Among these one must list the Histadrut (the General Federation of Jewish Labor), which serves the intellectual and cultural needs of the towns, villages, and settlements. One must also, of course, point to the great Hebrew University in Jerusalem, which shortly after the beginning of the state established its Adult Education Center (*Ha-Merkaz le-Haskolat ha-Am*). One of the first guiding spirits of this center was Professor Martin Buber. In tribute to his labors and to his memory, the Hebrew University is now building a Martin Buber Adult Education Center on its now Mount Scopus campus.[18] The Tel Aviv University and the other Israeli universities all have centers for adult education. In a class by itself is the important nationwide voluntary private agency, with headquarters in Jerusalem, called the Adult Education Association in Israel (*Ha-Hitagdut le-Hinnukh Mevugarim be-Yisrael*). It publishes an impressive monthly magazine in addition to a considerable literature in pamphlet form. Jointly with the Center for Adult Education of the Hebrew University, it also publishes an annual volume containing many learned articles and reports on special studies and research projects.

In this brief survey we have not included the many study circles in synagogues throughout Israel, as well as the public lectures and study groups in such synagogues as the Hekhal Shelomo, the Yeshurun Synagogue, and the new Center for Conservative Judaism and the School for Bible and Archaeology, all in Jerusalem.

(4) WORLD-WIDE PROJECTS FOR JEWISH STUDY

In order to complete and conclude the story of adult Jewish education in the twentieth century, we must report on a number of projects that reach out to the entire Jewish world.

The World Jewish Bible Society, centered in Jerusalem but reaching out to Jewish communities everywhere, is an affiliate of the World Zionist Organization's Department of Education and Culture in the Diaspora. Through its subsidiary, the Israel Society for Biblical Research, it publishes an excellent quarterly magazine in Hebrew called *Bet Mikra,* which presents the writings of the foremost Bible scholars of our times. Its most important work is the sponsorship of Bible Study Circles in both Israel and the lands of Jewish dispersion. The Central Bible Study Circle is held in the President's Mansion in Jerusalem. Other Bible Study Circles are held in hundreds of Jewish communities throughout the world. In order to stimulate the study of Bible, the World Jewish Bible Society also publishes a magazine in English called *Dor le-Dor* ("From generation to generation"), which, as stated on its title-page, is directed to the English-reading public and "to the interests of Jewish laymen who wish to deepen their understanding of their heritage through Bible study." Its articles on Bible themes are scholarly but popular and appealing.

Of special interest and value is another organization of the World Jewish Bible Society, the Bible Readers' Union, which is centered in London. It was founded in 1939 and publishes a monthly bulletin in English, a kind of study-guide for those who are committed to the daily study of one chapter of the Bible. Through an attractive and informative Triennial Bible Reading Calendar, all members of the Bible Readers' Union throughout the world simultaneously study the same chapter of the Bible. In so doing, each member completes the study of the entire Bible in three years.[19]

If the above society devotes itself to the spread of Bible study throughout the Jewish world, another society based in Jerusalem, the World Congress for Hebrew (*Ha-Brit ha-Ivrit ha-Olamit*), is dedicated to the worldwide study of the Hebrew language and Hebrew literature. Its quarterly magazine in Hebrew, *Am ve-Sefer* ("People and Book"), is rich in content and format. The foremost Hebrew authors, scholars, and literary figures write for it, and each issue gives a full picture of Hebrew happenings on every continent of the globe in addition to popular articles on Hebrew literary and linguistic themes. In addition, this world organization sends its staff of emissaries to all centers of Jewish life—large or small—in order to establish circles for the study of the Hebrew language and the reading and appreciation of Hebrew literature.[20]

It is necessary to list also the worldwide daily Mishnah study program which was established about the year 1950 as a memorial to the Six Million. The initiator of this program, Rabbi Jonah Shtenzel of Tel Aviv, called it *Ha-Mishna ha-Yomit* ("The daily Mishnah"). Every participant studies two prescribed chapters of the Mishnah each day, following a calendar for the order of study issued by Rabbi Shtenzel. Thus, all the students in this program are studying the same Mishnah chapters at the same time as a memorial tribute to the Jewish martyrs of our time.[21]

The oldest of the worldwide projects is the *Daf Yomi*—the daily study of a page of the Talmud. The originator of this program was the great rabbi of Lublin, Poland, Rabbi Meir Shapiro, who proposed it in 1924 at the Great Assembly (*Kenesiah Gedolah*) of the Agudat Yisrael in Vienna. It was approved, and since then there have been, and are, hundreds of synagogues where Jews gather each day to study the prescribed page. It takes seven years to complete the study of the entire Talmud, which consists of 2,702 pages. At the end of each cycle, a festive *siyyum ha-gadol*—a great feast—is held to celebrate the completion of the sacred and exalting experience of seven years of dedicated daily devotion to talmudic learning.[22]

NOTES

INTRODUCTION   **PAGES V–IX**

1. Sh. Y. Tscharno, *Le-Toledot ha-Hinnukh be-Yisrael,* pt. 3, *Tekufat ha-Geonim* (Jerusalem, 1939).

2. Moritz Guedemann, *Geschichte des Erziehungswesens und der Kultur der abendländischen Juden während des Mittelalters,* 3 vols. (Vienna, 1888).

This work came out in Hebrew as *Ha-Torah ve-ha-Hayyim be-Artzot ha-Maarav bi-Yimei ha-Beinayim,* trans. A. Sh. Friedenberg (Warsaw, 1896).

Dr. Guedemann published still another book, which might be considered a continuation of his first work. This is his *Quellenschriften zur Geschichte des Unterrichtswesens und der Erziehung bei den deutschen Juden* (Berlin, 1891).

3. Simhah Asaf, *Mekorot le-Toledot ha-Hinnukh be-Yisrael: Mi-Tehilat Yemei ha-Beinayim ad Tekufat ha-Haskalah,* 4 vols. (Tel Aviv, 1925).

4. Isidor Fischman, *The History of Jewish Education in Central Europe: From the End of the 16th Century to the End of the 18th Century* (London, 1944).

5. Emanuel Gamoran, *Changing Conceptions in Jewish Education,* vol. 1, Jewish Education in Russia and Poland (New York, 1924).

6. Zevi Scharfstein, *Toledot ha-Hinnukh be-Yisrael,* 3 vols. (New York, 1945).

7. *News of YIVO* 80 (October, 1961): 3, 6.

CHAPTER I   **PAGES 1–9**

1. Other passages from the Pentateuch that stress the importance of education are: Gen. 18:19; Exod. 12:26, 13:8–9, 14; Deut. 4:8–9, 5:1, 28, 6:20–25, 11:19, 31:10–13. Passages prescribing the promulgation of the laws, the writing of the laws, and the use of devices to keep the people reminded of them, are: Num. 15:37–41; Deut. 6:8–9, 11:18–20, 17:18–20, 20:12, 27:1–4, 8.

2. *Yalkut Shimoni,* ad loc.

3. Kid. 29a–b.

4. *Yalkut Shimoni,* ad loc.

5. Mishnah Sota 7:8; Tosefta, ed. Zuckermandel, p. 308; B. Sota 41a–b; Y. Sota, 6:7.

6. *Antiquities* 4. 8. 12.

7. *Hilkhot Hagigah* 3. 3.

8. For an excellent presentation of this entire subject and for a full bibliography, see E. Ben Ezra, "Le-Toledot Mitzvot Hakhel," *Hadoar* 38 (14 Tishri 5713): 802–3, and Shelomo Goren, "Mitzvat Hakhel le-Or ha-Halakhah," in *Torat ha-Moadim* (Tel Aviv, 5724), pp. 127–38.

9. Above in n. 8 and also: Sh. Z. Kahana, "Mitzvat Hakhel," *Hadoar* 34 (17 Av 5712): 700–701; David Flinker, "Sukkos Traditzie Vert Baneit in Yisroel," *Der Tog,* October 3, 1952; Issachar Yaakovson, "Taamei Mitzvat Hakhel," in *Binah be-Mikra* (Tel Aviv, 5713), pp. 209–12.

10. Max Radin, *The Life of the People in Biblical Times* (Philadelphia, 1929), pp. 84–87; Sh. Y. Tscharno, *Le-Toledot ha-Hinnukh be-Yisrael,* pt. 1, *Tekufat ha-Mikra* (Jerusalem, 1939), pp. 25–26, 57–62; Ben Zion Dinur, "Ha-Hinnukh biTkufat Ha-Mikra," *Mahnayim* 108 (Av 1966): 18–23.

11. George F. Moore, *Judaism* (Cambridge, Mass., 1927), 1:283.

12. *Against Apion* 2. 17.

13. Louis Ginzberg, *The Legends of the Jews* (Philadelphia, 1913), 1:70.

14. Ibid., 5:260, 274.

15. Ibid., 5:228.

16. Ibid., 5:265.

17. Ibid., 2:315.

18. Ibid., 1:297, 2:315, 5:264; also Shalom Spiegel, *The Last Trial* (Philadelphia, 1967), p. 4.

19. Ginzberg, *Legends,* 1:316, 326, 341, 350; 5:274, 289.

20. Ibid., 1:395; 5:291, 313.

21. Ibid., 2:5.

22. Ibid.

23. Ibid., 5:356.

24. Ibid., 3:116.

25. Ibid., 3:143; 6:61.

26. Ibid., 3:67, 68, 420.

27. Ibid., 3:89; 6:54.

28. Ibid., 3:439.

29. Ibid., 3:67, 68, 173, 209, 218, 274, 350; 6:70.

30. Ibid., 3:73; 6:70.

31. Ibid., 3:323.

32. Ibid., 6:2.

33. Ibid., 3:7.

34. Ibid., 4:97, 101, 113, 114; 6:260, 263.

35. Ibid., 6:242, 257, 260.
36. Ibid., 5:200; 6:289.
37. Ibid., 6:242.
38. Ibid., 3:48.
39. Ibid., 4:355.

CHAPTER II

1. Ber. 28b.
2. Louis Finkelstein, "The Origin of the Synagogue," *Proceedings of the American Academy for Jewish Research* 1 (1928–30): 52; idem, *The Pharisees* (Philadelphia, 1938), 2:563; Jacob Mann, *The Bible as Read and Preached in the Old Synagogue* (vol. 1, Cincinnati, 1940; vol. 2, New York, 1966).
3. Finkelstein, *The Pharisees*, 2:568–69.
4. George F. Moore, *Judaism* (Cambridge, 1927), 1:286–87.
5. Y. Meg. 75a.
6. *Yalkut Shimoni,* Vayakhel.
7. *Against Apion* 2. 7.
8. *Antiquities* 16. 2, 3.
9. Fragment (from the first book of the *Hypothetica*) in Eusebius, *Praeparatio Evangelica* 8. Philo, ed. Mangey, 2. 630 f.
10. Moore, *Judaism,* 1:306–7; *De Specialibus Legibus* 2; *De Septenario* 6. 62 f.; *Philo,* ed. Mangey, 2. 282.
11. Philo, *On the Ten Commandments* 20, quoted in Abraham Millgram, *Sabbath: Day of Delight* (Philadelphia, 1944), pp. 214–15.
12. Harry A. Wolfson, *Philo* (Cambridge, 1947), 2:260.
13. Acts 15:21; see also Matt. 4:23; Mark 1:21, 6:2; Luke 4:15, 16, 31, 6:6, 13:10; Acts 13:14, 27, 42, 44, 16:13, 17:2, 18:4; et al.
14. Y. Meg. 75a, B.K. 82a.
15. Y. Ket. chap. 1, par. 1.
16. Meg. 32a and Mishnah Meg. 3:4—6; see Ismar Elbogen, *Der Jüdische Gottesdienst* (Frankfurt a.M., 1931), pp. 156 f., 538.
17. Moore, *Judaism,* 1:299–300.
18. Ibid., 1:302; see also Elbogen, *Der Jüdische Gottesdienst,* pp. 186 ff.
19. Ned. 37b; Meg. 3a; Y. Meg. 4:1.
20. Meg. 4:4.
21. Y. Meg. 74d.
22. Moore, *Judaism,* 1:303–4.
23. Meg. 32a.
24. Shimon Yaakov Glicksberg, *Ha-Derashah be-Yisrael* (Tel Aviv, 1940), p. 10.
25. Ibid., p. 13; Israel Bettan, *Studies in Jewish Preaching* (Cincinnati, 1939), p. 9.

26. William G. Braude, trans., *Pesikta Rabbati* (New Haven, 1968), 1:1.
27. Israel H. Levinthal, "The Uniqueness of the Classic Jewish Sermon," *Conservative Judaism* 27, no. 2 (Winter 1973): 77.
28. Solomon B. Freehof, *Modern Jewish Preaching* (New York, 1941), pp. 30–32.
29. Ibid., pp. 39–40.
30. Git. 38b; Y. Sot. 1, 4.
31. Tos. Meg. 3:2.
32. Glicksberg, *Ha-Derashah be-Yisrael*, p. 11; Bettan, *Studies in Jewish Preaching*, pp. 11–12.
33. Glicksberg, *Ha-Derashah be-Yisrael*, p. 11; Bettan, *Studies in Jewish Preaching*, pp. 12–13.

CHAPTER III   **PAGES 23–30**

1. Ber. 64a.
2. Targum Yerus. to Gen. 22:19, 24:62, 35:22; Gen. R. 63.
3. Gen. R. 63:10.
4. Targum Onkelos on Gen. 25:27.
5. Targum Yerus. to Gen. 33:17.
6. Gen. R. 95, Tanh. Vayigash 11.
7. Targum Yerus. to Exod. 39:33.
8. Num. R. 21.
9. Targum to 1 Sam. 19:19.
10. Eccles. R. 2:4.
11. San. 94b.
12. Gen. R. 63:10.
13. Y. Meg. 3:73d; Lam. R., introd. 12, 2.2; Pesik. 14, 121b.
14. Louis Ginzberg, *Students, Scholars and Saints* (Philadelphia, 1928), p. 87.
15. Y. Ket. 8, 32c.
16. B.B. 21a.
17. Avot 1:4; see Emil Schürer, *A History of the Jewish People in the Time of Jesus Christ* (New York, 1886–90), 2:44–89.
18. Sot. 9:15; Ber. 4:7c; Taan. 4:67d; and elsewhere.
19. Avot 1:1.
20. Avot 1:2.
21. Avot 1:6.
22. See Louis Finkelstein, "The Origin of the Synagogue," *Proceedings of the American Academy for Jewish Research* 1 (1928–30): 55, and idem, *The Pharisees* (Philadelphia, 1938), 2:566.
23. George F. Moore, *Judaism* (Cambridge, Mass., 1927), 1:311–13.
24. Tos. San. 7:1; Suk. 53a.

25. Y. Meg. 3:1 (73d).
26. Y. Hag. 76c; *Pesikta,* ed. Buber, p. 120b.
27. Moore, *Judaism,* 1:316–17.
28. Mishnah Meg. 3:1.
29. Meg. 26b, 27a.
30. Git. 38b.
31. *Seder Eliyahu Rabba* 13, 14.
32. Ber. 17a.
33. Gen. R. 48.
34. San. 105b.
35. Pesik. K. 48b.
36. Moore, *Judaism,* 1:314.
37. *Mishneh Torah, Hilkhot Talmud Torah,* chap. 4 at end.
38. Solomon Ganzfried–David Feldman, *Kitzur Shulhan Arukh* (Leipzig and New York, 1924), p. 23, par. 13.
39. Moore, *Judaism,* 1:319–20; Eccles. R. on Eccles. 7:28.
40. Shab. 116b; also Tos. San. 7:1 and Suk. 53a.
41. Moore, *Judaism,* 1:309–10.
42. Eccles. R. 5:7; also Lev. R. 22:1.
43. R.H. 23a.
44. Trans. P. M. Raskin in *Book of Jewish Thoughts,* ed. Joseph Hertz (New York, 1932), pp. 94–95.

CHAPTER IV   **PAGES 31–41**

1. Lewis N. Dembitz, *Jewish Services in Synagogue and Home* (Philadelphia, 1898), pp. 193–202; Nathan Isaacs, "Study as a Mode of Worship," in *Jewish Library,* ed. Leo Jung (New York, 1943), 1:51–70; Max Kadushin, *Worship and Ethics: A Study in Rabbinic Judaism* (Evanston, Ill., 1964), pp. 78–89; Abraham Millgram, *Jewish Worship* (Philadelphia, 1971), pp. 15–16, 67–70, 108–20, 194–97, 554–56.
2. Taan. 27, 27b.
3. Men. 110a.
4. Leopold Zunz, *Gottesdienstliche Vorträge der Juden* (Frankfurt a.M., 1892), p. 2.
5. Millgram, *Jewish Worship,* p. 108.
6. Ber. 11b.
7. Ibid.
8. Ibid.
9. Mishnah Peah 1:1.
10. Ber. 11b.
11. Mishnah Zeb. 5.
12. Beginning of Sifra.

13. Kadushin, *Worship and Ethics*, p. 89.
14. William G. Braude, trans., *The Midrash on Psalms* (New Haven, 1959), 1:23.
15. *Midrash Shoher Tov*, Ps. 1.
16. Kadushin, *Worship and Ethics*, p. 84. Y. Ber. 1:8, 3c.
17. Ker. 6a.
18. Mishnah Tamid, end.
19. End of treatise Berakhot.
20. Meg. 31a.
21. Solomon Schechter, "Rabbi Elijah Wilna, Gaon," in *Studies in Judaism, First Series* (Philadelphia, 1911), pp. 85–86.
22. *Keter Shem Tov* (Jerusalem, 1968), p. 22b. Quoted in Louis Jacobs, *Hasidic Prayer* (Philadelphia, 1973), p. 17.
23. Jacobs, *Hasidic Prayer*, p. 20.
24. Ibid.
25. Ibid., p. 18.
26. Norman Lamm, "Study and Prayer: Their Relative Value in Hasidism and Mitnagdism," in *Samuel K. Mirsky Memorial Volume* (New York, 1970), pp. 40–41, 46.

CHAPTER V   **PAGES 43–68**

1. San. 94a. See Sh. Y. Tscharno, *Le-Toledot ha-Hinnukh be-Yisrael*, pt. 2, *Tekufat ha-Talmud* (Jerusalem, 1939); also A. Hefterman, "Ha-Hinnukh be-Sifrut ha-Talmudit," *Shevilei ha-Hinnukh* 5, no. 3; Ch. Z. Reines, "Haskalat ha-Am bitkufat ha-Mikra ha-Mishnah ve-ha-Talmud," *Shevilei ha-Hinnukh* 30, no. 2; M. Glick, "Hinnukh ve-Horaah al pi Talmud Bavli," *Bitzaron* 24, no. 8, and 26, no. 7; also Hermann Gollancz, *Pedagogics of the Talmud and That of Modern Times* (London, 1924).
2. Sifra on Lev. 26:44.
3. Ber. 61b.
4. Ber. 64a.
5. Avot 4:7.
6. Ibid.
7. Avot 1:17.
8. Kid. 40b.
9. A.R.N., ed. Schechter, chap. 2, p. 14.
10. Avot 4:6.
11. Avot 3:22.
12. Kid. 40b.
13. Ber. 17a.
14. Deut. R. 7:4.
15. Avot 5:14.

16. Yoma 86a.
17. Avot 2:6.
18. Avot 2:8.
19. Avot 3:21.
20. Ned. 41a.
21. Min. 69b.
22. Avot 2:8.
23. Avot 6:7.
24. Avot 2:2.
25. Ber. 35b.
26. Avot 2:17.
27. Avot 2:9.
28. Avot 4:12.
29. Avot 6:4.
30. Yoma 35a.
31. Avot 4:11.
32. Gen. R., chap. 1.
33. Avot 5:25.
34. Avot 6:6.
35. Avot 6:3.
36. Avot 6:10.
37. Avot 6:2.
38. San. 91b.
39. Lev. R., parshot Tsav, chap. 9, par. 3.
40. Mek., ed. Lauterbach, 2:198.
41. A.R.N., ed. Schechter, chap. 2, p. 14.
42. Avot 2:2.
43. Avot 1:1. For a full and excellent study of the teacher in talmudic times, see the following essays by Moses Aberbach: "Ha-Moreh ha-Ivri bitkufat ha-Talmud," *Shevilei ha-Hinnukh*, 31, nos. 1–2; "Ha-Yahasim bein ha-Rav ve-ha-Talmid," ibid., 34, no. 1; "Ha-Yahasim bein ha-Rav ve-ha-talmid bitkufat ha-Talmud," ibid., 34, no. 2; "Baayot Mishmaat ve-Onshin bitkufat ha-Talmud," ibid., 27, no. 4; 28, nos. 3–4; 29, no. 4. Also, Max Arzt, "The Teacher in Talmud and Midrash," in *Mordecai M. Kaplan Jubilee Volume* (New York, 1953), English sec., pp. 35–49.
44. R.H. 23a.
45. Deut. R. 2:18.
46. William G. Braude, trans., *Pesikta Rabbati* (New Haven, 1968), 1:455.
47. San. 91b.
48. Tanh., Hayei Sarah 6.
49. A.Z. 19a.
50. Ibid.
51. Braude, *Pesikta Rabbati*, 1:61.

52. *Yalkut Shir ha-Shirim*, ed. Greenhut.
53. Braude, *Pesikta Rabbati*, 1:54.
54. Avot 4:6.
55. Suk. 49a.
56. Ket. 103b.
57. San. 99a.
58. Kid. 30a.
59. M.K. 17a.
60. R.H. 34a.
61. Pes. 112a.
62. Avot 6:3.
63. Hor. 13a.
64. B.M. 33a.
65. Ibid.
66. Avot 4:15.
67. San. 110a.
68. Ber. 27b.
69. Ket. 66a.
70. Pes. 51a.
71. San. 100a.
72. Yoma 37a.
73. Yoma 53a.
74. Avot 4:15.
75. Meg. 21a.
76. Pes. 117a.
77. Erub. 13a, b.
78. A.Z. 19a, b.
79. Taan. 8a.
80. Erub. 54a.
81. Ibid.
82. Y. Hag. 1:76, and also Midrash Tehillim on Ps. 127.
83. Mishnah Ber. 4.
84. Hag. 3b.
85. Avot 2:17.
86. Erub. 54b.
87. *Yalkut Eliezer*, sec. on Torah, par. 81.
88. Avot 2:5.
89. Avot 1:15.
90. Y. Ber. at end.
91. San. 99a.
92. Hag. 9b.
93. Yoma 29a.
94. Hag. 15a.

95. San. 99a.
96. A.Z. 19a.
97. Taan. 7b.
98. Erub. 54b.
99. Sifri Ekeb, chap. 48.
100. Pes. 72a.
101. Erub. 54a.
102. Ibid.
103. Ibid.
104. Meg. 32a.
105. Erub. 54b.
106. Y. Ber. 5:1.
107. Min. 43b.
108. Avot 4:18.
109. Avot 1:6.
110. Avot 1:16.
111. Avot 2:15.
112. A.Z. 19a.
113. A.Z. 19a, b.
114. Erub. 54b.
115. Taan. 7a.
116. Ber. 63b.
117. Taan. 7a.
118. Ibid.
119. Ibid.
120. Ibid.
121. Avot 3:7.
122. Avot 3:3.
123. Avot 3:4.
124. Avot 6:6.
125. Taan. 7a, b.
126. Midrash Nelam, quoted in *Yalkut Eliezer,* sec. on Torah, par. 130.
127. Avot 1:4.
128. Avot 4:18.
129. Ibid.
130. Avot 6:9.
131. Avot 1:15.
132. Erub. 65a.
133. Ibid. In this connection it is worth recalling that Rabbi Moses Sofer (1762–1840) wittily interpreted the verse *Ke-hitzim be-yad ha-gibbor ken b'nei ha-neorim* (Ps. 127:4) to mean: "As arrows in the hand of the hero, so are the children [the results] of nights spent in wakefulness," with *neorim* meaning

both "youth" and "wakefulness." Quoted in Leo Jung, ed., *Jewish Leaders* (New York, 1953), p. 123.

134. Exod. R. 47:5.
135. Erub. 18b.
136. San. 92a.
137. *Yalkut Eliezer,* sec. on Torah, par. 62. A similar sentiment is quoted in Midrash Tehillim: "Rabbi Brechia said: 'Our forefathers instituted the practice of studying Mishnah at dawn and at dusk.'" Quoted in William G. Braude, *The Midrash on Psalms* (New Haven, 1959), 1:24.
138. *Yalkut Shimoni,* Vayakhel.
139. Pes. R. 117.
140. *Seder Eliyahu Rabba* 26.
141. Pes. R., sec. on Ten Commandments; see Braude, *Pesikta Rabbati,* 1:490.
142. Lev. R., chap. 9.
143. Midrash Mishle 31.
144. Git. 60a.
145. San. 26b.
146. A.Z. 19a.
147. San. 19a.
148. A.Z. 19a.
149. Ibid.
150. Hag. 3a, b; Tos. Sot. 7:9.
151. Meg. 28b.
152. Meg. 7a.
153. Shab. 31a.
154. Sifri, Vaethanan.
155. San. 99a.
156. Meg. 28b.
157. Exod. R. 41:5.
158. Exod. R. 47:1.
159. B.M. 33a.
160. Sot. 44a.
161. Soferim, chap. 16; halakhah 8, 9.
162. Kid. 30a.
163. Soncino Talmud, Kiddushin, p. 144, n. 6.
164. Sifre 84b.
165. Ned. 62a.
166. Taan. 7a.
167. Avot 6:1.
168. Ber. 17a.
169. Suk. 49b.
170. San. 99b.

171. Y. Sot. 1:4.
172. San. 94b.
173. Ber. 17a.
174. Ned. 50a. See Anne Goldfeld, "Women As Sources of Torah In Rabbinic Judaism," Judaism vol. 24, No. 2, Spring 1975, pp. 245-256.
175. Ber. 11a.
176. Ber. 16b.
177. Ibid.
178. Ibid.
179. Ber. 17a.
180. Ibid.
181. Ibid.
182. Midrash Tanhuma on Toledot.

CHAPTER VI   **PAGES 69–77**

1. Jacob Lauterbach, "The Name of the Rabbinical Schools and Assemblies," in *Hebrew Union College Jubilee Volume* (Cincinnati, 1925), pp. 211–22.
2. B.B. 12b.
3. Quoted in Abraham Zacuto, *Sefer ha-Yuhasin,* first published by Samuel Shullam. Reprinted in many subsequent editions.
For much of the material in this chapter, see: (a) Sh. Y. Tscharno, *Le-Toledot ha-Hinnukh be-Yisrael,* 3, *Tekufat ha-Geonim* (Jerusalem, 1939). This study appeared earlier in *Ha-Tekufah* 20 (1936): 228–60. (b) Chaim Karlinsky, in *Hadoar,* 23 Kislev 5723, p. 125, and ibid., 14 Marheshvan 5724, p. 9.
4. Tscharno, *Le-Toledot ha-Hinnukh be-Yisrael,* pt. 3, pp. 211–12, quoted from *Sefer ha-Yuhasin.*
5. Ibid., p. 213.
6. Ibid.
7. Salo W. Baron, *Social and Religious History of the Jews* (New York, 1937), 1:287.
8. Tscharno, *Le-Toledot ha-Hinnukh be-Yisrael,* pt. 3, pp. 217–18.
9. *Day–Jewish Journal,* September 19, 1960, p. 5.
10. Shelomo Dov Gotein, *Sidre Hinnukh: Bi-Yemei ha-Geonim u'be-et ha-Rambam; Mekorot Hadashim min ha-Genizah* (Jerusalem, 1962).
11. Ibid., p. 127.
12. Ibid.
13. Ibid., p. 128.
14. Ibid.
15. Ibid., p. 130.
16. Ibid., p. 137.
17. Ibid., p. 138.

CHAPTER VII   **PAGES 79–115**

1. For the material on Rashi, see Samuel H. Blumenfeld, *Master of Troyes: A Study of Rashi, the Educator* (New York, 1946), pp. 24, 25, 46–48, 80–83, 85–87, 93, 106–201.

2. Ad loc. Shab. 105b.

3. Ad loc. Pes. 49b.

4. Ad loc. Sot. 49a.

5. Ad loc. Avot 1:1.

6. Ad loc. Sot. 49a.

7. Ad loc. Shab. 30b.

8. Simhah Asaf, *Mekorot le-Toledot ha-Hinnukh be-Yisrael* (Tel Aviv, 1925), 1:4.

9. Ad loc. Tos. Meg. 23b.

10. See also Rashi on Num. 3:1, Ps. 127:3, Eccles. 4:8, Kid. 30b.

11. See also Shab. 119b.

12. Ad loc. Shab. 30a.

13. Sifre on Deut. 11:13.

14. Ad loc. Avot 3:9.

15. Shab. 99a.

16. Ad loc. A.Z. 19a.

17. Ad loc. Taan. 6a.

18. Ad loc. Yeb. 117a.

19. Ad loc. Shab. 63b.

20. Ad loc. Erub. 54a.

21. Ibid.

22. Ad loc. Hag. 9b.

23. Ad loc. Erub. 54a.

24. Ad loc. Suk. 46b.

25. Ad loc. San. 99b.

26. Ad loc. Shab. 63a, Hor. 12a.

27. Ad loc. Erub. 55a.

28. Ibid.

29. Ad loc. Erub. 54b.

30. Pes. 112a.

31. Ad loc. Suk. 46b.

32. Mekhilta.

33. Ad loc. Ber. 63b.

34. See also Rashi, ad loc. Taan. 7b–8a, Erub. 54a.

35. Ad loc. Shab. 31a.

36. Ad loc. Sifre on Deut. 32:2.

37. Ad loc. Taan. 4a.

38. Tosafot, Ber. 11b 2.

39. Quoted from *Sefer Hasidim* in Asaf, *Mekorot le-Toledot ha-Hinnukh be Yisrael*, 1:19–20.

40. Kid. 30a.

41. Ber. 35b.

42. See the beginning of *Sefer ha-Rokeah;* chap. entitled "Shoresh ha-Torah she-be-hilkhot Hasidut."

43. Quoted from his book *Vo-vei Ho-ammudim* in Asaf, *Mekorot la-Toledot ha-Hinnukh be Yisrael*, 1:70.

44. Quoted from the *Tokhahat Megillah,* which is attached to the *Sefer Reshit Bikkurim,* in Asaf, *Mekorot le-Toledot ha-Hinnukh be-Yisrael,* 1:176.

45. "The Good Heart," written by Isaac ben Eliakim of Posen and published in 1620 in Prague.

46. "The Commandment for Women," first printed in Venice, 1552.

47. "The Gross Mirror," written by Moses ben Henoch and first published in Basel, 1602.

48. "The Book of Moral Instruction," apparently by Joseph Yoseppa, shamash of Worms; printed in Amsterdam, 1690.

49. A very popular paraphrase of the Pentateuch, composed by Rabbi Jacob ben Isaac Ashkenazi of Janow, Poland, and printed in Cracow, in 1620.

50. Quoted from the *Amude Shesh* (1617) in Asaf, *Mekorot le-Toledot ha-Hinnukh be-Yisrael,* 1:63.

51. Quoted in Asaf, *Mekorot le-Toledot ha-Hinnukh be-Yisrael,* 1:76.

52. The famous Maharal.

53. Shlomo Katz, "An Aristocracy of Learning," *Commentary,* June 1947, pp. 578–82. The bracketed comments are Katz's. See also Abraham J. Mesch, *Abyss of Despair* (New York, 1950), pp. 110–16.

54. *Mahberet ha-Tofet ve-ha-Eden,* ed. Goldschmidt (Berlin, 1922).

55. Quoted in Asaf, *Mekorot le-Toledot ha-Hinnukh be-Yisrael,* 1:40.

56. Felix Giovanelli, "Learning among the Hebrews: A 17th Century Report," *Commentary* 13 (June 1952): 589–93.

57. Quoted from the *Teshuvot ha-Geonim* 4 (Lyck no. 87) in Asaf, *Mekorot le-Toledot ha-Hinnukh be-Yisrael,* 2:3.

58. Quoted from Asaf, *Mekorot le-Toledot ha-Hinnukh be-Yisrael,* 2:3, n. 7.

59. *Sefer ha-Ittim* of Rabbi Judah ha-Barzeloni, p. 267, quoted in Asaf, *Mekorot le-Toledot ha-Hinnukh be-Yisrael,* 2:62–63.

60. Quoted in Asaf, *Mekorot le-Toledot ha-Hinnukh be-Yisrael,* 2:12, n. 2.

61. From the *Sefer ha-Ittim* of Rabbi Judah ha-Barzeloni, p. 267, quoted in Asaf, *Mekorot le-Toledot ha-Hinnukh be-Yisrael,* 2:12–13.

62. Ibid., 2:21.

63. Quoted in ibid., 2:20–22.

64. Quoted in ibid., 2:21.

65. Quoted from the Testament of Judah ibn Tibbon in Israel Abrahams, *Hebrew Ethical Wills* (Philadelphia, 1926), 1:58.

66. Ibid., 1:62.

67. Ibid., 1:64.

68. Ibid., 1:63–64.

69. *Shivas Yisrael,* p. 113, quoted in *Mishlei Yisrael.* See Mordecai Waxman, *A History of Jewish Literature* (New York, 1938–47), 1:170.

70. Quoted from the *Iggeret ha-Teshuvah* in Asaf, *Mekorot le-Toledot ha-Hinnukh be-Yisrael,* 2:45–46.

71. Shab. 127a.

72. Sifri Ekeb.

73. Quoted in *Yalkut ha-Deot ve-ha-Midot,* Cecil Roth, *History of the Jews of Venice* (Philadelphia, 1930), pp. 171–72; see also p. 324, n. 75.

74. *Menorat ha-Maor,* ed. and trans. Hyman G. Enelow (New York, 1929–32), 1:16.

75. A.Z. 18b.

76. This explanation differs from the one in the Talmud, which explains this biblical phrase as meaning: "he who does not participate in evil plannings."

77. A.Z. 19b.

78. *Menorat ha-Maor,* 3:203–4.

79. Ibid., 3:212–23.

80. Ibid., 3:215–17.

81. Ibid., 3:221–23.

82. Ibid., 3:223–26.

83. Ibid., 3:226–38.

84. Ibid., 3:243.

85. Cf. Avot 6:9.

86. Cf. Shab. 31a.

87. *Menorat ha-Maor,* 3:247. Cf. A.R.N., ed. Schechter, p. 70.

88. Ibid., 3:248. Cf. Gen. R. 65:20.

89. Ibid., 3:254.

90. Ibid., 3:256.

91. A.Z. 3b.

92. *Menorat ha-Maor,* 3:287–99.

93. Ibid., 3:287–303.

94. Taan. 7a.

95. Erub. 54b.

96. *Menorat ha-Maor,* 3:202–16.

97. Ibid., 3:321.

98. Cf. *Seder Eliyahu Zuta* 14, ed. Friedman, pp. 195 f.

99. Avot 5:25.

100. Mishnah Kin. 3:6.

101. Yoma 86a.

102. *Menorat ha-Maor,* 3:316–21.

103. B.M. 33b.

104. B.B. 8a.

105. *Menorat ha-Maor,* 3:355–57.

106. Deut. R. 7:4.

107. Kid. 40b.

108. *Menorat ha-Maor,* 3:357–59.

109. For sources, see *Menorat ha-Maor,* fn. to "elel" 11. 9 ff, p. 359.

110. Ibid., 3:359–60.

111. Ibid., 3:360–70.

112. Avot 2:6.

113. Avot 5:21.

114. Introduction to *Maase Ephod,* quoted in Asaf, *Mekorot le-Toledot ha-Hinnukh be-Yisrael,* 2:68–72.

115. Ibid., 2:83.

116. Quoted in *Mishle Yisrael,* Waxman, *History of Jewish Literature,* 1:170.

117. Quoted in Asaf, *Mekorot le-Toledot ha-Hinnukh be-Yisrael,* 3:27; see also "Wege Nach Zion," in Kurt Wilhelm, *Von Jüdischer Gemeinde und Gemainschaft* (Berlin, 1938).

118. Asaf, *Mekorot le-Toledot ha-Hinnukh be-Yisrael,* 3:26.

119. Solomon Schechter, *Studies in Judaism: Second Series* (Philadelphia, 1908), p. 296.

120. Ibid., p. 298.

121. Quoted in Asaf, *Mekorot le-Toledot ha-Hinnukh be-Yisrael,* 3:10.

122. Ibid., 3:82–84.

123. Ibid., 3:5.

CHAPTER VIII   **PAGES 117–133**

1. Israel Abrahams, *Hebrew Ethical Wills* (Philadelphia, 1926), 1:63.

2. Ibid., 1:80–82.

3. Ibid., 1:85.

4. Quoted in ibid., 2:220.

5. Ibid., 2:222.

6. Ber. 8a.

7. Abrahams, *Hebrew Ethical Wills,* 2:226–28.

8. A. H. Freiman, "Sefer al Esek ha-Torah," in *Jubilee Volume in Honor of Professor Louis Ginzberg* (New York, 1964), Hebrew sec., pp. 355–61.

9. Ibid., pp. 361–63.

10. Avot 2:5.

11. Shab. 30a.

12. Shab. 30b.

13. Avot 5:23.
14. Mishnah Sota, end.
15. A.Z. 17b.
16. Avot 2:6.
17. Erub. 55a.
18. Ber. 63b.
19. Avot 4:12.
20. Avot 5:25.
21. Avot 6:4.
22. Erub. 22a.
23. Ket. 59b.
24. Eccles. R. 1:34.
25. Suk. 28a.
26. Avot 6:1.
27. Abrahams, *Hebrew Ethical Wills,* 1:118–25.
28. Ibid., 1:124.
29. Hag. 9b.
30. Erub. 65a.
31. Avot 2:14.
32. Ned. 81a.
33. B.K. 30a in reference to Mishnah Avot.
34. Avot 3:4.
35. Ber. 13a.
36. Abrahams, *Hebrew Ethical Wills,* 2:172–75.
37. Ibid., 2:203–4.
38. Simhah Asaf, *Mekorot le-Toledot ha-Hinnukh be-Yisrael* (Tel Aviv, 1925), 1:64.
39. Abrahams, *Hebrew Ethical Wills,* 2:253–54.
40. Ibid., 2:255.
41. Ibid., 2:256–57.
42. Franz Kobler, ed., *A Treasury of Jewish Letters* (Philadelphia, 1953), 2:450–53.
43. Ibid., 2:460–62.
44. Abrahams, *Hebrew Ethical Wills,* 2:285.
45. Asaf, *Mekorot le-Toledot ha-Hinnukh be-Yisrael,* 1:178–80.
46. Abrahams, *Hebrew Ethical Wills,* 2:290.
47. Asaf, *Mekorot le-Toledot ha-Hinnukh be-Yisrael,* 1:177–78.
48. See *Prince and Nazirite* (by Hisdai), chap. 10; cf. Israel Abrahams, *Studies in Pharisaism: First Series* (1917), p. 93.
49. Abrahams, *Hebrew Ethical Wills,* 2:322–23.
50. Tos. Kid. 30a.
51. Asaf, *Mekorot le-Toledot ha-Hinnukh be-Yisrael,* 1:272.

CHAPTER IX   **PAGES 135–165**

1. Louis Ginzberg, *Students, Scholars and Saints* (Philadelphia, 1928), p. 117.

2. The English translation of *Hilkhot Talmud Torah* in this chapter is from vol. 1 of Moses Hyamson's edition of the *Mishneh Torah* (New York, 1937). Chapter and section citations are given in brackets at the conclusion of each extract. The parenthetical references and comments are Hyamson's.

See also Shelomo Veisblit, "Darkei Horaah be-Mishnat ha-Rambam," *Mahnayim* 108 (Av 1966): 40–43; Zev Elifant, "Bi-Shevilei ha-Pilosofiah ha-Hinnukhit shel ha-Rambam," *Shevilei ha-Hinnukh* 34, no. 1 (Autumn 1973): 11–16; Yehoshua Veinshtein, "Ha-Rambam ha-Moreh le-Dorot," *Shevilei ha-Hinnukh* 31, no. 1 (Autumn 1973), continued in ibid. 34, no. 2 (Winter 1973): 81–89, and in subsequent issues.

3. This translation from the *Shulhan Arukh* was made by Dr. David de Sola Pool. It first appeared in *Menorah Journal* 10 (June–July 1924) and was reprinted in *Jewish Education* 16, no. 3 (May 1945). The parenthetical references and comments are from the notes appended by Dr. Pool to the translation; the annotations in smaller type were selected by Dr. Pool from the several commentaries on the basic text of the *Shulhan Arukh*.

CHAPTER X   **PAGES 167–171**

1. Louis Finkelstein, *Jewish Self-Government in the Middle Ages* (New York, 1924), p. 248.

2. Ibid., p. 349.

3. Ibid., p. 354; cf. also Abraham A. Neuman, *The Jews in Spain* (Philadelphia, 1942), 2:64.

4. Isaac Rivkind, in *Reshumot* 4 (1926): 345 ff., has published the two extant versions of this ordinance. See also Kurt Wilhelm, *Von Jüdischer Gemeinde und Gemeinschaft* (Berlin, 1938).

5. Simhah Asaf, *Mekorot le-Toledot ha-Hinnukh be-Yisrael* (Jerusalem, 1942), 4:62.

6. Israel Halpern, *Takkanot Medinat Mehrin (1650–1748)* (Jerusalem, 1952), p. 9.

7. Ibid., p. 7.

8. Regulation no. 45 in *Takkanot ha-Kehillah d'K.K. Ashkenazim—Amsterdam, 1737.*

9. Asaf, *Mekorot le-Toledot ha-Hinnukh be-Yisrael,* 4:66, quoted from *Pinkas ha-Medinah, O, Pinkas Vaad ha-Kehillot bi-Medinat Litta* (Berlin, 1925), p. 266.

10. Finkelstein, *Jewish Self-Government,* p. 350.

CHAPTER XI   **PAGES 173–195**

1. *News of the YIVO* 56 (March 1955): 5.

2. Jacob R. Marcus, *Communal Sick Care in the German Ghetto* (Cincinnati, 1947), chap. 2, "The Origin of the Hebra Kaddisha"; also Appendix 8, "The Origin of the Term Hebra Kaddisha." In both of these places, full and copious references are given to the entire literature on this subject.

3. Ber. 98b, R.H. 19b, Bet. 14b, 27a.

4. Isidore Epstein, *The Responsa of Rabbi Solomon ben Adreth of Barcelona* (London, 1925), pp. 66–68.

5. Marcus, *Communal Sick Care*, p. 61.

6. Ibid., pp. 80–87, for an analysis of the differences between Jewish and Christian religious guilds; also, Isaac A. Levitats in *Hadoar* (8 Tevet 5716), p. 147, and idem in *Hadoar 35th Jubilee Volume* (New York, 1957), p. 234.

7. For an excellent presentation of this subject, see Mark Wischnitzer, *A History of Jewish Crafts and Guilds* (New York, 1965); Michael Hendel, *Melakhah u-Vaalei Melakhah be-Am Yisrael* (Tel Aviv, 1955), especially chap. 5, "Hevrot Baalei Melakhah be-Polin Bemeah Hasheh Esreh ad ha-Shmoneh Esreh"; Yaakov Katz, *Masoret u-Mashber ha-Hevrah ha-Yehudit Bemotzaei Yemei ha-Beinayim* (Jerusalem, 1958), especially chap. 16, "Havurot ve-Hayyei ha-Hevrah," pp. 174–84.

8. Hendel, *Melakhah u-Vaalei Melakhah*, pp. 62–74.

9. Ibid., pp. 74–75, and Katz, *Masoret u-Mashber ha-Hevrah ha-Yehudit*, p. 188.

10. Hendel, *Melakhah u-Vaalei Melakhah*, pp. 76–77.

11. Ibid., p. 77.

12. Avot 1:2.

13. Marcus, *Communal Sick Care*, p. 117; Isaac Levitatas, *The Jewish Community in Russia 1772–1844* (New York, 1943), pp. 118 and 190.

14. Jacob R. Marcus, "The Triesch Hebra Kaddisha," *Hebrew Union College Annual* 19 (1945–46): 189.

15. *Pinkas ha-Takkanot . . . min Hevrah Kaddisha d'Kabronim b'Altona,* p. 19; MS in Dubnow Collection of YIVO Library.

16. "Statutes of the Benevolent Society Rodfei Zedakah, Frankfurt, 1786," in *Jahrbuch der Jüdische, Litterarischen Geselschaft* 3 (1904): 241 ff.; A. Sulzbach, quoted by Kurt Wilhelm in *Von Jüdischer Gemeinde und Gemeinschaft* (Berlin, 1938), p. 105.

17. *The Takkanot of the Hevrah Kaddisha Tiferet Bahurim, Amsterdam, 1778;* MS in Elkan Adler Collection, Jewish Theological Seminary Library, takkanah 17.

18. *The Takkanot of the Hevrah Kaddisha Talmud Torah, Amsterdam, 1804,* no. 37.

19. Ibid., no. 20.

20. Hendel, *Melakkah u-Vaalei Melakhah*, p. 74.

21. Ibid., p. 75.

22. Levitats, *Jewish Community in Russia*, p. 190.

23. *Ha-hevrah Kenessiah le-Shem Shamayim of Venice, 1611–1843*, MS in Elkan Adler Collection, Jewish Theological Seminary.

24. See catalogue of MSS in Adler Collection no. 2774.

25. MS pp. 18b and 19a.

26. MS p. 20b.

27. MS, p. 21a.

28. MS, p. 22b.

29. MS, p. 20a.

30. MS, p. 23a.

31. Ibid.

32. MS, p. 23b.

33. Wischnitzer, *Jewish Crafts and Guilds*, pp. 184–90, 283–85.

34. Max Grunwald, *History of the Jews in Vienna* (Philadelphia, 1936), pp. 384–85.

35. Marcus, *Communal Sick Care*, p. 118.

36. Max Grunwald, "Altjudische Gemeindleben" in *Mitteilungen Zur Jüdischen Volkskunde* (Vienna, 1926), p. 599, quoted in Wilhelm, *Von Jüdischer Gemeinde und Gemeinschaft*, pp. 98–99.

37. Wilhelm, *Von Jüdischer Gemeinde und Gemeinschaft*, p. 101.

38. Ibid., pp. 106–7.

39. Marcus, *Communal Sick Care*, p. 118.

40. *Pinkas ha-Takkanot . . . min Hevrah Kaddisha b'Altona*, pp. 23–24.

41. *The Pinkas of the Verein Holcha Tom in Kempen in Posen*, in the Yeshiva University Library, MS no. 86.

42. Wischnitzer, *Jewish Crafts and Guilds*, pp. 110–13.

43. These statutes have frequently been referred to and reprinted. See Max Grunwald, "Kleine Beitrage zur jud. Kulturgeschichte," *Mitteilugen zur judischen Volkskunde* 21 (Vienna 1920), p. 21, and Wilhelm, *Von Jüdischer Gemeinde und Gemeinschaft*, pp. 92–93.

44. MS in Elkan Adler Collection, Jewish Theological Seminary Library, on p. 47, no. 1126.

45. MS in Dubnow Collection, YIVO Library. *Takkanot shel ha-Hevrah Kaddisha Agudat Bahurim* (Amsterdam, 1790).

46. *Pinkas Vaad ha-Kehillot ha-Rishonot bi-Mdinat Litta*, ed. Shimon Dubnow (Berlin, 1925), p. 34.

47. Avraham Hayyim Shabad, *Sefer Toledot ha-Yamim she-Avru al Hevrah Kaddisha Shivah Keruim ve-al Bet ha-Midrash ha-Gadol Asher be-Ir Pinsk, 1763–1903, Pt. 1, 1763–1794* (Vilna, 1904).

48. In *Yeda Am* (Tel Aviv) 13, nos. 23, 24; also in the column by Menashe Unger in the *Day–Morning Journal* (date cannot be determined).

49. MS in Jewish Theological Seminary Library, accession no. 63964.

50. Michael M. Zarchin, "Tailors' Guild of Kurnik, Province of Posen," *Jewish Quarterly Review* 28 (1937–38): 47–56.

51. Samuel Winter, "Minute-Books of Societies," *YIVO Bleter* 13 (January–February 1938): 86, 88.

52. Hendel, *Melakhah u-Vaalei Melakhah,* pp. 267–69.

CHAPTER XII   **PAGES 197–207**

1. Taan. 7a.

2. Israel Abrahams, *Jewish Life in the Middle Ages* (Philadelphia, 1896), p. 357, n. 2.

3. L. Rabinowitz, *The Social Life of the Jews in Northern France in the XII–XIV Centuries* (London, 1938), pp. 218–19, quotes Tos. Ber. 11b, 2.

4. Ibid., pp. 218–19.

5. Isidore Epstein, *The Responsa of Adreth* (London, 1935), pp. 64–65.

6. Responsum 84, quoted in Abrahams, *Jewish Life in the Middle Ages,* p. 324.

7. Isidore Epstein, *The Responsa of Rabbi Simon ben Zemach Duran* (London, 1930), p. 77.

8. Chaim Tchernowitz, *Toledot ha-Poskim* (New York, 1946), 3:127–28. Also quoted in Simhah Asaf, *Mekorot le Toledot ha-Hinnukh be-Yisrael* (Tel Aviv, 1925), 1:26.

9. "Gur Aryeh" on Rashi for Deut. 6:7.

10. Asaf, *Mekorot le-Toledot ha-Hinnukh be Yisrael,* 1:63.

11. Morris S. Goodblatt, *Jewish Life in Turkey in the 16th Century, Based on the Responsa of Rashdam* (New York, 1952), pp. 64 and 107.

12. Franz Kobler, ed., *A Treasury of Jewish Letters* (Philadelphia, 1953), 2:393–95.

13. Asaf, *Mekorot le-Toledot ha-Hinnukh be Yisrael,* 4:117.

14. Ibid., 4:62.

15. Ibid., 1:70.

16. Ibid., 4:115.

17. Max Grunwald, *History of the Jews in Vienna* (Philadelphia, 1936), pp. 383–84.

18. Adolf Kober, *History of the Jews in Cologne* (Philadelphia, 1940), p. 282.

19. *Meor Einayim,* chap. 57 of *Helek Yemei Olam;* also *He-Asif,* 3:214, 220. These sources are quoted in Moses Shulvas, *Hayyei ha-Yehudim be-Italya Bitkufat ha-Rinesans* (New York, 1955), p. 197.

20. Cecil Roth, *History of the Jews in Venice* (Philadelphia, 1930), pp. 155–56.

21. Abrahams, *Jewish Life in the Middle Ages,* p. 327.

22. A. H. Shabad, *Sefer Toledot ha-Yamim mi-Pinkasim shel Shivah Keruim,* 2nd ed. (Vilna, 1904), p. 93.

23. Ibid., p. 106.

24. Ibid., p. 107.

25. Ibid., p. 124.

26. MS in library of Jewish Theological Seminary, p. 8a.

27. Ibid., pp. 8a, 17a.

28. Ibid., p. 66a.

29. *Takkanot me-ha-Havurah ha-Kedoshah Anshei Maamad,* organized by Rabbi Joseph Saul Nathanson of Lemberg, takkanah no. 8.

30. Tchernowitz, *Toledot ha-Poskim,* 3:123.

31. *YIVO Bleter* 13 (January–February 1938): 77.

32. Israel Cohen, *History of the Jews in Vilna* (Philadelphia, 1943), p. 108.

33. Ibid., pp. 182–83.

34. Daniel Shternfeld, *Sefer ha-Hukim ve-ha-Takkanot ha-Yeshivah Torat Hayyim,* printed in *Husiatin* (n.d.).

35. *News of YIVO* no. 32 (April 1949): 5, 8. There is a reproduction of a page, from an eighteenth-century book, bearing the stamp of this association.

36. The account of this incident given here is by Mrs. Saul Lieberman. See Louis Finkelstein, ed., *Thirteen Americans* (New York, 1953), pp. 172–73.

CHAPTER XIII   **PAGES 209–260**

1. The list of these manuscripts in the library of the Jewish Theological Seminary is as follows:

a. *Pinkas min ha-Havurah Magidei Tehillim u-Gemilut Hasadim* (Kiev, 1895). This is a beautifully bound large volume written with letters like those of a Sefer Torah but in much larger script and in inks of various colors.

b. *Pinkas me-ha-Havurah Shas of the Bet ha-Midrash of Rabbi Vilkovski* (Bialystok, 1865).

2. Mainly in Isaac Levitats, *The Jewish Community in Russia 1772–1844* (New York, 1943), chaps. 6 and 9; Samuel Winter, "Minute-Books of Societies," *YIVO Bleter* 13 (January–February 1938): 77–94; A. Lipman, *Le-Toledot ha-Yehudim be-Kovno* (Keidany, 1934); Simhah Asaf, *Mekorot le-Toledot ha-Hinnukh be-Yisrael* (Tel Aviv, 1925), 4:234–37.

3. MS in library of Jewish Theological Seminary.

4. Levitats, *Jewish Community in Russia,* pp. 194–96.

5. Winter, "Minute-Books of Societies," pp. 78–80, 93.

6. Ibid., pp. 80–83.

7. Ibid., p. 93.

8. Ibid., pp. 82–83.

9. Lipman, *Le-Toledot ha-Yehudim be-Kovno,* pp. 208–9.

10. Levitats, *Jewish Community in Russia,* p. 195 and table 1, facing p. 110.

11. MS in library of Jewish Theological Seminary; see Y. L. Zlotnik, "Seridim mi-Kehillat Gombin," *Reshumot*, n.s. 3 (1947): 217–28.

12. Two MSS entitled *Pinkas Hevrah Mikra of Gombin, 1792–1892* in library of Jewish Theological Seminary.

13. MS I, p. 3b. See also Zlotnik, "Seridim mi-Kehillat Gombin."

14. MS I, p. 4a.

15. MS I, p. 5a.

16. MS II, end fly-leaf.

17. MS II, p. 47.

18. Winter, "Minute-Books of Societies," pp. 77–78.

19. Levitats, *Jewish Community in Russia*, pp. 194, 197, and table 1, facing p. 110.

20. Ibid., p. 194 and table 1, facing p. 110.

21. Lipman, *Le-Toledot ha-Yehudim be-Kovno*, pp. 214–16.

22. Levitats, *Jewish Community in Russia*, pp. 193–94.

23. Winter, "Minute-Books of Societies," pp. 83–84.

24. Levitats, p. 193 and table 1, facing p. 110.

25. Asaf, *Mekorot le-Toledot ha-Hinnukh be-Yisrael*, 4:236–37.

26. Levitats, *Jewish Community in Russia*, p. 197.

27. Aryeh Newman, "An Almost Forgotten Chapter in Jewish Adult Education," *Jewish Affairs* (Johannesburg, S.A.), February 1957, pp. 44–48.

28. *Jewish Encyclopedia*, s.v. "Maggid," 3:252–54.

29. A. R. Meyers, *England in the Late Middle Ages*, p. 62, quoted in C. Hartley Grattan, *In Quest of Knowledge* (New York, 1955), pp. 57–58.

30. G. R. Owst, *Literature and Pulpit in Mediaeval England* (Cambridge, 1933), quoted in Grattan, *In Quest of Knowledge*, p. 58.

31. *Commentary* 11, no. 5 (May 1951): 480–84, introduction by Dr. Nahum N. Glatzer.

32. Levitats, *Jewish Community in Russia*, p. 192, and table 1, facing p. 110.

33. Ibid., pp. 118–19, 192–96, and table 1, facing p. 110.

34. Zlotnik, "Seridim mi-Kehillat Gombin," pp. 219–23.

35. Asaf, *Mekorot le-Toledot ha-Hinnukh be-Yisrael*, 4:234–36.

36. Lipman, *le-Toledot ha-Yehudim be-Kovne*, pp. 210–13.

37. MS in library of Jewish Theological Seminary. See note 1, item b, above.

38. Levitats, *Jewish Community in Russia*, p. 191 and table 1, facing p. 110.

39. Ibid.

40. A copy of this pinkas is in the author's possession.

41. *Sefer Shaarei Torah u-Tefillah me-Hevrat Yeshivat Bar Yohai*, organized in Safed, 1890 (Jerusalem, 1903).

42. Isaac Levitats, "Hevrot Yehudiyot be-Amerika," in *Sefer Hadoar 35th Anniversary Volume* (New York, 1957), pp. 234–40.

43. Bernard Segal, "A Providence Pinkas," *Providence Passover Journal,* p. 8.

44. *Providence Jewish Herald,* October 15, 1948.

45. Bernard Segal, "The Pinkas," *Rhode Island Jewish Historical Notes* 1, no. 3 (June 1955): 193–226.

46. From the minute-books of the congregation. Reprinted in *Chizuk Amuno Bulletin* 17, no. 22 (January 27, 1956).

47. A copy of this pinkas is in the author's possession.

CHAPTER XIV

1. Maurice Samuel, *In Praise of Yiddish* (New York, 1971), p. 38.

2. Max Grunwald, "Das Lernen," in *Jahrbuch fur Jüdische Volkskünde* (Berlin and Vienna, 1925), pp. 98–110.

3. Zevi Hirsch Halevi Kolk, *Sefer mi-Dor le-Dor* (Warsaw, 1901), pp. 82–84.

4. Yaakov Lipschitz, *Zichron Yaakov* (Kovno, 1927), p. 67.

5. Ibid., p. 72.

6. Ibid., p. 195.

7. Ibid., p. 150.

8. Ibid., p. 149.

9. Zevi Scharfstein, *Toledot ha-Hinnukh be-Yisrael be-Dorot ha-Aharonim* (New York, 1945), 1:14–15.

10. Avot 4:11.

11. A.R.N. 28.

12. Quoted in Scharfstein, *Toledot ha-Hinnukh be-Yisrael,* pp. 15–16.

13. Simhah Asaf, *Mekorot le-Toledot ha-Hinnukh be-Yisrael* (Tel Aviv, 1925), l:x.

14. Solomon Simon, *My Jewish Roots* (Philadelphia, 1956), p. 40.

15. Ibid., p. 135.

16. Ibid., pp. 98–99.

17. Ibid., p. 157.

18. Israel Matz, "Memories of Kalvaria," *Menorah Journal* 48, nos. 1–2, pp. 82–83.

19. Daniel Persky, *Hadoar* 38, no. 1 (November 1, 1957).

20. There is a monograph on Reb Isser's Heder in *Yiddishe Neshomos* by A. Litwin. It also appeared in a Hebrew translation published by *Am Oved* in Tel Aviv.

21. Yitzchak Nisenbaum, *Alai Heldi* (Warsaw, 1929), p. 93.

22. Ibid., p. 75.

23. Eliezer Eliyahu Friedman, *Sefer ha-Zikhronot* (Tel Aviv, 1906), p. 146.

24. Ibid., p. 23.

25. Ibid., p. 137.

26. Ibid., p. 226.

27. S. I. Fin, *Kiryah Ne'emanah* (Vilna, 1860), p. 234.

28. In *Vilner Zamelbuch,* ed. D. Shabad (Vilna, 1916), 1:158–61.

29. Ben Zion Alfas, *Maasei Alfas: Toladah ve-Zikhronot* (Jerusalem, 1941), p. 51.

30. Quoted in Simcha Kling, *Nachum Sokolow: Servant of His People* (New York, 1960), p. 146.

31. Aryeh Zeev Rabiner, "The City of Boisk and Its Rabbis," *Sinai* 9, nos. 1–4 (1945): 68. For more information on Rabbi Kook in Boisk, see Jacob Agus, *The Banner of Jerusalem* (New York, 1946), p. 120.

32. Isaac Hirsch Weiss, *Zichronosai* (Warsaw, 1895), p. 76.

33. Yehezkel Kotick, *Meine Zichronos* (Berlin, 1922), pp. 238–39.

34. Jacob Mazeh, *Zikhronot* (Tel Aviv, 1936), 2:35.

35. J. L. Fishman, *Sarei ha-Meah* (Jerusalem, 1947), 4:43.

36. Zalman Shazar, *Morning Stars* (Philadelphia, 1967), pp. 7–10.

37. *Maasei Alfas: Toladah ve-Zikhronot* (Jerusalem, 1941).

38. Ibid., pp. 19–20.

39. Hyman Grinstein, *The Rise of the Jewish Community in New York* (Philadelphia, 1945), p. 252.

40. Moshe Davis, *Yahadut Amerika be-Hitpathukah* (New York, 1951), p. 117, referring to *Occident* 20, no. 1 (April 1962): 44–45.

41. Isaac Levitats, "Hevrot Yehudiyot be-Amerika," in *Sefer Hadoar 35th Anniversary Volume* (New York, 1957), pp. 236–37.

42. Zevi Hirsch Masliansky, *Zichronos* (New York, 1924), p. 224.

43. Ibid., pp. 251–253.

CHAPTER XV   **PAGES 285–303**

1. Various aspects of the general theme of this chapter are dealt with in a number of books and articles:

   a. The following articles all appeared in vol. 106 (1966) of the magazine *Mahnayim,* published by the Israel Defense Forces, a special "Hebrew Book" issue ed. by Menahem Ha-Kohen: Avraham Arazi, "Ha-Sefer ve-ha-Sofer be-einei Hazal" (pp. 14–21); Avraham Broides, "Devarim al ha-Sefer" (pp. 58–61); Yosef Nedavah, "Gezerot al Sefarim Ivriyim" (pp. 84–87); Mordechai Kukis, "Be-Maalot ha-Sefer ha-Ivri (pp. 84–87); G. Kresel, "Otzarot Sifrei Yisrael ba-Olam" (pp. 62–71).

   b. A. M. Haberman, *Toledot ha-Sefer ha-Ivri* (Jerusalem, 1945).

   c. Shimon Federbush, "Hibat ha-Sefer," in *Hikrei Yahadut* (Jerusalem, 1966).

   d. Naftali ben Menahem, *Gevilei Sefarim* (Jerusalem, 1947).

   e. Cecil Roth, "Jewish Love of Books," *Jewish Book Annual* 3 (1944–45).

2. *Sefer Hasidim* 691; and *Bet Yosef, Yoreh Deah* 282.

3. *Yoreh Deah* 277; *Sefer Hasidim* 754.

4. *Massekhet Soferim* 83.

5. *Likutei Maharil* 118.

6. This item, together with those cited in nn. 2–5 above, is from Federbush, *Hikrei Yahadut,* pp. 20–22.

7. Solomon Simon, *My Jewish Roots* (Philadelphia, 1956), p. 39.

8. Y. Meg. 4:1; B. Kid. 33b.

9. M.K. 26a.

10. Meg. 26b.

11. Rambam, at end of *Hilkhot Sefer Torah* 10:4.

12. Ibid.

13. San. 21b.

14. Min. 30b.

15. Ibid.

16. B.B. 16a; Rambam, *Hilkhot Sefer Torah* 10:1.

17. See Arazi, "Ha-Sefer ve-ha-Sofer be-einei Hazal."

18. Erub. 13b; Sot. 20a.

19. Suk. 26a.

20. *Yoreh Deah,* 270.

21. See Haberman, "Toledot ha-Sefer ha-Ivri."

22. *Sefer Yesharim,* 50.

23. *Teshuvot Hakhmei Tzarfat ve-Loteiz,* 84.

24. *Responsa Maharam Rotenburg,* ed. Prague, nos. 119, 250.

25. *Pesakim u-Khetavim,* 112.

26. *Responsa Rivash,* 137.

27. *Tzavaot Geonei Yisrael,* vol. 1, p. 57.

28. *Mahzor Vitry,* 321.

29. Arazi, "Ha-Sefer ve-ha-Sofer be-einei Hazal," pp. 18–19.

30. Ket. 50a; *Yalkut Shimoni* on Ps. 106.

31. *Sefer Hasidim,* 671.

32. *Responsa Harash* 93:3.

33. *Leket Yosher,* vol. 2, p. 59; *Shulhan Arukh, Hoshen Mishpat,* 292:20.

34. *Responsa Maharam Rotenburg,* ed. Prague, 346.

35. Ad loc. Shev. 40b.

36. Quoted in Haberman, *Toledot ha-Sefer ha-Ivri,* p. 13.

37. Ibid.

38. Israel Davidson, *Thesaurus of Mediaeval Hebrew Poetry* (Philadelphia, 1924), no. 1082.

39. *Sefer Hasidim,* 648.

40. Ibid., 647.

41. Ibid., 648.

42. Israel Abrahams, *Hebrew Ethical Wills* (Philadelphia, 1926), 1:82.

43. Zevi Leipnik, *Kav ve-Naki,* chap. 54.

44. Quoted in Federbush, *Hikrei Yahadut*, p. 33.

45. In introduction to *Responsa R. Akiba Eiger*.

46. Quoted in Federbush, *Hikrei Yahadut*, p. 33.

47. Quoted in Ben Menahem, *Gevilei Sefarim*, p. 11.

48. Federbush, *Hikrei Yahadut*, pp. 18–19.

49. Tos. B.B. chap. 1.

50. *Magen Avraham, Orah Hayim*, 150.

51. *Pinkas ha-Vaad*, no. 502.

52. Ibid., no. 739.

53. S. D. Goitein, "The Social Services of the Jewish Community as Reflected in the Cairo Genizah Records," *Jewish Social Studies* 26, no. 1 (January 1964): 13.

54. Quoted in Haberman, *Toledot ha-Sefer ha-Ivri*, p. 13.

55. Introduction to his book *Novelot Hakhmah*, quoted in Federbush, *Hikrei Yahadut*, p. 14.

56. *Hatzofeh* (Tel Aviv), December 12, 1955, quoted in Federbush, *Hikrei Yahadut*, p. 19.

57. Kresel, "Otzarot Sifrei Yisrael ba-Olam." Also, Cecil Roth, "Famous Jewish Book Collections," *Jewish Book Annual* 25 (1967–68); Carl Alpert, "Libraries in Israel," ibid., vol. 15; idem, "Community Libraries, ibid., vol. 18; idem, "The Hebrew Union College Library," ibid., vol. 20; Nahum M. Sarna, "The Library of the Jewish Theological Seminary," ibid., vol. 21; Jacob I. Dienstag, "The Mendel Gottesman Library of the Yeshivah University," ibid., vol. 22; Abraham Berger, "The Jewish Division of the New York Public Library," ibid., vol. 23; idem, "The Library of the Dropsie College," ibid., vol. 24; Dina Abramowicz, "The YIVO Library," ibid., vol. 25; Charles Berlin, "The Judaica Collection at Harvard," ibid., vol. 26; Shimeon Brisman, "The Jewish Studies Collection at UCLA," ibid., vol. 27; idem, "The Library of the American Jewish Historical Society," ibid., vol. 28; Max Kreutzberger, "The Library and Archives of the Leo Baeck Institute in New York," ibid., vol. 29.

See also A. R. Malakhi, "Otzerot Ruakh Olu Be-esh," *Bitzaron* 54, no. 6, pp. 68–80; Solomon Farber, "Selected Private Jewish Library Collections," *Jewish Book Annual*, vol. 29.

58. Max L. Margolis and Alexander Marx, *A History of the Jewish People* (Philadelphia, 1927), pp. 571–72.

59. Nedavah, "Gezerot al Sefarim Ivriyim."

60. 1 Macc. 1:53–56.

61. Taan. 4:6.

62. A.Z. 18a.

63. Quoted in Roth, "Jewish Love of Books," p. 3, and in Nedavah, "Gezerot al Sefarim Ivriyim," p. 60.

64. Roth, "Jewish Love of Books," pp. 3–4.

65. Quoted in Federbush, *Hikrei Yahadut*, p. 23.

66. Trans. by P. M. Raskin in *A Book of Jewish Thoughts*, ed. Joseph Hertz (New York, 1932), pp. 94–95.

67. Rav Hai Gaon, *Musar ha-Sekhel*, ed. A. H. Weiss (Warsaw, 1893), par. 32–33, quoted in Roth, "Jewish Love of Books," p. 4.

68. Ibid., par. 128.

69. Israel Abrahams, *Hebrew Ethical Wills* (Philadelphia, 1926), 1:63–64, n. 23.

70. Ibid., 1:64.

71. Ibid., 1:57, 81–82.

72. Roth, "Jewish Love of Books," p. 6.

73. Israel M. Goldman, *The Life and Times of Rabbi David ibn abi Zimra* (New York, 1970), p. 32; also Federbush, *Hikrei Yahadut*, p. 28.

74. Ber. 11b.

75. "Lifnei Aron ha-Sefarim," *K 1 Kitvei H. N. Bialik* (Tel Aviv, 1939), p. 47.

76. *Kitvei Agnon*, vol. 3, chap. on "Shas al Bet Zikni."

77. L. Kupershtein, "Kedushat ha-Sefer ve-ha-Lashion be-Yetzirat Agnon," *Am ve-Sefer* 45–46 (1971): 32–37.

78. Broides, "Devarim al ha-Sefer," p. 26.

79. *He-Hafetz Hayyim ha-Yov u-Fealav*, vol. 1, chap. 4, quoted in Kukis, "Be-Maalot ha-Sefer ha-Ivri."

80. Ben Menahem, *Gevilei Sefarim*, pp. 67–69.

CHAPTER XVI PAGES 305–318

1. Nahum N. Glatzer, "The Frankfort Lehrhaus," *Leo Baeck Institute Year Book* 1 (1956): 105–22.

2. Franz Rosenzweig, *On Jewish Learning*, introduction by N. N. Glatzer (New York, 1955), pp. 10–11.

3. Ibid., p. 59.

4. Ibid., p. 67.

5. Glatzer, "Frankfort Lehrhaus," pp. 105–22.

6. Ibid. For the full text of this address, see Rosenzweig, *On Jewish Learning*, pp. 95–102.

7. Glatzer, "Frankfort Lehrhaus," p. 105, etc.

8. Ernest Simon, "Jewish Adult Education in Nazi Germany as Spiritual Resistance," *Leo Baeck Institute Year Book* 1 (1956): 68–104.

9. Glatzer, "Frankfort Lehrhaus," pp. 105–22.

10. Israel M. Goldman, "Objectives in Adult Jewish Education," *Proceedings of the Rabbinical Assembly of America* 5 (New York, 1939): 435–47. "Jewish Educational Content in Terms of Contemporary Needs," *Proceedings of the Rabbinical Assembly of America* (New York, 1943), 191–199. "Adult Jewish Education in the Structure of Conservative Judaism," *Proceedings of*

the *Second Annual Rabbinical Assembly Conference on Jewish Education* (New York, 1947), 87–96. "We Must Search Our Ways," *Proceedings of the Rabbinical Assembly Conference on Reshaping the Structure of Jewish Education in America* (New York, 1946), 6–9.

11. Louis Finkelstein, "The National Academy for Adult Jewish Studies," *American Hebrew,* October 25, 1940.

12. Mordecai M. Kaplan, "Don't Be Your Own Enemy: Jews Who Are Ignorant of Their Heritage Lack Self-Respect Because They Have Nothing in Common Save Anti-Semitism," *National Jewish Monthly,* October 1940.

13. Samuel I. Cohen, "Adult Jewish Education," *American Jewish Year Book* 66 (1965): 279–90.

14. Mordecai M. Kaplan, *The Future of the American Jew* (New York, 1948), pp. 468–79.

15. Mordecai M. Kaplan, "Adult Jewish Education," printed in full in Dr. Samuel Margoshes's column in the *Day,* April 26 and 27, 1956.

16. Cohen, "Adult Jewish Education," pp. 279–90; also idem, "History of Adult Jewish Education in Four National Organizations" (Ph.D. diss., Yeshiva University, 1967).

17. Hayim Naḥman Bialik, *Devarim She-b'al Peh* (Tel Aviv, 1935), 2:87–91.

18. Gideon G. Freudenberg, "Adult Education in Israel," *Jewish Education* 28, no. 3 (Spring 1958): 52–57.

19. See publications of World Jewish Bible Society.

20. See publications of Ha-Brit ha-Ivrit ha-Olamit.

21. David Edelsberg, "Monument far die Sechs Million Yiddishe Kedosim," *Day–Jewish Journal,* May 11, 1956, p. 7.

22. Nisan Gordon, "Yiden Vos Lernen a Blatt Gemara Yeden Tog," *Day–Jewish Journal,* September , 1960, p. 5; David Edelsberg, "Mazel Brocho fun ein Idee," *Day–Jewish Journal,* September 16, 1960, p. 5; "Mahzor Hashvii shel Daf ha-Yomi," *Ha-Pardes* 42, no. 4 (January 1968): 38.

BIBLIOGRAPHY

1. *Primary Sources*

The Bible.
The Mishnah.
The Babylonian Talmud.
The Jerusalem Talmud.
The Mekilta de-Rabbi Ishmael, ed. Lauterbach. 2 vols., Philadelphia, 1933.
Midrash Rabbah.
Midrash Tanḥuma.
Midrash Tehillim, trans. Braude. 2 vols., New Haven, 1959.
Pesikta Rabbati, trans. Braude. 2 vols., New Haven, 1968.
Yalkut Eliezer
Yalkut Shimoni
Yalkut Shir ha-Shirim
Avot de-Rabi Natan, ed. Schechter. New York, 1945.
Yad Hazakah, Maimonides.
Shulḥan Arukh, Joseph Karo.
Massekhet Soferim, ed. Miller. Leipzig and Vienna, 1878.
Maḥzor Vitry, ed. Hurwitz. Nuremberg, 1923.
Sefer Hasidim, ed. Wistinetzki and Freimann. Frankfurt a.M., 1924.
Menorat ha-Maor, Israel ibn Al-Nakawa, ed. and trans. Enelow. 4 vols., New York 1929.
Josephus, trans. Whiston. Philadelphia, 1857.
Philo, trans. Colson and Whitaker. Loeb Classical Library, 10 vols., New York 1929–32.

2. *Manuscripts*

1. In the library of the Jewish Theological Seminary:
   Ha-Hevrah Kenessiah le-Shem Shamayim of Venice, 1611–1843.
   The Pinkas of the Hevrah Kaddisha Tiferet Bahurim, Amsterdam 1778.

347

The Pinkas of the Hevrah Mikra of Gombin, 1792–1892.

The Pinkas of the Havurah Maggidei Tehillim u-Gmiluth Hassadim. Kiev, 1895–1905.

The Pinkas of the Havurah Shas shel Harav Vilkovsky.

The Takkanot of the Hevrah Kaddisha Talmud Torah of Amsterdam, 1804.

2. In the library of the Yeshiva University:

The Pinkas of the Verein Holche Tom in Kempen, Posen.

3. In the library of YIVO:

The Takkanot of the Hevrah Kaddisha Agudat Bahurim, Amsterdam 1790.

The Pinkas ha-Takkanot min Hevrah Kaddisha de-Kabronim be-Altona.

4. In Possession of the Author:

The Pinkas of the Hevrat Yeshivat Bar Yochai.

The Pinkas of the Hevrah Mishnah shel Bais Hakneseth Tifereth Yisroel de-Baltimore.

The Minute-Book of the Beth ha-Midrash Association of the Chizuk Amuno Congregation, Baltimore.

3. *In Hebrew and in Yiddish*

אברבך, משה: התפתחות החנוך העברי. שבילי החנוך, שנה כ"ו, חוברת ב'־ג'; 1966.
שנה כ"ז, חוברת ב'־ג' 1966־67.

אברבך, משה: בעיות משמעת ועונשין בתקופת המקרא והתלמוד. שבילי החנוך, שנה
כ"ז, חוברת ד'; שנה כ"ח, חוברת ג'־ד'; שנה כ"ט, חוברת א'־ד', 1967־9.

אברבך, משה: המורה העברי בתקופת התלמוד. שבילי החנוך, שנה ל"ב, חוברת
א'־ב', 1971.

אברבך, משה: היחסים בין הרב והתלמיד. שבילי החנוך, שנה ל"ד, חוברת א'
1973.

אברבך, משה: היחסים בין הרב והתלמיד בתקופת התלמוד. שבילי החנוך, שנה ל"ד,
חוברת ב'־ד', 1974.

אליפנט, זאב: בשבילי הפילוסופיה החינוכית של הרמב"ם. שבילי החינוך, שנה ל"ד,
חוברת א', 1973.

אלפס, בן ציון: מעשי אלפס; תולדות וזכרונות. ירושלים, תש"א.

אסף, שמחה: מקורות לתולדות החנוך בישראל; מתחלת ימי הבינים עד תקופת
ההשכלה. תל אביב, תרפ"ה. ד' כרכים.

ארזי, אברהם: הספר והסופר בעיני חז"ל. מחניים, חוברת ק"ו, תמוז, תשכ"ה.

ביאליק, חיים נחמן: דברים שבעל פה. תל אביב, תרצ"ה. כרך ב'.

בן מנחם, נפתלי: גוילי ספרים, ירושלים, תש"ז.

בן עזרא, ע.: לתולדות מצות "הקהל". הדואר, גליון ל"ח, תש"ג.

ברוידם, אברהם: דברים על הספר. מחניים, חוברת ק"ו, תמוז, תשכ"ו.

גוטיין, שלמה דוב: סדרי חנוך בימי הגאונים ובית הרמב"ם; מקורות חדשים מן הגניזה. ירושלים, תשכ"ב

גורן, שלמה: תורת המועדים. תל אביב, תשכ"ד.

נידעמאנן, משה: ספר התורה והחיים בארצות המערב, העתקת א"ש פריעדבערג. ווארשא, תרנ"ו, ג' כרכים.

גליק, מ.: חנוך והוראה על פי תלמוד בבלי. בצרון, שנה כ"ד, חוברת ח'; שנה כ"ו, חוברת ז', תשי"א-ב'.

גליקסברג, שמעון יעקב: הדרשה בישראל, תל אביב, ת"ש.

דובנוב, שמעון: פנקס ועד הקהלות הראשונות במדינת ליטא. ברלין, תרפ"ה.

דייוים, משה: יהדות אמריקה בהתפתחותה. ניו-יורק, תשי"א.

דינור, בן ציון: החנוך בתקופת המקרא, מחנים, חוברת ק"ח, אב, תשכ"ו.

דרוק, דוד: ר' לוי גינצבורג. ניו-יורק, תרצ"ד.

דרייזין, נחום: תולדות החנוך היהודי; מתחילת הבית השני עד חתימת המשנה. ירושלים-תל אביב, תשכ"ה.

הברמן, א. מ.: תולדות הספר העברי. ירושלים, תש"ה.

היילפרין, ישראל: תקנות מדינת מעהרין; 1748—1650. ירושלים, תשי"ב.

הירשענזאהן, חיים: ספר תורת החנוך בישראל. סעאיני, תרפ"ז.

הנדעל, מיכאל: מלאכה ובעלי מלאכה בעם ישראל. תל אביב, תשט"ז.

הפטרמן, א.: החנוך בספרות התלמודית. שבילי החנוך, שנה ה' (סדרה שניה), חוברת ג', 1945.

וואכסמאן, מאיר: דור דור ומחנכיו. ניו-יורק, תרפ"ז.

וויזיל, נפתלי הערץ: ספר דברי שלום ואמת; על תורת האדם ותורת החנוך לנערי בני ישראל. ווארשא, תרמ"ו.

וויים, יצחק הירש: זכרונותי, ווארשא, תרנ"ה.

וינשטין, יהושע: הרמב"ם — המורה לדורות. שבילי החנוך, שנה ל"ד, חוברת ב'-ג', 1974.

ויסבליט, שלמה: דרכי הוראה במשנת הרמב"ם. מחנים, חוברת ק"ח. אב, תשכ"ו.

זלוטניק, י. ל.: שרידים מקהלת גומבין, הוצאת 1923. הוצאה חדשה 1947. רשומות, כרך ג'.

טשרנא, ש. י.: לתולדות החנוך בישראל. ירושלים, תרצ"ט. ג' חוברות.

טשרנוביץ, חיים (רב צעיר): תולדות הפוסקים. ניו יורק, תש"ח. ג' כרכים.

יודילוביץ, מ. ד.: ישיבת פומבדיתא. ניו-יורק, תרצ"ה.

יעקובסון, יששכר: טעמי מצות „הקהל" בינה במקרא, תל אביב, תשי"ג.

יערי, א.: מחקרי ספר. ירושלים, תשי"ח.

כהנא, ש. ז.: מצות „הקהל". הדואר, גליון ל"ד, תשי"ב.

כהנא, יצחק זאב: קניית ומכירת ספרים בהלכה. בתוך מחקרים בספרות התשובות. ירושלים, תשל"ג.

כ"ץ, יעקב: מסורת ומשבר; החברה היהודית במוצאי ימי הבינים. ירושלים, תשי"ח.

לאם, נחום: תורה לשמה במשנת ר' חיים מוולוזין ובמחשבת הדור. ירושלים, תשל"ב.

לויטטס, יצחק: חברות יהודיות באמריקה. בתוך: ספר הדואר למלאות לו ל"ה שנה. ניו-יורק, תשי"ז.

לייפנוק, צבי ונקי: קב ונקי.

ליפמאן, א.: לתולדות היהודים בקאוונא. קיידאני, תרצ"ד.

מאסליאנסקי, צבי הירש: זכרונות. ניו-יורק, תרפ"ד.

מזא"ה, יעקב: זכרונות. תל אביב, תרצ"ו. ד' כרכים.

מלאכי, א.ר.: אוצרות רוח עלו באש. בצרון, שנה נ"ד, חוברת ו', תשכ"ז.

מרקין, יצחק: תולדות החנוך וההוראה. ניו-יורק, תרפ"ד.

נאטאנזאהן, יוסף שאול הלוי: תקנות מהחבורה הקדושה אנשי מעמד לבוב. תש"ד.

נדבה, יוסף: גזרות על ספרים עבריים. מחניים, חוברת ק"ו, תמוז תשכ"ו.

ניסנבוים, יצחק: עלי חלדי. ווארשא, תרצ"ט.

ספר שערי תורה ותפלה: מחברת ישיבת בר יוחאי, נוסדה בעיר הקודש צפת, תר"ו.

פדרבוש, שמעון: חיבת הספר; חקרי היהדות. ירושלים, תשכ"ו.

פישמאן, יהודה ליב הכהן: שרי המאה. ירושלים, תש"ד. ד' כרכים.

פלינקער, דוד: סוכות; טראדיציע ווערט באנייט אין ישראל נאך צוויי טויזענט יאהר. דער טאג — פרייטאג, דריטער אקטאבער, 1952.

פריעדמאן, אליעזר אליהו: ספר הזכרונות. תל אביב, תרס"ו.

קאטיק, יחזקאל: מיינע זכרונות. ברלין, 1922.

קולק, צבי הירש הלוי: ספר מדור לדור. ווארשא, תרס"א.

קופרשטיין, ל.: קדושת הספר והלשון ביצירת עגנון. עם וספר, מ"ה-מ"ו, ירושלים תשל"א, 1971.

קוקיס, מרדכי: במעלות הספר העברי. מחניים, חוברת ק"ו, תמוז, תשכ"ו.

קרסל, ג.: אוצרות ספרי ישראל. מחניים, חוברת ק"ו, תמוז, תשכ"ו.

ראבינער, אריה זאב: העיר בויסק ורבניה. סיני, שנה ט', חוברת א'-ד', 1941.

ריבקינד, יצחק: הספר העברי. רשומות, כרך ד', ירושלים, תרפ"ז, 1925.

ריינס, ח. ז.: השכלת העם בתקופת המקרא, המשנה והתלמוד, שבילי החנוך, שנה ל', חוברת ב', 1969.

שאבאד, ד': ווילנער זאמעלבוך, ווילנע, 1916.

שבד, אברהם חיים: ספר תולדות הימים שעברו על חברא קדישא שבעה קרואים ועל
ביהמ"ד הגדול אשר בעיר מינסק; התקכ"ז — התרם"ד. ווילנא, תרם"ד.

שרפשטיין, צבי: תולדות החנוך בישראל בדורות האחרונים; משנת 1789 עד 1914.
ניו-יורק, תש"א. ג' כרכים.

שרפשטיין, צבי: החדר בחיי עמנו. ניו-יורק, תש"ג.

שרשפטין, צבי: ארבעים שנה באמריקה. תל אביב, תשט"ז.

שרפשטיין, צבי (עורך): יסודות החנוך היהודי באמריקה. ניו-יורק, תש"ז.

שולוואס, משה: חיי היהודים באיטליה בתקופת הריניסאנס. ניו-יורק, תשט"ו.

שטערנפעלד, דניאל: ספר החוקים והתקנות . . . הישיבה תורת חיים בעיר בראדשין,
הוסיאטין.

תקנות דחברא קדישא דק"ק אשכנזים באמשטרדם, תקל"ו.

תקנות דח"ק תלמוד תורה באמשטרדם, תקם"ד.

תקנות הקהלה דקהל אשכנז אשר באמשטרדם, תצ"ז.

תקנות להשומרים אצל הנבינות — אמשטרדם, תר"ו.

תקנות מח"ק גמילות חסדים של בחורים מק"ק אשכנזים האללאנדיא אמשטרדם,
תקע"ה.

4. *In German and French*

Bacher, W. "Das Altjüdische Schulwesen." *Jahrb. f. Jüd. Gesch. u. Lit.,* vol. 6.
Blach-Gudensberg. *Das Padagogische im Talmud.* Halberstadt, 1881.
Durr, L. *Die Erziehung im Alten Testament,* 1932.
Duschak, M. *Schulgesetzgebung und Methodik d. alten Israeliten.* Vienna, 1872.
Elbogen, Ismar. *Der Jüdische Gottesdienst.* Frankfurt a.M., 1931.
Fischel, Walter. *Die Jüdische Padagogik in der Tannaitischen Literatur.* 1928.
Frankfurter, S. *Das Altjüdische Erziehungs und Unterrichtswesen im Lichte moderner Bestrebungen.* 4th ed., Vienna, 1910.
Goldfeld, Anne. "Women as sources of Torah in the Rabbinic Tradition" *JUDAISM* 94:2. 1975, New York pp. 245-256.
Grunwald, Max. "Das Lernen." In *Jahrbuch fur Jüdische Volkskünde.* Berlin and Vienna, 1925.
Guedemann, Moritz. *Geschichte des Erziehungswesens und der Kultur der abendländischen Juden während des Mittelalters.* 3 vols., Vienna, 1888.
———. *Quellenschriften zur Geschichte des Unterichtswesens und der Erziehung bei den deutschen Juden.* Berlin, 1891.
Guttmann, J. *Die Scholastik des XIII. Jahrhunderts in ihren Beziehungen zum Judentum und zur jüdischen Literatur.* Breslau, 1902.
Herner, S. "Erziehung und Unterricht in Israel." *Haupt Oriental Vol.* pp. 58–66.

Hirsch, S. R. *Aus der Rabbinische Schulleben inbesonders im Talmudischem Zeit.* 1971.

Kottek, H. "Die Hochschulen in Palastina und Babylonia." *Jahrb. f. Jud. Gesch. u. Lit.*

Lewit, J. *Darstallung der theoretischen und praktischen Padagogik im Jüdischen Altertume nach dem Talmud.* Berlin, 1896.

Marcus, Samuel. *Die Padagogik des israelitischen Volkes von der Patriarchen- zeit bis auf den Talmud.* 2 vols., Vienna, 1877.

Perlow, T. *Léducation et l'enseignement chez les Juifs a l'époque talmudique.* 1931.

Rosenberg, E. *Die jüdische Volkschule der Tradition,* 1890.

Schargorodzka, F. *Die padagogischen Grundlagen des Pharisaischen Judentums des tannaitischen Zeitalters in Palastina,* 1913.

Schwarz, Ad. "Hochschulen in Palastina und Babylonien." *Jahrb. f. Jud. Gesch. u. Lit.,* 1899.

Simon, Joseph. *L'éducation et l'instruction des enfants chez les anciens Juifs d'après la Bible et le Talmud.* Paris, 1879.

Stein, Solomon. *Schulverbaltnisse, Erziehunglehre u. Unterrichtsmetboden in Talmud.* Berlin, 1901.

Stern, J. *Die Talmudische Padagogik.* 1915.

Strassburger, Baruch. *Geschichte der Erziehung und des Unterrichts bei den Israeliten, Von den Vortalmudischen Zeit bis auf die Gegenwast.* Stuttgart, 1885.

Van Gelder, E. *Die Volkschüle des jud. altertums noch Talmud, u. rab- binischem Quellen.* Berlin, 1872.

Wiesen, Joseph. *Geschichte und Methodik des Schulwesens im talmudischen Altertume.* Strassburg, 1892.

Wiesner, L. *Die Jugendlehrer in der talmudischen Zeit.* Vienna, 1914 .

Wilhelm, Kurt. *Von Jüdischer Gemeinde und Gemeinschaft.* Berlin, 1938.

Zunz, Leopold. *Gottesdienstliche Vorträge der Juden.* Frankfurt, a.M., 1892.

5. *In English*

Abrahams, Israel. *Hebrew Ethical Wills.* 2 vols., Philadelphia, 1926.

Abramowicz, Dina. "The YIVO Library." *Jewish Book Annual,* vol. 25.

Agus, Jacob. *The Banner of Jerusalem.* New York, 1946.

Almond, D. *Hebrew Religious Education.* 1922.

Alpert, Carl. "Community Libraries." *Jewish Book Annual,* vol. 15.

———. "Libraries in Israel." *Jewish Book Annual,* vol. 18.

———. "The Hebrew Union College Library." *Jewish Book Annual,* vol. 20.

Arzt, Max. "The Teacher in Talmud and Midrash." In *Mordecai M. Kaplan Jubilee Volume.* New York, 1953.

Baron, Salo W. *A Social and Religious History of the Jews.* vols. 1 and 2, Philadelphia, 1942.

———. *The Jewish Community.* 3 vols., Philadelphia, 1942.

Berger, Abraham. "The Jewish Division of the New York Public Library." *Jewish Book Annual*, vol. 23.

————. "The Library of the Dropsie College." *Jewish Book Annual*, vol. 24.

Berger, J. *Elementary Education in the Talmud*. Montreal, 1929.

Berlin, Charles. "The Judaica Collection at Harvard." *Jewish Book Annual*, vol. 26.

Bettan, Israel. *Studies in Jewish Preaching*. Cincinnati, 1939.

Blumenfeld, Samuel M. *Master of Troyes: A Study of Rashi, the Educator*. New York, 1946.

Braude, William G., trans. *The Midrash on Psalms*. 2 vols., New Haven, 1959.

————, trans. *Pesikta Rabbati*. 2 vols., New Haven, 1968.

Brisman, Shimeon. "The Jewish Studies Collection at U.C.L.A." *Jewish Book Annual*, vol. 27.

————. "The Library of the American Jewish Historical Society." *Jewish Book Annual*, vol. 28.

Cohen, Israel. *History of the Jews in Vilna*. Philadelphia, 1943.

Cohen, Samuel I. "Adult Jewish Education." In *American Jewish Year Book* 66 (New York, 1965).

————. "History of Adult Jewish Education in Four National Organizations." Ph.D. diss., Yeshiva University, 1967.

Cornill, Carl Heinrich. *The Culture of Ancient Israel*. Chicago, 1914.

————. "Education of Children." *Ancient Israel Monist.*, vol. 13, pp. 1–22.

Davidson, Israel. *Thesaurus of Mediaeval Hebrew Poetry*. 4 vols., Philadelphia, 1924.

Dembitz, Lewis N. *Jewish Services in Synagogue and Home*. Philadelphia, 1898.

Dienstag, Jacob I. "The Mendel Gottesman Library of the Yeshivah University." *Jewish Book Annual*, vol. 22.

Drazin, Nathan. *History of Jewish Education from 515 B.C.E. to 220 C.E.* Baltimore, 1940.

Ellis, G. Harold. "Origin and Development of Jewish Education." *Ped. Seminary* 9 (1902): 50–62.

Enelow, Hyman G. *Adult Education in Judaism*. Cincinnati, 1927.

————, ed. and trans. *Menorat Ha-Maor (The Book of Illumination)* by Rabbi Israel ibn Al-Nakawa. 4 vols., New York, 1929.

Epstein, Isidore. *The Responsa of Rabbi Simon ben Zemach Duran*. London, 1930.

————. *The Responsa of Rabbi Solomon ben Adreth of Barcelona*. London, 1925.

Faber, Solomon. "Selected Private Jewish Library Collections." *Jewish Book Annual*, vol. 29.

354 LIFELONG LEARNING AMONG JEWS

Feldman, William Moses. *The Jewish Child: Its History, Folklore, Biology, Sociology.* London, 1917.

Finkelstein, Louis. *Akiba: Scholar, Saint and Martyr.* New York, 1936.

———. *Jewish Self-Government in the Middle Ages.* New York, 1924.

———. "The National Academy for Adult Jewish Studies." *American Hebrew,* October 25, 1940.

———. "The Origin of the Synagogue." *Proceedings of the American Academy for Jewish Research* 1 (1928–30): 49–59.

———. *The Pharisees.* 2 vols., Philadelphia, 1938.

———, ed. *Thirteen Americans.* New York, 1953.

Fischman, Isidor. *The History of Jewish Education in Central Europe: From the End of the 16th Century to the End of the 18th Century.* London, 1944.

Freehof, Solomon B. *Modern Jewish Preaching.* New York, 1941.

Freudenberg, Gideon G. "Adult Education in Israel." *Jewish Education.* 28, no. 3 (Spring 1958).

Gamoran, Emanual. *Changing Conceptions of Jewish Education.* New York, 1924.

Ginzberg, Louis. *Students, Scholars and Saints.* Philadelphia, 1928.

———. *The Legends of the Jews.* 7 vols., Philadelphia, 1911–38.

Giovanelli, Felix, trans. "Learning Among the Hebrews: A 17th Century Report." *Commentary* 13 (June 1952).

Glatzer, Nahum N. Introduction and trans. "Rules for the House of Study by Moses Hayyim Luzzatto." *Commentary* 11, no. 5 (May 1951).

———. "The Frankfort Lehrhaus." *Leo Baeck Institute Year Book* 1 (London, 1956).

Goitein, S. D. "The Social Services of the Jewish Community as Reflected in the Cairo Genizah Records." *Jewish Social Studies* 26, no. 1 (January 1964).

Goldman, Israel M. "Objectives in Adult Jewish Education." *Proceedings of the Rabbinical Assembly of America* 5 (1939), 435–449.

———. *The Life and Times of Rabbi David ibn abi Zimra.* New York, 1970.

———. "Jewish Educational Contest in Terms of Contemporary Needs," *Proceedings of the Rabbinical Assembly of America* (New York, 1943), 191-199.

———. "Adult Jewish Education in the Structure of Conservative Judaism," *Proceedings of the Second Annual Rabbinical Assembly Conference on Jewish Education* (New York, 1947), 87-96.

———. "We Must Search Our Ways," *Proceedings of the Rabbinical Assembly Conference on Reshaping the Structure of Jewish Education in America* (New York, 1946), 6-9.

Gollancz, Hermann. *Pedagogics of the Talmud and That of Modern Times.* London, 1924.

Goodblatt, Morris S. *Jewish Life in Turkey in the 16th Century, Based on the Responsa of Rashdam.* New York, 1952.

Grattan, C. Hartley. *In Quest of Knowledge.* New York, 1955.

Graves, Frank P. *A History of Education Before the Middle Ages.* New York, 1919.

Greenberg, Simon. "Jewish Educational Institutions." In *The Jews: Their History, Culture and Religion,* ed. Louis Finkelstein. Philadelphia, 1949.

Grinstein, Hyman. *The Rise of the Jewish Community in New York.* Philadelphia, 1945.

Grunwald, Max. *History of the Jews in Vienna.* Philadelphia, 1936.

Herford, R. Travers. *The Pharisees.* New York, 1924.

Hertz, Joseph. *Jewish Religious Education.* London, 1924.

Hoffman, Justin. "The Ends of Education in Classical Judaism," *Jewish Education* 32, no. 2 (Winter 1962).

———. "The Student in Classical Judaism." *Jewish Education* 38, no. 1 (January 1968) : 50–58.

Hyamson, Moses, trans. *Mishneh Torah.* New York, 1937.

Imber, N. H. "Education and the Talmud." In *Report of the U.S. Commissioner of Education, 1894–95,* 2:1795–1820.

Isaacs, Nathan. "Study as a Mode of Worship." In *Jewish Library,* ed. Leo Jung. 2nd ed., New York, 1943.

Jacobs, Louis. *Hasidic Prayer.* Philadelphia, 1973.

Josephus. *Antiquities of the Jews, Contra Apionem,* trans. William Whiston. Philadelphia, 1857.

Kadushin, Max. *Worship and Ethics: A Study in Rabbinic Judaism.* Evanston, Ill., 1964.

Kaganoff, Nathan M. "The Library of the American Jewish Historical Society." *Jewish Book Annual,* vol. 28.

Kaplan, Mordecai M. "Adult Jewish Education." *The Day,* April 26–27, 1956.

———. "Don't Be Your Own Enemy." *National Jewish Monthly,* October 1940.

———. *The Future of the American Jew.* New York, 1948.

Katz, Shelomo. "An Aristocracy of Learning." *Commentary,* June 1947.

Kent, Charles Foster. *The Makers and Teachers of Judaism.* New York, 1911.

Kling, Simcha. *Nachum Sokolow: Servant of His People.* New York, 1960.

Kober, Adolf. *History of the Jews in Cologne.* Philadelphia, 1940.

Kobler, Franz, ed. *A Treasury of Jewish Letters.* 2 vols., Philadelphia, 1953.

Kretzmann, Paul Edward. *Education Among the Jews from the Earliest Times to the End of the Talmudic Period, 500 A.D.* Boston, 1916.

Kreutzerger, Max. "The Library and Archives of the Leo Baeck Institute in New York." *Jewish Book Annual,* vol. 29.

Lamm, Norman. "Study and Prayer, Their Relative Value in Hasidism and Mitnagdism." In *Samuel K. Mirsky Memorial Volume.* New York, 1970.

Lauterbach, Jacob Z. "The Name of the Rabbinical Schools and Assemblies in Babylonia." In *Hebrew Union College Jubilee Volume.* Cincinnati, 1925.

Leipziger, Henry M. *Education of the Jews.* New York, 1890.

Levinthal, Israel H. "The Uniqueness of the Classic Jewish Sermon," *Conservative Judaism* 27, no. 2 (1973): 77–80.

Levitats, Isaac. *The Jewish Community in Russia 1772–1844.* New York, 1943.

Lowenthal, Marvin. "On Community Libraries." *Jewish Book Annual,* vol. 18.

Maller, Julius B. "The Role of Education in Jewish History." In *The Jews: Their History, Culture and Religion,* ed. Louis Finkelstein. Philadelphia, 1949.

Mann, Jacob. *The Bible as Read and Preached in the Old Synagogue.* Vol. 1; Cincinnati, 1940; vol. 2; New York, 1966.

Marcus, Jacob R. *Communal Sick Care in the German Ghetto.* Cincinnati, 1947.

———. "The Triesch Hebra Kaddisha." *Hebrew Union College Annual* 19 (1945–46).

Margolis, Max L., and Marx, Alexander. *A History of the Jewish People.* Philadelphia, 1927.

Marx, Alexander. *Essays in Jewish Biography.* Philadelphia, 1947.

Matz, Israel. "Memories of Kalvaria." *Menorah Journal* 48, nos. 1–2.

Maynard, John Albert. *A Survey of Hebrew Education.* Milwaukee, 1924.

Mesch, Abraham J. *Abyss of Despair,* New York, 1950.

Mielziner, M. *Introduction to the Talmud.* Cincinnati, 1894.

Millgram, Abraham E. *Jewish Worship.* Philadelphia, 1971.

———. *Sabbath: The Day of Delight.* Philadelphia, 1944.

Moore, George Foot. *Judaism in the First Centuries of the Christian Era: The Age of the Tannaim.* 3 vols., Cambridge, Mass., 1927.

Morris, Nathan. *The Jewish School from the Earliest Times to the Year 500 of the Present Era.* London, 1937.

Neuman, Abraham A. *The Jews in Spain.* 2 vols., Philadelphia, 1942.

Neusner, Jacob. *History and Torah: Essays on Jewish Learning.* New York, 1965.

Newman, Aryeh. "An Almost Forgotten Chapter in Jewish Adult Education." *Jewish Affairs* (Johannesburg, S.A.), February 1957.

News of YIVO, October 1960, no. 80.

Owst, G. R. *Literature and Pulpit in Mediaeval England.* Cambridge, 1933.

Pearce, Clarence. *The Education of Hebrew Youth from the Earliest Times to the Maccabean Period.*

Pool, David de Sola. "The Traditional Code of Jewish Education." *Menorah Journal* 10 (June–July 1924); reprinted in *Jewish Education* 16, no. 3 (May 1945).

Rabinowitz, L. *The Social Life of the Jews in Northern France in the XII–XIV Centuries.* London, 1938.

Radin, Max. *The Life of the People in Biblical Times.* Philadelphia, 1929.

Rawidowicz, Simon. "On Jewish Learning," *Studies in Jewish Thought.* Philadelphia, 1975.

Rosenberg, Meyer J. *The Historical Development of Hebrew Education from Ancient Times to 135 C.E.* New York, 1927.

Rosenzweig, Franz. *On Jewish Learning.* Introduction by N. N. Glatzer. New York, 1955.

Roth, Cecil. "Famous Jewish Book Collections." *Jewish Book Annual* 25 (1967–68).

———. *History of the Jews in Venice.* Philadelphia, 1930.

———. "Jewish Love of Books." *Jewish Book Annual,* 1944–45.

Samuel, Maurice. *In Praise of Yiddish.* New York, 1971.

Sarna, Nahum M. "The Library of the Jewish Theological Seminary of America" in *Jewish Book Annual,* vol. 21.

Schechter, S. *Studies in Judaism.* 3 vols., Philadelphia, 1896–1924.

Shapiro, Joseph. "Education among Early Hebrews with Emphasis on Talmudic Period." *Abstracts of Thesis Researches Completed and Bibliography of Publications.* University of Pittsburgh, 1938.

Shazar, Zalman. *Morning Stars.* Philadelphia, 1967.

Shurer, Emil. *History of the Jewish People.* 5 vols., Edinburgh, 1908.

Simon, Ernest. "Jewish Adult Education in Nazi Germany as Spiritual Resistance." *Leo Baeck Institute Year Book* 1 (London, 1956).

Simon, Solomon. *My Jewish Roots.* Philadelphia, 1956.

Spiegel, Shalom. *The Last Trial.* Philadelphia, 1967.

Spiers, Baer. *The School System of the Talmud.* London, 1898.

Strack, Hermann L. *Introduction to the Talmud and Midrash.* Philadelphia, 1931.

Swift, Fletcher H. *Education in Ancient Israel from Earliest Times to 70 C.E.* Chicago, 1919.

Waxman, Meyer. *A History of Jewish Literature.* 2nd ed., New York, 1938.

Winter, Samuel. "Minute-Books of Societies." *Yivo Bleter* 13 (January–February 1938).

Wischnitzer, Mark. *A History of Jewish Crafts and Guilds.* New York, 1965.

Wolfson, Harry Austryn. *Philo.* 2 vols., Cambridge, Mass., 1947.

Zafren, Herbert C. "The Hebrew Union College Library." *Jewish Book Annual,* vol. 20.

Zarchin, Michael M. "Tailors Guild of Kurnik, Province of Posen." *Jewish Quarterly Review* 28 (1937–38).

INDEX

358